MW01626994

PostScript. July 2013 £16.99

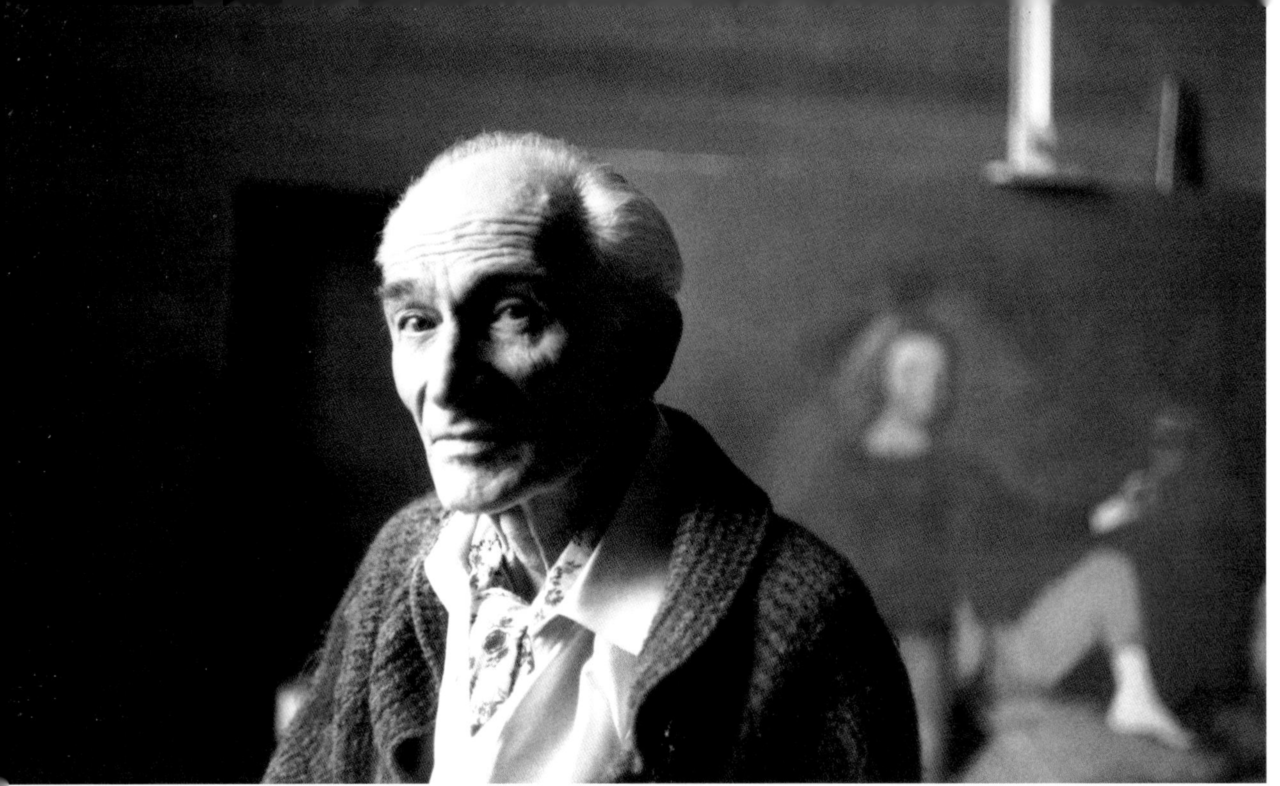

Balthus at his home, 1990.
Photo: Henri Cartier-Bresson.

Balthus

Balthus

Works and Interview

Mieke Bal

Ediciones Polígrafa

Photographic credits:

The Art Institute of Chicago, Chicago (p. 130); Henri Cartier-Bresson / Magnum Photos (p. 2); Catedral de Toledo (p. 27); County Museum of Art, Los Angeles (p. 136 bottom); Loomis Dean (cover and p. 8 / Getty Images); Elkon Gallery Inc., New York (p. 105); Martine Franck / Magnum Photos (p. 154); Fundación Thyssen Bornemisza, Madrid (pp. 66, 122); Galleria degli Uffizi, Florence (p. 45 bottom); Galleria dell'Accademia, Venice (p. 142); Gemäldegalerie, Berlin (p. 89); The Hirschhorn Museum and Sculpture Garden, Washington D. C. (pp. 79, 85, 93, 119); Indianapolis Museum of Art, Indianapolis (p. 59); The Lefevre Gallery, London (p. 41); The Metropolitan Museum of Art, New York (pp. 87, 88, 94, 97); The Minneapolis Institute of Art, Minneapolis (pp. 48, 82, top); Moderna Museet, Stockholm (p. 115); Musée d'Art moderne, Troyes (p. 54, 107); Museo de Bellas Artes, Granada (p. 74); Museum Boijmans Van Beuningen, Rotterdam (p. 67); The Museum of Modern Art, New York (pp. 19, 49, 81, 83); National Gallery, London (pp. 45 top, 92, 136 top); Pinacoteca Communale, Sansepolcro (p. 113 top); Réunion de Musées Nationaux (pp. 10, 13, 17, 21, 28, 30, 55, 63, 64, 78, 96, 126); Giorgio Soavi (p. 144); Staatliche Museen, Berlin (p. 44 bottom); Tate Gallery, London (p. 132); Ubu Gallery, New York (p. 113 bottom); Vassar College, Poughkeepsie, New York (p. 102); Walter Art Gallery, Baltimore (p. 44 top); Wadsworth Atheneum Museum of Art, Hardfort, Connecticut (p. 125).

Balmes, 54. 08007 Barcelona (Spain)
www.edicionespoligrafa.com

Concept of the Collection: Francisco Rei
Coordination and proof reading: Montse Holgado
Translation (Interview): Sue Brownbridge
Copy editing: John Barrass
Design: Estudi Polígrafa / Carlos J. Santos
Color separation: Estudi Polígrafa / Borja Ardite
Printing and binding: Indústria Gràfica Domingo, Barcelona

Available in USA and Canada through D.A.P./Distributed Art Publishers
155 Sixth Avenue, 2nd Floor, New York, N. Y. 10013
Tel. (212) 627-1999 Fax: (212) 627-9484

ISBN: 978-84-343-1165-7
Dep. legal: B. 12.310 - 2008 (Printed in Spain)

Contents

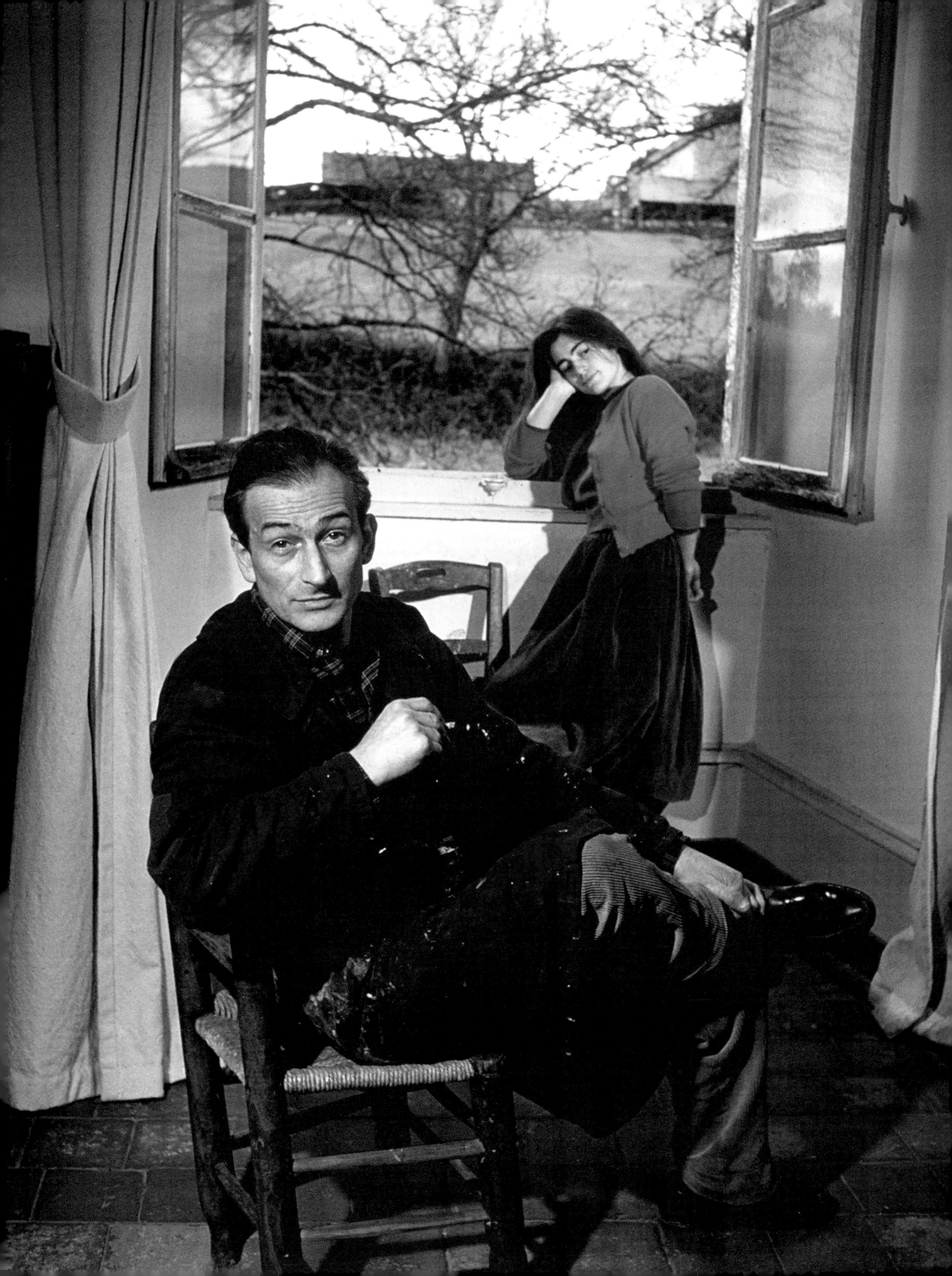

Balthus: Other Realities

MIEKE BAL

Introduction[1]

In 1980-1981 the French painter Balthus (1908-2001) painted a large work, now in the collection of the Centre Georges Pompidou in Paris, which can be seen as a summation of his many artistic preoccupations. The large, almost square canvas *Le Peintre et son modèle* (The Painter and His Model, p. 10) shows a man standing at a window, perhaps looking out, and slightly more to the front, a girl reading a green double sheet. The painting has a subdued yet vibrant color scheme reminiscent of old frescos; none of the colors are brilliant but the coloring is. The ambiance of the scene is peaceful, silent. I have, recently, had the opportunity to study this painting in detail and have realized how limitless its appeal is as it refuses to give itself up even after hours of voracious looking. Its subject is self-referential, and it contains many topics that recur in the artist's oeuvre. For these reasons I propose this work as an entrance into this presentation of Balthus's painterly world.

1. This essay was written with the generous support of the Dutch Royal Academy of Arts and Sciences. I owe the staff of the Clark Art Institute, as well as the Institute itself, the warmest gratitude for their hospitality and help during the drafting of this text.

The predominant color is a greenish yellow that summons a sense of antiquity. The tone of old walls intimates the ambition to paint for eternity, or at least, for a long duration of time. The color is not uniform; its nuances travel across the entire surface. This makes the surface vibrant even if the color scheme is close to monochromatic. The background walls and floor divide the space with indirect interior light that appears to come through the windows and has a gentle impact. Accents of light give the scene life as, for example, on the wooden dowels of the simple chair on which the girl leans, and on the other chair, quite different in style, standing to the left, on which elements of fabric, perhaps the girl's outdoor clothes, are casually flung.

Color is also the main tool of composition. Different tones of yellow place enlivening accents on the far left, in the bright squares on the box, used to mark the artist's signature. And a fuller, golden yellow on the far right, on the outside of the little stepladder, offsets both the glowing orange of the inside of one of its vertical supports, and the brighter, light-touched front of both supports, as well as the top. The greenish side of things, meanwhile, also traverses the entire field. Its dominant portion appears on the upper left of the wall, descending to the chair whose curved legs contrast with the browner straight chair in the center, and onto the girl's skirt. None of these surfaces are evenly green; the color is modulated according to shape, light, and volume. The skirt, for example, is brighter or darker according to the way the girl's body fills the wide garment, which is otherwise rather shapeless. The far right picks up the accent in the milk pail. Here, the sheen on the metal is responsible for the modulation of color.

Such nuances of color as we see in this picture are indicative of the artist's deep commitment to the craft of painting. His entire oeuvre could be considered from the perspective of color only, and in this sense, it could even be treated as abstract, disregarding the figures and the fantasies, the architectures and the landscapes, the furniture and the earthenware pots, the fruits and the fabrics. It is with color that Balthus creates all these contents. But not color alone. Texture is a great aid in giving color its vivacity. Some of the colors emerge from superimpositions of layers of paint and glaze. At times, the canvas comes through, and often the paint is made coarse by means of the addition of sand or other granular substances, as in the case of *Le Peintre et son modèle*. The rough surface harmonizes with the kind of colors, the mute, old-looking, cool colors that manage, with the help of soft light, to produce an ambiance much warmer than the palette would suggest.

Balthus and his niece Frédérique Tison at the Chateau de Chassy, 1956. Photo: Loomis Dean.

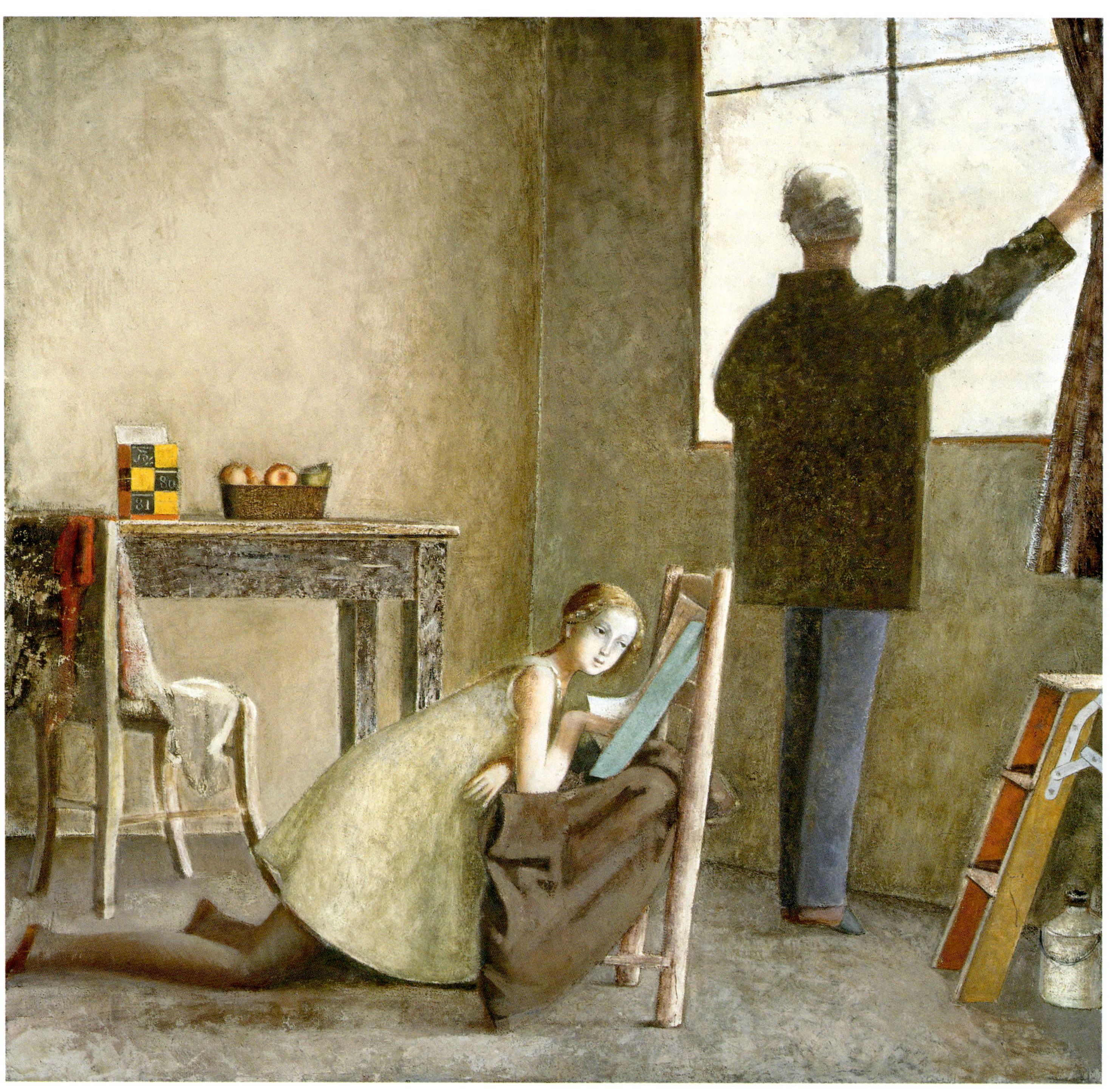

But this is not an abstract painting. Two figures populate the quiet scene, the standing painter and the leaning girl. Both are signature figures, the latter more famously than the former. The standing painter recurs throughout the long career of the artist, from the lone stroller in the 1929 *Les Quais (la berge près du pont Neuf)* [The Quays (The Riverside near the Pont Neuf), right] or the man holding a baguette in the 1952-1954 *Le Passage du Commerce Saint-André* (The Passage of the Commerce Saint-André, p. 12) to the man walking up the scene on the lower left corner in the 1960 *Cour de ferme à Chassy (Grand Paysage avec arbre)* [Farmyard at Chassy (Great Landscape with Tree), p. 13]. In all these cases the painter, or the man walking away, whom critics have tended to identify as the painter, is a highly simplified figure. Wearing blue trousers and a darker smock, here brown, he always looks like someone on his way to work. He is invariably shown from the back. Most characteristically, he lifts one of his heels. In the other paintings, this lifted heel indicates the movement of walking. Here, a different meaning suggests itself. The man is standing on his toes to reach the curtain he wishes to open, to let in the light. The heel alone gives the flat figure an aura of activity. It brings the scene to life, much in the way the color modulation brings the wall to vibrancy.

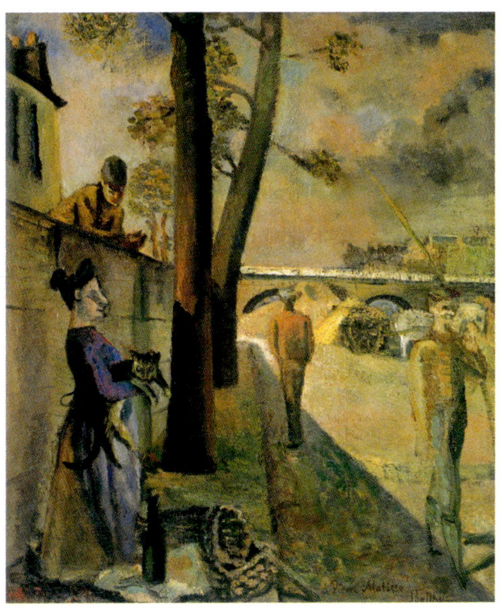

Le Peintre et son modèle, 1980-1981.
The Painter and His Model.
Casein and tempura on canvas, 226.5 × 230.5 cm.
Musée National d'Art Moderne, Centre Georges Pompidou, Paris.

Les Quais (la berge près du Pont Neuf), 1929.
The Quays (the riverside near the Pont Neuf).
Oil on canvas, 73 × 59.8 cm.
Private collection.

The other figure is a young girl. She seems to be reading, although several details make that assumption questionable. The cover of the paper positioned on the chair is colored in a bright green. This color contains more blue than the other shades of green and thus draws attention to itself. The brighter green also indicates that the paper consists of only one double sheet. Yet, while it is not a book, it doesn't seem to be a newspaper either. Nor is any writing or printing visible on its inside. Moreover, the girl's head, the centre where the light converges, is turned slightly to the viewer. Her eyes are focused neither on the paper nor directed to the viewer, which makes her look vague and dreamy. This, as well as her tender age, is a recurring feature of Balthus's figures of girls. Her slightly spread legs—another characteristic of Balthus's girls—make her pose a bit implausible, considering both the unlikely pose itself, as well as the somewhat strange shape of, in this case, her right hand.

These two figures are incarnations of the two main characters that occupy Balthus's figurative world. I mean this in two senses of the word "world": the real world in which he models his figures, if we are to believe he is a realist artist, and the art world, if we pay attention to the dual particularity of the window the figure of the painter is clearing for us. The window has a grid, and it is opaque. The grid divides it into four almost equal, square parts. This play with squares gains more importance if we realize that it mirrors the format of the canvas. Its opaqueness is also striking, and the paint that has been spilled over the wood, which divides the window into squares, draws additional attention to it. As opposed to other windows, as well as that legendary window-on-the-world that representational art is supposed to be, this window offers no view to the world outside, none of the landscapes the artist paints so often. And then, the painter makes us aware of the opaqueness by his sideways glance, not even pretending to look through the window.

The figure of the painter, then, comes with a programmatic statement against transparency; one that nods to abstract painting, which was the fashion of the day when the young Balthus was trying to make a name for himself, and being a figurative painter was not really the royal road to success. In the 1980s, this was no longer an issue. But the division between figurative and abstract, or representational and self-referential painting has never entirely disappeared. Making the figure of the painter appear to ponder about the meaningfulness,

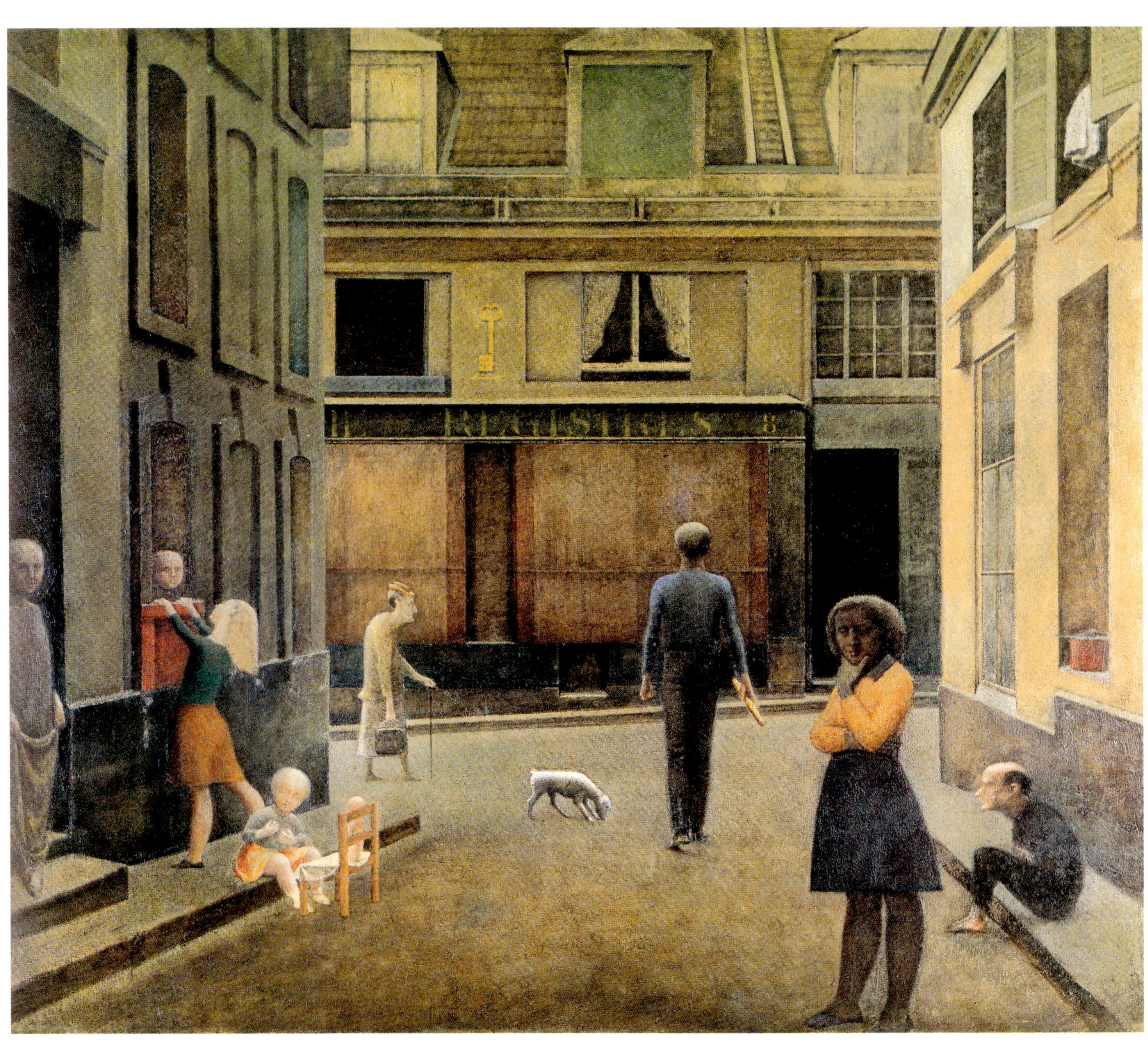

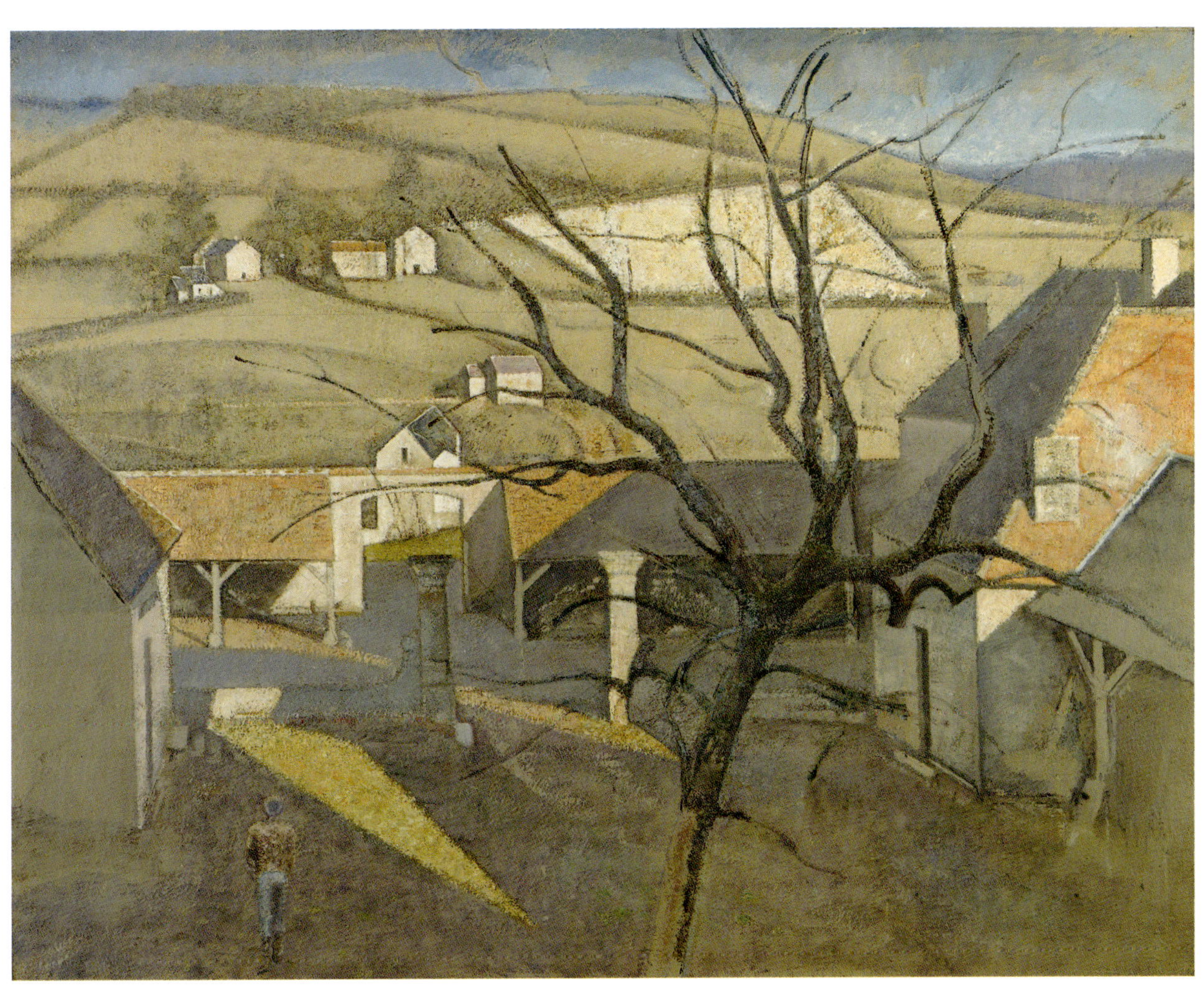

Passage du Commerce Saint-André, 1952-1954.
Passage of the Commerce Saint-André.
Oil on canvas, 294 × 330 cm.
Private collection.

Cour de ferme a Chassy (Grand paysage avec arbre), 1960.
Farmyard at Chassy (Great Landscape with Tree).
Oil on canvas, 130 × 162 cm.
Musée National d'Art Moderne, Centre Georges Pompidou, Paris.

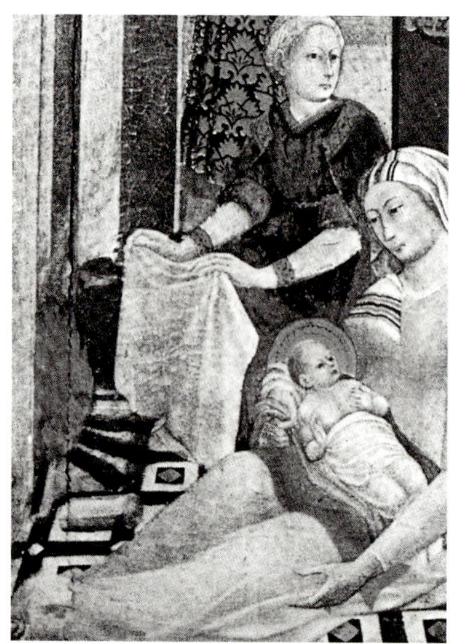

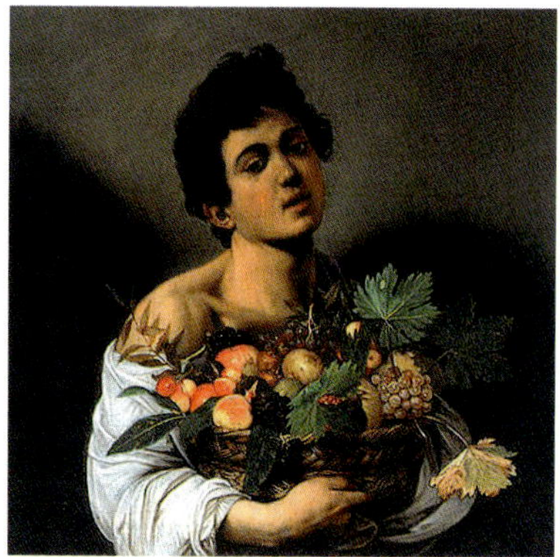

or the meaninglessness, of this binary opposition is, I submit, a pointed way of addressing painting itself in this work. Hence, the lifted heel indicating effort and movement comes to stand for the effort to overcome, and the move away from this binary opposition. If I consider this a programmatic work by a very ambitious artist, the figure of the painter, looking critically at the opaque canvas, standing on tiptoe, is reaching for the stars. Now we can see that the line we had automatically assumed to be the window frame, in fact does not cut through the wall but is superposed on it. Hence, it is a picture frame.

The figure of the girl is equally programmatic. The reputation of the artist as an erotic and even perverse painter who sometimes depicted adolescent girls in sexually inviting positions, is well known. In this painting, the girl we see is young indeed. At the same time, her hair, framing a face that could come from a Renaissance fresco and refer to Renaissance images, establishes a tension between different durations. The girl is simultaneously young—her age as a human being—and old—her shape and colors as pertaining to age-old art. The shape of the face and the hair that frames it are, indeed, quite like the midwife behind the Virgin (left, top) in the Sasetta's *Nativity*, which Jean Clair has evoked in the most convincing iconographic analysis of Balthus's work I know (2001).

This tension turns the girl, like the figure of the painter, into a programmatic figure. As such she makes a statement about the relation of painting to the past, the tradition within which, as the fresco-like color and surface already intimate, the artist seeks to insert his work. In terms of the eroticism of the girl figures, for which many people know and judge the artist's oeuvre, this reference also diverts or at least frames the issue of the erotic in art. From a personal obsession it becomes a much more widely practiced way of, as the painters would allege, honoring the beauty of creation. This is not to say that the issue is moot; I will have occasion to return to this in several later chapters. But in the face of this painting, it cannot be easily viewed as an explicit case of a male artist exploiting the young female body, as a somewhat cliché judgment would have it.

In addition to raising the young-old tension, the girl figure exhibits another concern. The girl is reading, but not really. In this (non-)activity she is also raising an aesthetic issue. This pose of reading is especially significant in the case of an artist who uses literary allusions in titles and subject matter [*La Toilette de Cathy* (p. 30), *Alice dans le miroir* (p. 21), *Les Beaux jours* (p. 93)] so as to evoke "the other" of the so-called sister arts, painting and literature, and then obeys the laws of neither quite properly. The girl is depicted in great detail, but nothing points to an ambition to depict her realistically. The ambiguity of her (not) reading, as I will argue, is also programmatic for Balthus's vision of the art of painting. It is part of the larger issue of narrative in painting. With the two figures' intense preoccupation with something invisible and the lack of interaction between them, together with the silent quality of the painting, we get a glimpse of other aesthetic themes that recur in the oeuvre. I would sum these up as "the mise-en-scène of the invisible".[2]

As if to enhance the issue of figuration as an intervention in the history of art, the painting contains some exquisite still-life elements. The basket of fruit, in which each apple and pear is endowed with its own individual existence, the texture of its own skin, the shades of its colors, the sheen or matte surface, performs that intimate integration of keen vision and masterly craft—in addition to other elective affinities to old masters such as Caravaggio and

Chardin (p. 14, bottom). Next to it, a checkered cardboard box, reiterating the grid pattern on the window, flaunts its mission of offsetting the basket of fruit. Round forms are juxtaposed to squares, subdued colors to bright ones. These still-life elements not only indicate one of the genres in which Balthus excelled. They are also programmatic of his fascinating and, perhaps, fascinated attention to the details of texture. The fabrics on each of the two chairs emulate renaissance drapery. The stepladder and pail on the right, along with the curtain, seem exercises in illusionism. The rough wood of the table has been captured so as to harmonize with the simple form of the carpentry.

Over the course of this exploration of Balthus's work I will return to this painting as a summation of the artistic program underlying the oeuvre. And if I chose a rather late work as my anchor, this is because such a choice undercuts some tendencies in art criticism I prefer to bracket for this study. In this I follow the artist's own wish. The most frequently quoted line pronounced by the artist is this: "Balthus is a painter of whom nothing is known. Now, let's look at the paintings". The point is well taken. Whether or not he abided by his own rule is immaterial; later in life he did yield to the pressure to give interviews. However, the excerpts printed in this book clearly demonstrate his reluctance to do so. He diverts attention from the questions, abducts them into different directions, mystifies or refuses to answer, asking his own questions instead. This seems quite fitting to me. If we are interested in Balthus, it is in his paintings. Even if all those critics who quote the famous line—and I have read little scholarship about the artist where it is not quoted—proceed to disobey its injunction and probe the enigmatic myths he has spun himself around his biography, I contend that the best way to come up with a new vision of this artist is to finally leave his life to himself and look at his paintings.[3]

In addition to the constant, ritualized references to artists' life stories and anecdotes, much writing on art, even if not biographically inclined, follows the chronological "development" of artists and divides their career in stages or "periods". "Early works", "mature works", "late works" are terms only too well known in art writing. They follow a vision of life in terms of development, and in this respect contain qualifications I do not wish to endorse. I contend that especially in the case of Balthus, such implicit qualification would be even more inappropriate than for most, given that he was a premature "Wunderkind" and painted recognized masterpieces well into his very old age. His work spans most of the twentieth century. Hence, while there is, naturally, a distinction to be made between the very touching *Mitsou* drawings (p. 142) made when he was eight to ten and published at twelve, and some of the very last few paintings do seem to give the viewer pause compared to all the rest, the larger bulk of the oeuvre does not gain from a mechanical development narrative. And, just in practical terms, so many writings following the chronological format have been published on Balthus that adding another one would be the most futile of repetitions.[4]

Nor can I appeal to the genre-based divisions usually applicable, and again, for reasons pertaining to the works themselves. Balthus has painted landscapes and still lives, portraits and scenes, but more often, he has painted works that contain elements of all these genres. Moreover, the genres are very unevenly distributed among his works, even if we disregard, as I shall do in this text, the chronological order in which he has made them. Finally and most importantly, I feel that the artist has deliberately pitted genres against one another. These negative arguments leave me with the task of choosing an approach that will contribute to understanding the pictures.

Sassetta,
detail of *Naitivity of the Virgin*,
1432-1436.
Collegiata, Asciano.

Caravaggio,
Boy with a Basket of Fruit,
ca. 1593.
Oil on canvas, 70 x 67 cm.
Galleria Borghese, Rome.

2. Both the window as grid and the girl's failure to read are discussed by Garrett Stewart (2003). He develops these themes further in his book on the depiction of reading in Western art (2006).

3. The line is so frequently quoted that it makes no sense to even cite sources for it. The biography by Nicholas Fox Weber quotes it several times (1999). And while it seems almost masochistic to allege such a stark, forbidding vision against biography in the genre of the biography, in the end the author has obeyed at least the second sentence, if not the first. Paradoxically, of all critical writings on the artist, this alleged biography offers the best collection of detailed readings of the paintings. I will freely profit from Weber's thoughtful analyses, referencing them in brackets in the text, even if, here and there, I will also feel compelled to diverge.

4. Again, it is almost pointless to cite examples. Let me just allege one of the very accessible books, the one by Claude Roy (1996). While this book does look at the paintings, and does so with a keen and sensitive eye, the division of the chapters follows the "periods" of the artist's career as well as the artist's statements. In the case of Balthus, these periods tend to coincide with his places of dwelling.

La Phalène, 1959-1960.
The Moth.
Casein and tempura on canvas,
162 × 130 cm.
Musée National d'Art Moderne,
Centre Georges Pompidou, Paris.

Although Balthus has painted slowly and his oeuvre is not exceedingly voluminous, there is little unity in it, even in mode of painting. His painting goes by the label of realism, and although there are many ways in which realism can be achieved, including those that establish tensions between it and its alleged counterpart, characterizing Balthus as a realist is both undeniably sensible and utterly uninformative. This paradox of realism manifests itself also when a few oeuvres combine a realistic mode of painting with a more fanciful, imaginative, fictitious approach to reality. He painted stories and poems, lyrical outbursts and stark tragedies, dramas and descriptions. Note that in the case of this artist, the literary genre labels seem easier to handle than any of the standard art-historical genre labels.

Instead of following the formats that have amply been used to present Balthus's work, I will proceed in waves, or circles. In the same vein as my beginning, I will present artistic issues through paintings that I consider exemplary of them. These works, and the ideas they trigger, will return in ever-wider circles of ripples. The general focus is on the eerie sense of very real and very unreal that the paintings emanate. We have already seen this in the depiction of the girl in *Le Peintre et son modèle*. I consider this ambiguous relationship to "reality" the heart of Balthus's work. It both invites viewers in and holds them at bay at the same time. We get access to a world of his own, but without clearly being told what there is to see, think and feel about whatever we think we are seeing. Thus, the works labor against assumptions of representation and appropriation.

The primary means of this labor—figuration—is indispensable for the effect. Although figurativity is supposedly the royal road to realism, in Balthus's case it is not at all. I argue that, instead, the paintings draw the viewer into a world we know not to exist. This canny fictionality makes allegations of erotic visual appropriation, in any general sense, naïve and prudishly censoring. It also throws the viewer inclined to such responses back to him- or herself. Moreover, reducing Balthus's work to the painting of nude adolescent girls is ignoring his many works that are not in the least focused on this theme but on other subjects, equally fictional, or at least, equally dependent on one's vision.

I will explore this paradox in the chapters to follow. In the first three chapters I will examine the means, the techniques the artist uses to produce his make-believe pictures. In chapters four, five and six I will analyze the visible world of the images. Finally, the invisible world of everything that cannot be represented will become, if not visible, at least imaginable. The tension between visibility and invisibility is, I contend, what Balthus sought to stage with his elaborate painting technique, composition, and poses.

Out of three aspects of this technique—color, space, and figuration—the first two counter the third. During his tenure as director of the Villa Medici in Rome, Balthus has put his sense of color, the theme of the first chapter, to the use of restoration of the villa (1961-1975). Perhaps because of his early interest in Piero della Francesca and other Italian Renaissance painters, he was able to assess the effect of color on chalk walls. In his paintings, including those from long before the Rome period, colors were used intensely, materially, and substantially. In the painting that I took as my starting point, this was obvious in the yellows and greens, with the few accents of red and orange, and, less conspicuously, in the applications of blue and a different shade of green. The texture with which the colors of the paintings are applied is more sculptural than colorist alone.

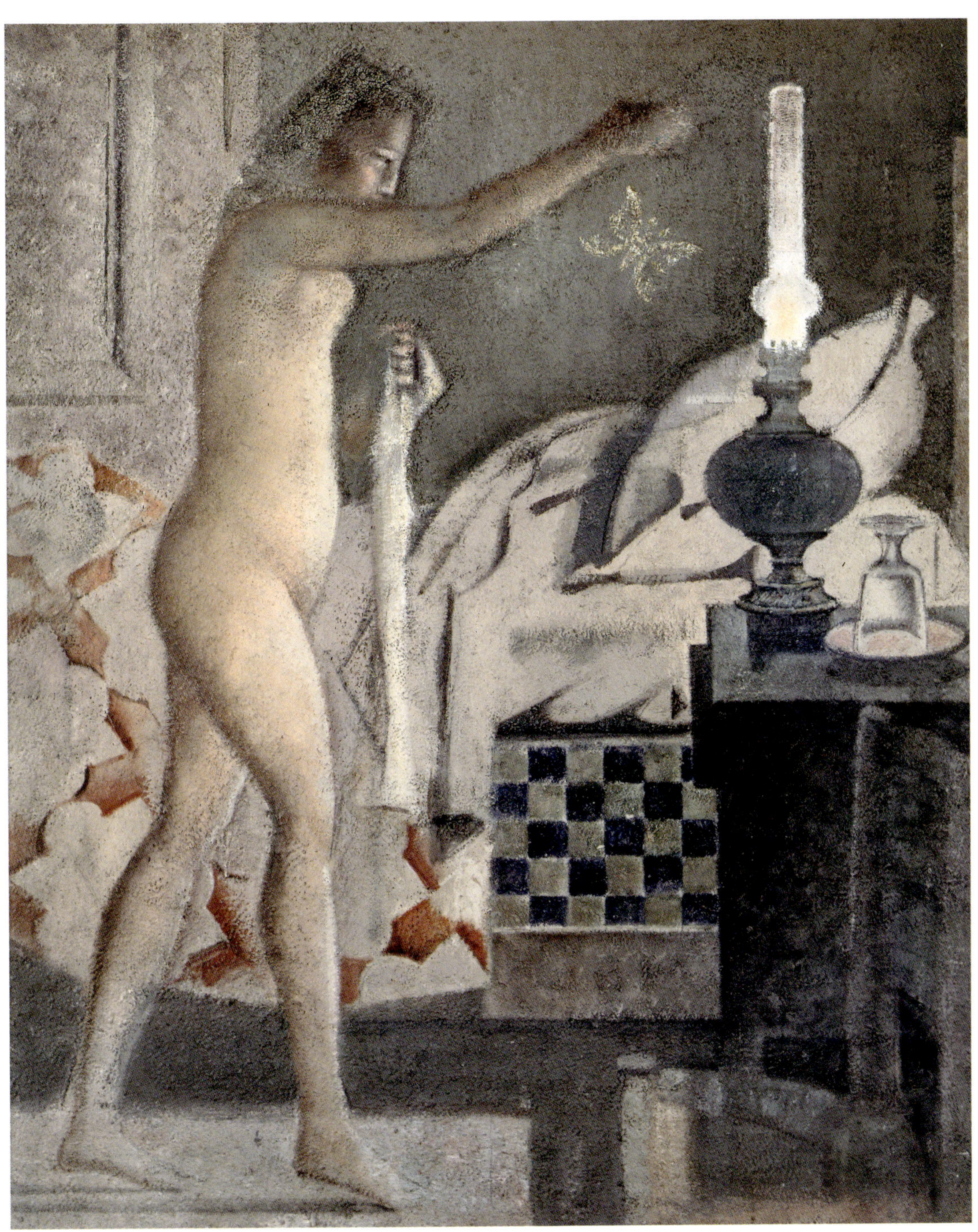

5. "Diegetic" is a term in narrative theory derived from diegesis, or narrative content. In antiquity, diegesis was the opposite of mimesis, a term which, usually mistranslated as "imitation", is more adequately understood as "representation". I use the term "diegetic" for narrative content here to acknowledge narrative expectation without claiming reality status for narrative content. This distinction is crucial for Balthus's work. For all narratological terms, see Bal (1997).

La Rue, 1933.
The Street.
Oil on canvas, 195 x 240 cm.
The Museum of Modern Art, New York. James Thrall Soby Bequest.

Color as substance will be, therefore, the first issue to be studied in this book. In the work *La Phalène* (The Moth, p. 17) for example, the rough surface, no stranger to his once-contemporary Fautrier, is applied in cool and subdued colors, with only small accents of more striking tints. But while the combination of pastel hues is integrated extremely carefully, the semi-transparency of the moth itself, the focus of the scene, leaves the narrative, "diegetic" existence of the insect ambiguous. The animal is painted on a surface so rough that it seems both de-realized and emphatically presented as painted only, on a flat surface. That flatness connects this art with that of his contemporary abstractionists, whose work he scorned and deliberately defied.[5]

In chapter two I analyze Balthus's approaches to space. The spaces Balthus puts before us are willful distortions of the reality we would see when looking at the spaces he depicts. In *Le Peintre et son modèle* we have already seen how the opaqueness of the window makes it impossible to see the natural extension of the space into the outside world. But the room in which the scene is set also seems distorted. The wide angle of the corner makes the room shallow, so that the combination of the table and chair on the left on the one hand, and the chair and girl in the middle on the other, seems implausible. The left-hand wall is extended farther than a right angle would allow, while the other wall, against which the painter stands, should normally come forward more at the right hand side. This distortion in the direction of shallowness is more than a way to clear space for the elements of the scene—although it is also that. It is a pointed act, almost an activism, against the illusory depth of linear perspective. In this sense, it alerts us to the fact that Balthus's painterly decisions are not easily dismissed as either arbitrary or simply technical procedures of realism. On the contrary; they often counter the very realism he first sets out to present.

This is especially obvious in his landscapes. But also in the still lives, the rooms, and the other settings of scenes, space is not to be considered real at all. The effect of de-reality is achieved partly through contrived cropping, partly through the insertion of figures (or their absence where one would expect them), partly through the interaction between figures and space.
The search for infinity in mighty landscapes, for example, is countered by means of flatness, cropping, the deletion of horizons, the use of unexpected formats, and the representation of rocks as rows of flat sheets. These come in addition to the relationship to Chinese landscapes.

In light of these two manners—substantial colors and distorted, flattened spaces—in which the artist deliberately de-realizes the worlds he depicts, the obstinate figurativity of his works becomes an act of defiance. In chapter three I therefore look at the imaginative worlds staged in the scenes. The focus is on the utter lack of communication between figures. We have already seen this in *Le Peintre et son modèle*. Not only is the painter turning his back to the model, while she, in turn, looks away from him. Moreover, each figure is emphatically engrossed in a contemplative activity that leaves no space for the other—even in thought. This is what undermines any attempt to read these pictures realistically in a simple way. Even a cityscape, such as *La Rue* (The Street, p. 19) turns into a somber fairy tale for adults prone to philosophize about the modern world. Figures of stiff body poses refuse to interact with one another. No meeting takes place on the street.

One could surmise that the interior of rooms is better suited for encounters. But even in the scenes set there, communication between figures is studiously avoided. In *Le Peintre et son modèle* the painter turns his back to the girl, ostensibly to perform the simple—though

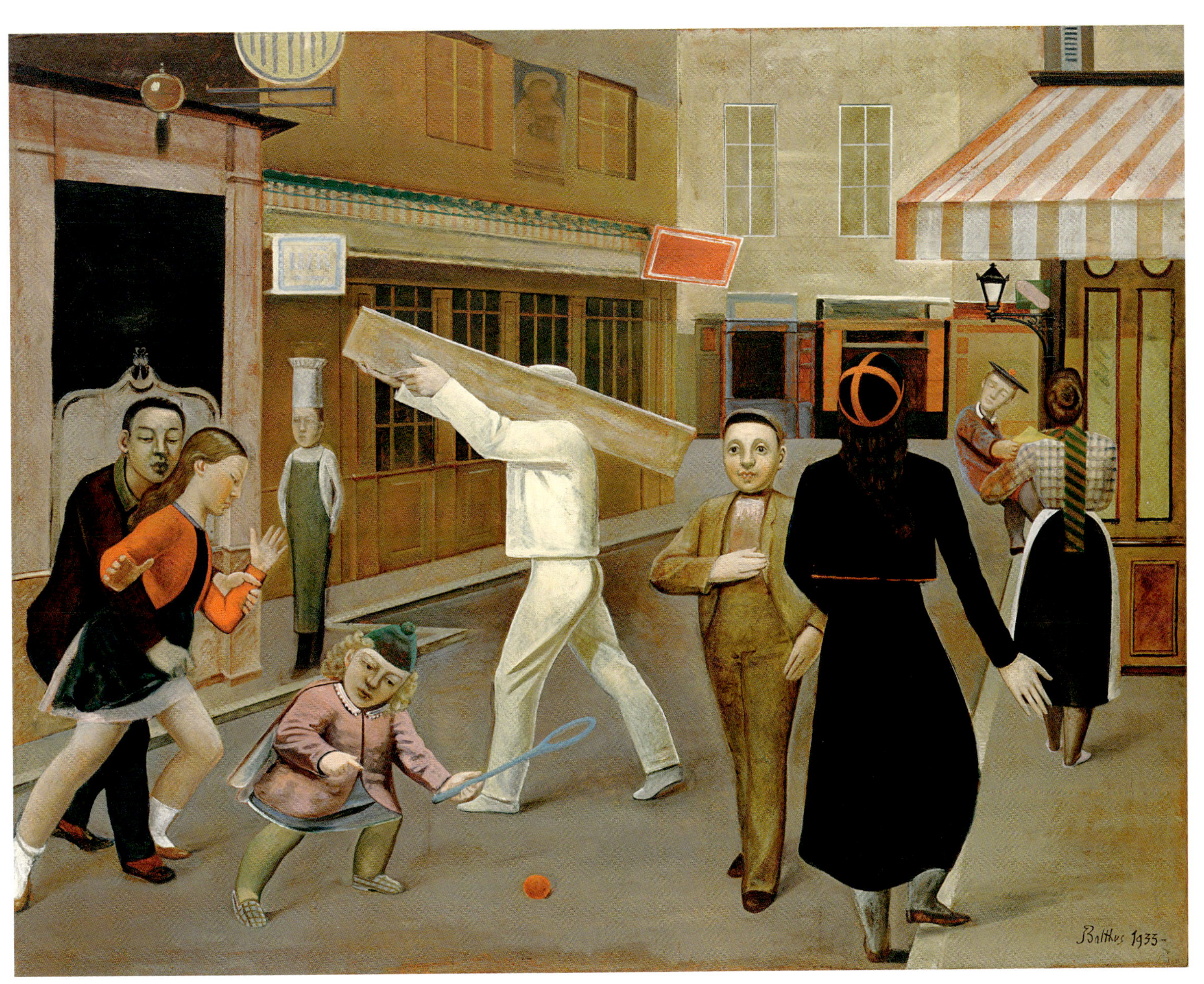
Balthus 1933-

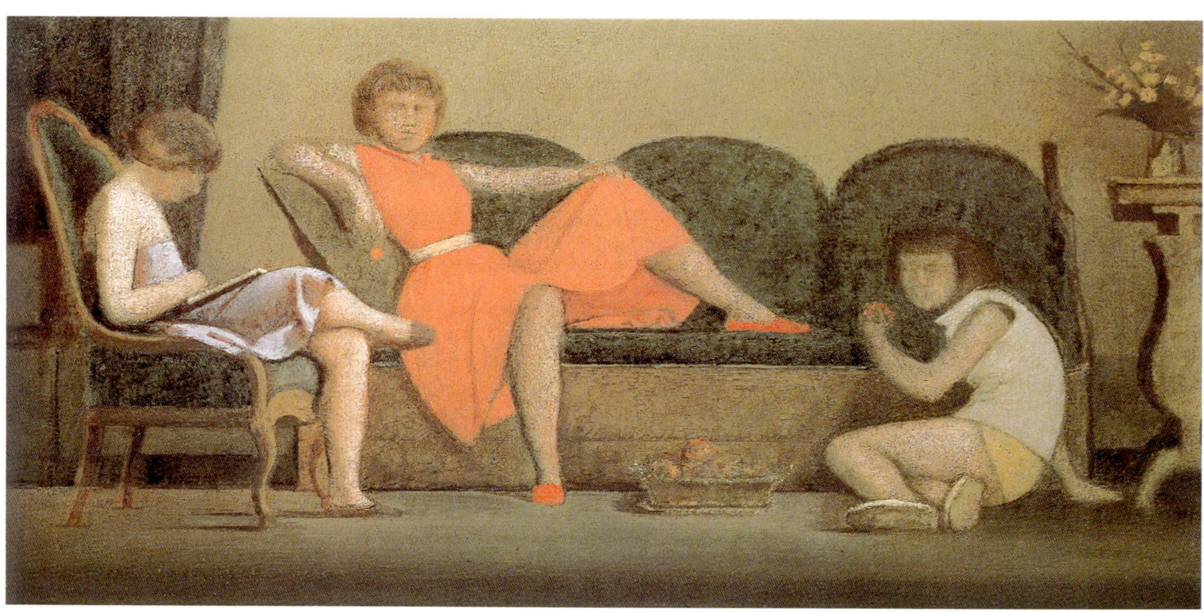

Les Trois sœurs (Sylvia, Marie-Pierre et Béatrice Colle), 1954-1195.
The Three Sisters.
Oil on canvas, 130 × 196 cm.
Private collection.

Alice dans le mirroir, 1933.
Alice in the Mirror.
Oil on canvas, 162 × 112 cm.
Musée National d'Art Moderne, Centre Georges Pompidou, Paris.

consequential—action of opening the curtain to let in the light, but as I have suggested, more likely to address an issue of representation in its opposition to abstraction. In *Les Trois sœurs* (The Three Sisters, above) each of the three protagonists is immersed in her own activity. No contact happens.

In the subsequent chapters, the outcome of the inquiry into Balthus's techniques is brought to bear on the visible world offered to the eye. I contend that we never quite get to see what we think is, or must be represented and in this sense we don't get access to the diegetic world. Balthus achieves this in two ways, discussed in chapter four and five. In chapter four I will show how, time and again, the usual deployment of genre categories as a mode of understanding visual images goes awry. As I mentioned above, Balthus has worked in many of the classical genres, such as landscape, still life, portraiture, the nude, history painting or, in this case, its domestic version, which I simply call scenes. For Balthus, genre labels are deceptive. Invariably, using them to understand a painting makes a crucial aspect of the work near-invisible. Thus, Balthus seems to tease his viewers with a strategy of concealment. Landscapes contain figures that change the view offered to the viewer of the painting. Scenes are emphatically un-dramatic; they foreground neither movement nor events, but stillness and the total lack of events. Nothing ever happens. In *Le Peintre et son modèle* the catalogue of genres appears to be fully deployed in order to stop them all in their tracks, while the total blockage of landscape where we would expect it calls forth that genre in its very invisibility.

The second lack of access to the diegetic world that is so teasingly put forward, is foregrounded in the range of traditional pictorial motives such as the mirror, the window, glass objects, i.e. objects that stand for transparency and hence can also be deployed to signify the lack of it. In chapter five I will describe how here, too, Balthus refuses to comply with the traditions he also venerates and emulates. Mirrors, in his work, are instruments

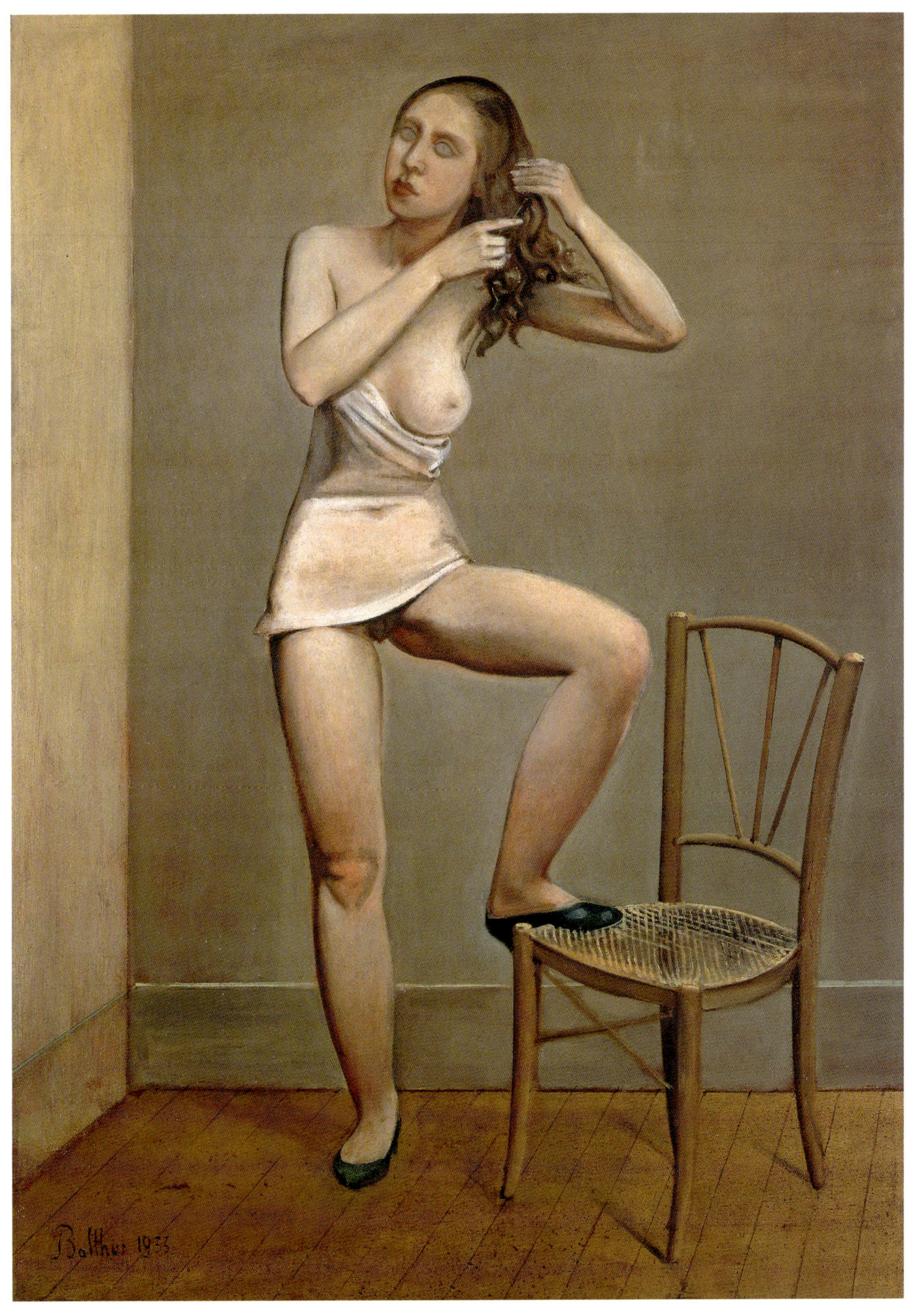
Balthus 1933

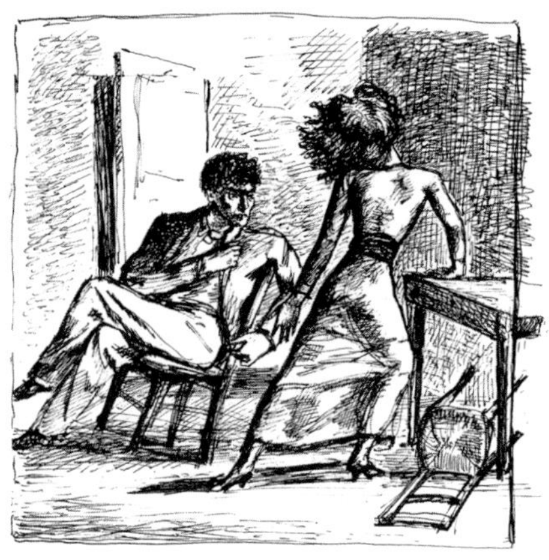

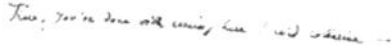

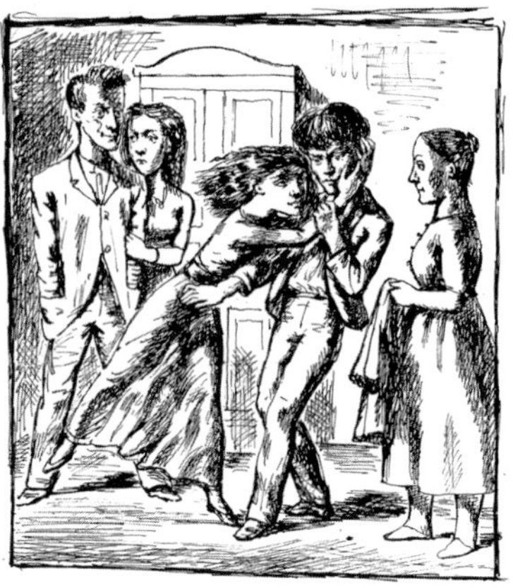

Je vous refuserai à l'avenir l'accès de cette maison, 1933-1935.
There you've done with coming here! cried Catherine.
Ink on paper, 35 × 26.5 cm.
Legacy Alexina Duchamp.

Tu n'avais qu'à ne pas me toucher, 1933-1935.
You needn't have touched me.
Ink on paper, 35 × 26.5 cm.
Legacy Alexina Duchamp.

Grande composition au corbeau, 1983-1986.
Grand Composition with Raven.
Oil on canvas, 200 × 130 cm.
Private collection.

neither of vanity nor of self-reflection. Instead, like the window in *Le Peintre et son modèle*, they partly block our view of the scene, in those cases where we do not see the reflection, so that the act of looking in the mirror becomes futile. Or, they block our view entirely, so that only the reflection is visible. This is why in *Alice dans le miroir* (meaning Alice in the mirror; not Alice au miroir, or at the mirror!) the mirrored young woman, like her namesake, is no longer of our world (p. 21). The play with mirrors raises the question of the locus of desire—a question never answered unambiguously.

As a result, the dramaturgy of the paintings is always contrived. This is especially the case with the ostensibly erotic subjects. Two features characterize these. One is the stillness, the utter lack of movement I just mentioned. Rather than snapshots, the images offer movie stills. The second feature is the untenable, physically impossible poses. The iconography of unreality is consistent throughout Balthus's long career; it is already in place in the early drawings after *Wuthering Heights* (above).

But if all Balthus's skill, imagination, and visual sophistication are deployed to push the viewer out of an assumed represented world, what is there to see instead? I contend in chapter six that Balthus's work, while obsessed with visual depiction, is primarily a long experiment with invisibility, or rather, other-visibility. His project is to depict what defeats depiction, to represent what is only vaguely present as an intuition, a feeling, a fleeting emotion; a fantasy. Dreams are the most obvious instance of the visuality of the invisible. As Freud has elaborated theoretically but we all know experientially from our own dreams, the starkly visual nature of dreams does not make them any easier to grasp. They are narrative (they refuse to be still), they are incoherent, or "other-coherent" (they are enigmas, or rebuses) and they are insensitive to censorship. The unreality of the depictions, in spite of the realist technique and the figurative nature of the images, glosses all scenes with a sense of distance from ordinary presence.

But dreams can be nightmares, and in Balthus's work, in spite of the erotically displayed adolescent girls, there is not much happiness in the dreams. And if there is, the shadow of a melancholic underside remains visible. The predominant feeling is a sense of estrangement.

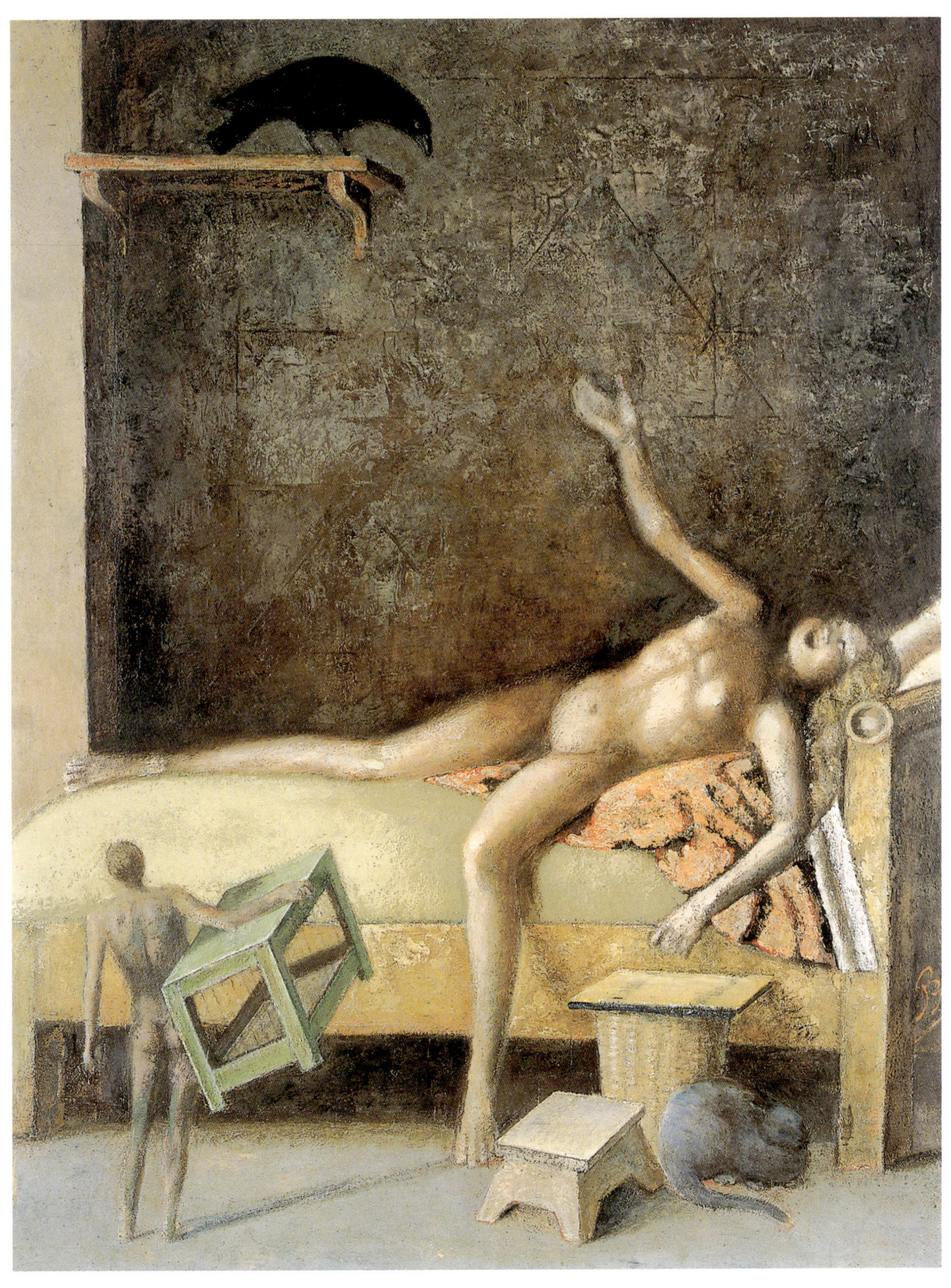

Sensations of what has been called, in three very different translations, das Unheimliche, the Uncanny, and l'inquiétante étrangeté, will be taken to lie at the heart of many of Balthus's paintings. On the condition, though, that these three phrases of the languages in which Balthus was fluent, remain present and resonate with one another. *Grande composition au corbeau* (Grand Composition with Raven, p. 23) from which we cannot eliminate the shadow of Edgar Allan Poe, stands for the literary imagination in the artist' work. Even the most fairy-tale inspired scenes foreground the less-than-happy sense of not-belonging that infuses this corpus of images. Through a variety of disparities and mismatches, the art shrouds the magic of childhood so often invoked in relation to art.

It is tempting to seek an explanation for such a feeling in the artist's life history—of which "nothing is known". For example, some have attempted to see in this uncanniness of the paintings the influence of the harrowing experiences of World War II. Yet, nowhere in his work is there a representation of events related to that war. Still, the war may offer an excellent entrance into the relationship between fiction and reality as Balthus has it. I speculate that the consistent effort to de-realize the visible world and to clear away its primary mode of reading—realism—has made it impossible to envision any form of representation of such suffering. At the same time, precisely because this effort was so consistent, the challenge of dealing with a world of anxiety and fear was not so strange to this artist.

I will use this paradox to meet the challenge of history in the face of painting. In the deliberately speculative chapter seven, I will look at some landscapes and scenes that may or may not, depending on the beholder, harbor and repress such anxiety. Seen in this way, we can consider the possibility that partly in acknowledgment of, partly in a hoped-for compensation for, the atrocities happening on a daily basis, landscapes such as *Paysage de Champrovent* (Landscape of Champrovent, p. 25) embody the double exposure to a land in suspension between erupting violence and peaceful but always precarious refuge.

Finally, it is in this context of fantasy that I consider the issue of the adolescent girls, so off-putting to many and the object of censoring ambivalence for others. My claim is that the work of Balthus is not perverse in the ordinary sense in which scenes of pornography often are. What is perverse is not the scenes, the vulnerability, the immanent violence, or the victimization of some of the figures. What constitutes the perversion of these dream worlds and nightmares is, instead, the consistent refusal to accept and endorse the categories our culture has adopted to reassure us concerning the possibility of perversion. The "polymorphous perversion" of the infant according to Freud is a more suitable model than the fear of pornography that is so frequently deployed to dismiss allegedly erotic art. Balthus's one-time close friend Antonin Artaud—like him, an opponent of surrealism's strategies to counter stereotypes of gender and sexuality—has amply written about the need to liberate Western culture of its Oedipal obsessions. It is in line with this view that I seek to characterize Balthus's images, including the ones that, at first sight, are the most disturbing.[6]

This book will show, therefore, images made by this artist in a combination and an order made by their critic. The images are ordered according to the ever-wider circle I cast around key issues in the art of Balthus. This may seem unusual for a monograph, hence, a bit disconcerting. But it is consistent with how we see art. Rarely are we able to follow the

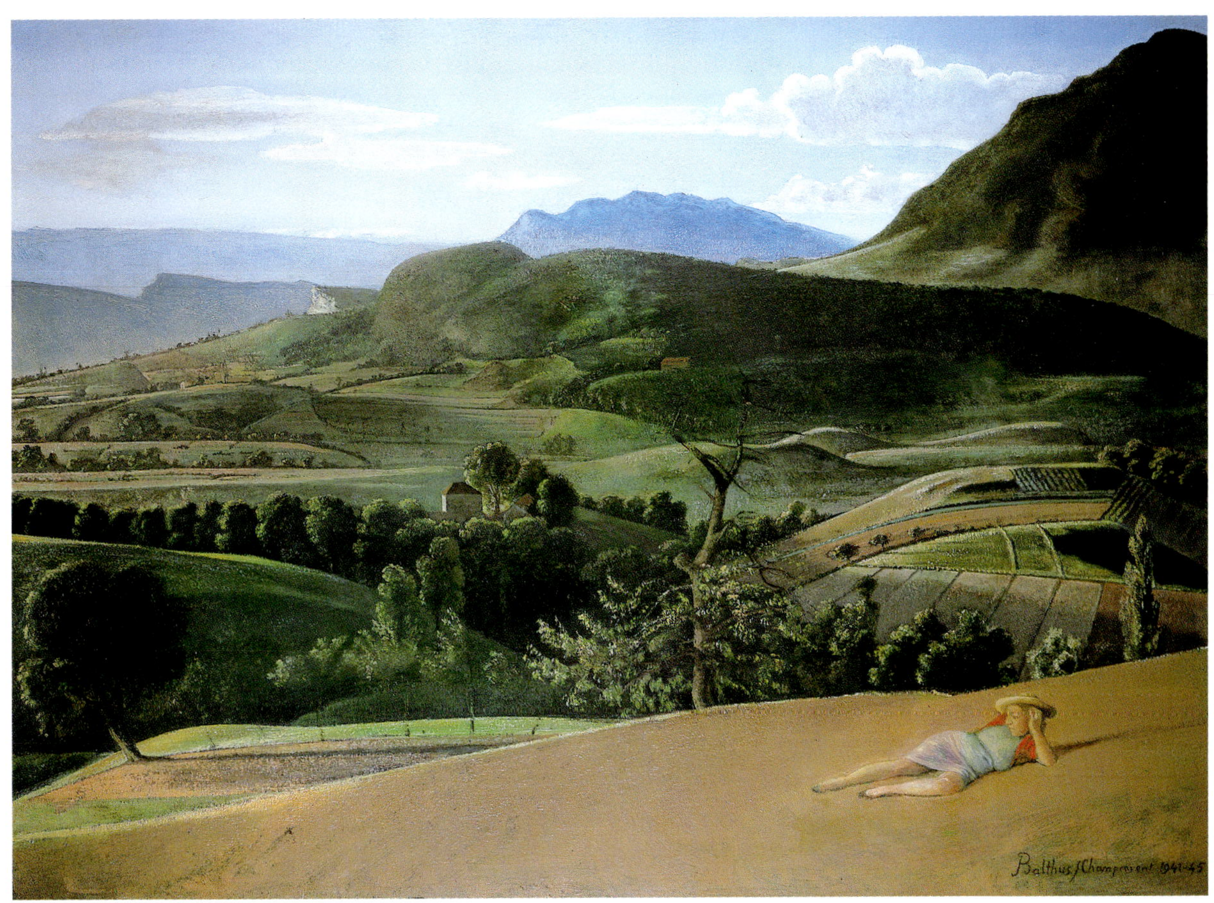

Paysage de Champrovent, 1941-1943.
Landscape of Champrovent.
Oil on canvas, 96 × 130 cm.
Private collection.

itinerary of an artist, not because we cannot reconstruct the chronology of their making—we can do that all too easily!—but because we don't have access to the person's mind. And if modern psychology is right, neither does the artist himself. Instead of speculating why he made the images he made, what they tell us about his personal obsessions, I prefer to speculate on what these images can mean to the very diverse people who see them in different places, or when browsing a book, such as this one.[7]

6. Artaud wrote several articles on Balthus, reprinted later (1983a, b and c). These are worth reading, not in spite of but also because of the increasing mental destabilization of this author.

7. In order to facilitate reading, all note call numbers are put at the end of the paragraphs in which the annotated term or name occurs.

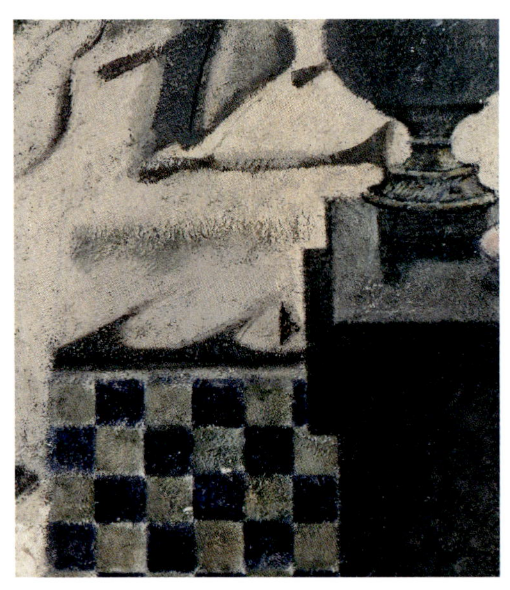

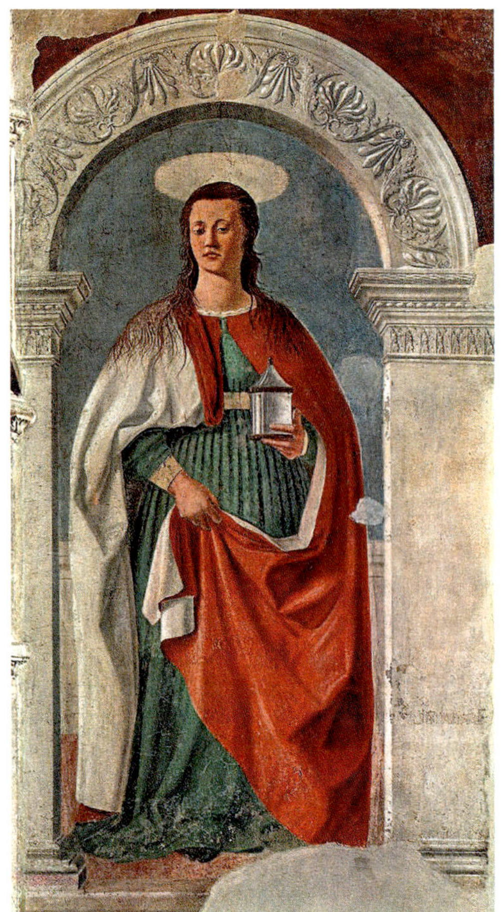

1. Color, the Stuff of Painting

I began the discussion of *Le Peintre et son modèle* (p. 10) with an analysis of the colors as tools of composition. As I went in search of the paintings, I have become entirely riveted by the artist's use of color: almost minimalist, monochromatic, and mostly cool, with very few main colors, all subtle and subdued on the one hand, with only very few accents to harmonize the painting and bring it to life, on the other. And yet the colors are vibrant, as if in movement. They make the surface alive, and diverse, as I have already suggested for the work known as *La Phalène* (p. 17).

The colors of this work are quiet, pastel but not at all sweet; reminiscent of old frescoes rather than of watercolors. The red pattern on the blanket verges on orange; the grayish blue in the checkered pattern on the support of the bed alternates with an off-white going toward a very pale green. The lamp stand is more gray than blue. The wall in the background is of the same gray with a nuance of blue as is the top of the bed stand at the lower right near the picture plane. Sheets are not white but off-white, beige almost. The closest the painting comes to white is in the light in the glass top of the oil lamp. The flame is not orange but yellow. And the skin tones of the nude figure are beige with outlines in reddish brown.

Most critical commentaries fill in the narrative content of the scene. The woman is allegedly trying to capture the moth, perhaps protecting it from burning in the flames to which it is flying. But what does this painting look like if, in agreement with the most recent arrangement in the Centre Pompidou, we put it in a section of semi-abstract, "rough" painting, along with, for example, Fautrier? Let us first look at that primary figure of the narrative, the butterfly after which the painting is titled. This figure deserves such privileged treatment because it is very different from the other figurative elements. It is more ornate and detailed in its figuration than the volumes and planes that surround it. It is slightly brighter in color. And most importantly, it barely touches the surface on which it is affixed either temporarily (as a narrative element), or permanently (as an ornament). The gray-blue wall remains visible through its delicate wings, even through its body. It could be a lone stencil of formerly decorated wallpaper, as if it had remained after all others have been removed (left, above).

Once we have noticed the slight application of paint of this figure, the entire painting becomes a study in precariously flat planes. The square, checkered side of the bed is just a board, entirely flat, without the slightest hint of the distortion attributable to distance. The rumpled bedding shows the virtuosity of a painter who excels in Renaissance drapery, with folds that, compared to baroque drapery, remain just darker patches, harmoniously distributed, not illusionistic at all (left, bottom and p. 27). The lamp lacks the sheen that would have given it volume. And the body of the young woman with its grainy outline, brighter in front, darker at the back, reminds us of Matisse's flat images that he radicalized in his cutouts. The most conspicuous indication of flatness is the arm. Stretched out in front, it ends in a stump that can barely pass for a hand. Even a painter whose notorious weakness is hands could have done better than this wooden stump if the idea was to suggest the woman is chasing the moth and seeking to capture it.[8]

In order to set the stage for a new approach to Balthus, one that will deal with the paintings' interaction with their viewers rather than with the latter's presuppositions, I now confront this description with a piece of critical discourse. Nicholas Fox Weber, author of the Balthus biography and in general, one of his finest critics, seems to start from an assumption of realism when he writes:

> The woman in *The Moth* has a body made real by the modeling of its flesh but artificial by its pose. The warm, bright glow of the oil lamp is convincing, and other details ring true. One superb, highly finished vignette of painting—the upside-down drinking glass—is fixed and immobile, the air trapped within it, the light established inside as well as out. But then, everything is thrown into disarray. A tempest-like force has blown into the normal world. The bedclothes are freshly rumpled. The woman and the moth disrupt the stasis (1999: 479; emphasis added).

The interest of this passage lies in the way the realism of the reading—"a body made real by the modeling of its flesh"—leads to an interpretation that, to me at least, seems entirely fanciful. The bedclothes are perhaps rumpled, but not freshly so, and the diagonals formed by the creases are too evenly disposed. Instead of "disarray" I see a harmonious composition of diagonal and square forms. This dialogue of shapes is foregrounded, for example, by the diamond pattern on the blanket and the square checkered bed next to it. Two planes, each with a pattern, contain the only colors that are not a variation of gray and beige. The author of the quoted description makes the image narrative by means of the sentence beginning with "But then". A storm, no less, disrupts a scene so still that the air inside a glass is almost visible.

I find the latter observation indicative of a keen eye for the details of a painting made up of just that: details, elements, of a series of flat surfaces. This critic knows how to look. Thus, while I find the leap to realism unconvincing and potentially damaging in the way it under-illuminates the predominant work with color, I also see how the painting, ever so subtly, solicits such a narrative mode of looking. It does so by means of unification. The surface, rough, grainy, sandy, that, in addition, emphasizes the importance of surface as such, also further unifies the painting in terms of flatness. This is the paradox of rough surfaces à la Fautrier, Masson, and other abstractionists with whom Balthus rubbed elbows during his formative years in Paris. While these techniques make the surface visible and even voluminous, they also enhance the fact that it remains just that: a surface. And in a surface no tempest blows.

Does this mean that Weber made it up? Not quite. Instead of criticizing him for bad looking—an accusation to which his descriptions throughout his book would give the lie—I suggest he is going along with the thrust of the painting, and thus unwittingly demonstrates what the point of the technique is. Even if, falling for it perhaps too quickly, he cannot see what caused it. Oblivious to the technique that produces flatness, he understands the purpose of it. True: by way of taking away the reality of the representation, the painter entices the viewer to step into the fantasy. But instead of using realism to that effect, the artist deploys the techniques of flatness to make the painting like images in illustrated books, demonstrating that adults are not immune to the images that feed children's imagination.

Jean Clair, another superb connoisseur of Balthus's work and co-editor of the *Catalogue raisonné* (Clair and Monnier, 2001), went in the same direction when he wrote in an older text, reprinted in the catalogue for the large retrospective at the Centre Pompidou in 1983-1984, that "the large butterfly is flittering around the lamp" (1983: 105). When we take another look at the semi-transparent image of the butterfly on the rough wall, its wings spread out to form yet another flat surface, we immediately see how wrong this is as an observation of the painting, yet how right as a vision of what we imagine we see when we step into the tale. My first proposal for an approach to Balthus, then, is to consider the

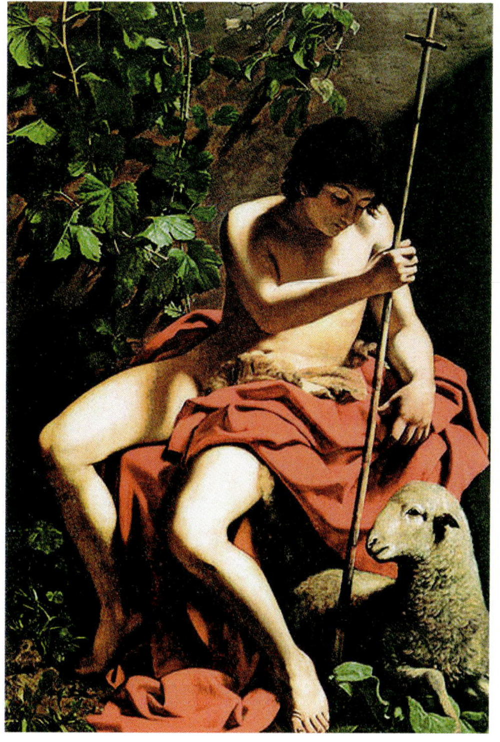

Detail of *La Phalène* (p. 16).

Renaissance folds:
Piero della Francesca,
Mary Magdalene.
Cathedral, Arezzo.

Baroque folds:
Caravaggio,
John the Baptist, c. 1598.
Oil on canvas, 169 × 112 cm.
Museo Tesoro Catedralicio,
Toledo.

8. On the specificity of baroque drapery, see Deleuze (1993). I have offered detailed analyses of these folds (1999). Balthus's folds remain rigorously on the more formal side of Renaissance folds. Nicholas Fox Weber's detailed analyses of the paintings unfailingly point out the weakness in the depiction of hands (1999).

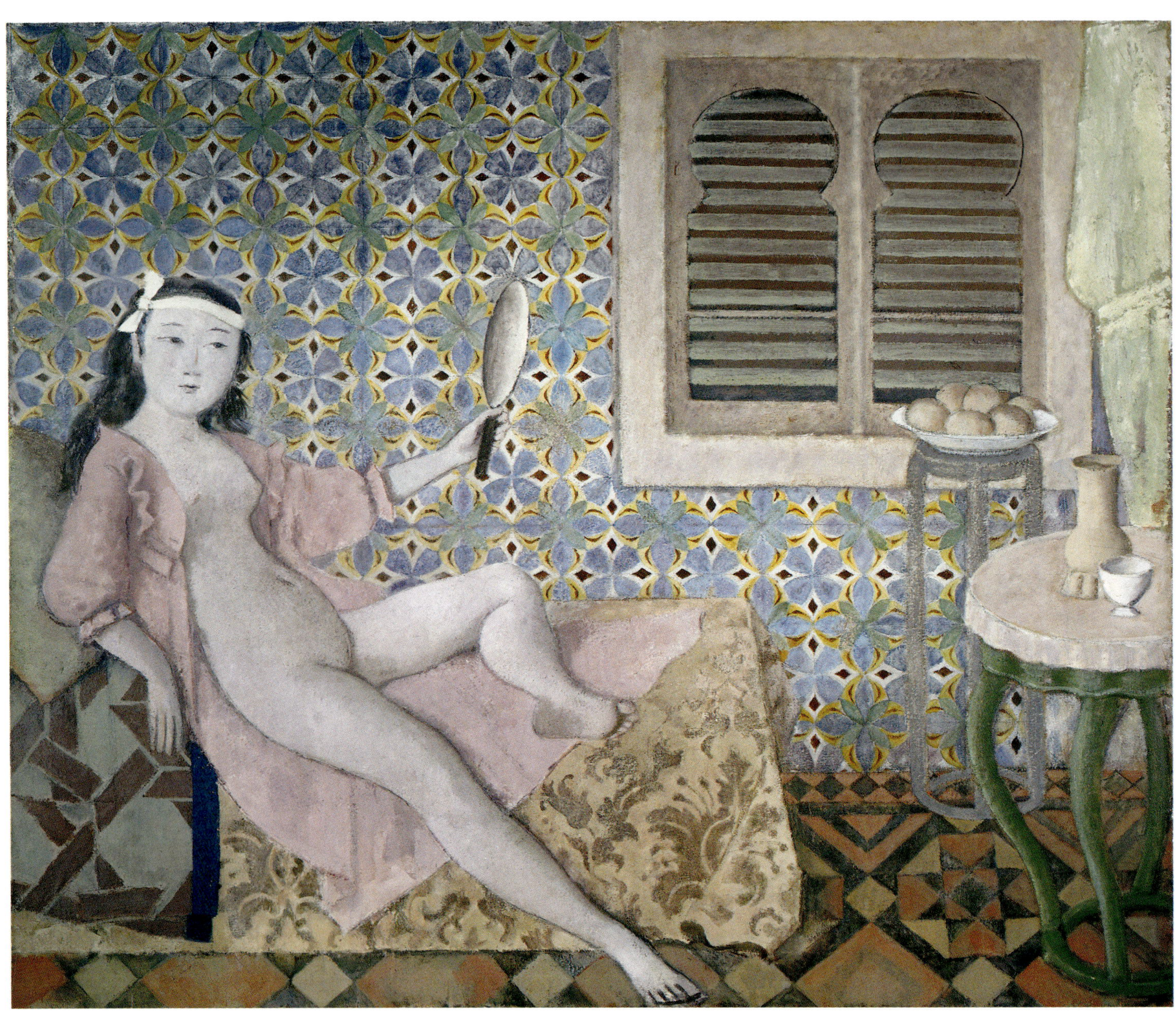

emphatic flatness produced by substantive color as a kind of mirror for a viewer—an opaque one. As we will see in chapter five, sometimes, mirrors also appear as motifs, and then they are opaque as well.

There are many other paintings in which color is the primary tool to achieve the plausibility of fantasies that fly in the face of reality. This is a first and most important qualification of Balthus's subject matter. Three works in the collection of the Centre Pompidou represent fantasies of the kind for which Balthus is famous: young women on display. In the museum's storage room, I saw two of these three juxtaposed in a way they will never be displayed in the gallery, and the juxtaposition made the work with color even more conspicuous. In addition, there is an opaque mirror that supplements the subtle play with color. Both are visible in the overall pink *La Chambre turque* (The Turkish Room, p. 28) and the yellow *La Toilette de Cathy* (Cathy Dressing, p. 30). Unlike the figurations, both colors are far from realistic. [The third painting I saw in conjunction with this topic was *Alice dans le miroir* (Alice in the Mirror, p. 21), which was exhibited in the gallery.][9]

The former nude was painted when Balthus lived with his Japanese lover and future wife at the Villa Medici where the Turkish Room of that building inspired this interesting combination of two exotic elements—Turkishness and Japaneseness—which cancel each other out. The Japanese sitter also fits in the oriental room, except that the room is not Japanese at all. The woman and the room show the disparity between two cliché forms of orientalism—the "Turkish" one from the eighteenth century and the "Japanese" one from the nineteenth. But for this discussion of color in its relationship to narrative, the fact that an overall color scheme of unlikely, sweet pastels sets the scene for a look into a totally opaque mirror is most to the point.

The latter work, *La Toilette de Cathy*, shows a nude next to what must be a round, framed mirror on a chest of drawers, visible on the far right side of the work. Except that that mirror is not even visible; it is just indicated at the edge of the painting. Instead, a fully clothed man sits, implausibly, in the middle of the bedroom where a pedestrian-looking servant is combing the hair of an entirely nude, evenly yellow female. And if this description seems unclear, this is exactly the trouble with this painting.

The title bears no secrets: this is Cathy, the object of erotic fascination of the wild romantic hero Heathcliff in Emily Brontë's novel *Wuthering Heights*. The artist, usually so reluctant to speak about himself, has never hidden his fascination with this novel, which he read as a young boy. Balthus had already drawn the scene depicted in this painting in a series of drawings he made to illustrate the first part of the novel. Here, however, the female figure is fully dressed, albeit in thin-enough fabric to show her nipples and legs (right and p. 22).

In the drawing, she is also a giant, compared to the man she dwarfs. Her legs are elegantly, although artificially crossed, with the man's legs turned the other way. Both turned toward the right side of the image, the heads of the two figures rhyme. What color does in the painting, line does in the drawing. The third figure, ostensibly the servant Nellie Dean—the implausible, pedestrian narrator of the story in the novel—has her head entirely turned, so that we only see her profile. Heathcliff appears to be arguing, as if to match the line quoted: "Why have you that silk frock on, then?". In the painting, the title is looser and so is the relationship to the story. Here, although the main lines of the composition are similar, things have changed dramatically. There is no longer an argument. Characteristically, no communication between the figures occurs.[10]

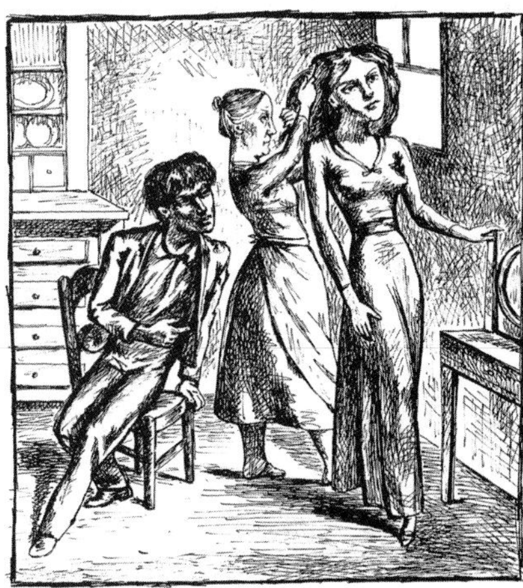

La Chambre turque, 1963-1966.
The Turkish Room.
Oil on canvas, 180 × 210 cm.
Musée National d'Art Moderne, Centre Georges Pompidou, Paris.

Alors, pourquoi as-tu cette robe de soie?, 1933-1935.
Why have you that silk frock on, then?
Indian ink and pencil,
39.8 × 31 cm.
Succession Alexina Duchamp.

9. I am deeply grateful to Catherine Duruel and Jean-Marc Gilletta and the staff of the MAMCGP storerooms for making this experience possible at a time that, for them, was hectic and difficult.

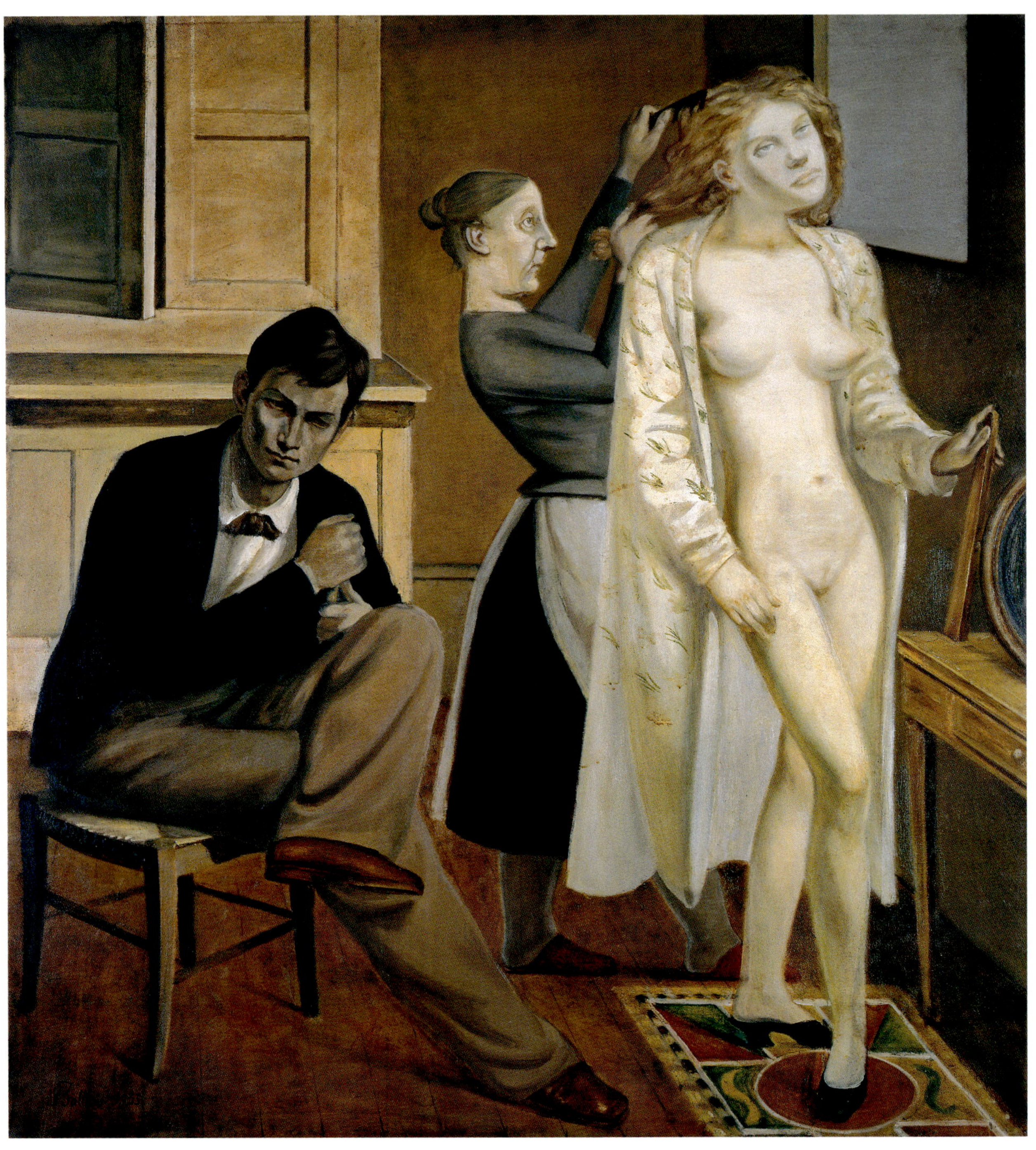

The man has the face of the artist. The dissatisfied mouth is shaped similarly to that in *Le Roi des chats* (The King of Cats, p. 32). There, it expresses pride, even arrogance. Here, just disgruntled frustration. Yet, it is the identical face. Even in the classical self-portrait of 1940, (p. 33) the same mouth refuses to open. Balthus represents himself consistently as brooding, not speaking, and even when the literary quotation of a direct discourse accompanies the work, such as for p. 29, the world is silent. In the 1940 self-portrait, the classical pose of the painter with a brush in front of a canvas—either already filled, or dauntingly empty—does not entirely follow the rules of the game. The artist is painting, holding a brush, but neither palette nor easel makes the act plausible. He is applying the brush on a dark grayish-blue wall, a darker version of the one in *La Phalène*. His claim to fame as an artist, this self-portrait seems to say, is color, not figuration; realism is not the first principle of this art, even if it is one of its tools.[11]

Heathcliff in *La Toilette de Cathy* still has the full cheeks of the artist on a photograph when he was eighteen (right). In spite of his adult and rather chic clothes, there is something boyish about him. His face is also colored in a sickly gray. Perhaps that boyishness matches the subject better than any other feature; and perhaps the color is pointing that meaning out for us. For, the nude woman standing at the painting's right is not for him to look at. The consequence of this also pertains to the representation of the space. Here, the room has more depth than in *Le Peintre et son modèle*. That depth is just enough to signify that he is dreaming, or fantasizing about the woman, but not nearly is she in his orbit.

The primary method of endowing her with that status of fantasy is color. Both her body and the robe she is barely wearing are yellow. The robe is, in fact, white on the inside, suggestive, perhaps, along with the masterfully painted sheen of satin on the outside, of the ermine worn by royalty—and painted by ambitious old masters. But the matching color of robe and body turn her definitely into an image, far removed from reality. This fantasy character of the figure as an image of the imagination is also indicated in the figurative elements of the image. Her genitals are those of a child, her head and face that of an adult, a giant adult even. But the yellow that sets her apart frames that deformation of scale.

With the man sitting in the darkness that turns his face gray, his hand no longer arguing but closing its fist in frustration, one may wonder where the light comes from that illuminates the female figure and colors it yellow. Here, the somewhat greater depth of the representation fulfils its anti-realistic function again. The light cannot come from the window, which is behind her. It might come from anything that, we can imagine, is on the side of the mirror, but the mirror itself, of which we see only the edge, is too small for such evenly frontal light. The light is emphatic; the shadow on her legs delimits its power and thus brings it into visibility. The feet crossed, the front one put exactly in the center of the elaborate pattern of the rug: it all suggests that the display is for whoever is in the space before the picture plane to which she is standing so close. Not Heathcliff-Balthus, but the viewer is allowed as well as forced to see this naked body. And, aware of its discrepancies, the viewer is invited to think about what it is he sees. An image, a fantasy. Whose?

Together, the *La Chambre turque*, with its glowing pink figure on the left, and the yellow Cathy on the right side of the painting form a strange pair of "colored women". Both adult women with their child's sex and their artificial pose do not see anything in the mirror that recalls a long tradition of iconographically related pictures. Instead, they *are* the mirrors, or, as the title of

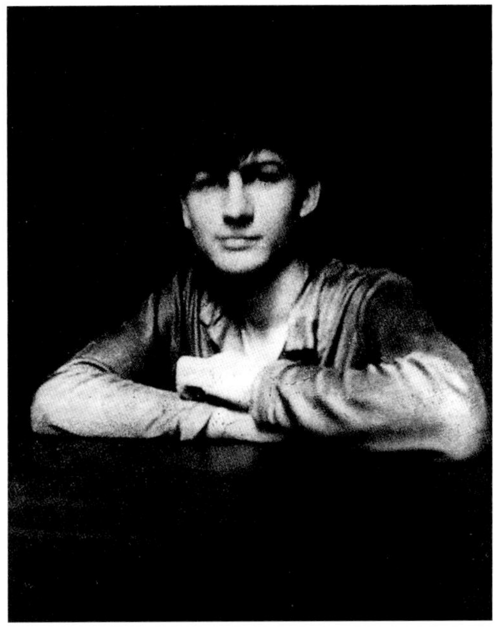

La Toilette de Cathy, 1933.
Cathy Dressing.
Oil on canvas, 165 × 150 cm.
Musée National d'Art Moderne, Centre Georges Pompidou, Paris.

Photograph of Balthus at age 18.

10. With the depiction of Nellie, Balthus conforms to class cliché about working women as well as an age and gender based one, already evident in the seventeenth century. See Salomon (2004) for a fine analysis of such clichés in domestic painting.

11. Charles A. Riley offers an ironically relevant aristocratic perspective on the *Le Roi des chats* (2001).

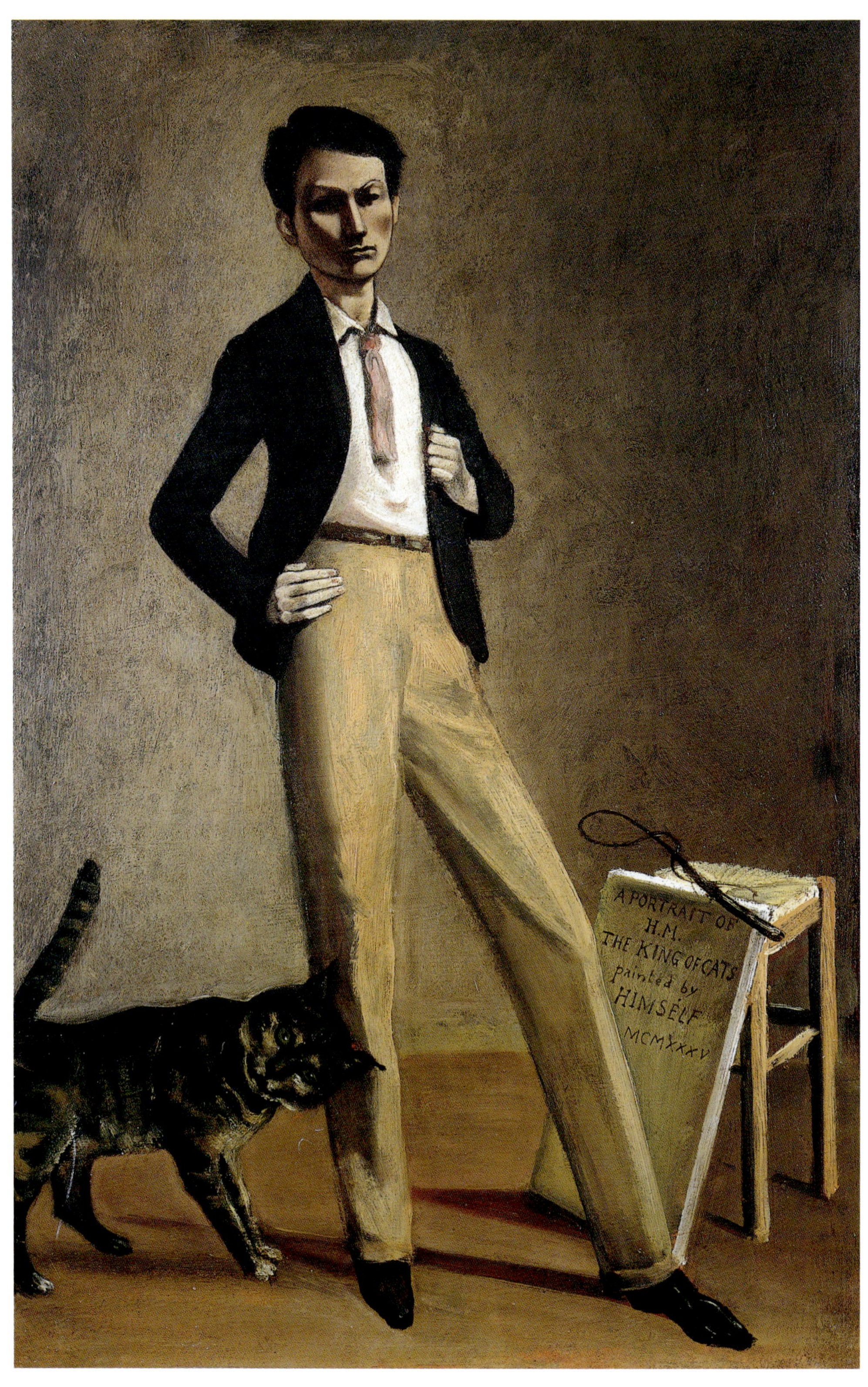
A PORTRAIT OF
H.M.
THE KING OF CATS
painted by
HIMSELF
MCMXXXV

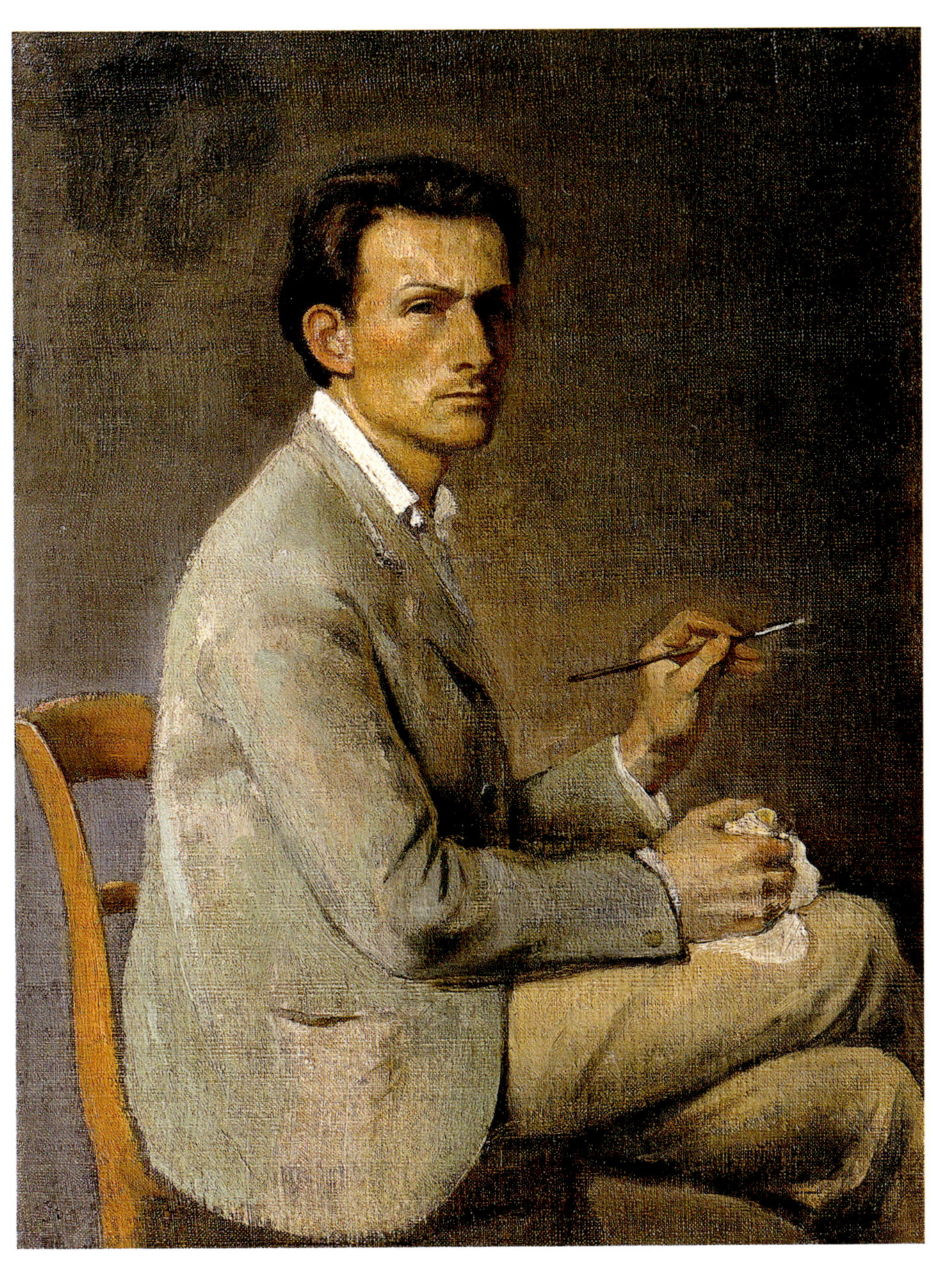

Le Roi des chats, 1935.
The King of Cats.
Oil on canvas, 71 × 48 cm.
Collection of the artist.

Autoportrait, 1940.
Self-Portrait.
Oil on canvas, 44 × 32 cm.
Private collection.

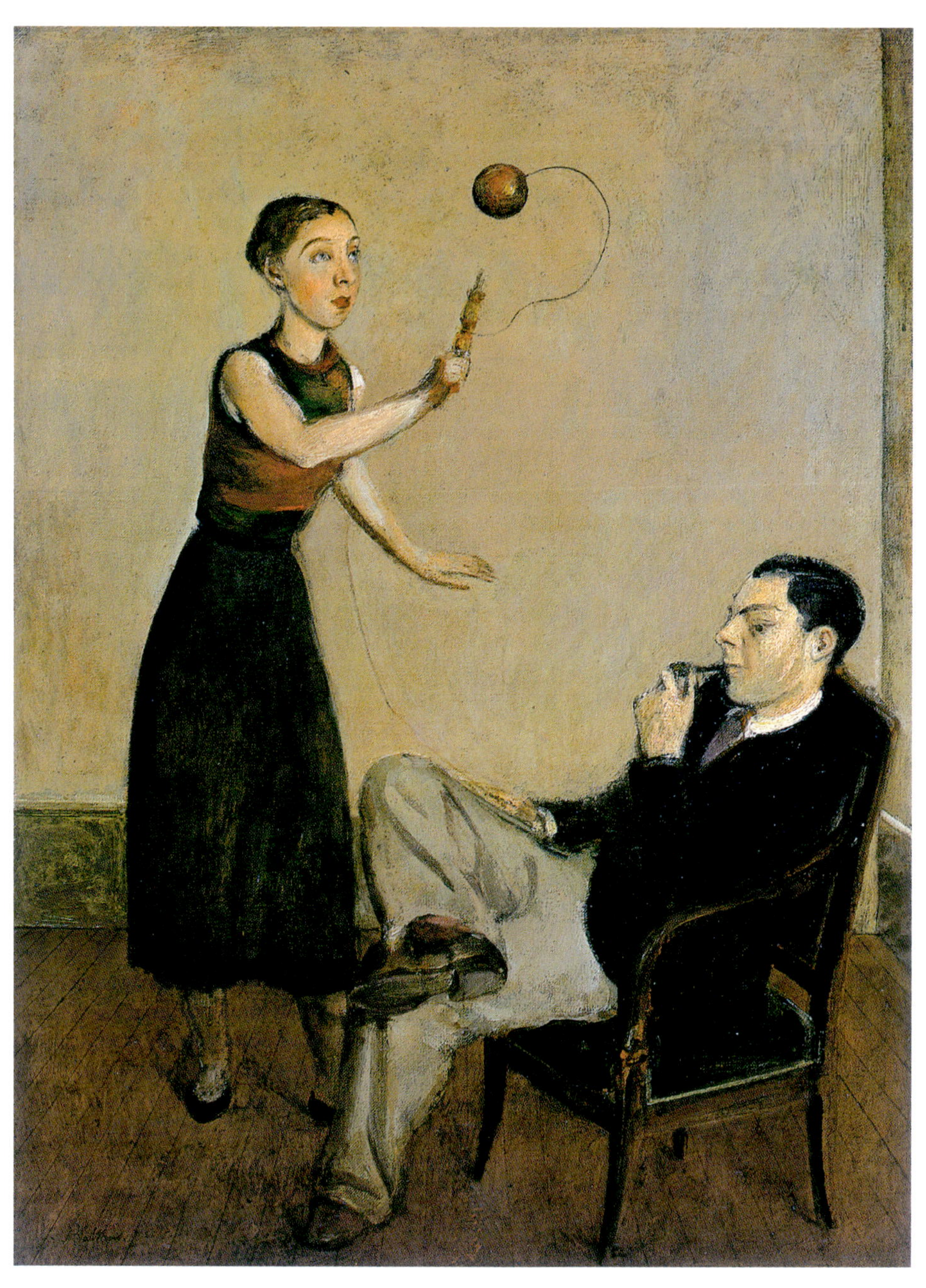

Alice has it, they are in the mirror. Prior to that visit to the storerooms, I had already seen that most "erotic" of Balthus's paintings that would ever be displayed, *Alice dans le miroir*, in the galleries of the newly refurbished Centre Pompidou, and it, too, has an eerie, de-realizing color. With a canny sense of theater, but also with a keen understanding of the theoretical import of the painting, the curators have hung the painting across from the entrance of the gallery and at the exact height that makes an adult visitor look right at the genitals of the woman.[12]

The sitter for Alice was a well-known figure in Paris at the time, and therefore, the painting was more scandalous than it is today. Balthus also depicted this woman fully dressed, but no less disturbing, since there she is as tall as they come but utterly infantilized by the game she is playing (p. 34). But what the curators did in their act of hanging, the painter had already done with his palette: foreground the visitor's inevitable collusion in any erotic obsession he or she might impute to the artist. How did he do that?

As in *Cathy*, the predominant color, not only of the figure but of the entire painting, is yellow. Not the fresco-like greenish yellow of *Le Peintre et son modèle*, but a morbid, even yellow. There is something dead about this Alice, whom the title places neither in front of, nor at the other side of, but within the mirror. As opposed to Louis Carroll's figure, this is an Alice for adults.

Color is not the only technique to achieve the deadness of this standing figure. Her body is monstrously deformed, with uneven breasts—one huge and the other small, and a waist no larger than her hefty thigh. Both anomalies are emphasized, the large breast by being naked and the waist by means of a totally transparent gauzy garment that hangs next to it, which at some distance also foregrounds it. Furthermore, as the wall caption suggests, she is combing the wet hair of a drowned Ophelia, and her veiled, dead green eyes complete the killing.

The painting, including its title, lends itself to such fantasies as, for example, that by Pierre Jean Jouve, who owned the painting, and wrote a story about it; one day, the figure from the hanging painting above Jouve's bed, disappeared (1983). The almost monochrome color scheme, in collaboration with the figurative elements and the title, offers an opaque screen for the viewer. Again, realism is only a trap, an entrance into fantasy. But here, due to the figure's pose enhanced by the hanging, that fantasy is both more disturbing and less easily avoidable or naturalized than in *La Phalène*. Alice is, indeed, in the mirror.

Being forced, as by both painter and curator, to look into the crotch of a naked female figure is a confrontation with one's own desires and/or taboos. This would turn the canvas into a mirror and the image seen in it, into a self-image. Hanging the painting at such a disturbing eye-level, the curators have foregrounded this theoretical implication of the uniform colors. Most mirrors in Balthus's work are just as opaque. As I have already suggested apropos of the *La Chambre turque* and *Cathy*, mirrors never mirror the figure, but are only indicative of the act of mirroring, and are proposed to the viewer for that reflection. The opacity of substantive color is the paradoxical means to intimate this reflexivity.[13]

Let me give a few examples of the way color inflects the motif of the mirror that offers no visual reflection, and thereby shifts the meaning of reflection from visual mirroring to intellectual thought. In all these cases, color replaces transparent reflection. The mirror in *Japonaise au miroir noire* (Japanese Woman with Black Mirror, 1967-1976, p. 36) and *Japonaise*

Pierre et Betty Leiris, 1932-1933.
Pierre and Betty Leiris.
Oil on canvas, 70 × 50 cm.
Present location unknown.

12. The most explicitly erotic painting, *La Leçon de guitare*, (p. 144) was painted in order to scandalize. It is in a private collection and never on display. I visited the storeroom and the exhibition at the Centre Pompidou in 2007.

13. *Alice dans le mirror* is also among the paintings where the figure is much more mature in age than Balthus's reputed adolescents. It is the only one where the figure has pubic hair.

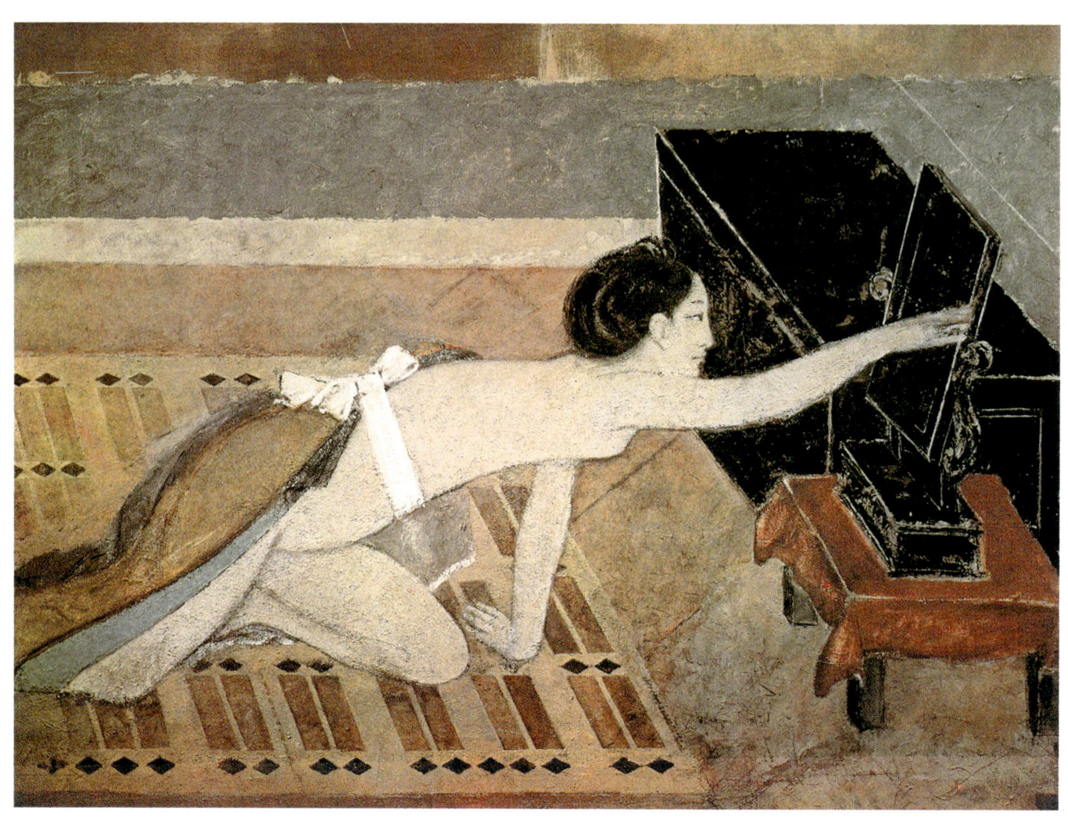

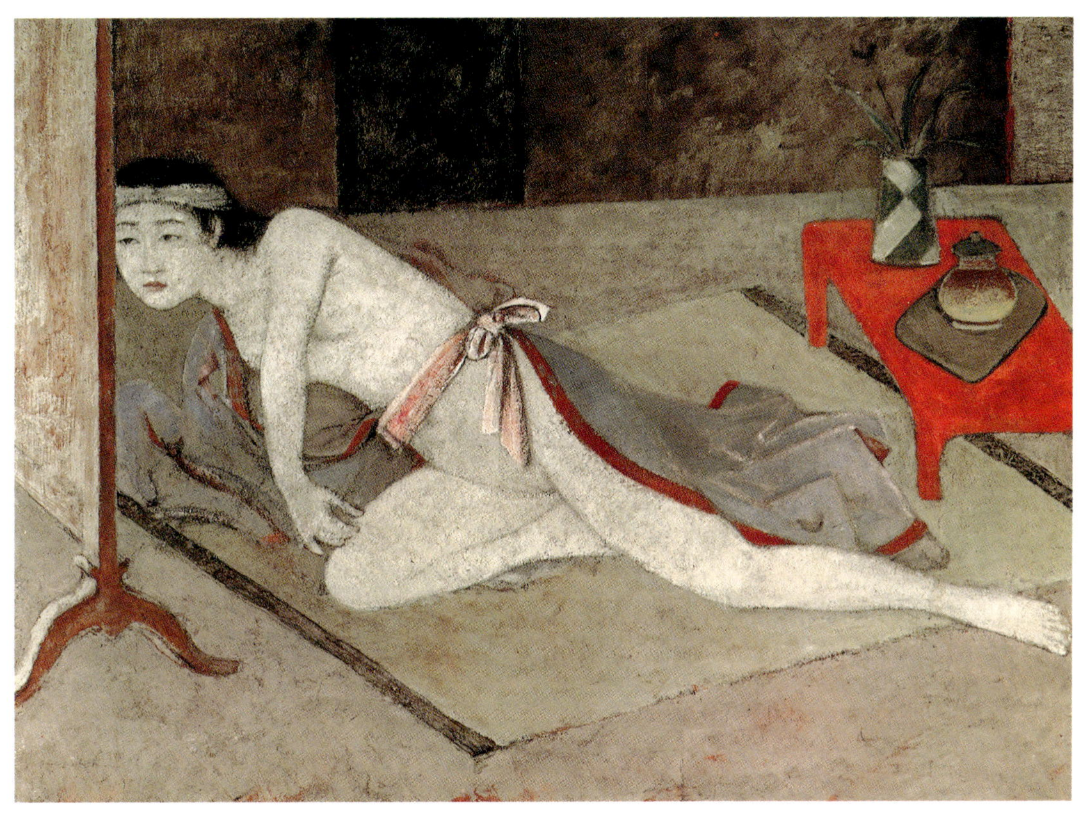

Japonaise au miroir noir, 1967-1976.
Japanese Woman with Black Mirror.
Casein and tempura on canvas,
157 × 195.5 cm.
Private collection.

Japonaise à la table rouge,
1967-1976.
Japanese Woman with Red Table.
Casein and tempura on canvas,
145 × 192 cm.
Private collection.

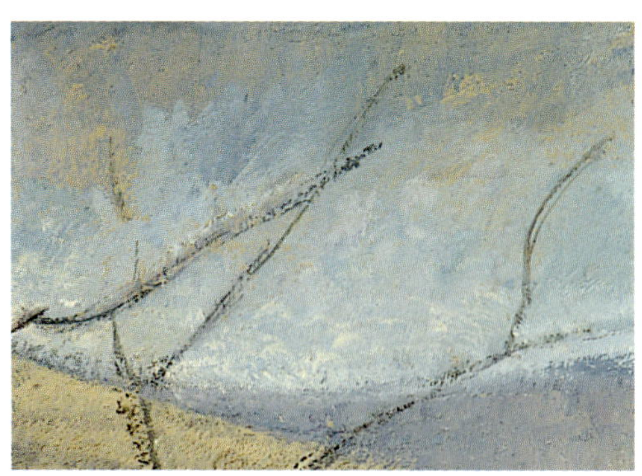

Detail of *Cour de ferme à Chassy (Grand paysage avec arbre)*, p. 13.

Le Chat au miroir I, 1977-1980.
Cat with a Mirror I.
Casein and tempura on canvas, 180 × 170 cm.
Private collection.

à la table (Japanese Woman with Red Table, 1967-1976, p. 37) show two symmetrically disposed figures reaching out to a mirror in which nothing can be seen. The former is black, the latter out of reach of the viewer, with red the suggested color. The three versions of *Le Chat au miroir* (Cat with Mirror, pp. 39, 40, 41), with the third one being among the artist's most "colorful" works, play with the opacity of the mirror in humorous ways—a humor that is undermined by the artist's dead-serious attitude toward cats. Here, the naked girl is not, as the traditional Venus, gazing at her own beauty but is rather indifferent to the effect of her nude body, holding the mirror up to the small animal at the other side of the bed. Her action draws attention away from her nudity.

And so does the color, unreal in all three paintings. The first version is painted in the fresco-like pastels so typical of the artist; the last one is so brightly colored that it seems almost a self-parody. Full of bright reds and greens, the red cheeks of the boy/girl figure match the incandescent yellow of the cat's eyes. In-between, the hand mirror with shades of brown, orange and yellow establish the visual connection between the two figures and the obstacle to visibility between them.

Color is a consistent technique that de-realizes whatever Balthus sets out to depict. This deployment of his palette is by no means restricted to those paintings that directly represent fantasy images. The *Cour de ferme à Chassy (Grand paysage avec arbre*, p. 13*)* is a composition in nuances of lavender, with a touch of green offsetting the general hazy color of the morning. Like the butterfly in *La Phalène*, branches of the tree for which the work is named are drawn as if in crayon on top of thick layers of paint, so that they take the color of their background (left). The *Grand paysage avec vache* (Great Landscape with Cow, p. 42) is, strangely, a landscape painted in a vertical format, what the English language calls a portrait format, deployed to paint four distinct bands of color. Colorwise, this painting looks more like the *La Chambre turque* than like the greener pastures usually depicted in the landscape tradition. An electric blue sky occupying almost half of the picture sets off a clear pink triangle and rectangle, both flat images of buildings. A lavender-orange row of woolly trees occupies the middle band below these building. An eggplant-color band of earth follows. Below that, a grayish-green field on which a pink cow and a tiny man in a blue shirt repeat the accents of the upper half of the painting, filling the rest of the horizontal bands. Verticals come from curved, near-black tree trunks.

And if this is not convincing enough to make the case for Balthus's use of color against reality, *Grand paysage aux arbres (Le Champ triangulaire)* [Great Landscape with Trees (The Triangular Field), p. 43] even fleetingly evokes the shape of a palette. A narrow portion at the top left and broadening a bit toward the right, is devoted to a sky that, although cloudless, changes color at least four times. Almost parallel to this sky, the bottom consists of a triangular shadow, cut toward the right by a brick wall. Trees with heads of leaves figure blots of paint. The top of the triangle has a darker spot that looks like the hole through which painters hold their palette with their thumb. Splatters of white here and there—tree trunks struck by the light, and cows—complete the illusion that this landscape harbors within itself a shadow of the artist choosing his colors. But in order for color to take over so strongly, space, the illusionary three-dimensionality of painting, needs to be underplayed. This idea will be elaborated on in the following chapter.[14]

14. Like most things and concepts, color is a historical category. In relation to Balthus, I can recommend two books. One is on color in the Middle Ages (Pley 2004), the other on color in the classical age (Lichtenstein 1993). Not that the periods are particularly relevant for Balthus's use of color, although they are in fact also that. But the approaches—one really looking at color, the other analyzing the discourse surrounding it—are complementary and, together, illuminate much of what the artist's work performs.

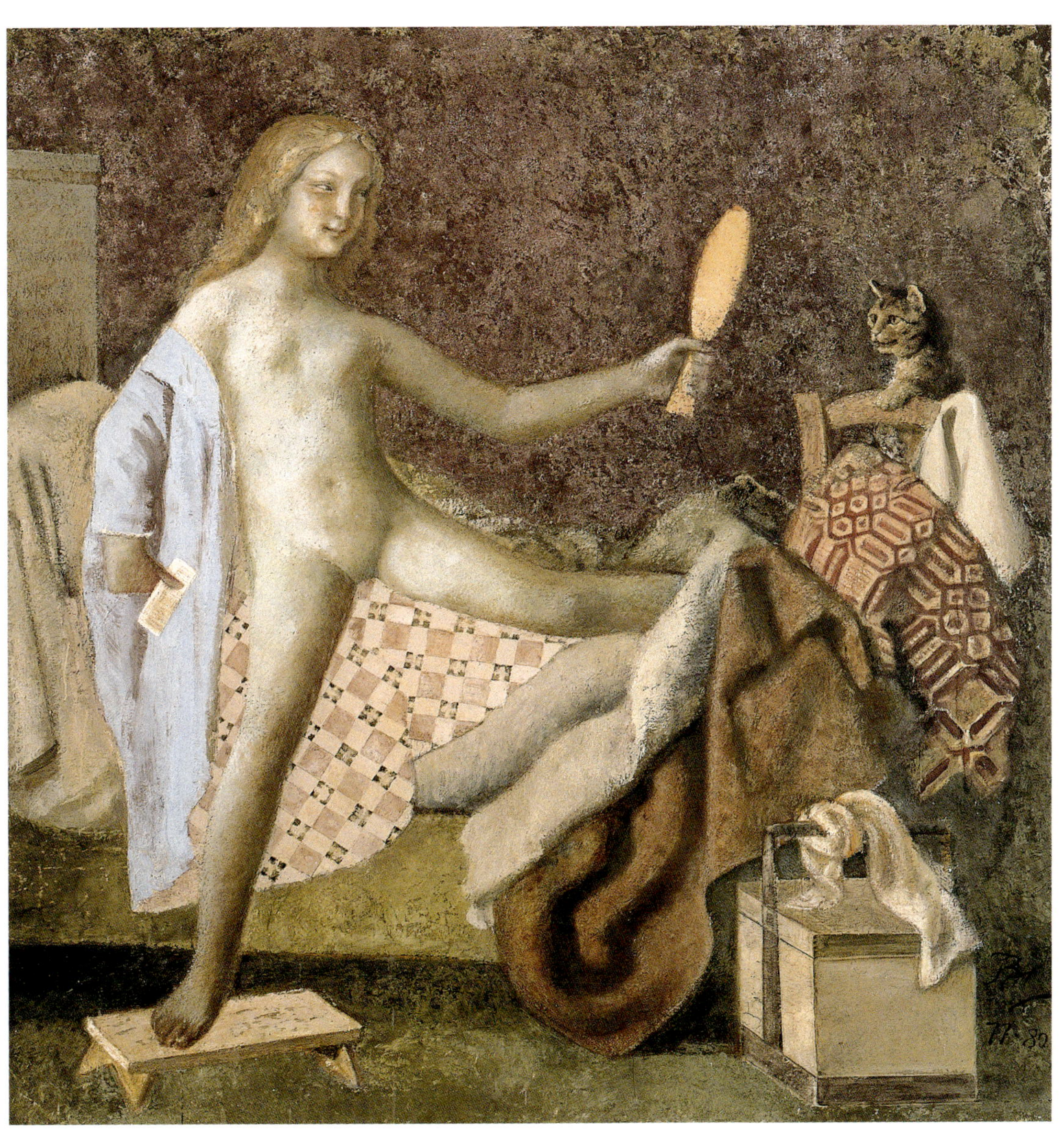

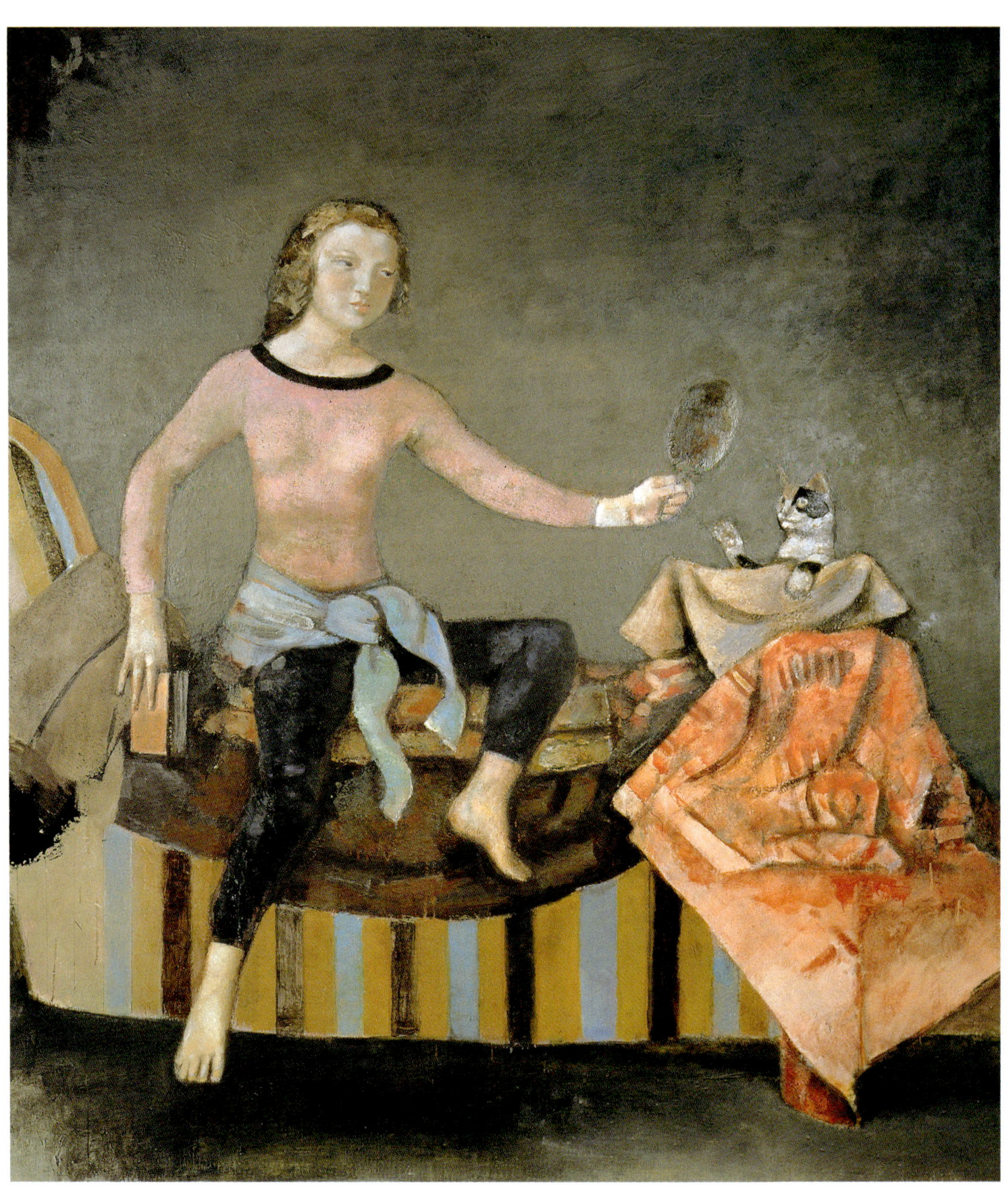

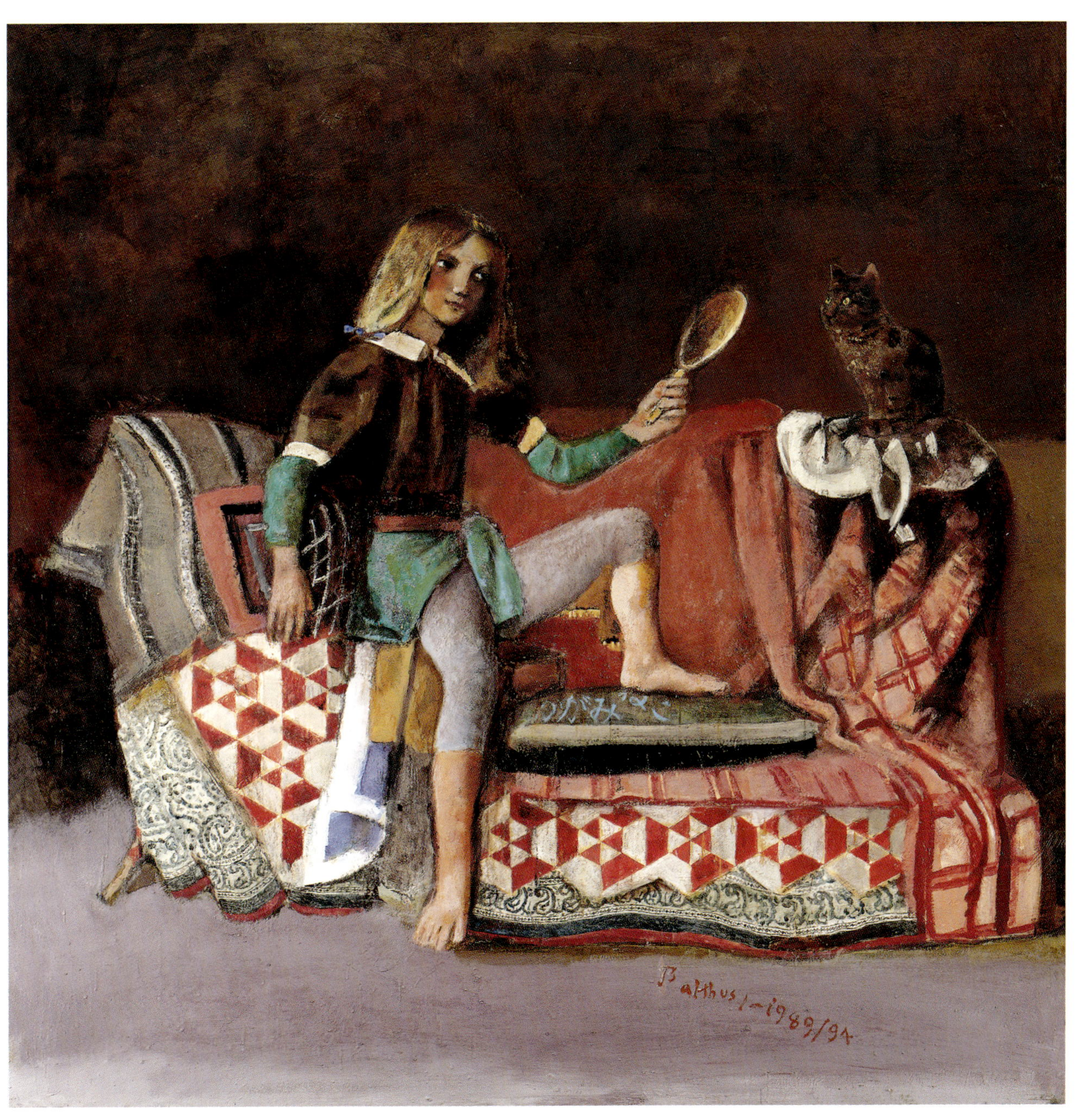

Le Chat au miroir II, 1986-1989.
Cat with Mirror II.
Oil on canvas, 200 × 170 cm.
Private collection.

Le Chat au miroir III, 1989-1994.
Cat with Mirror III.
Oil on canvas, 220 × 195 cm.
Collection of the artist, represented by
The Lefevre Gallery, London.

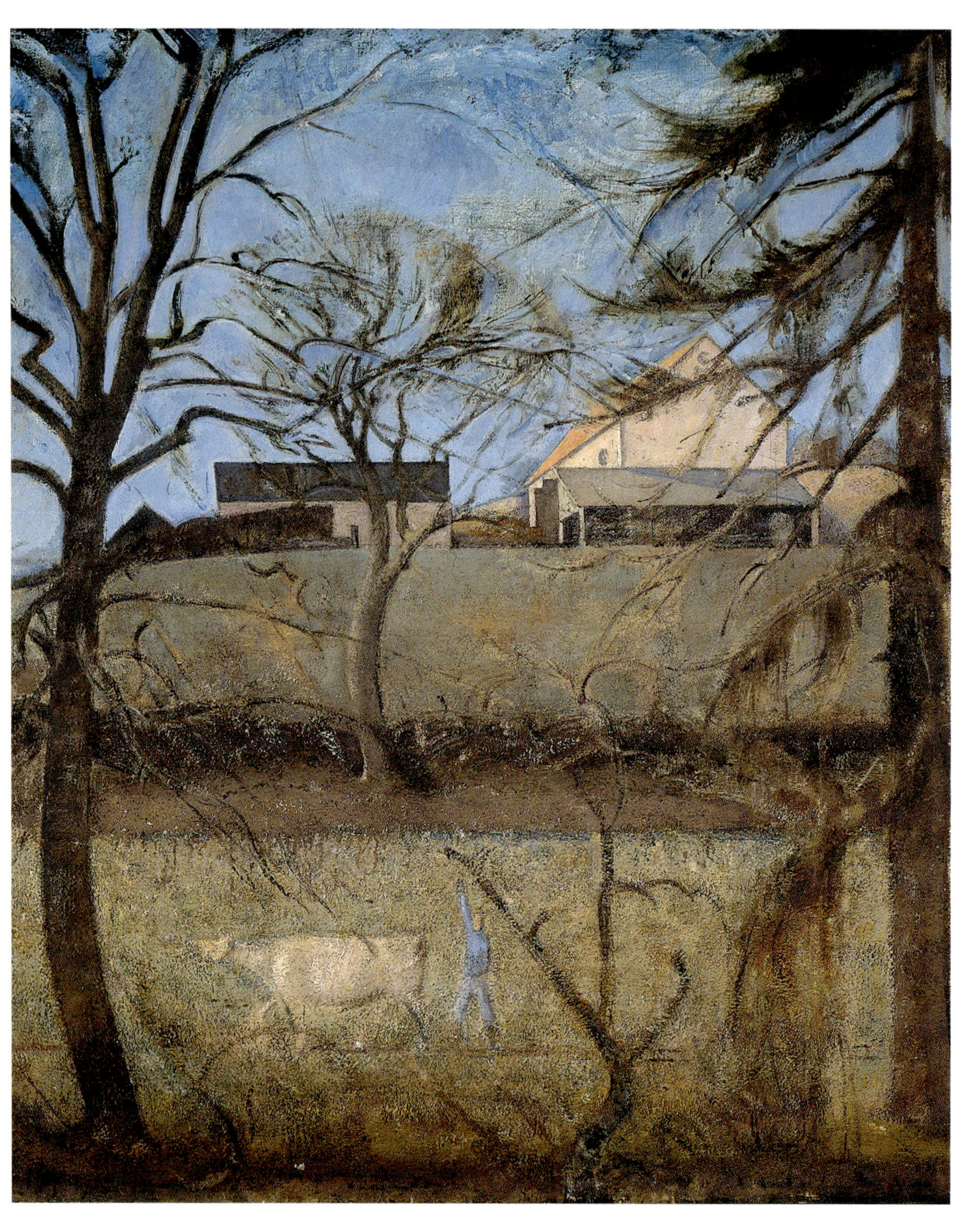

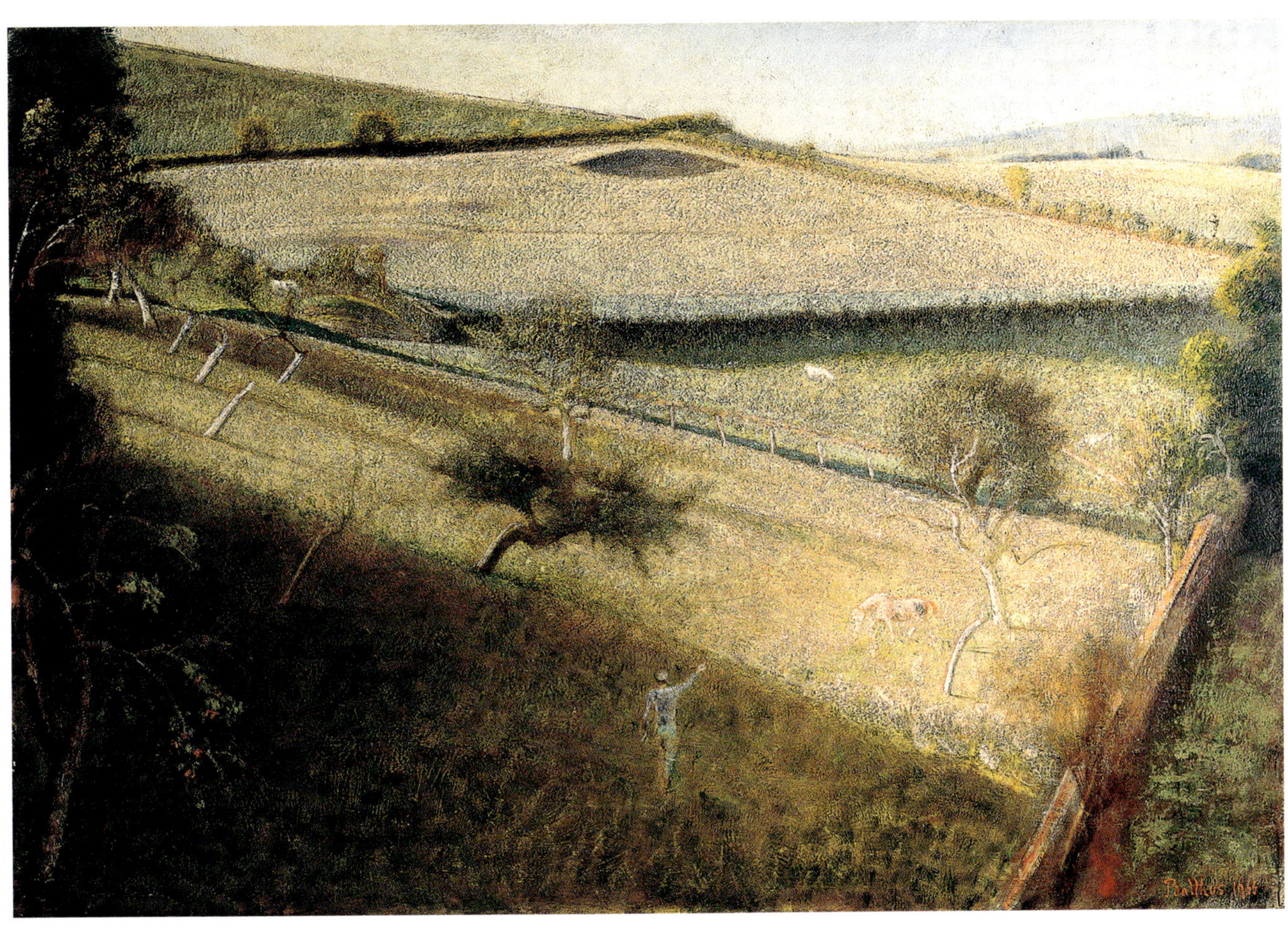

Grand paysage avec vache, 1959-1960.
Great Landscape with Cow.
Oil on canvas, 162 × 130 cm.
Private collection.

Grand paysage aux arbres
(Le Champ triangulaire), 1955.
Great Lanscape with Trees,
(The Triangular Field).
Oil on canvas, 114 × 162 cm.
Private collection.

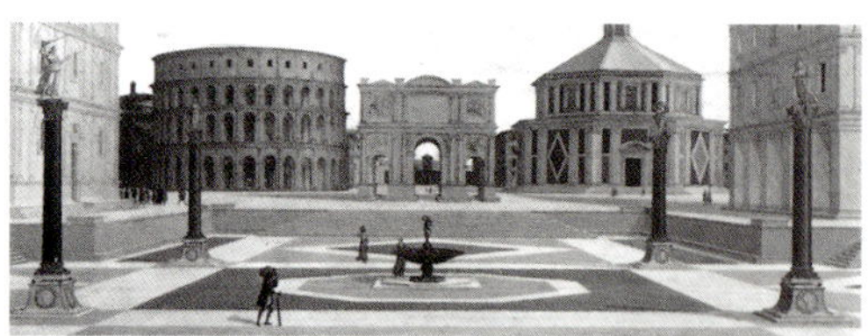

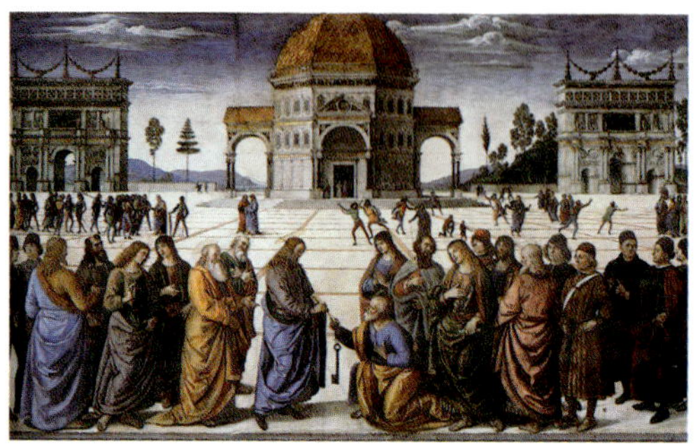

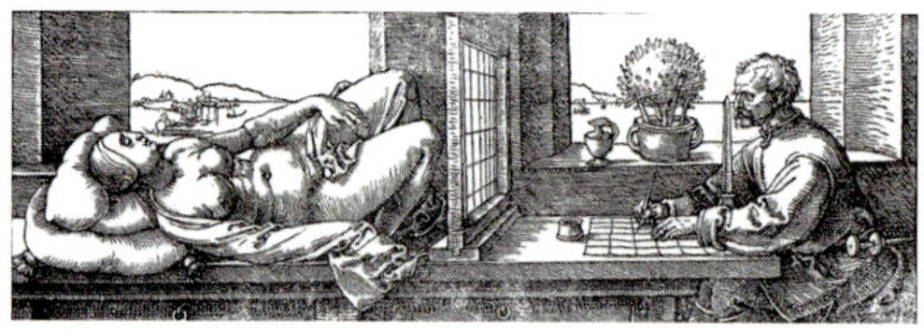

Detail of *Architectual Perspective*. Known as the Baltimore panel. Walter Art Gallery, Baltimore.

Pietro Perugino, *Christ Handing the Keys to St. Peter*, 1481-1482. Fresco, 335 x 550 cm. Sistine Chapel, Vatican.

Albrecht Dürer, *Draughtsman Drawing a Recumbent Woman*, 1525. Woodcut, 8 x 22 cm. Graphische Sammlung Albertina, Vienna.

2. Shallow Spaces

In art that aims to depict something—representational art—the tension between the two-dimensional surface of the support and the three-dimensional world depicted has traditionally been a source of inventiveness and creativity. In Western art, linear perspective conquered the flat image during the Renaissance (left). Before that, and in different artistic cultures, sometimes scale would be the means of suggesting space: objects at a distance would be made smaller than objects close to the picture plane (p. 45, top). Other modes of creating space or rather, its illusion, include color, with darker colors receding, brighter ones coming forward. Caravaggio, for example, suggested convex or concave forms by the use of white and black, bright and dark colors (p. 45, bottom).

With all such means, and many more, at the disposal of painters and draughtsmen, artists who seem to insist on the ambiguity, even the impossibility of depicting space convincingly, can be assumed to do so for a reason relevant to their art. When discussing *Le Peintre et son modèle* (p. 10), I have already remarked on the compressed or shallow space in some of Balthus's paintings. I will further explore this shallowness, and confront it especially with the genre of paintings that are entirely based on the representation of space, namely landscapes. I will argue that the effect of—and, I speculate, the motivation for—the insistent shallowness of the spaces lies in the simultaneous acts of going along with the fantasy, and stopping to consider painting.

But first, this argument requires more than the technical flatness we have seen so far. Indeed, there are paintings where flatness is produced by means different from the shallow perspective mentioned in the introduction—angles that become blunter, walls that extend farther than strictly realistic representation would allow. The flatness Balthus emphasizes so frequently by means of color sometimes mingles with another strategy that achieves flatness—this time through figuration. Through this, the painting comes to resemble Matisse's paintings, where ornate wallpaper dominates and the figure in the room seems just another piece of wallpaper. But while there is a continuity between such paintings and the artist's cut-outs in Matisse, in Balthus's work, figures appear as cut, sometimes quite roughly so, even though he never used the technique.

The figure of the girl in his large, square *Golden Afternoon* (p. 46) is sleeping in a pose that would make a realistic viewer squirm, but as a two-toned orange diagonal she nicely offsets the yellow and blue planes around her. Between the still life on the excessively tilted coffee table and the varied patterns on the sofa, floor, and pillow, she seems just another ornament. The curtains evoke the theater and its own deceptions of depth. The window with its blue open shutters doubles up that frame. The perspective is such that the landscape behind it, bleached white but for the two bands of green foliage, looks like a painting. If the woman figure is so uncomfortably posed, it is because she literally does not have enough space. She does not lie on the sofa; she is stuck to an image of it, like the butterfly in *La Phalène* (p. 17).

Something similar can be said of the imaginary figure flying by the sleeper in *Le Rêve II* (The Dream II, p. 47). Here, the space has definitely more depth, but even so, the oriental rugs on the floor and the table are drawn with a crammed perspective, while the bowl on the table seems to float, like another cut-out ornament. The right arm of the sleeper looks like a loose limb juxtaposed to her body. Everything in this painting works to foreground the imaginary character of the scene. And it is imagined as split. There are two scenes, the images of which appear as two distinct planes. Both the scene of the dream as well as the scene in which we see her dreaming are imaginary. Superimposed on the background, the two scenes are glued together as if in a collage. The seams of this collage are clearest where the two skirts meet, the brown one of the sleeper implausibly cutting off the lavender and blue one of the figure her sleep conjures up.

In *Le Salon* (The Living Room) I and II (pp. 48 and 49), the scene requires enough space to position the sleeping girl with the reading girl in front of her, as well as, in the second version, a cat. But the piano, whose curved leg reiterates the curve of the sofa's back, emphasizing lines that delimit planes, is placed at an angle blunt enough to reduce the depth of the room. The still life element in the first version, as a result, is absent in the second where there is really no room for a table between the sofa and the reading girl. Instead, the velvet drapery that supposedly represents a tablecloth is a beautifully painted regular set of folds—renaissance, not baroque ones—that harmoniously break the otherwise visually monotonous flat sofa. The glass bowl of fruit looks more like a painting that, however, is not hung on the wall but rather on the curved frame. Levels of superimposed planes make a realistic assessment of the room impossible. Needless to say, this further glosses the unlikely pose of the sleeper and the reader.

In the second version, both the sleeping and the reading are more insistent. The sleeper leans backwards, her throat thick, so that it pains us to anticipate her stiff neck when she awakes. The reader reads in such a position that we only see her profile. Her pink dress is just a tone off from the skin tones of her legs. The still life is reduced to a single item, a dark silver pot and the sheen distinct from the softer one of the velvets. The new element is a very Balthusian cat—like an Egyptian god, or a sphinx, with his eyes closed, a pose in which cats do not sleep. Like the doll-like central figure in *La Rue* (p. 19), its human mouth is curled upwards, as if almost grinning, but not quite. Color composes the scene again. Accents of red interrupt brown-orange: the sleeper's slippers, the red tassel on her left, her red sweater. In the lower part of the painting there are accents of white: the cat, the book, the reader's sock, the inside of the tablecloth. Then, on the right, the keys of the piano, covered by a cloth, and the score.

The feet of the sleeper are too small, due to an ostensive foreshortening, reminding us of the image's two-dimensionality. The candle on top of the piano is painted so lightly that the band of wall molding is visible through it. A 7 cm wide band defines the top of the painting; the bottom, under the rug, leaves 5 cm. The result is a painting that looks wider than it is. And the paint is consistently matte, even where the silver pot shines. If this painter emulates Caravaggio here, he stops short of imitating the latter's surfaces. Clearly, Balthus has a stake in this. Again, this stake is to foreground the flatness that qualifies illusionism.

Keeping in mind this tendency to flatten space—both through color and through design—I now propose to look at some landscapes. I have already mentioned a few that display the artist's coloristic tendency without necessarily having a flattening effect. In *Grand paysage avec vache* (p. 42) that effect does emerge, but rather than being due to color, it is as much or more to the result of the unusual vertical ("portrait") format and the division in horizontal bands. *Le Champ triangulaire* (p. 43) looks flat due to the starkly geometrical design and the tension in scale that emerges when the large but distant landscape flips over to become a huge palette. *Cour de ferme à Chassy* (*Grand paysage avec arbre*, p. 13) has a similar geometrical design—including a triangular field in the back. The Triangle in *Paysage à la tour* (Landscape with Tower, p. 50) might well be a depiction of the same field of *Cour de ferme à*

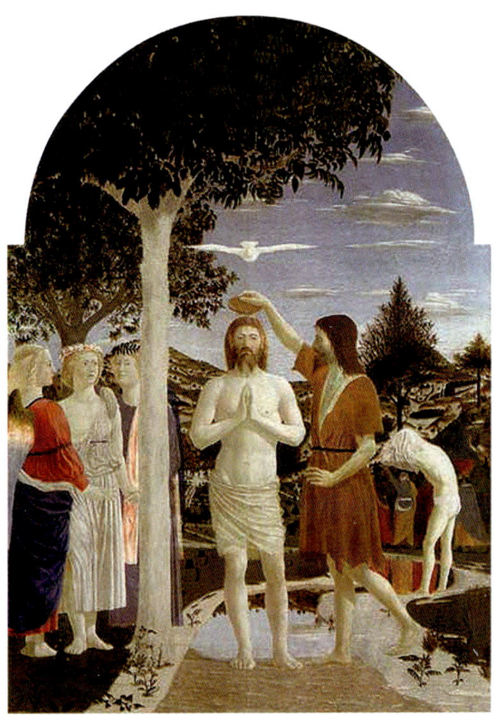

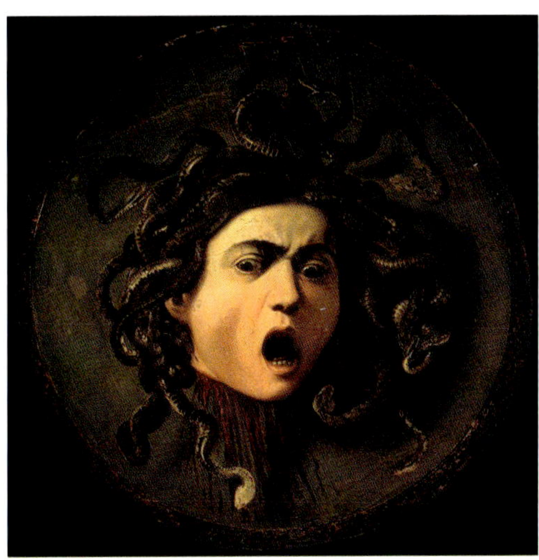

Piero della Francesca,
Baptism of Christ, 1448-1450.
Tempera on panel, 167 x 116 cm.
National Gallery, London.

Caravaggio,
Medusa, 1598-1599.
Oil on canvas mounted on wood, 60 x 55 cm.
Galleria degli Uffizi, Florence.

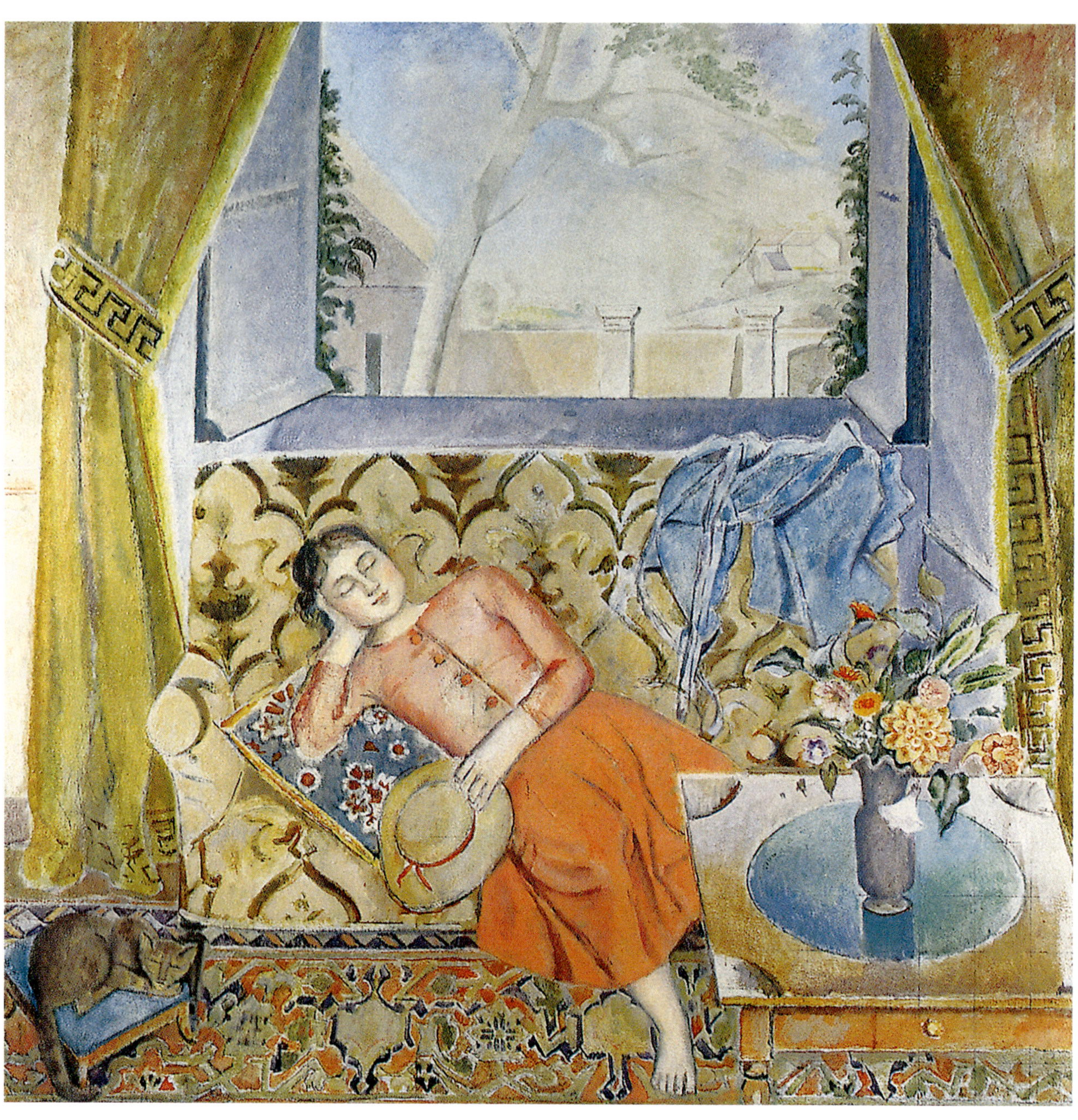

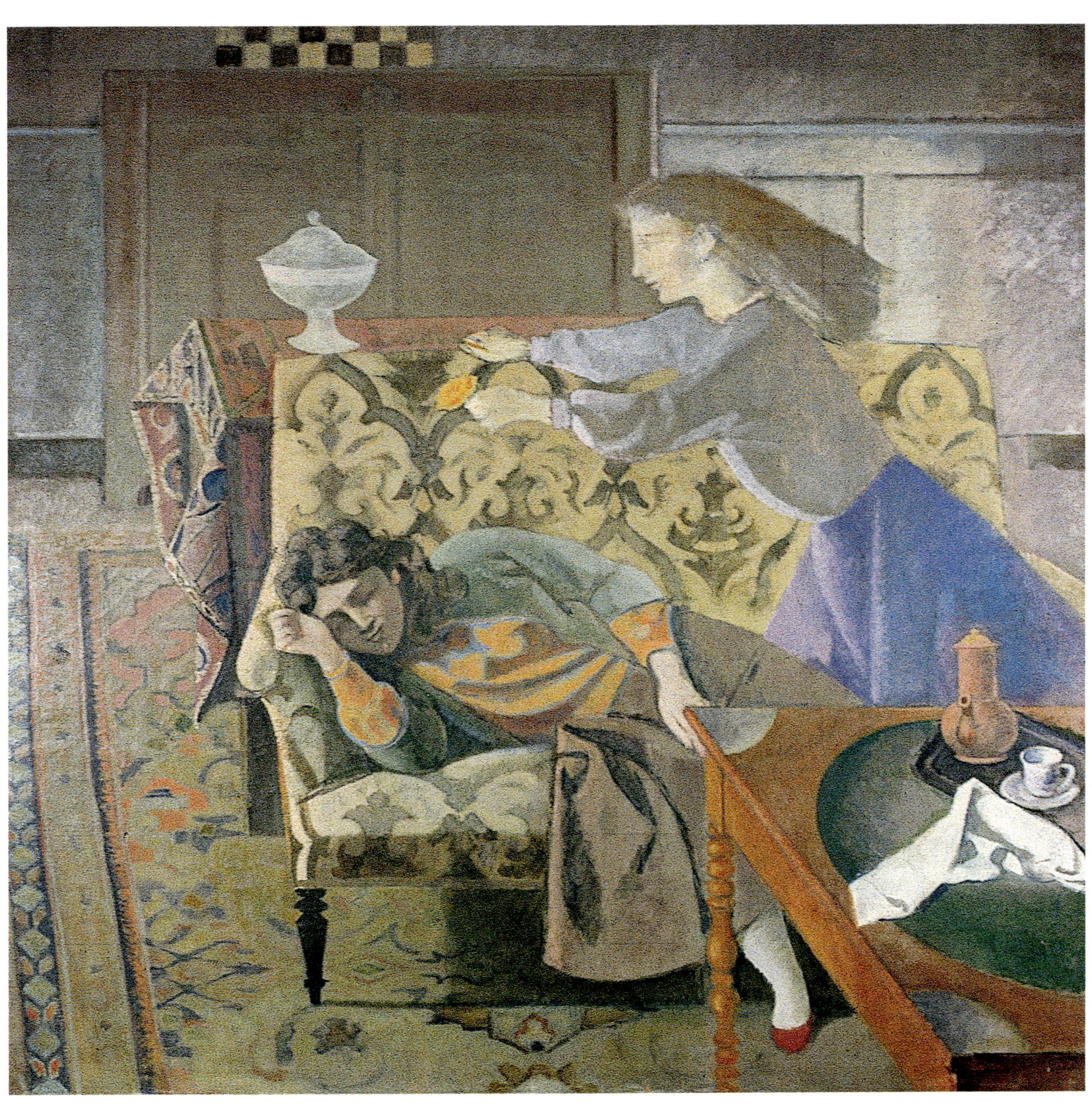

Golden Afternoon, 1957.
Oil on canvas, 198.5 × 198.5 cm.
Private collection.

Le Rêve II, 1956-1957.
The Dream II.
Oil on canvas, 198 × 198 cm.
Private collection.

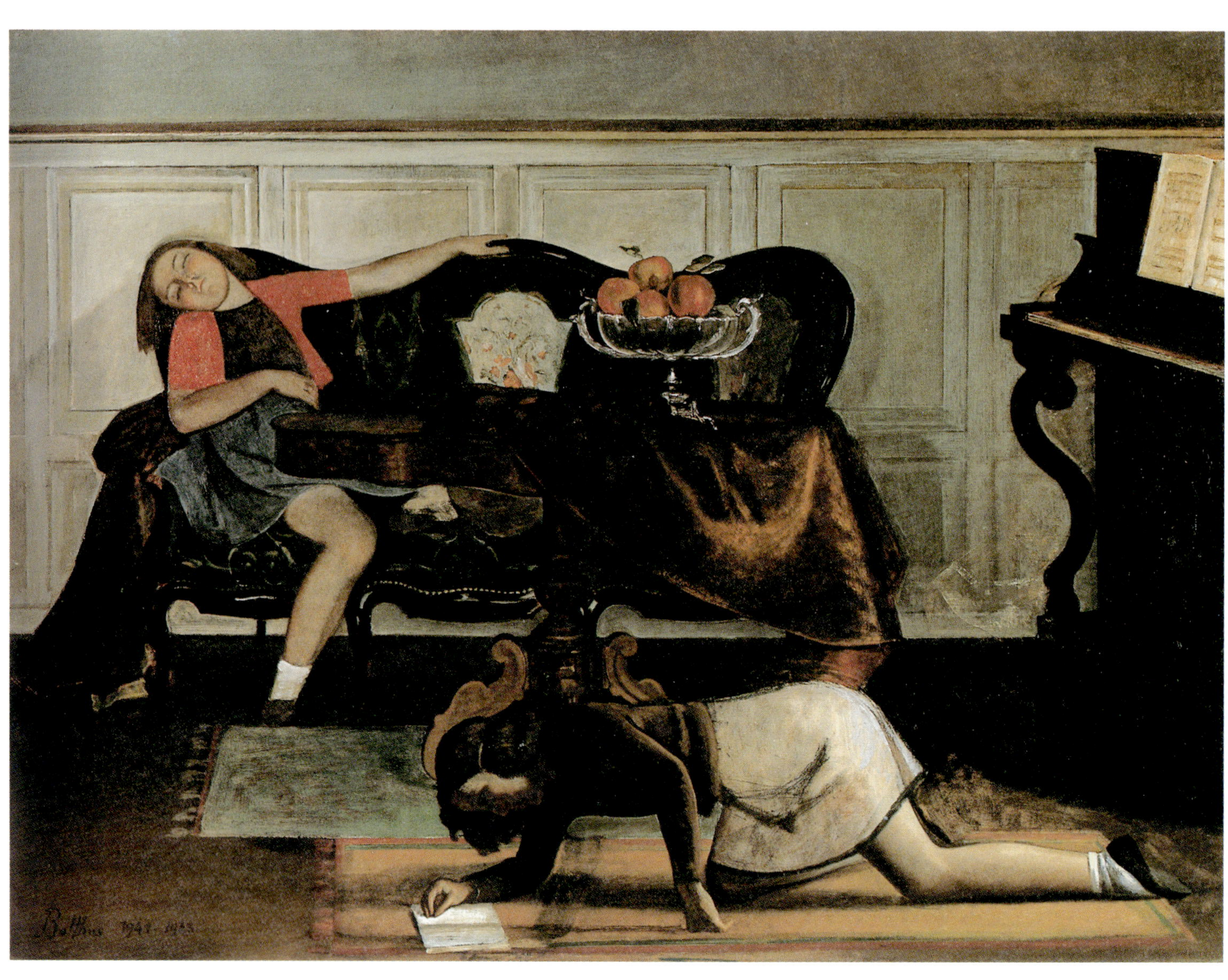

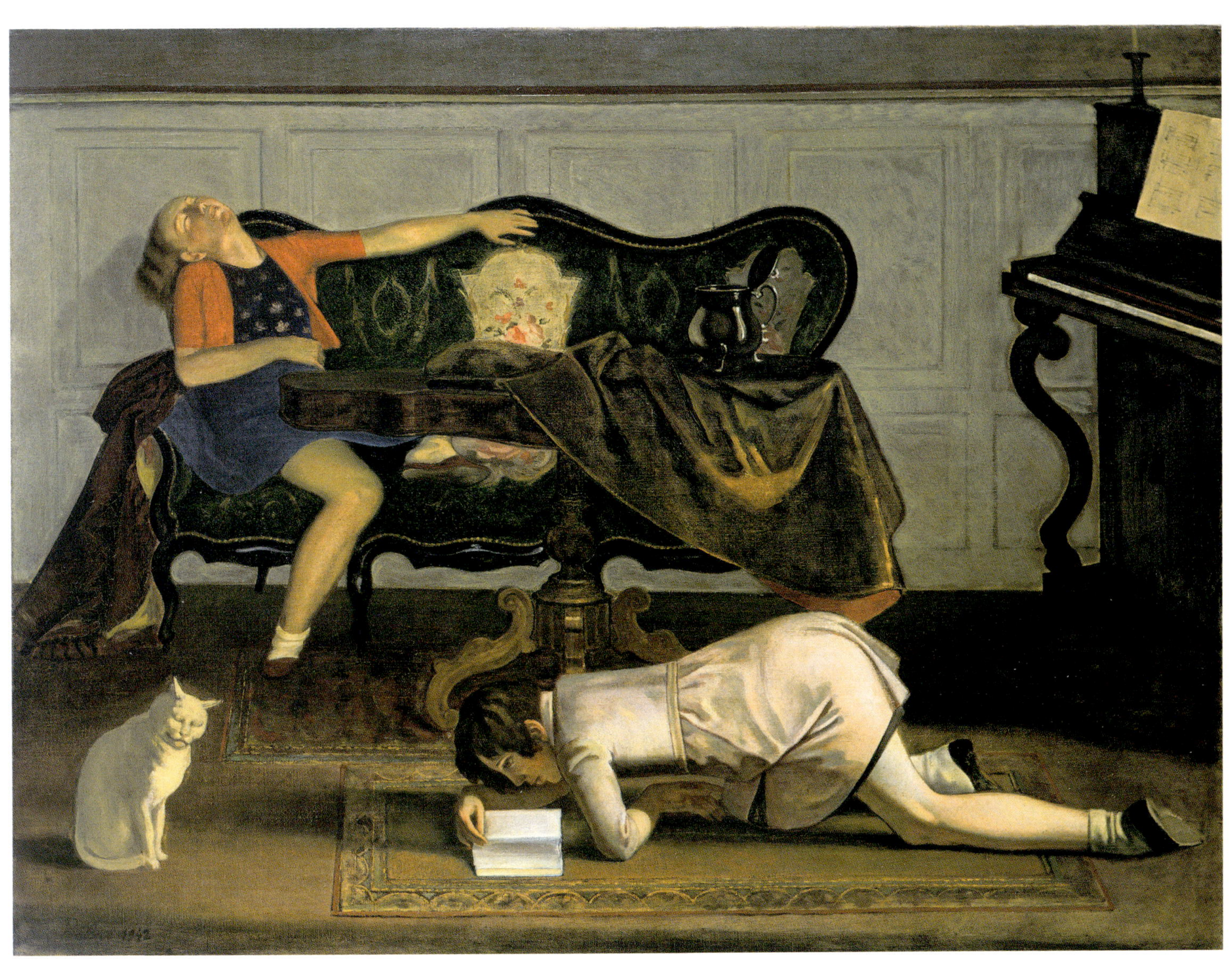

Le Salon I, 1941-1943.
The Living Room I.
Oil on canvas, 114 × 147 cm.
The Minneapolis Institute of Art,
Minneapolis.

Le Salon II, 1942.
The living Room II.
Oil on canvas, 114.8 × 146.9 cm.
Museum of Modern Art, New York.

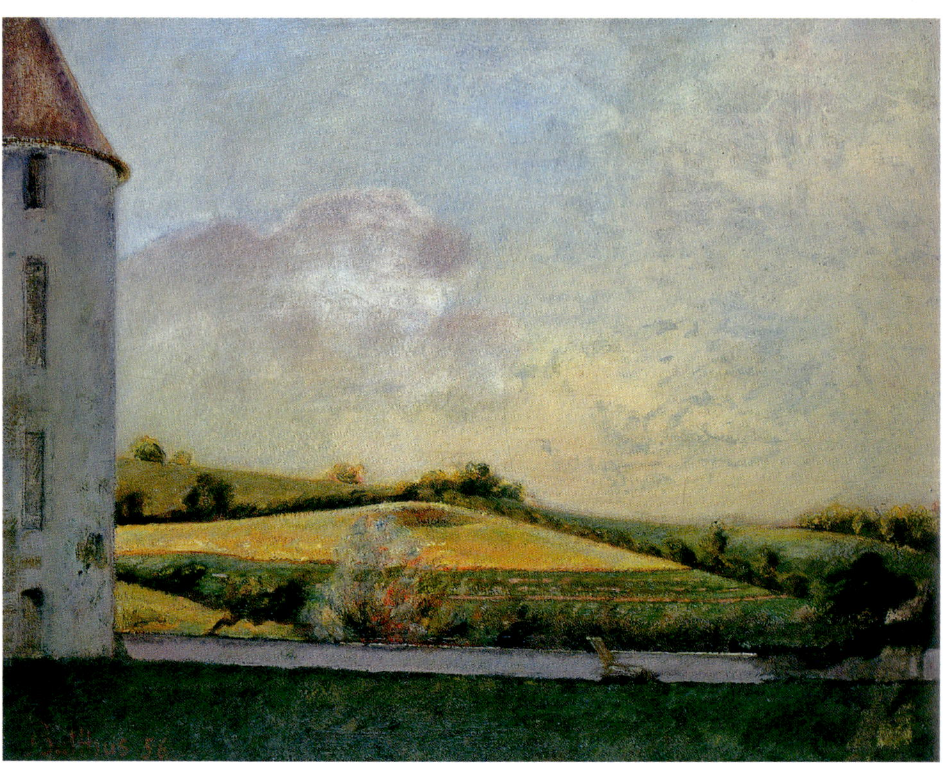

Chassy (Grand paysage avec arbre). The triangular form with the blunt angle, stretching the shape sideways, with or without a tower, (p. 50 and 13 respectively) makes the landscape look flattened. As with the division in the horizontal planes of the *Grand paysage avec vache*, it is as if geometrical forms, starkly drawn, make the landscape tilt forwards.

In each case, the sense that space is not "real" and competes with the flat surface of the painting, is produced in different ways that all converge. In p. 13 and 42, the very narrow space left for the sky unbalances the horizon and thereby makes the landscape ominous, as if tilted forward. In p. 13 this geometrical effect is not so pronounced. But here, the planes of lavender, yellow-green, orange and, farther away, beige compose a field of angular planes, comparable to Cézanne's 1885-1885 *Hamlet at Payannet, near Gardanne*. There, the mountain is lavender, with green in the foreground, quite like the small triangular patch of very bright and intense green right outside the gate in Balthus's work. The cardboard box shape of houses is also similar to Balthus's paintings. The tree draws capriciously curved lines across the color fields. The tree trunk ends below the edge, while the upper branches cross the sky so that the tree appears larger than the canvas. Here, the design of planes and lines overrules the composition of the landscape.

If the narrowness of the band of sky already flattens the landscape, those landscapes where no horizon is visible at all make it even more difficult to see three-dimensional space. These paintings are sometimes presented as images seen through a high window,

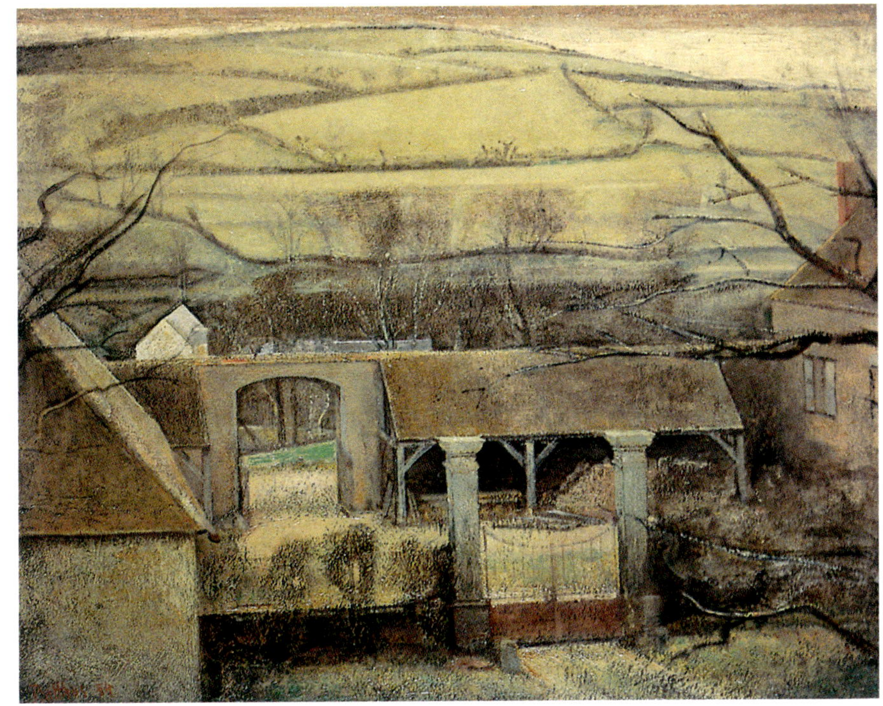

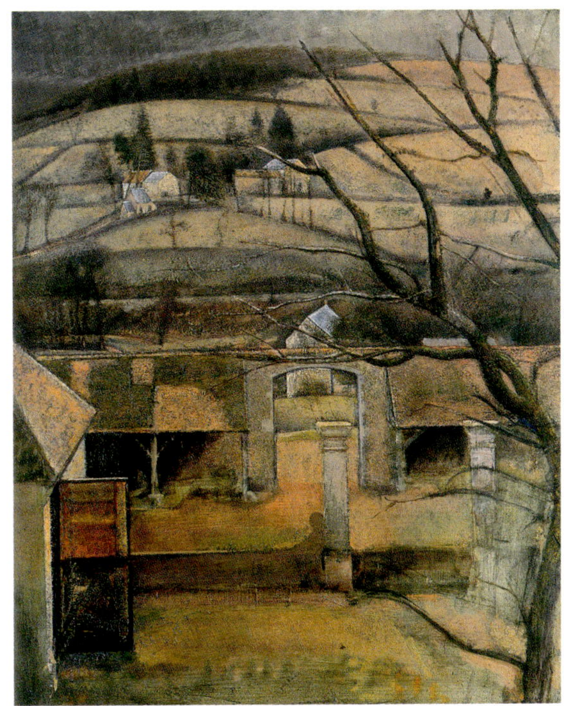

as in *La Cour de ferme à Chassy* (The Farmyard at Chassy, above, left). The colors are, again, remarkably subtle, all shades of green and brownish beige. The shape of the "palette" of the *Le Champ triangulaire* seems to have been deployed to the full. The absence of sky enhances the lines delimiting the different plots, the buildings on the close front, depicted from above, are reduced to planes, and again capriciously curved branches of a tree pose the only accent in the otherwise near-monochromatic painting.

Some of these landscapes are in portrait format. This makes another version of the view from above at Chassy so different from the other (above, right). Here, there is a hint of a horizon, with ominous darkened clouds just above a group of pine trees. But the vertical format, together with the black, slim tree branches, evokes Chinese landscape painting. It is affiliated with *Cour de ferme à Chassy (Grand paysage avec arbre)* in the depiction of buildings, the gate with a patch of grass beyond it, and distant toy houses, but, due to the format, it is very different in atmosphere, The verticality brings it in affinity with a work like *Paysage de Monte Calvello* (Landscape of Monte Calvello, p. 52) *and Paysage de Monte Calvello II* (Landscape of Monte Calvello II, p. 53), the latter being Balthus's last known work. This affinity may sound strange, since the former is not vertical in format. But what is vertical, here, are the rocks.

Indeed, in *Paysage de Monte Calvello* the left part of the painting is dominated by rocks that go up in vertical bluffs, almost white, above which green bushes lead up to a vertical ruin of a tower. The atmosphere of the painting, its unity as a surface, is enhanced by the use of

Paysage à la tour, 1956.
Landscape with Tower.
Oil on canvas, 65 × 81 cm.
Private collection.

La Cour de la ferme à Chassy, 1954.
The Farmyard at Chassy.
Oil on canvas, 75 × 92 cm.
Private collection.

Paysage de Chassy (La Cour de la ferme), 1954.
(Landscape at Chassy – The Farmyard)
Oil on canvas, 100 × 81 cm.
Private collection.

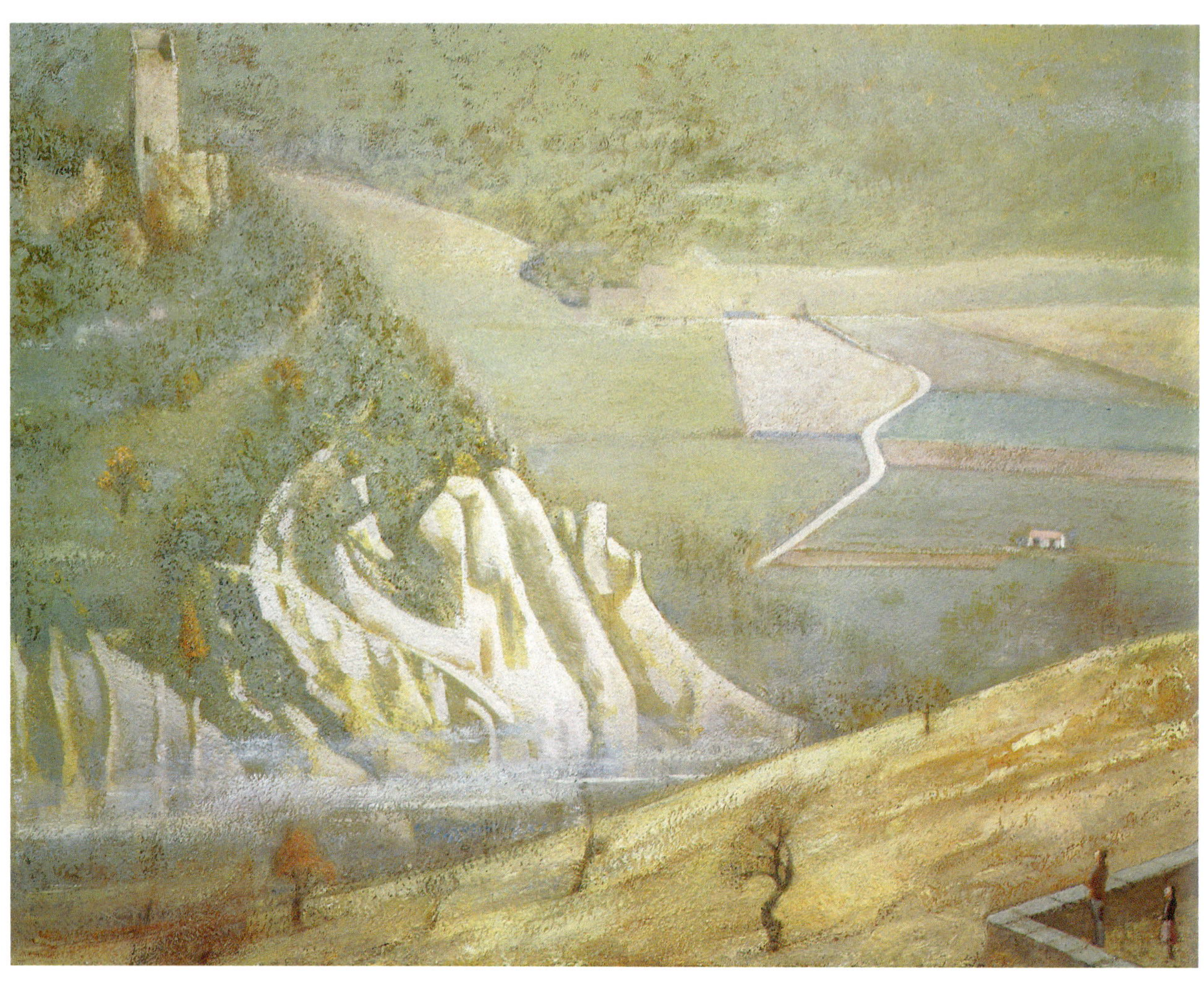

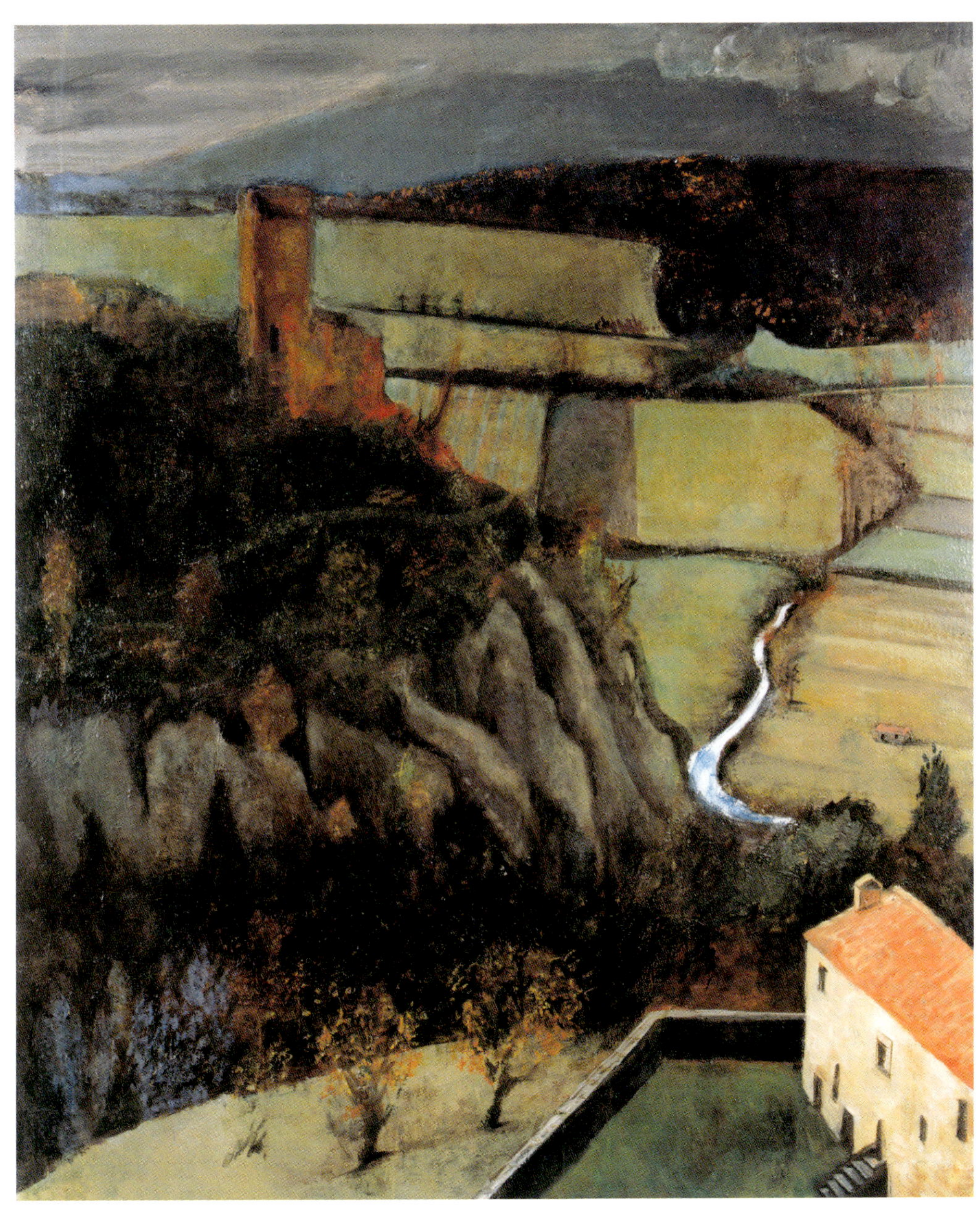

Paysage de Monte Calvello, 1979.
Landscape of Monte Calvello.
Casein and tempura on canvas,
130 × 162 cm.
Private collection.

Paysage de Monte Calvello II,
1994-1998.
Landscape of Monte Calvello II.
Oil on canvas, 162 × 130 cm.
Collection Setusko Klossowska de Rola.

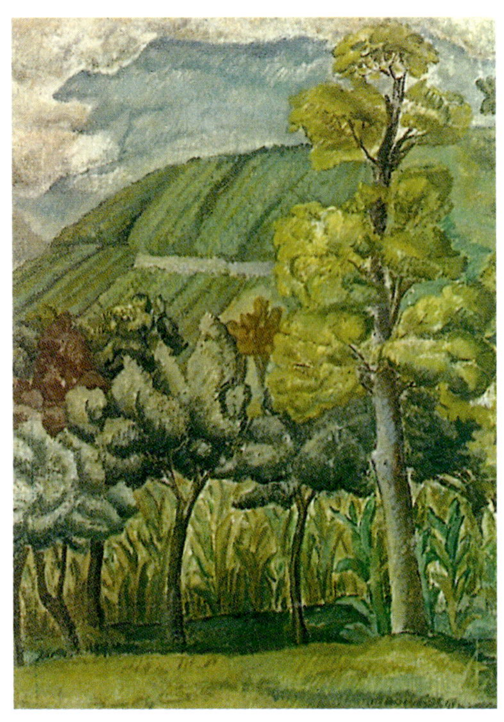

Paysage (Muzot), 1923.
Landscape (Muzot).
Oil on cardboard, 49.5 × 37.5 cm.
Private collection.

Paysage Provençal, 1925.
Provençal Landscape.
Oil on panel, 77 × 51 cm.
Musée d'Art moderne, Troyes.

plaster dust in the paint. The resulting gritty texture evokes the morning mist. The use of glazure, producing both thickness and transparency, gives the painting its unique early morning light when the sun has risen but has not yet chased away the humid air of dawn. Through the gauze of that air, the sandstone rocks swirl upwards. Shaped by rain and wind, they evoke both the long-term process of rock formation in nature and the process quality of painting. This analogy between nature's long duration and the slow process of a painter like Balthus is meaningful beyond the representation. It draws the referent—the real, nature-shaped rocks—back into the painting, but a painting that honors nature's work.[15]

Paths curve through the bushes in visual continuity with the curves of the rocks. From the middle outward another curved path or road cuts through the fields. Trees, again moving in curves that rhyme with the others, dot a field in the foreground that would form a triangle if it weren't interrupted, at the very close, lower right corner, by a terrace. The angle is sharp and the portion of the terrace we see is very tiny. Without clues as to what it is attached to, it appears to be a roof terrace. But it hosts two standing figures; one male close to the wall, and one female a bit behind him. It is a tribute to the consistent verticality of the image that the figures, although standing at the very bottom of the image, appear to be standing high. The total absence of a horizon makes the landscape with its insistence of vertical, curved lines tilt forward. And this effect occurs even though a darker triangular edge separates the flat field from the rising mountain.[16]

In order to demonstrate the idea that verticality as a tool to create flatness is a very specific artistic program, the comparison by counterpoint with Balthus's last painting is helpful. This work is vertical in format but less so in composition. All the elements of the alleged reality depicted in both works are there. The rocks, the paths, more vague, and the road; the terrace and, as we now see, the house of which it is the courtyard. The angle of the terrace is blunt, not sharp, and the figures have disappeared. And with all these changes, the verticality that was so reminiscent of Chinese landscapes in the earlier painting, is gone. Even though this canvas is vertical in format, due to the tension between format and depiction it seems square. Just as it seems square, it is also flat. But the tension that the use of verticality enhanced has vanished.

And to make the case that the tendency to use verticality to achieve flatness is an ongoing preoccupation, two very early landscapes fit the bill just as well. At the time when he was still busy copying Piero's frescos, at the age of fifteen he painted a landscape in portrait format and apparently without horizon, using color and line to start out with linear perspective, (left) then a combination of two fields looking like pieces of a jigsaw puzzle to break with this linearity. These two fields are, in fact, a strange hue of blue surrounded by a brownish tone, and even if they cannot really be construed as a horizon, they are in fact a piece of sky. The painting's variations of greens are already remarkable. Quite different in tone, more blue with touches of pink and orange, is the *Paysage provençal* (Provençal Landscape, p. 55) from two years later. This painting is also vertical, as well as with a small band of sky.

Then, there is the most extraordinary instance of "verticalization" against all odds. The *Paysage d'Italie* (Landscape of Italy, p. 56) is made in landscape format, rather small. It is perhaps the most "abstract" of the artist's landscapes. The misty quality, resembling *Paysage de Monte Calvello*, is not achieved by means of plaster dust but is painted, and as a result, the mist is

15. For a fine analysis of this painting, see Weber (1999: 559-563).

16. Weber sees in this painting a merging of Swiss landscapes and Italian and Chinese traditions of landscape painting. Many critics have written on the influence of Chinese landscapes on these works, see in particular Xing Xiaozhou (2001).

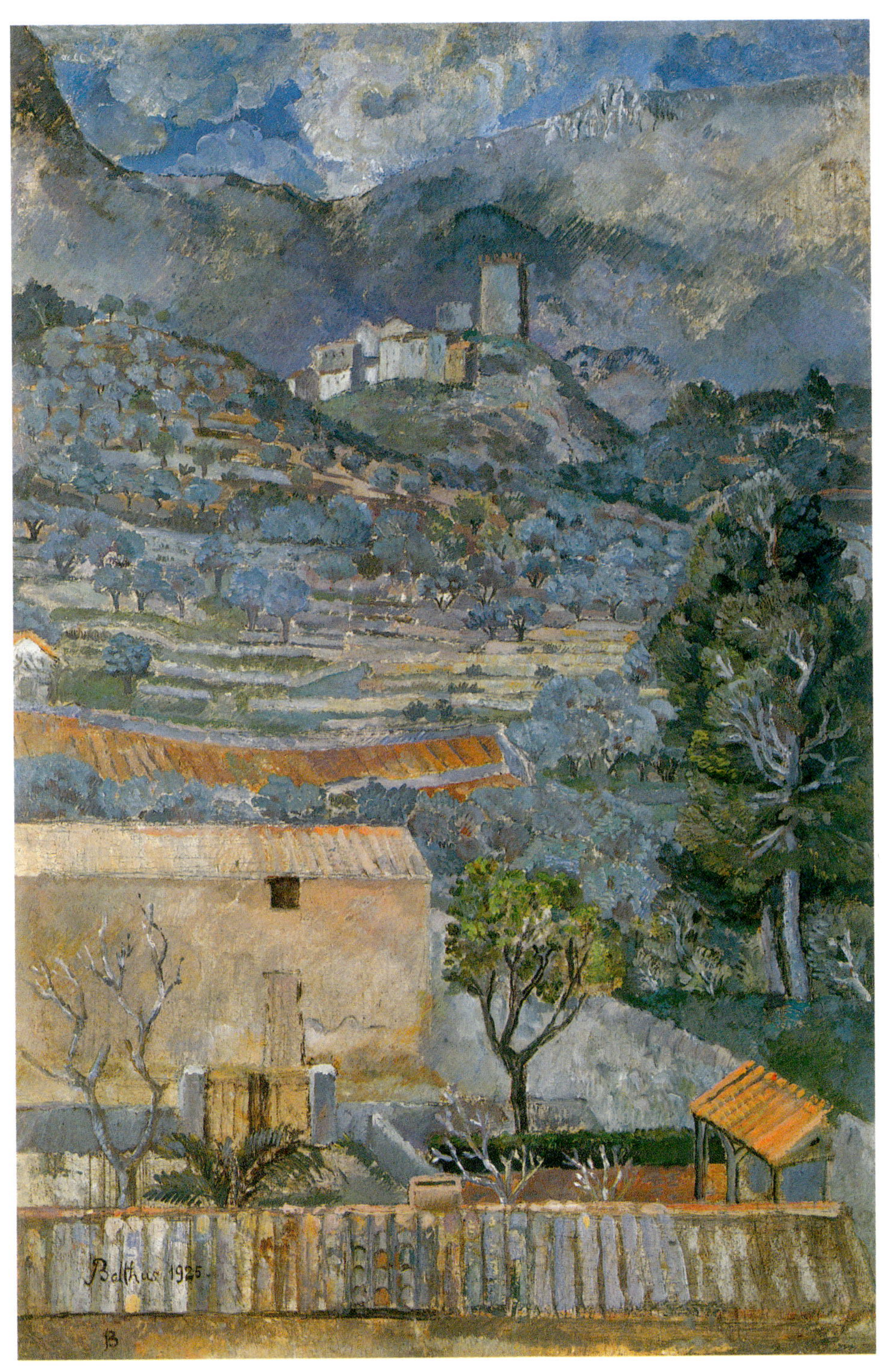
Balthus 1925.

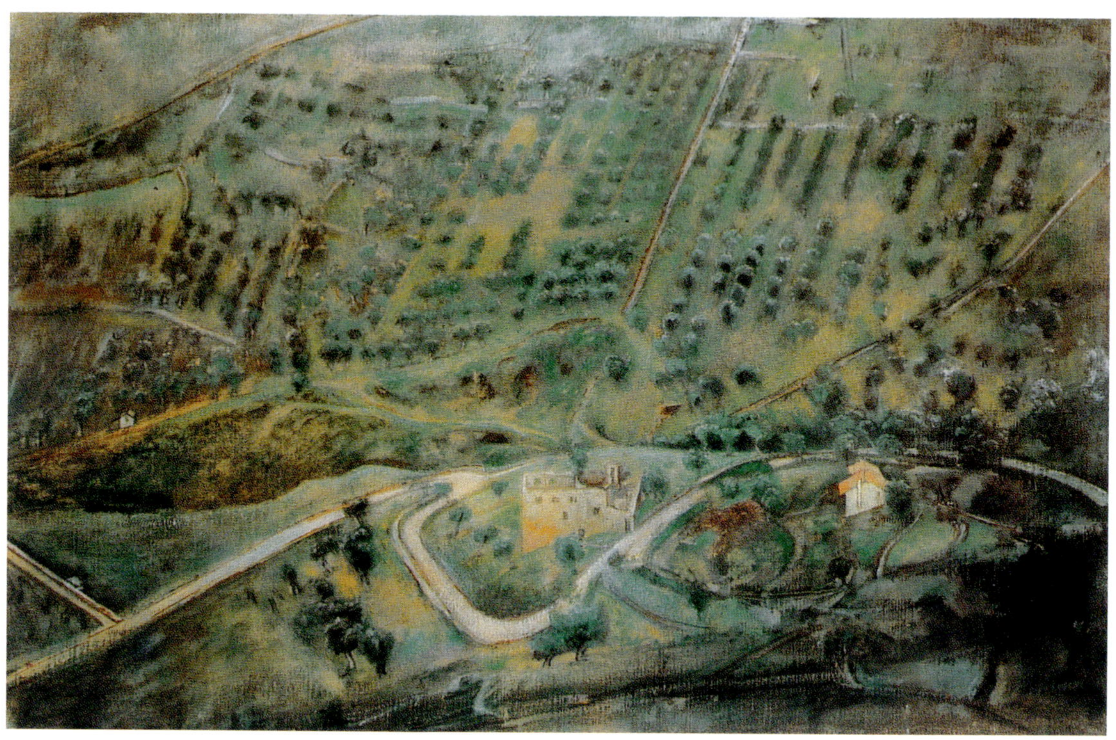

more concrete. What makes it almost abstract is the arrangement of the landscape as fundamentally distant, so that a division of color fields and lines predominate. The rows of dots forming trees turn the image almost into a grid. The neatness of these rows of dots sets this landscape off against the one where nature's hand is so strongly present (*Paysage de Monte Calvello*).

There is a temporality to this. The veil of mist is arrested but in a second it will lift, and dissolve. The shortest duration, a certain sense of momentariliness, appears here, and contradicts the long duration of the painting's making. Spatially, at the heart of the painting—but a low heart—there is the castle surrounded by a road that curves around it and then moves on, toward the right, to curve around a house. Here, the landscape is vertical not due to any of the other means discussed but to the high viewpoint. This landscape does not tilt forward but is "really" very steep. Or is it? The painter must have stood—or pretend to have stood—on a gigantic mountain in front of the picture plane, on the near side of the stream that forms the painting's lower edge. This makes the viewer a tourist, a mountain climber. A dizzying sense of height is the result.

One more landscape without horizon will caution us, however, against any assumption of a systematic connection between a technical and an aesthetic aspect. Take the gorgeous *La Bergerie* (The Sheep Farm, p. 57), entirely horizontal, both in format and in design. From a distance this painting strikes the viewer as a monochromatic color field painting—if such a truism may be permitted. The tints are all those earthen tones that go with the landscape, but within that general tone all kinds of hues alternate to form an abstract pattern. The lines are predominantly triangular, with blunt angles, and in the middle ground, to the right, stands the

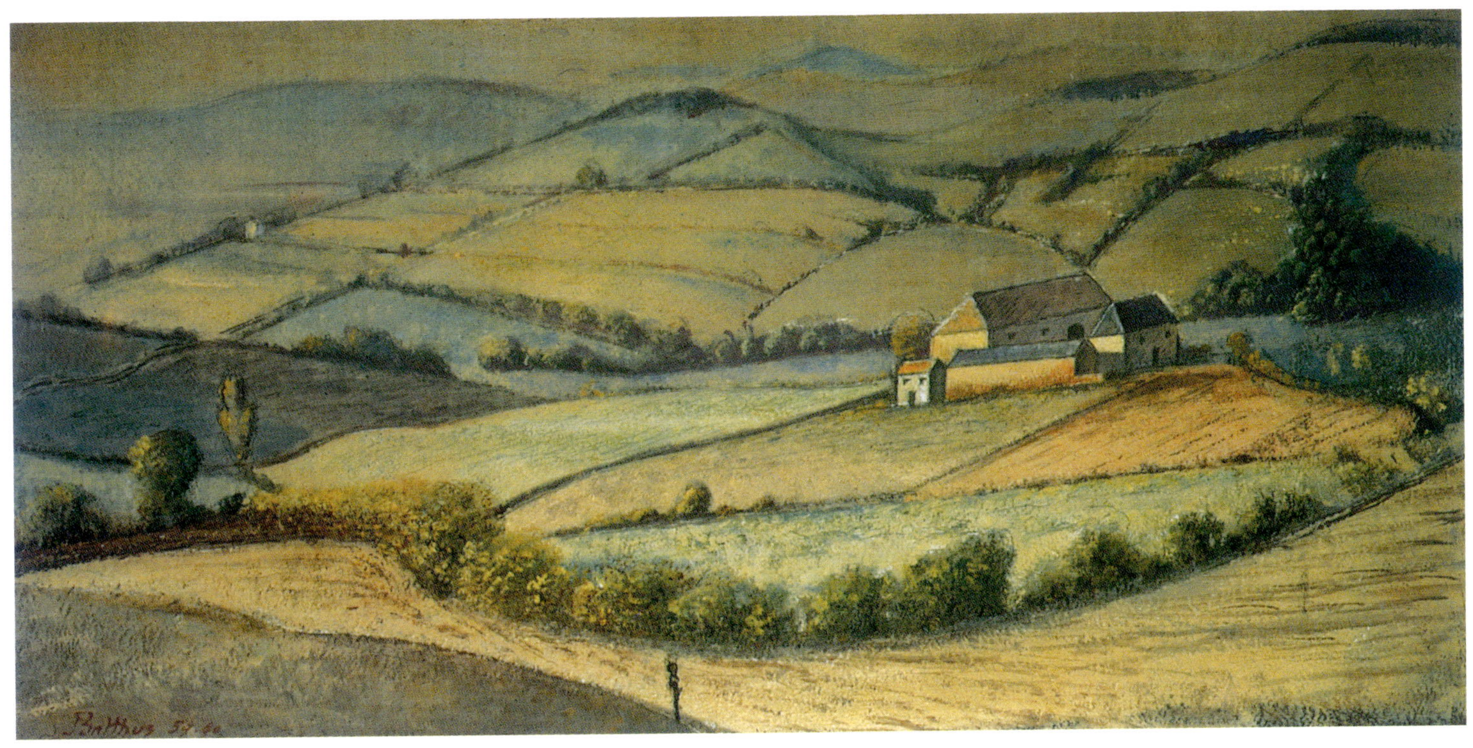

low building of the farm. A few of the triangular fields are lavender, others tend toward ochre, and in the foreground, on the right of the farm is a near-orange field, on its left a bright green one. The latter color is repeated below the orange, before a row of darker green bushes functioning as a hedge, before which a cornfield is yellowish again. On the left, a darker triangle suggests shadow. Despite the fact that the landscape itself extends beyond the upper edge of the painting, the differences in hue are utterly effective in evoking a flat surface.

Balthus has painted many more landscapes than the few I have called upon here. Some of these will come up in later discussions. For now, the point I have been making is that the artistic imagination of this painter produces images that are primarily and crucially two-dimensional. In many of these paintings there may be a very real object the artist has depicted in the most realist mode he could muster, but something in his artist's imagination would always present the vision as an image. And that utterly imaginative, "imaging" way of looking at reality compelled him to make pictures that would never let us forget that they are just that; pictures, beautifully crafted, but before all, imagined. Indeed, it is in the craft that he appropriates the visions, and then offers them for view.

Paysage d'Italie, 1951.
Landscape of Italy.
Oil on canvas, 59 × 87 cm.
Private collection.

La Bergerie, 1957-1960.
The Sheep Farm.
Oil on canvas, 50 × cm. 101.5 cm.
Private collection.

17. That discussion will have to wait for another time and place. For interested readers I can refer to Ernst van Alphen (2004) who re-envisions abstraction along Deleuzian lines, relying on John Rajchman's discussion (1995). Balthus has always denied he was anything but a realist, but as I have mentioned, I am not interested in appealing to his statements, only those in paint, ink and pencil.

18. For convenience's sake I will avoid the clumsy "his or her" formulations, even when speaking of artists and viewers in general, except when issues of gender are explicitly at stake.

3. Figuration in an Age of Abstraction

When the artist André Masson entered the first exhibition of the then 25 years-old Balthus at the Pierre gallery in Paris, he was flabbergasted. "But this is figurative!" he exclaimed, as if the young artist had committed a crime. This anecdote, cited almost as frequently as the artist's rebuttal of biography, is the starting point for an inquiry into figuration and its relation to realism by the French author Evelyne Grossman on Artaud, Beckett, and Michaux, (2004). These three artists, all contemporaries of Balthus and evolving in the Paris art milieu of the time, couldn't be more different from our painter. Yet, if the critic evokes Balthus in the context of this awesome threesome, it is for a good reason. Although in a very different mode, he, like them, explored the ins and outs of figuration as a way into an anti-realism that could serve the cause of art. For, Balthus, as earnestly as these colleagues, had a religious belief in the value of art in a world that was crumbling around him.

Grossman uses the term "de-figuration" to characterize the attempt of these artists to deploy figuration against itself. Balthus was involved with something similar but on very different terms. He firmly adhered to figuration but deployed it against realism and, rejecting what he considered the laziness of many abstract painters, also refused to be adopted by surrealism, which he considered too subjective. I argue, however, that his deployment of figuration is not exactly in the service of realism—at least not if we understand it as the adequate representation of a reality outside the painting. I can put the thesis of this chapter in very simple terms. For this artist, realism is a mode, not content; a visual discourse, not subject matter. A mode, that is, to do what he is obsessively doing: to make what he sees. In all its apparent simplicity, this is a great paradox, the central one in Balthus's art.

But that is only displacing the question from subject matter to seeing. He paints his imagination, his visual desire, excitement, and pleasure; or his fear, frustration, and inexplicable dreams. He paints what he sees in his mind. In this chapter I will continue the analysis of the ways in which "realism" is the wrong term to understand this work. Of course, it would be ludicrous to make the opposite claim, that Balthus is an abstract painter. Instead, the very notion of abstraction, in its binary opposition with figuration, might be up for revision.[17]

Figuration is not the imitation of reality. It is making, not copying figures, in sculpture, drawing or painting, that have shapes to which we, viewers, can give meanings that are connected with our own world. Limiting myself to two-dimensional images here, the task of the viewer is to connect images on flat surfaces with things, people, and pieces of the outside world we know. The artist offers such surfaces. But if he or she can claim that certain images are "his" or "hers" it is because the artist saw them, then made them. And in that making he put his "soul": his craft, skills, materials, and visions. These visions may be entirely imaginative, or based on things he, in turn, sees. But the artist's acts of seeing are always combinations of perception and imagination. As are our own visions. To vary on a well-known saying, the artist proposes, the viewer disposes; for better or for worse. This is what the very specific hanging of *Alice* (p. 21) in the Centre Pompidou brought home to the visitors.[18]

Continuing the discussion of color and space, now in relation to figuration, I begin with two paintings, *Bouquet de fleurs sur la fenêtre* (Bouquet of Roses on the Windowsill, p. 59) and *La Rue* (p. 19). The former stands in visual continuity with the landscapes discussed in the previous chapter. The latter will introduce new themes for our discussion. *Bouquet de fleurs* combines the genres of still life and landscape. We recognize the triangular shapes and the

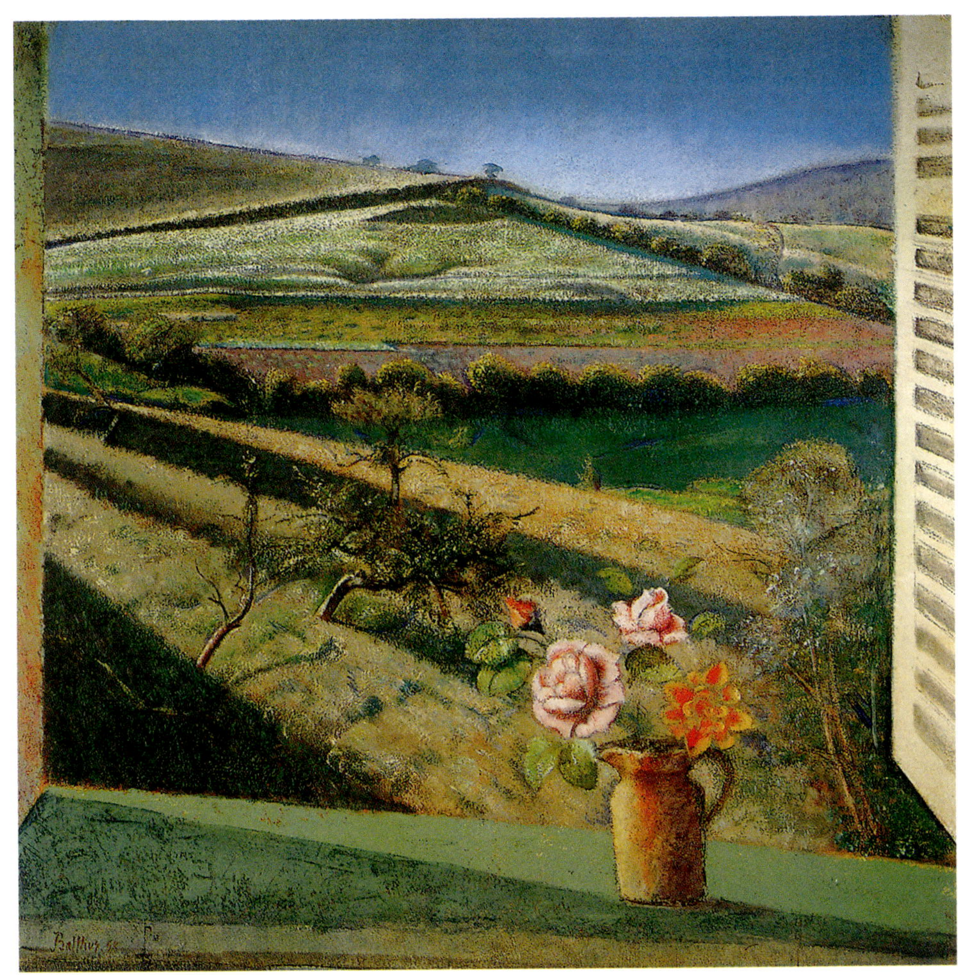

rigorous geometry of *Le Champ triangulaire* (p. 43). The shutters remind us of those images of rooms with views where the window frames the view to become a painting on the wall. *La Rue*, a work that is both rather exceptional and very famous, is connected with the issue of shallow space in different ways, and presents the issue of human figures in a new light.

Bouquet de fleurs sur la fenêtre, 1958.
Bouquet of Roses on the Windowsill.
Oil on canvas, 134 × 131 cm.
Indianapolis Museum of Art, Indianapolis.

The painting *Bouquet de fleurs* frames nature within the domestic setting where so much of Balthusian dramaturgy is set. It is set inside, but on the edge—in more senses than one. The color of the sky is a daring dark though powdery blue that is totally different from the sky in the *Le Champ triangulaire* (p. 43). The portion of the painting set outside has a similar although busier color scheme, including even the shadowed triangle on the left, which is repeated at a sharper angle on the green windowsill. The vase of flowers introduces new colors: yellow and ochre on the jug, yellow and orange on the one flower that is not a rose. And, of course, the most delicate shades of pink, capturing the light of the fleeting moment. As Weber remarks in the context of this painting, Balthus "painted flowers on a windowsill as they exist at only one brief moment of the morning. Canvases that he took years to complete evoke fleeting instants" (1999: 50). This temporal aspect is crucial to the understanding of figuration in this art. We have seen it already, for example, in the mist floating above the steep slope of *Grand paysage avec vache* (p. 42).

The biographer seems to concur with my earlier contention about viewing the visions offered up by artists. "Everything else disappeared from my thoughts as I succumbed to the vision before me", he writes. And he continues to describe the way the painting erased everything else from his mind (487-488). He even speaks of "intoxication" and "paradise" (488). The writer's adventures with this painting are worth reading for the power of the painting it first extols, and then questions. Seeing eroticism in the vase (as I do not) and the passage of time in the flowers (as I do too), he reflects on the futility of citing sources (Bonnard, Courbet) in preference to looking with what can be summed up as his body-and-soul. What seems at first a wordy description of a personal, idiosyncratic moment ends up as a convincing self-reflection on the "the artist proposes, the viewer disposes" maxim.

The precariousness of time in the fleeting moment that these pink petals captured, just that afternoon when light is no longer stable, coincides with an equally precarious spatial positioning. This is due to a flatness effect. What is ostensibly a shadow—the darker triangle of green on the windowsill—cuts the green color field in symmetrical halves of a surface, thus establishing their flatness. The jug stands right on the line that separates these two triangular fields. The narrow shadow on its right just confirms the realism but is so tiny that it is barely noticeable, only subtly breaking the otherwise monotonous division of the green fields. This subtlety is remarkable; it is where flatness and figuration join forces to produce emotions such as Weber describes. The jug itself is equally subtly both convincing in its illusion of three-dimensionality as it is a flat image, cut out with utter precision, its bottom disposed in that green/green line like just another dark, brown line.

Nothing, in this painting, makes it comparable to the robust and enigmatic early *La Rue* from 1933. As a cityscape, that work is more appropriately juxtaposed with the earlier *Les Quais* (p. 11) from 1929 or the later *Passage du Commerce Saint-André* from 1952-1954 (p. 12). What I seek to enhance by the association, however, is the ambiguity in the figuration as both flat and three-dimensional at the same time. In other words, along with that still life with landscape, combining two utterly realistic genres, *La Rue* can be taken as another instance of a realistic mode of painting in the service of the creation of a world of the imagination, one offered for a viewing which is conceived of as making connections. This may be paradoxical when we consider the figures. These bizarre figures—all of them are peculiar—are painted in great detail to enhance the way they fail to connect. Or do they?

Many critics have written interesting things on this strange painting. Jean Starobinski's article on Balthus's dramaturgy suggests that this painting exemplified the difference between classical history painting and this "stilled dramaturgy" of film stills where figures are immobilized and look like "mannequins". Starobinski also mentions the boy on the left whose assault on the girl announces Balthus's consistent erotic preoccupation, on which I will elaborate more later. For Starobinski, this boy's closed eyes and the resulting undetermined look constitute the "psychological vanishing point" of the painting. This point contrasts, geometrically as well as psychologically, with the alleged vanishing point that constructs the illusion of space. That point, however, is obliterated by the distorting and distorted walls, windows, and signs (1996: 25).

Citing sources—most notably Piero della Francesca in certain figures and Seurat for the composition and the stilled nature of the scene, but also surrealist fantasy and futurist mechanical dolls—again seems besides the point of what most keenly defines this painting. But the critical foci on modernist atmosphere (Clair 1999), dramaturgy (Starobinski 1996), dreamscape (Verschaffel 2004), and tableau vivant (Pierre Klossowski 1983) raise the issue of figuration in its relation to the modernity of the days. But if this is dramaturgy, what a strange play is staged! The only possible connection—physically aggressive, but no eye contact—is that between the assailant and his victim on the lower left, although her closed eyes and face don't reveal much either. Whether the physical contact is consensual or not remains indeterminate.[19]

The carpenter in white carrying a plank is on his way elsewhere. The automaton of Italian futurism, that moon-faced doll on his way to the picture plane and oblivious to the activities around him, is holding his arms for a split second before swiping his left arm at the woman who seems to step on the sidewalk to avoid a collision. While he looks like the empty-eyed figure in Massaccio's *History of Theophile* of Clair's engaging iconographic analysis, he also simply looks like a wind-up doll (right). The nurse carrying an adult baby looks ahead, while the alleged child looks in the opposite direction. The dwarf-like girl playing in the foreground is looking at her finger, not her ball. Verschaffel sees in this creature the ultimate evidence for his interpretation of the "probing gaze"—probing the lower belly, as he calls it (2004: 54). Clair, jollier, just sees the mirror image of a Robbia putto (1983: 260). The chef standing in front of a restaurant is the site of dimensional indeterminacy. He can be either a figure—but then, what is he doing there, in the street?—or a sign advertising the dishes of the day on his apron/blackboard. As the mise en abyme of this tension between realism and fantasy, and between three- and two-dimensionality, he/it is like the jug in *Bouquet*.[20]

The street is painted in great detail, but the fresco-like green-yellow wall in the back closes it off as a shallow, claustrophobic space, somewhere beyond the opposition between interior and exterior. This effect is further enhanced by the absence of the line demarcating the sidewalk. If seen as an interior—if not of a home, then of a dream—the decorator has done a fabulous job with the color scheme again. Take the reds, for instance. The red touches distribute the accents over the image, from the sweater of the assault victim, the ball rolling away from the dwarf, the sign near the upper middle, the stripes on the awning, going from red to orange and pink, rhyming with the pink-and-green sign next to it, the pompom on the "baby's" sailor's cap to, most remarkably, the crossed ribbons on the hat of the woman in elegant black, fitting exactly in the red frame of the window in the back wall. The skirt of the black costume of the woman in near-collision with the round-faced machine-man is repeated in the skirt of the nurse, whose white apron makes her seem more slender than her bulk as a whole suggests. The two sides of this apron cast an imagined connection with the carpenter in white, although the two figures are rigorously oriented in different directions, at a right angle from each other.[21]

As the chef, or sign, already indicates, even in this very full and lively picture the shallowness of space is charged with reflections on picture making. And as the marionette with its stiff arms further intimates, another ambiguity is superimposed on this one, shifting the reflection from painting to cultural philosophy. I am referring to the ambiguity between the formal perfection of automatons as the products of human ambition, the hybrid of modernity, on the one hand, and the human condition of loneliness, emptiness, and always-

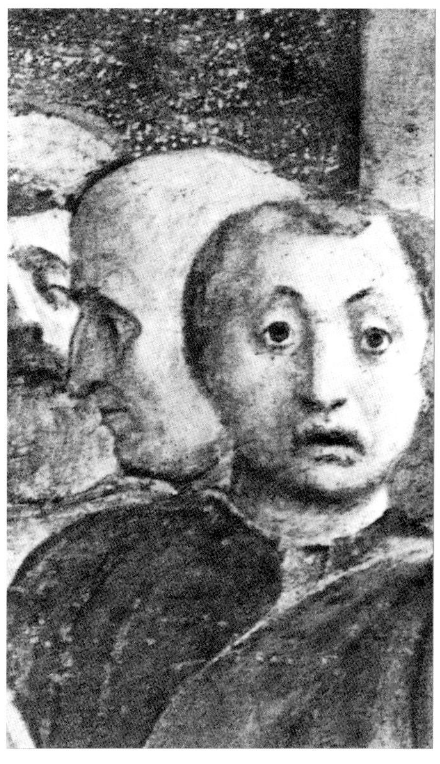

Masaccio,
detail of *History of Theophile*,
1426-1927.
Fresco.
Cappella Brancacci, Santa Maria del Carmine, Florence.

19. The painting itself still shows the traces of revisions, made at the request of the American owner, in the gesture of the young man on the lower left. In the first version, the arm was lower and he grabbed the skirt of the girl to raise it. The gesture in the revised version is just a fraction more ambiguous.

20. All this and much more has been noticed by, among others, Jean Clair (1983; 1999; 2001), Yves Bonnefoy (1983), Bart Verschaffel (2004), and Claude Roy (1996), to cite only the most interesting texts. "Mise en abyme" is a term from literary theory, although it originates in visuality. Derived from heraldry by André Gide, it theorizes the insertion, within a larger work, of one of its main elements, such as a mirror image. Usually, the term indicates self-reflexivity. See Dällenbach (1989).

21. Jean Clair (1999: 7) invokes Walter Benjamin's view of the streets of Paris as ambiguously domestic (for the stroller) in his book on Baudelaire, (1974) or his unfinished work on the Parisian *Passagen* (1999).

imminent catastrophe, on the other. Both tendencies are located in the city, and the absence of cars underlines what the shallow space already demonstrated: that busy city life draws impenetrable circles around individual lives.

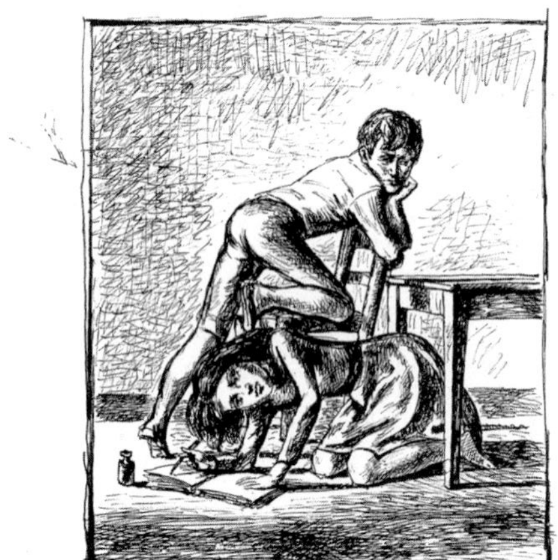

Artistically, the rigidity of doll-like figures is not softened but complicated, by the aliveness, activity, and grace with which the realist mode of painting infuses it. One symptom of their living-dead quality is the feet. All the female figures have obese thick legs, but small feet, wearing indoor slippers—the nurse's ones are pink, as part of a secondary color chain. The "child" playing has an old face, the boy being carried is reading the paper and has a very un-chubby, elongated triangular face. Rather than sitting on the nurse's arm, he appears to be climbing a mountain. Producing flatness and suggesting depth, fashioning man-made puppets and deferring to outside reality: both sides of both ambiguities are necessary to achieve the implication of the viewer, which is imperative for making art meaningful. They are also necessary for the strange fantasies of Balthus's dreams to be "convincing" while at the same time becoming "other-realities".

This otherness of Balthusian reality is even more conspicuous in the two related paintings I mentioned earlier, *Les Quais* and *Passage du Commerce Saint-André*. Already in 1929, barely twenty-one years old, Balthus made the city the setting of non-communication. The figure of the lone man walking away in *Les Quais*, usually considered as the artist (in his refusal to be visible, turning his back) walks in the opposite direction from the fisherman, who is walking to the lower right corner of the picture. There is a still life standing at the feet of the old woman with the cat. She looks rigidly ahead of herself, at no one. The boy leaning above her may look at her, at her cat, or at her basket, but his gaze is not returned.

The only figure looking at anyone—at the viewer, that is—is the cat. Is he appealing for help, or sympathy, in the impossibly uncomfortable grip of the woman who seems unwilling to move, hence, to let go of him? Or is this just an instance of the all-too-brief moment, and the cat will jump away right after? The cat's despair returns in that of the baby-man in *La Rue*, who appears also to be trying to escape from the firm grip that holds him. Yet, the stillness of these cutout figures is not that of durability. The ominous clouds in the sky indicate that the moment is a fleeting one, like the light on the rose petals in *Bouquet* and the mist on the *Paysage d'Italie* (p. 56).

The later *Passage* is the third work in this small series, and to all accounts and purposes, the series' "Masterpiece". The old woman with her witch-like appearance returns here, now in the background but intensely lit. So does the slender man-artist, now holding a baguette which the light foregrounds and magically transforms into a wand. Neither of these figures is in *La Rue*. The space is similar, but the atmosphere is not at all. While the earlier work seemed to be a meditation on the emptiness of city life, the Passage conjured up a cast of ominous announcers of hopelessness. Bonnefoy calls this "une œuvre de détresse"; a distraught work (1983: 91).

The shallow space is more or less similar to that of *La Rue*, and so is the lack of interaction, but although there is no violence here, the solitude is more radical. The pensive young woman with her timeless blue skirt and her firmly planted feet remains in the shadow, a darkness that the narrow band of light on top of her hair only enhances. Her eyes are cast down. Although her feet are cropped at the lower edge, her closeness to the picture plane doesn't bring her closer to us, for, as we know by now, this is "only" an image. Nor is she close to the straight-backed man who has just an instant before passed her—but theirs is a failed encounter. Bonnefoy speaks of the passage being "l'étouffement du possible"—the suffocation of the possible (91).

The old woman, whose hunchback the light mercilessly emphasizes, walks as straightly as the man with the blue shirt—one painful step at a time. But no encounter seems likely there either. The baby-man on the nurse's arm is now an old dwarf, sitting hunched on the sidewalk, and the light, just as mercilessly, shines on his bald head. He is not about to establish contact with any of his fellow-loners. In the middle of the street a dog—exceptional in Balthus's fauna, almost exclusively populated by cats—sniffs at the ground, carrying all the light.

What happened to the round-faced automaton? He is now an equally round-faced baby, or doll, or portrait, above the only red accent of an otherwise opaque window on the left. He is the carrier or the confrontational gaze, along with his half-cropped twin standing in the door opening, and perhaps, half-heartedly, the small child playing with her doll but not quite looking at it. The red shutter establishes—in the sense of an establishing shot in cinema—the more muted, but spectacularly beautiful ancient red of the central empty screen of closed shutters of the background shop. In these paintings, drawing is done by means of colors, and the figuration of a sociogram of lonely people stands in tension with the overt figuration. The parts of the painting, like the individuals in a world, do not add up to the whole.

This red of the closed shutters belongs to history, the history of painting as consolation, not to the world of 1954. "Registres" says the sign in the center of the image. Registers, as in settling accounts, paying your dues, or as in different registers of reality? For, it is as such that we best look at the figurative representations that are set indoors. The children in *Les Enfants Blanchard* (The Blanchard Children, p. 64) are oblivious to the sparse furniture of their room, to the indication of cold in the stack of coals near the doorway, and to the discomfort of their poses. This is one of those scenes for which the artist is famous—and which makes viewers hesitate on the threshold of enchantment. No eye contact, neither with the viewer nor with each other, breaks the isolation. The boy may simply be pensive, the girl reading. But he looks straight ahead, while she looks neither at her book nor at us. This is very different from the frank and annoyed look of the boy at the girl, and her almost appealing look at the viewer, in the drawing on the same subject (p. 62). The difference demonstrates purpose and meaning.

The simple, bare kitchen table is painted with utter precision and detail. The variation of brown in the wooden legs, the shadows and light bands, the tiny accent of light where the leg is affixed by a craftsman to become part of a table: it is a celebration of two crafts that come together here, carpentry and painting. Between flat and bodily, the children have volume. The bodies in their clothing, especially the torso and buttocks, foreground this. Yet, their outline also makes them cutouts, images, a collage. And these children, who look younger than their counterparts in ink, are portraits of real children as much as they are dolls, taking on poses designed for the image.[22]

Or take those unreal figures of the *La Partie de cartes* (The Game of Cards, p. 66) or their nasty successors of *Les Joueurs de cartes* (The Card Players, p. 67). Both paintings emanate that reference to ancient art, although in very different manners. They stand in the tradition of *Cheaters*—Caravaggio comes to mind, who turned the cheating into a class issue, and Georges

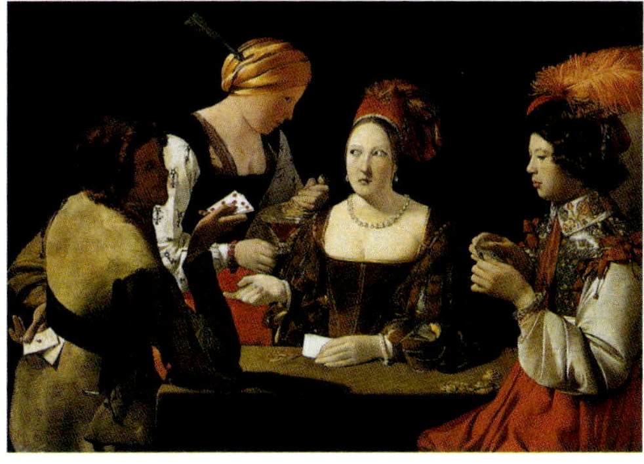

Parce que Cathy lui enseignait tout ce qu'elle apprenait, 1933-1935.
I have got the time on with writing for twenty minutes.
Ink on paper, 38.8 × 31 cm.
Legacy Maxina Duchamp.

Georges De la Tour,
Le Tricheur à l'as de carreau, 1635.
Cheater with the Ace of Diamond.
Oil on canvas, 106 x 146 cm.
Musée du Louvre, Paris.

22. Something of this order may have made Picasso purchase the painting.

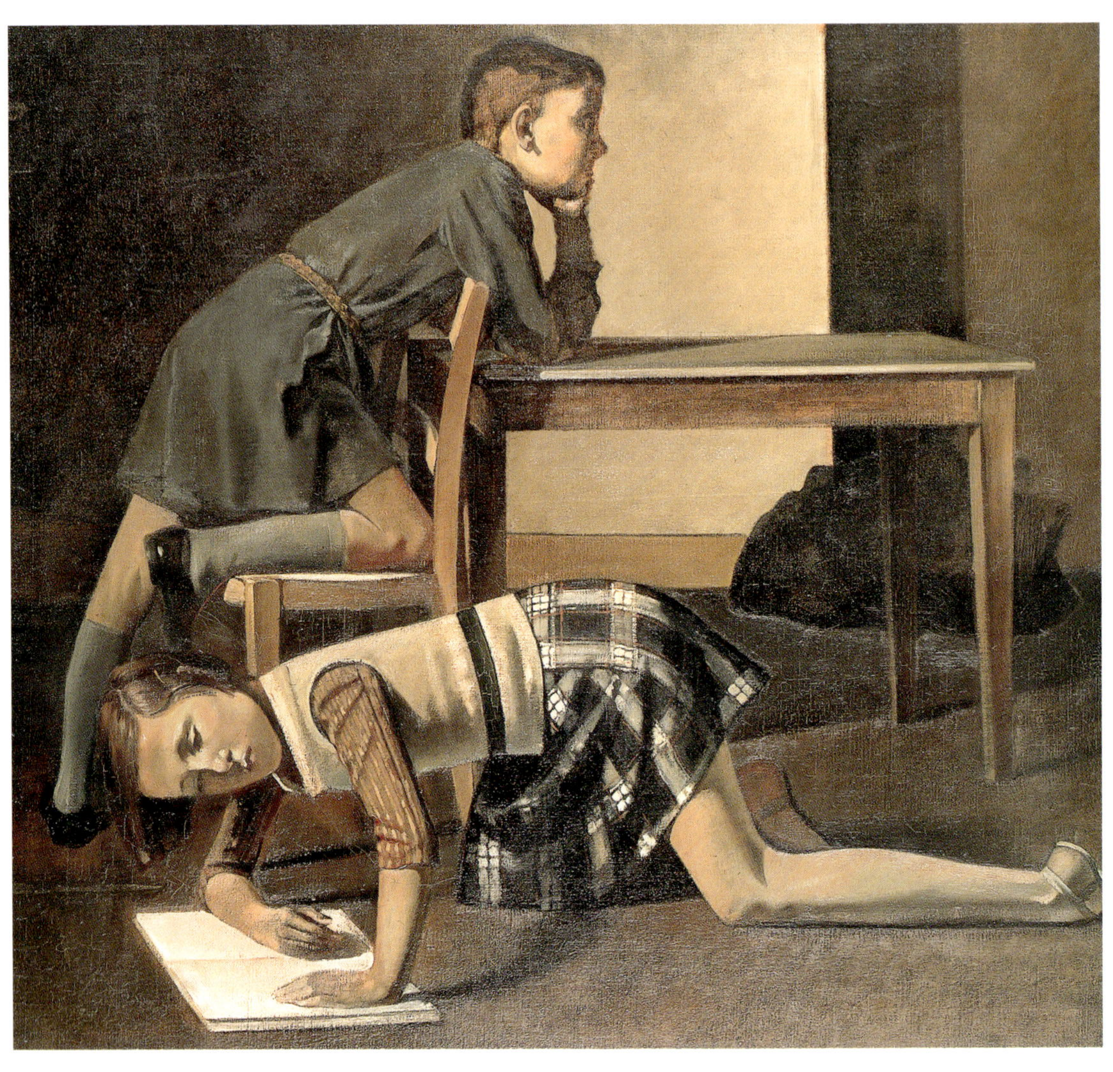

de la Tour, who liked the chiaroscuro atmosphere (p. 63), both elements that are, I suggest, emphatically absent in *La Partie*. The candle is there, but it is not lighted. The light comes from the right, and it is daylight. It enhances the cheater's buttocks, so that he looks almost naked, as well as the flatness of the victim's chest. Her elegantly stretched leg cannot help it: this figure is gender-ambiguous. The beautiful greens that dominate the furniture, the interior painting, and the victim's dress, the golden brown of the wall and the lighter version of the cheater's pants—if that's what they are—and other shades of it in both figures' hair and faces, are a harmony in ancient coloring. The red of the shirt is the only different color, unless we count the white shoes of the one figure and the white stockings of the other.

Les Enfants Blanchard, 1937.
The Blanchard Children.
Oil on canvas, 125 × 130 cm.
Musée du Louvre
(Musée Picasso), Paris.

Gender ambiguity is also obvious in the figure in blue in *Les Joueurs de cartes*. Moreover, in this painting the ancient quality comes from the use of casein and tempura, which gives the large background wall the aspect of an old fresco, or used paper, or ashes, with the added advantage of seeming close to the picture plane. The light is dusk. The head on the left is triangular, the one on the right is square; both look like cutouts. And what is the empty chair at the front doing there, other than those two typical jobs, of displaying the meticulously detailed mode of painting, especially displayed in humble, crafted furniture, and narrowing the space even more?[23]

The ambiguities that I have alleged to characterize Balthus's work so far are the primary ones of a whole range of other ambiguities. One is of scale. The strange picture *La Famille Mouron-Cassandre* (The Mouron-Cassandre Family, p. 68) recalls the man-baby in *La Rue* and the old dwarf in *Passage*. The old woman there can hardly be as small as she is compared to the painter merely because of perspective, since she is barely a few steps farther away. In the Mouron-Cassandre family portrait, the boy quietly sitting on the table reading a book is less than half the size of his gigantic sister, who, in turn, has an exceptionally small head in this oeuvre of hydrocephalic figures, compared with the head of her mother. The ensemble of five pale legs, however, suggests all figures are of the same size. We have already seen how unlikely the proportions are in *Alice dans le miroir*. In the same manner, the woman about to fly away like an antique angel in *Lady Abdy* (p. 69) has a body so elongated that she may not be able to haul it out of that window. In all these cases of problematic scale, the space is impossibly narrow.

Let me wind up this discussion through one of the works that deploy many strategies of figuration in the service of fantasy and thus sums up what is at stake in calling Balthus a realist—*La Chambre* (The Bedroom, pp. 70 and 72). This ambitious work, huge in size, is among those that have oriented the reputation of the artist in the direction of scandal, although by the time he painted it, he was no longer seeking scandal to establish his name. The sleeping nude girl extended on the chaise longue counts among the most provocative Balthusian nudes. Her legs are spread, although not towards the viewer. The light caresses her flesh. White socks and slippers indicate that her undressing is incomplete and this can mean anything the viewer may wish to imagine.

Let me offer a few examples of what they may imagine. Bart Verschaffel wrote an extensive iconographic analysis to demonstrate that "the principal source" of the painting is a piece of Renaissance erotic art, to wit, an engraving by Augustino Carracci (p. 71). The author makes a strong claim of methodology, attempting to differentiate painting from literature in terms

23. Significantly, the ancient colors and this "shallowing" chair are the subject of an article by abstract artist François Rouan, who discusses it in combination with Mondrian, Duchamp, and his own work (1993).

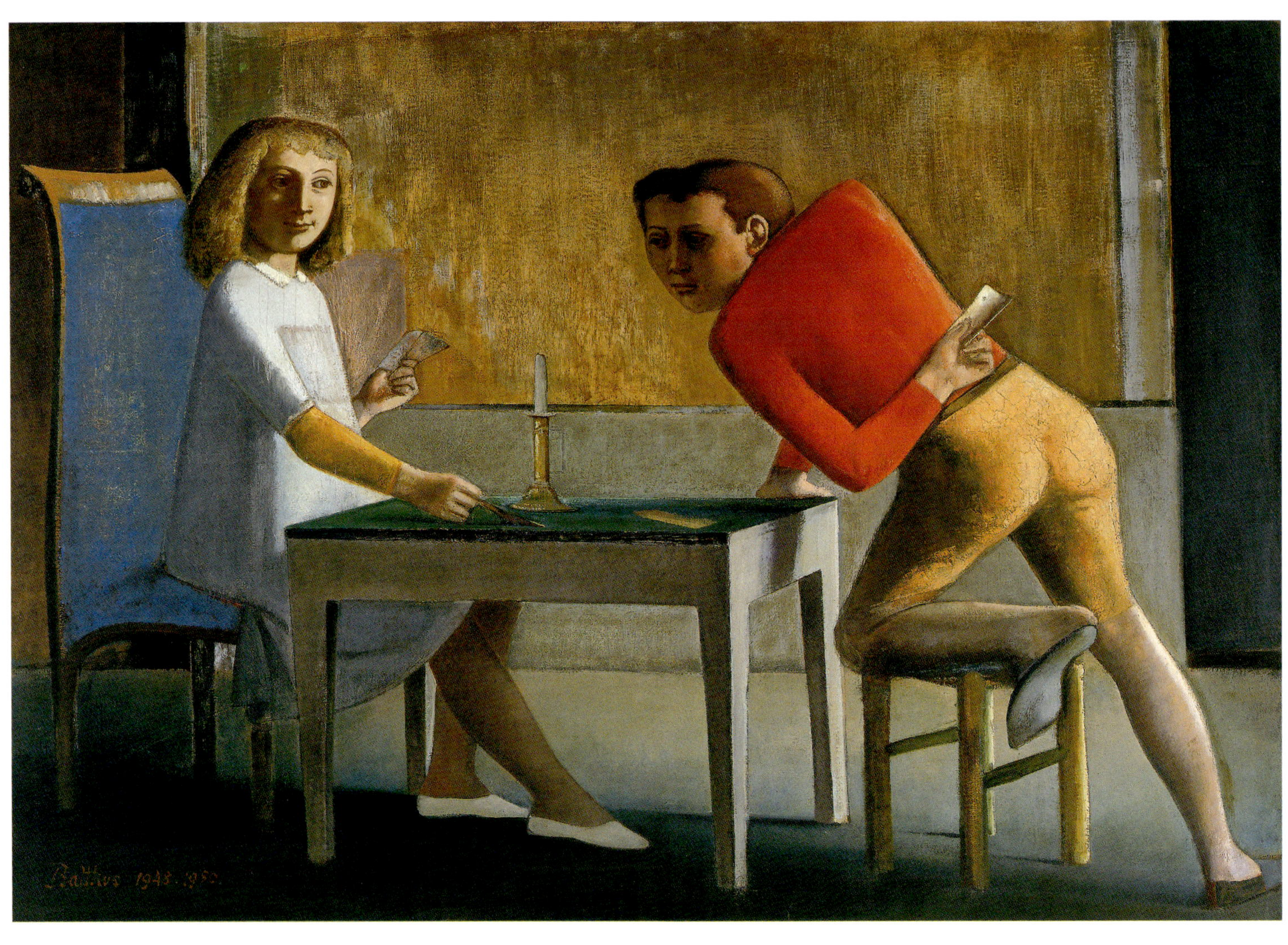

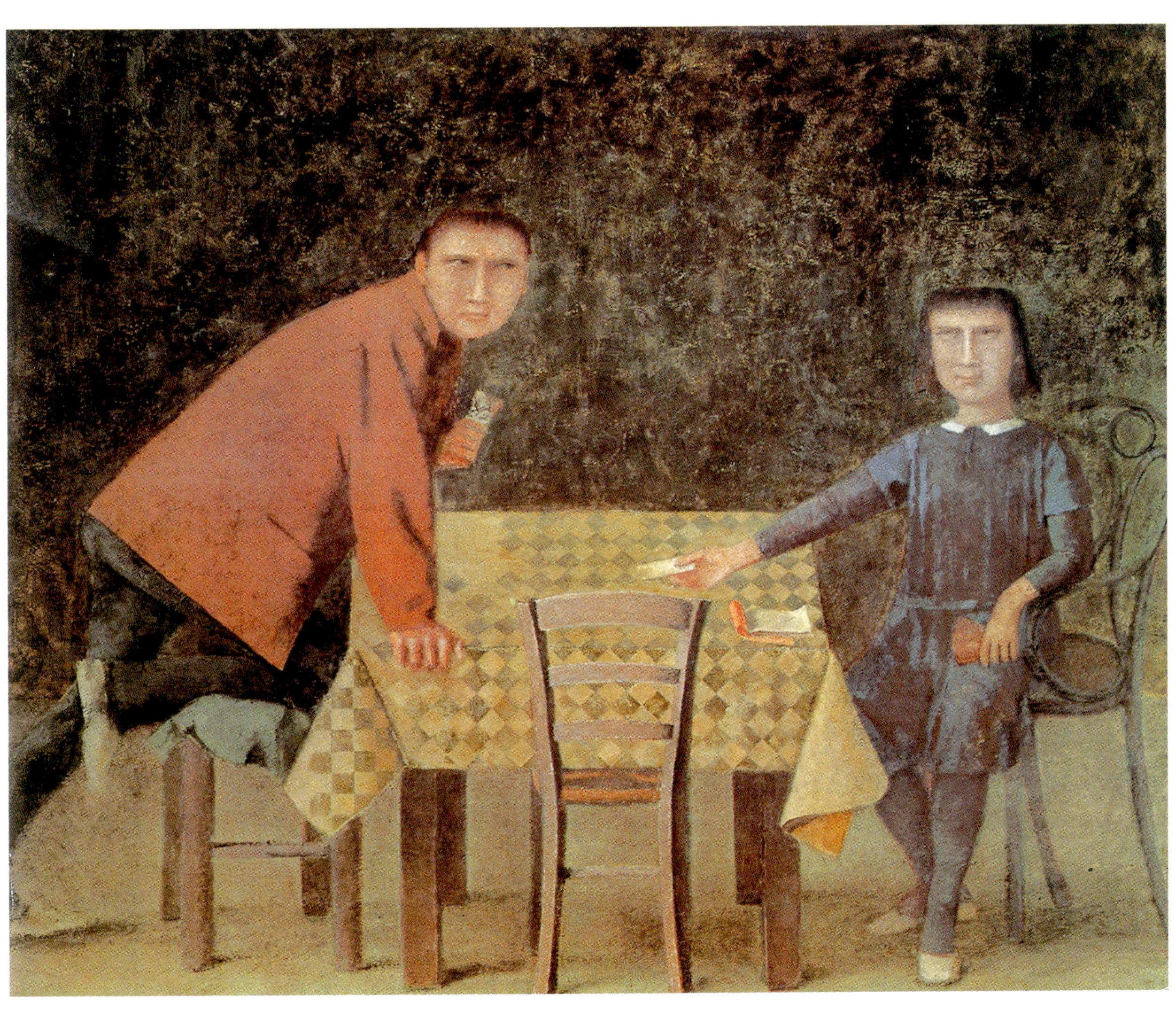

La Partie de cartes, 1948-1950.
The Game of Cards.
Oil on canvas, 139.7 × 193.7 cm.
Thyssen Foundation, Madrid.

Les Joueurs de cartes, 1966-1973.
The Card Players.
Casein, oil, and tempura on canvas, 190 × 223 cm.
Museum Boimans-van Beuningen, Rotterdam.

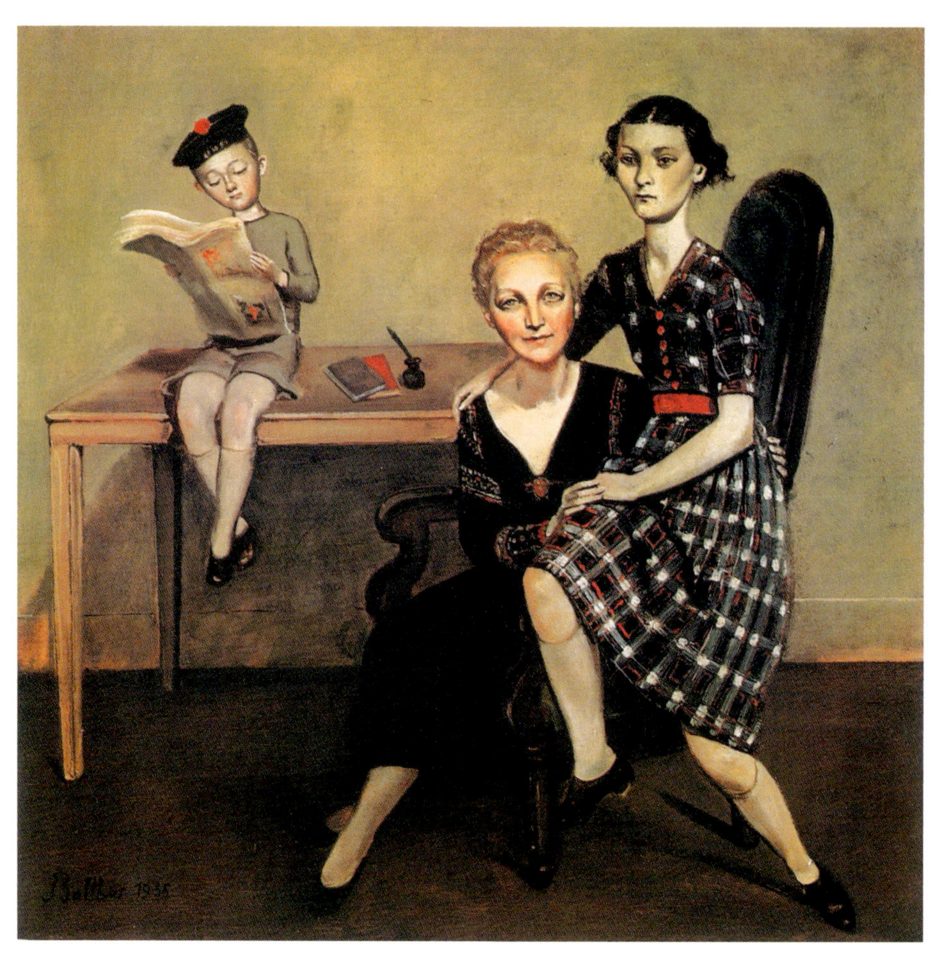

La Famille Mouron-Cassandre, 1935.
The Mouron-Cassandre Family.
Oil on canvas, 72 × 72 cm.
Private collection.

Lady Abdy, 1935.
Oil on canvas, 186 × 140 cm.
Private collection.

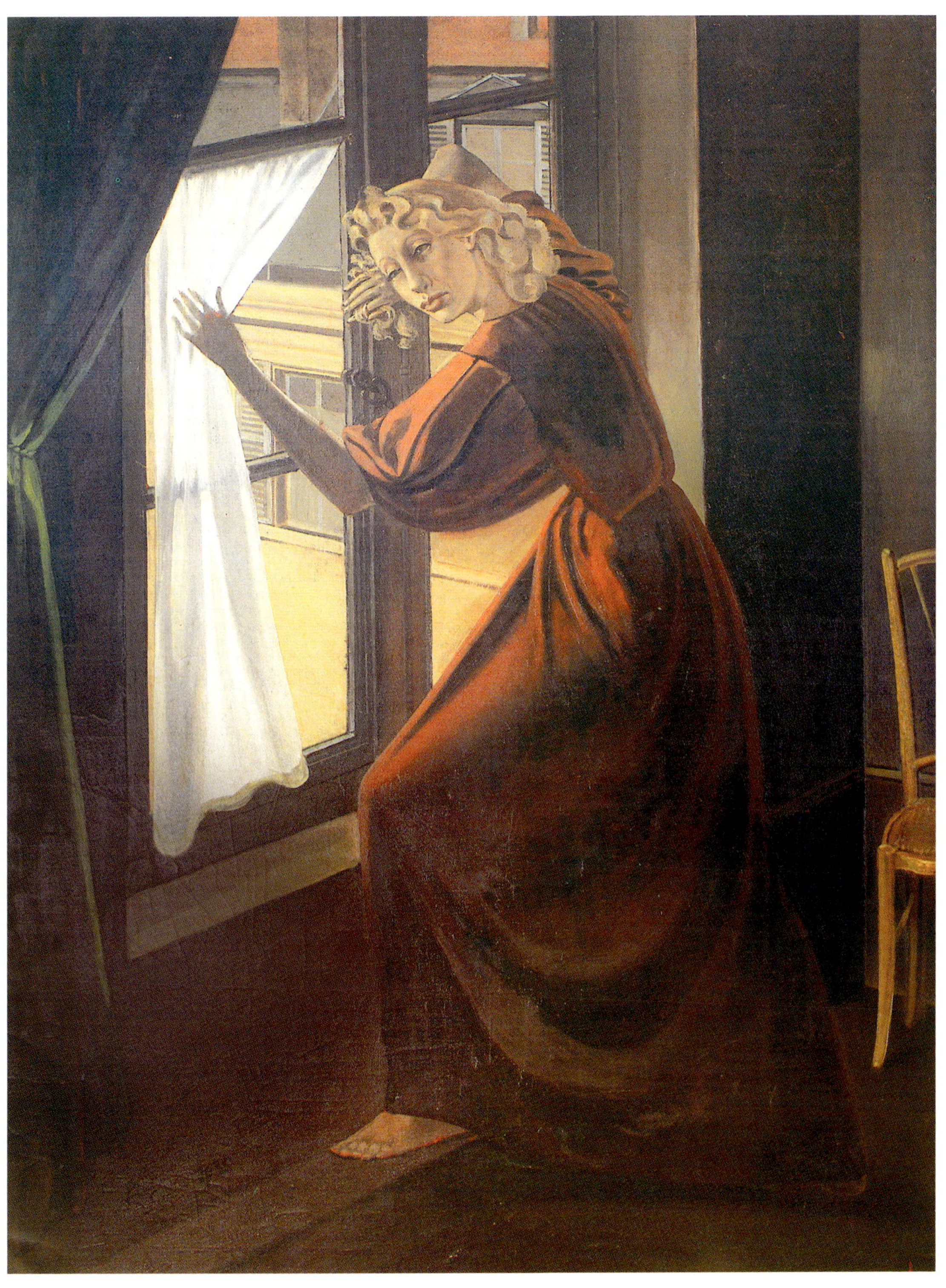

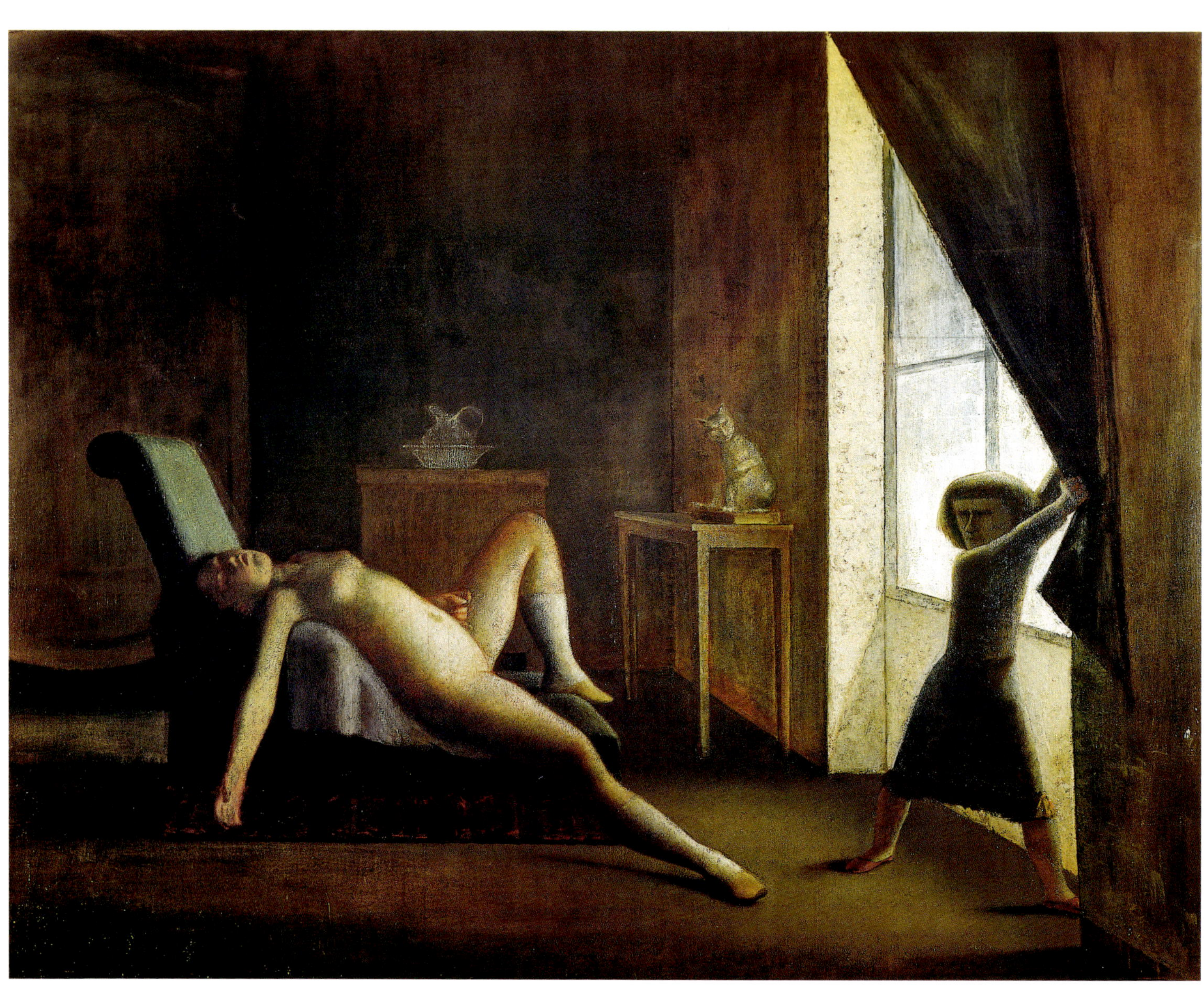

of temporality. Painting is an arresting of an apparition, and thus becomes an object of meditation. The religious vocabulary may surprise, but our artist used it himself as well (2004: 23). After first arguing that we should not look at painting as narratives (23-24), the critic ends up with a strong narrative reading.

The main figure of such reading is the holder of what he calls the "probing gaze". When he reaches the stage of putting together secondary sources, however, the critic becomes entangled in his own narrative impulse when he narrates what happens in the image (44). He ends this excursion into story-telling with the conclusion: "The engraving by Carrachi was made for the voyeur" (44). Voyeurism, indeed, is not only offered as a position for the viewer, but actually staged. But what figure is this, who is standing in for the viewer? Weber calls it a "demonic amalgam of little girl and old man" (30). The figure of the dwarf-like, gender-ambiguous creature in a blue skirt opens the curtain to let in the light. Light, so that he/she, and we, can see the nude girl.

This work is also central in a text by Balthus's brother, the writer Pierre Klossowski, whose key term is "tableau vivant", a paradoxical term for an actual painting. Tableaux vivants are supposed to be live enactments of the poses represented in paintings, while Klossowski is clearly referring to something else: not just the reverse, the depiction of still poses, but rather the depiction of poses held precariously, in a fleeting moment, a temporal cut-out from a drama that will resume its course right after. The point he is trying to make through this term is the sense of arresting a process, of the temporality of the still, as well as the artificiality of the pose—he calls it the excess of the pose. The scene is utterly dramatic, so that Klossowski's term rings true, in spite of the fact that it doubles up the tension between real and depicted: a tableau vivant is a live representation of a painting that represents a live scene. Theater returns to theater. But what is lost in the cycle is language; what is gained is silence.[24]

In that silence, the viewer is reduced to the sense of sight. This sense opens the realm of the imagination. Critics give evidence of this effect. I'll allege three responses. The first is of Klossowski, who is sensitive to the temporality and the representational paradox. Between the first and the last moment of theatricality, reality never intervenes, but temporality does—movement, arrest, antique resonances, and modern sensibility. The second is by Verschaffel, whose response is suggestive of a preoccupation with voyeurism that he brings to bear on a painting that may be asking for it, but does not impose the simple version that the critic alleges. The third critic is Weber, whose response is the most fanciful. He hints that the girl might be pregnant. The resulting iconographic exercise brings in Piero della Francesca's "equally baffling *Madonna del Parto*" (1999: 123; also 126). For me, these three responses are evidence of the image's imaginative power, rather than being evidence of any real source—as if that mattered; as if meaning, let alone affective effect, was transferred wholesale with figurations.[25]

I may as well add my own response: the somewhat chubby belly of the girl is an indication of her pre-adolescent age, and, along with her stockings, a disturbing confrontation with childhood sexuality—as a question, not a statement. The dwarf might be about to violate her or he or she might have just done that, as some fanciful readings have it; it may be male or female or both. Or, the girl might just be taking a nap on a hot afternoon. Clair (1999: 14) writes that the body, in such works as this,

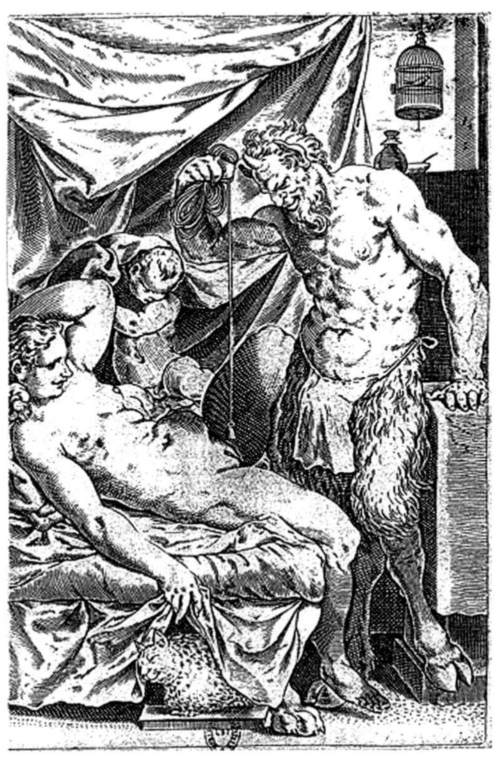

La Chambre, 1952-1954.
The Bedroom.
Oil on canvas, 270.5 × 335 cm.
Private collection.

Agustino Carracci,
The probing Satyr.
Engraving, 20.1 x 13.4 cm.

24. Klossowski's text was first published in 1957, reprinted in 1983. Verschaffel's book is recent (2004).

25. I have discussed this issue at length in the introduction to my book on Caravaggio and contemporary art (1999).

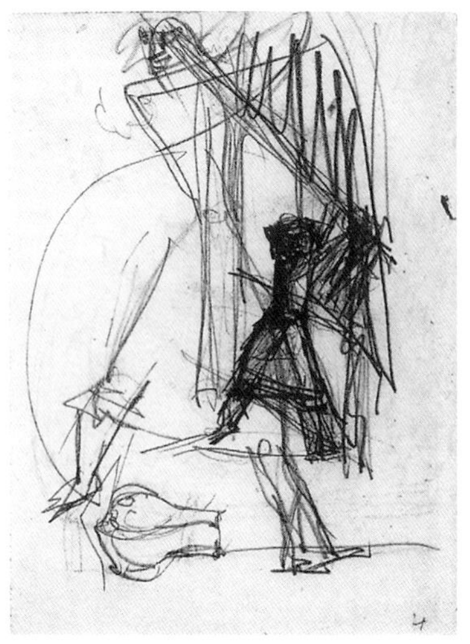

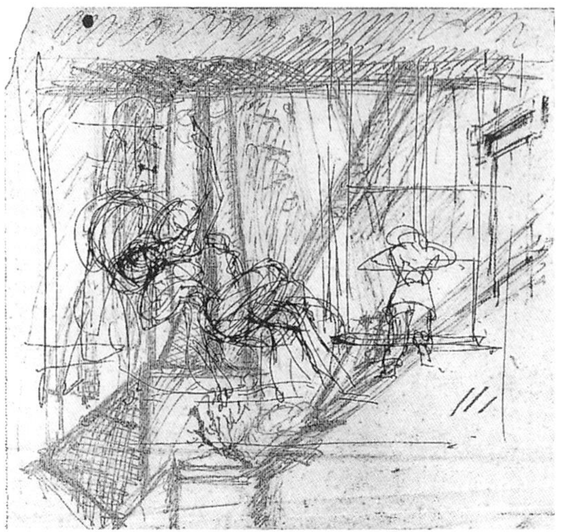

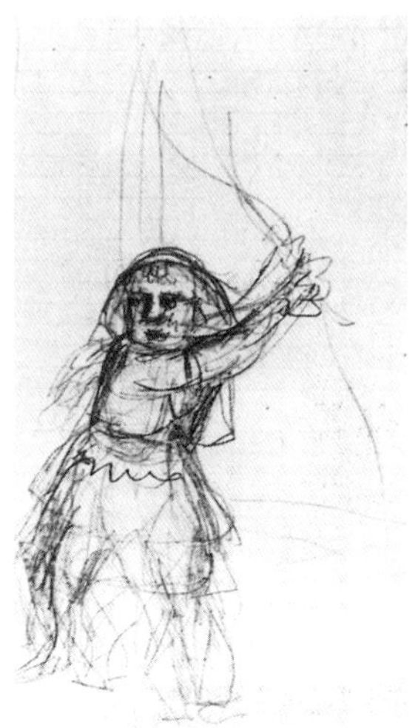

> ... appears to partake of both orders, that of the perfection of the marionette, which ensures its capacity unthinkingly to obey the laws of gravity, and that of the vulnerability of the flesh, which opens it to a higher awareness, an unlimited grace ... It is their fusion that produces this bizarre anatomy, as surprising and moving to us as were, in their day, the nudes of Lucas Cranach or Gustave Courbet.

Although I don't see the divinity in these bodies that Clair places there, the point of this ambiguity is articulated sharply: perfection without will, and vulnerability with grace. Fused, they lead to something that, before this painting, did not exist; and something that needs a witness. And it has one.

The cat, that favorite animal in Balthus's universe, is a silent witness to whatever happens, and the presence of such a witness does several things to the image. Cats can remain still forever, but you cannot count on it. They may jump up at any time. They are silent, although they can scream like hungry infants, which they do especially when in heat, when being hurt, or when something seriously shocking happens in their orbit. Cats are the animal realm's answer to the film still. None of the drawings related to this huge, life-size painting resolve its enigma for us.

Esquisse pour «La Chambre» (Sketch for *The Bedroom*, above left) examines the sole act performed before us: the drawing of the curtain. But the nude is not there. *Étude pour «La Chambre»* (Study for *The Bedroom*, above center), in contrast, studies the composition, the two figures standing in oblique and vertical lines, but the dwarf turns its back to the girl. *Étude pour «La chambre»* (Study for *The Bedroom*, above right), gives the figure of the dwarf a portrait, a face, though now the study concerns the pose of the legs and feet of that creature. The facial features are drawn in strong, bold lines, the lower part of the body in tentative thin and light ones. What is it, then, that frames this picture as rigorously fantastic, not realistic?

It is its size, for a start, which precludes an encompassing gaze. The viewer must come close in order to see more than shapes, with the effect that the painting can no longer be surveyed in its entirety. The sense of spatial restriction: the image may be huge, but the represented room is not. The two side walls converge at the narrow back wall. The still life behind the girl: are we going to see this, hence, look at a painting, or skip it, and dream away? It's our call. The simple kitchen table the cat is sitting on is such a well-crafted piece of painting that its very realism fails to make us fall for it; instead, it attracts attention to itself as painting. The cat's gaze: looking at the dwarf, it is endowed with human eyes.

Finally, the windows, cut-through with a grid, as in *Le Peintre et son modèle* (p. 10), give access to a patch of incredible color, but no outside view. That light that shines on the body before us, this window tells us, comes from painting, not from the sun. And once the perception has shifted from reality to paint, the illuminated side of the wall next to the window begins to rhyme with the oblique body. When I see this painting, I find myself unable to process it as the image of a scene. It may be a tableau vivant, but not an image for safe and quiet voyeurism. If it were just that, wouldn't we see a little more? The way the opened legs do not face us may be either a teaser, or a caution; a provocation or an act of censorship. Asking what it is, however, makes the painting a figuration of viewing.

Clearly, the three technical aspects—color, space, and figuration—that so far may make my analysis seem rather formalistic, all lead up to, and frame, the question of what it is that this strange, unfashionable oeuvre represents: the question of content. If I have postponed that discussion until after a good "formal" look at the works, it is in order to frame this discussion within an awareness of what looking at art amounts to; of our own contribution to any effect a work of art may have; of art as encounter, not passive consumption; of art as relation, neither objective nor subjective. In the case of Balthus, I realize that this may seem defensive, and please rest assured that I will not shy away from the discussion of what it is that may be disturbing. But I also find it important to address those issues with a sense of every viewer's complicity in any possible disturbance. And that collusion is not only individual, but also cultural. Whoever looks at Balthus has looked at, say, Cézanne's bathers, Degas's dancers, Renoir's blushing girls, and Manet's insolent naked woman. Among many, many others. In the following, I will switch gears and discuss what is there to see in Balthus's images, including what is the most problematic aspect of his reputation—if not of his work as a whole.

Esquisse pour «La Chambre», 1952-1953.
Sketch for *The Bedroom*.
Crayon gras on paper, 21 × 15 cm.
Private collection.

Étude pour «La Chambre», 1953.
Study for *The Bedroom*.
Ink on paper, 29.5 × 30.5 cm.
Private collection.

Étude pour «La Chambre».
Study for *The Bedroom*.
Pencil on paper.

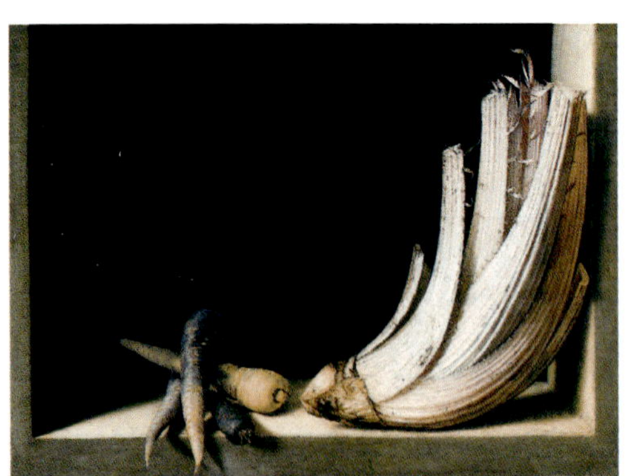

Juan Sánchez Cotán,
Bodegón con cardo y zanahorias,
1603-1627.
Still Life with Thistle and Carrots.
Oil on canvas, 62 x 82 cm.
Museo de Bellas Artes, Granada.

Fruits sur le rebord d'une fenêtre,
1956.
Fruits on a Windowsill.
Oil on canvas, 66.5 × 86.5 cm.
Private collection.

4. Genres and Their Discontents

What we see is framed by expectations. These, in turn, are shaped by conventions, such as those of genres. Genres are labels that give us an entrance into what we are going to see. Facing a landscape we expect to see nature, and the figures that sometimes populate it may already surprise. The signs, or symptoms of the human, social world remain tiny, easy to overlook, and irrelevant, absorbed in the might of nature that is the primary object of our gaze. A still life attracts our attention to the creatural aspects of things. Craftsmanship may be highlighted in multiple ways. Often, through the craft of depiction attention is drawn to the craft of making the objects. The craft of depiction is also used to enhance the appeal of the texture of bread, the inside of a lemon peel, or the ostentation of a rich bourgeois breakfast table. Portraits raise the question of individuality and likeness. Do we recognize the sitter, already known, do we get to know him or her, or do we encounter an image? History painting brings back into our memory the grand adventures of humanity as our culture has imagined them, with the examples from mythology, or the lessons of faith. And then, there is the nude, allegedly the celebration of human beauty, usually female, depicted, usually, by male artists. These works are sometimes voyeuristic, sometimes suggesting sexual exploitation.

Balthus has worked in many of the classical genres. We have already seen some of his exquisite landscapes, and although the formats of these works tend to be unusual—vertical, near-square, or extremely horizontal—we have no trouble identifying, then judging them as what that genre label tells us they are. In this sense, genres are discursive frames, directions for use, didactic tools to the same extent as artists' names, dates, indications of artistic movements to which they belonged, and summaries of content. Some of this information may be affixed next to the paintings on the museum wall; some may emerge from the sheer juxtaposition of works that, the curators presumably decided, are similar to one another, belong together in one respect or another. We may, once more, take the example of the landscape. As critics have noted, the olive trees at Monte Calvello (p. 52) are painted with "Chinese restraint" (Roy 1996, p. 133) and the curving movement from bottom to top is announced by the trees that look as flat as fans. The curves of the rocks are continued by those of the greenery, and end up surrounding the tower in ruins. Expecting a landscape, we get what we want. Its primary characteristic is fields—man-tended fields of labor transformed into color fields so subtle that they appear touched by the light, and by a very tender brush. Yet, between the lower right and the upper left a gaze is staged. The tall man and his short companion—she could be a child—gaze up at that tower and see its state, its age. Thus, history makes its appearance, and so do social conditions. The genre label has deceived us into a sense of awe before nature that makes us oblivious to those conditions. The tiny figures on the terrace remind us of them.

Still life, as a genre, predisposes us differently. Balthus has also practiced this genre, in works solely devoted to the depiction of things, as well as in corners or sections of works primarily belonging to other genres. Here, it is less nature that distracts us from social conditions, but craftsmanship. We admire the stunning fugitive finesse of the rose petals (p. 59), and the delicacy of the skin of apples and pears (p. 75), and suddenly the landscape and its disturbing symptoms of social conditions recede, literally, into the background. Painted in oil on canvas, this work suggests the same tender brush and slight, Chinese indication of trees and folds in the hills as in *Bouquet de fleurs*, the same

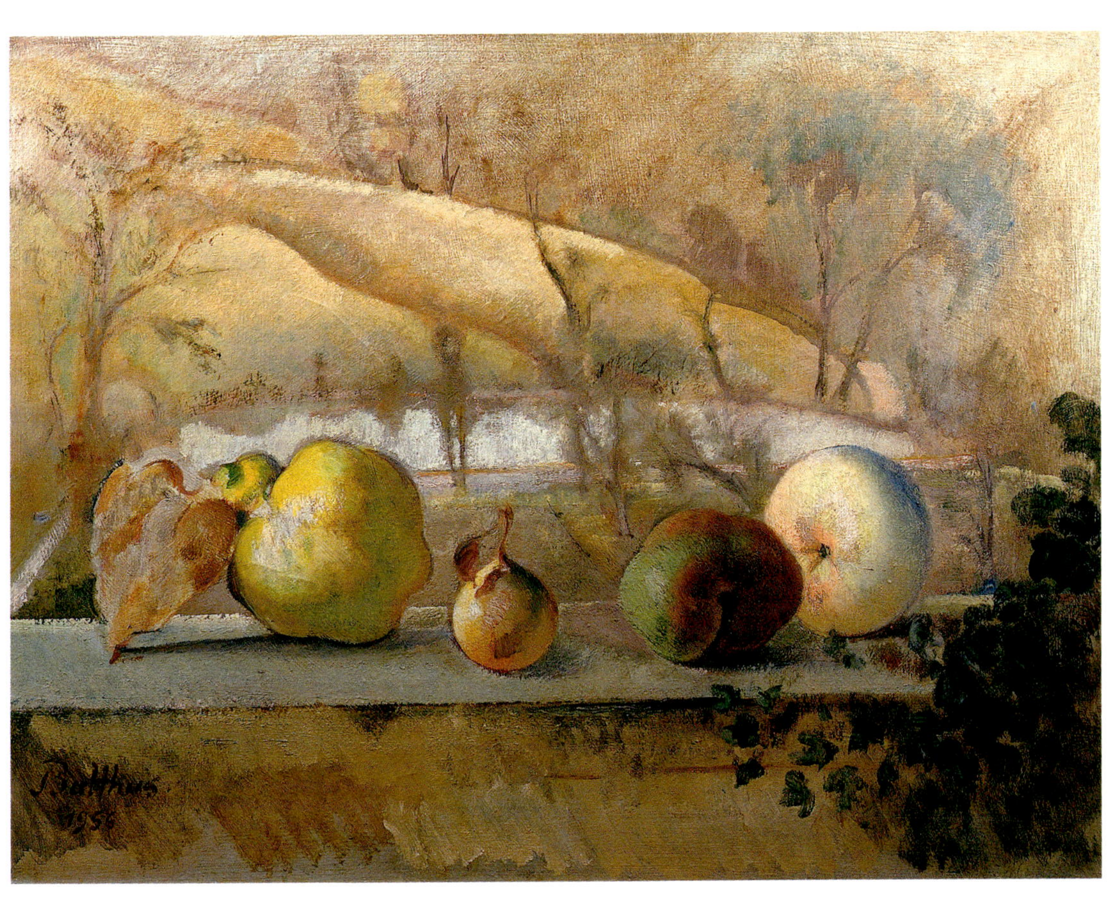

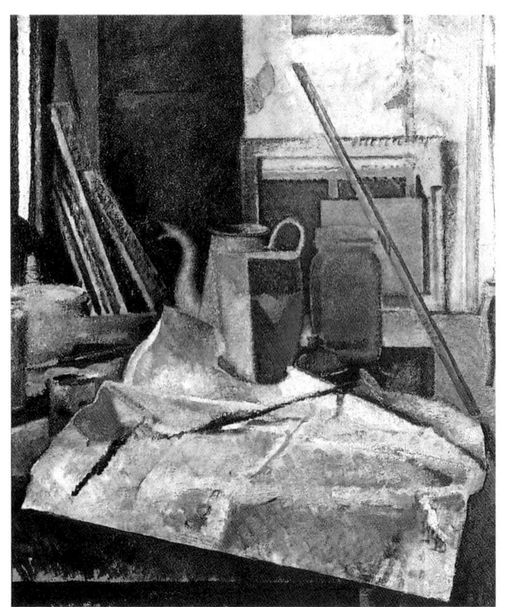

Nature morte dans l'atelier, 1958.
Still Life in the Studio.
Oil on canvas, 73 × 60 cm.
Private collection.

Jeune fille à la fenêtre, 1955.
Girl at a Window.
Oil on canvas, 160 × 162 cm.
Private collection.

detailing of the fruits' surfaces as the small still life in *Le Peintre et son modèle* (p. 10), and the humility of the object manages to invoke still lives from the Spanish seventeenth century by, for example, Sánchez Cotán (p. 74).[26]

Yet, while it is undeniably a member of that genre, the placement of the fruits balances the edge between exterior and interior that invokes not only the visible and delicately included landscape outside, but also the invisible scene inside. There is always something more, something else that genre categories obliterate. Shift the view, step back, and something else happens (p. 77). Move forward, and the interior, the human habitat, disappears altogether. Let in a touch of cubism and there is no longer the world, only the making of images (left).

Balthus also made numerous portraits. The portrait is classically the genre of individualism and the search for likeness, the presupposition that the model "behind" the portrait is just that person. Sometimes we know who the sitter is, sometimes we don't, but, nevertheless, we feel he or she is being presented to us. Balthus does not obey the rules of portraiture; he uses our expectations to wreak havoc with the genre. *Roger et son fils* (Roger and His Son, p. 78) is the portrait of a man and his son, and most of us have no other source to get to know the face of these two persons than through this painting. So, meet Roger and His Son. But this is not an identity picture. As we look longer, things begin to shift. The painting becomes uncomfortable, even ominous. The father looks unsmiling but not unkind. Compared to his healthy complexion the boy's face is grayish, sickly; a pale mask. Then we see how the father's hand seems to crush him down. His little fist held up to his father, in appeal or protest perhaps, but to no avail. His other hand loosely holds the ball with which he is not allowed to play during the long sittings. His feet are too small to carry his body, and his legs, spread and x-shaped, with one sock falling down, don't reassure. The portrait begins to move, or move us into spinning tales about these people.[27]

But sometimes, Balthus is just a portraitist, capturing something about a person beyond the visible, yet showing it for us to see. At the age of twenty-eight, he painted the single-figure portrait that, for me, has more psychological depth than any other (p. 79). The first thing that struck me was the sadness in her eyes. This made the violin, so meticulously painted, almost a gloss to the enigma of the human face. Is the violin an instrument of consolation, or is the sadness due to its inadequacy, or her inadequacy in relation to it? We will never know. The dark, unequal eyes, the slightly graying, curly hair, the thin lips and the lined mouth are all subtle signs of age. Her left hand firmly holds the violin, the right hand lies dead, at the end of the loose limb that is her lower arm. All this, along with the great shadow around her neck and the collar that stands up at the back, contributes to the question whether this woman going toward middle age is deeply grieving—but it refrains delicately from answering it.
The fabrics of the dark green jacket, the green-red tartan plaid, are not simply among those masterful details, so astounding for a painter so young, but are also compositional devices and harbingers of mood. Does the plaid that covers her entire lower body indicate illness or incapacitation? We will never know, or are not supposed to know, but for a fleeting moment, we may enter into the orbit of this woman's life and break the loneliness.

And this, no less, is a portrait, supposedly without a hint of the temporality of human events. This should make it similar to the contemporary *Portrait de la Vicomtesse de Noailles* (Portrait of the Vicomtesse de Noailles), but how different they are! The sponsor and muse

26. Still life has benefited from two brilliant studies lately. Sánchez Cotán is discussed in a study of still life by Norman Bryson, a book that completely changed my view of still life as a genre (1988). Hanneke Grootenboer (2005) discusses still life as a genre that proposes its own philosophy of perception.

27. For an excellent critique of the genre of portraiture, see Ernst van Alphen (1997).

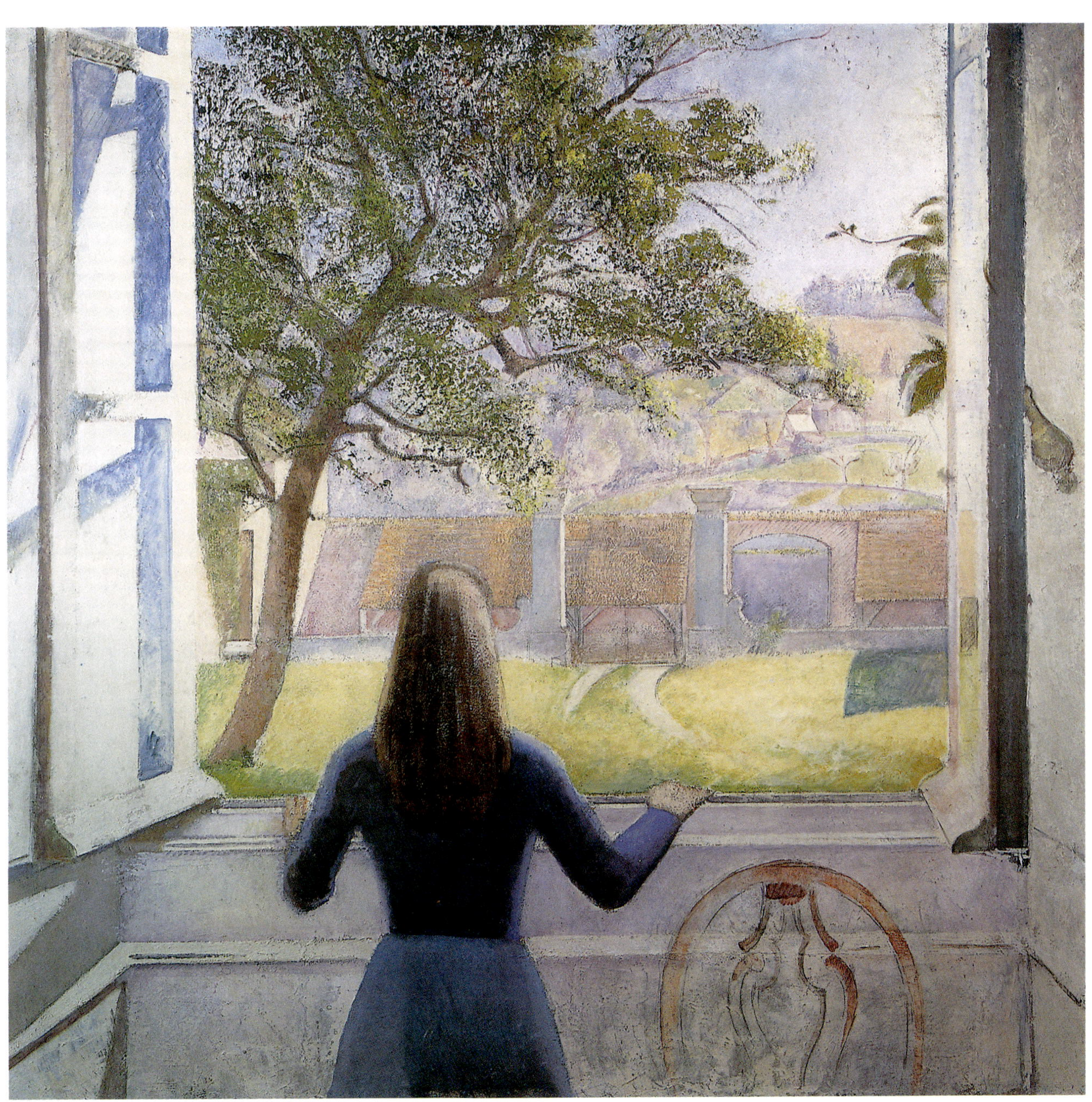

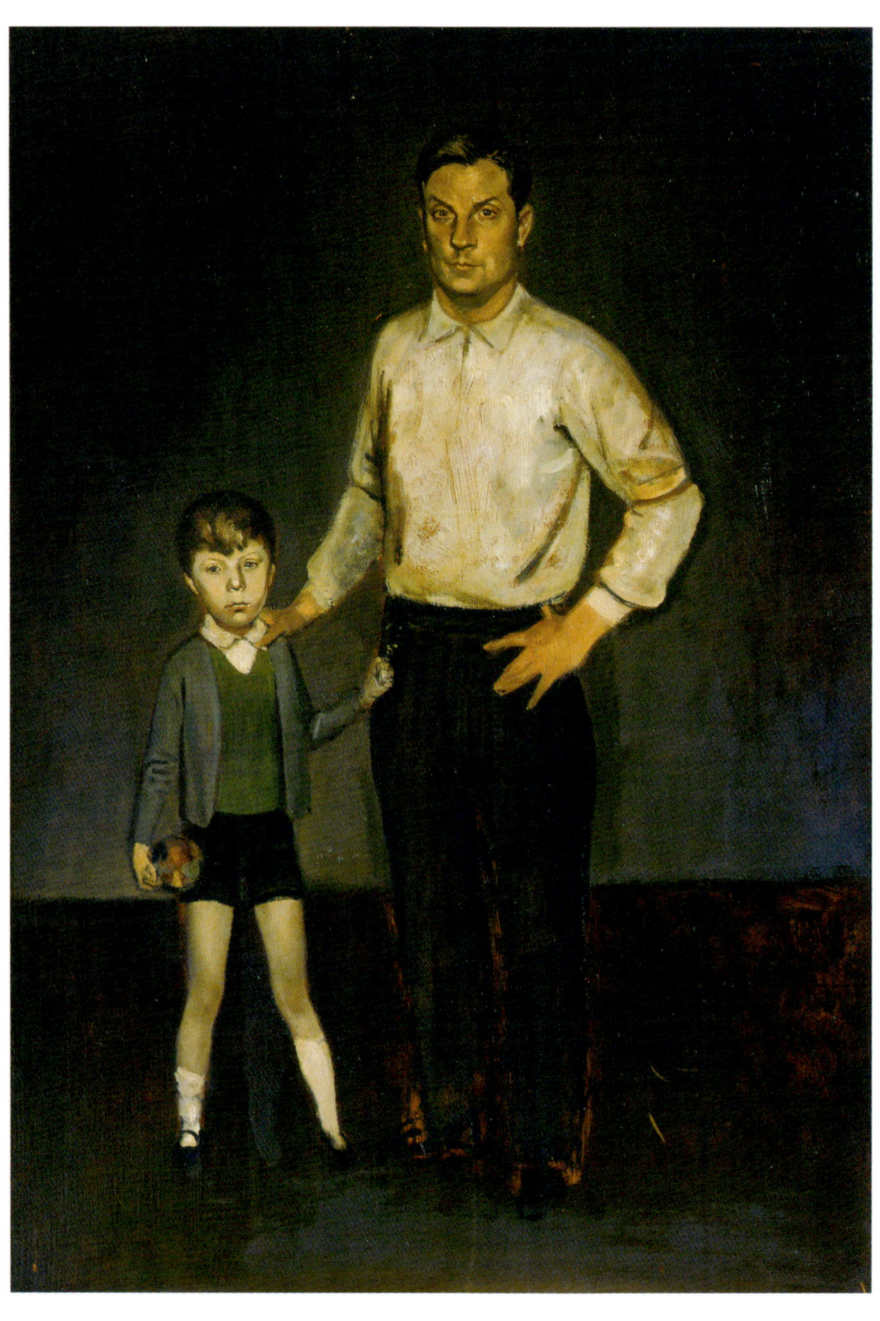

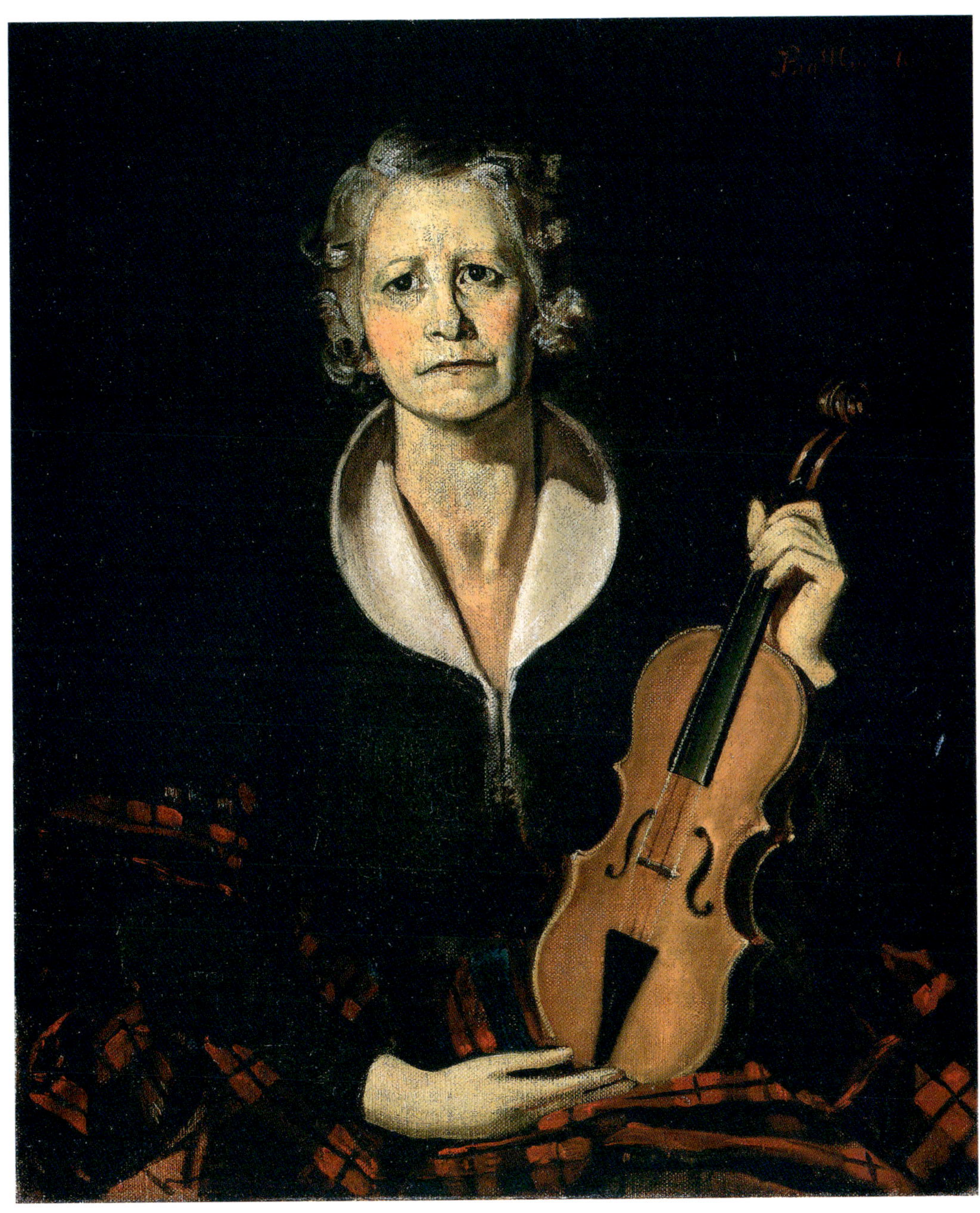

Roger et son fils, 1936.
Roger and His Son.
Oil on panel, 125 × 89 cm.
Musée National d'Art Moderne,
Centre Georges Pompidou, Paris.

Portrait de femme au violon (Lady Schuster), 1936.
Portrait of Woman with Violin
(Lady Schuster).
Oil on burlap, 81 × 65.4 cm.
The Hirschhorn Museum
and Sculpture Garden, Washington D.C.

28. Weber's detailed description (1999: 323-325) and his apt concluding phrase that Balthus uses his brush to assault, not to caress (328) is followed by a revelling description of the model that I find, again, an example of the collusion of the viewer when he writes: "in part because of the way Derain's finger connects visually to the model's hand between her bare knees, so close to her crotch that we feel as if we have been invited to investigate beneath her lifted skirt" (329). The "we", here, ignores differentiation among viewers and avoids responsibility for what each of us sees.

***Portrait de Joan Miró et sa fille Dolores*, 1937-1938.**
Portrait of Joan Miró and His Daughter Dolores.
Oil on canvas, 130.2 × 88.9 cm.
Museum of Modern Art, New York.

of Balthus and many of his friends, a real vicomtesse no less, is depicted sitting uncomfortably on a hard wooden kitchen chair at a bare, small kitchen table. These pieces fulfill several functions at once. First, they offer the usual opportunity to boast by merging the humble craft of carpentry with the lofty one of painting. The overall yellowish palette, interrupted and thus accented by that one patch of red of the sitter's blouse, cannot obscure the finesse of the painting of furniture, simple wall moldings, plinth, and the straw of the chair's seat. Second, these elements also place this Parisian celebrity in a space that can hardly be assumed to be in her own house. Is he punishing her for being wealthier than him, and showing how his humble economic status still allows him to be the Master? The third effect they have is the way the surrounding depiction submerges the sitter, making her just an additional image, flat and superimposed. Vastly different from the *Portrait de femme au violon* (Portrait of Woman with Violin, p. 79), this portrait gives nothing away of the sitter's psyche. Here, then, the painting does not depict the individuality, nor the social conditions (except by antiphrasis); it rather tells us that it won't.

How different this painting is from the sketchy portrait of the remarkable face of a child with a ghostly, skeletal hand. The crushing hand of the father in *Roger* returns to my mind and makes me feels uncomfortable. So does the hand that holds the little girl in the *Portrait de Joan Miró et sa fille Dolores* (Portrait of Joan Miró and His Daughter Dolores, p. 81) . Here, too, the firm hand of the father makes the girl seem to sag, and her legs, again, seem barely able to carry her body weight. The temporality of the long sittings becomes visible. Her unsmiling face and her hands that seek support on her father's (right) knee and (left) hand make the child's dress with its merry stripes—but in un-childish black and white—seem strangely out of order. And the left knee of that plump, distorted leg with the foot too small looks unsettlingly reddish, as if scraped. Again, the virtuoso monochromatic palette frames and inflects the simple idea that these are just individual people we get to see and know. Social conditions appear, but do so below the threshold of narrative meaning.

The genre becomes even more disturbed with the *Portrait d'André Derain* (Portrait of André Derain, p. 83) This work is surely strikingly small compared to the imposing presence of its main figure. Derain's face looks very different from his own self-portraits, where he looks more like Gauguin (p. 82). Not that it proves anything; Rembrandt, after all, in his sixty-some self-portraits, never managed to look the way others, such as his studio-mate Jan Lievens, saw him. But Lievens's portrait, obviously, is not about likeness. It is about how the artist saw his friend and colleague. And that vision included social conditions, after all.

The portrait is mercilessly critical of the giant. It gives him a pasty, ashen face with mask-like eyes, an over-sized head, and under-sized hands. It puts his hand on his chest, one finger inside his open shirt, as if his heart was worrying him. It gives his other hand the placement where one good tug on the loosely knotted belt would make the bathrobe drop. Above all, it puts him so close to the picture plane, massive like a pillar. It makes him stand at a distance from the model with her bared breast and blushing cheeks. And the stacked up empty frames against the wall suggest that the painter keeps himself busy with things other than painting. In all this I see a complex form of jealousy, complicated by identification, from the superior painter to the superior lover. According to Weber, this is a double fantasy portrait, of Derain and of Balthus—of Derain as Balthus as he would have lived had he been Derain. In revenge, he turns his colleague into a corpse.[28]

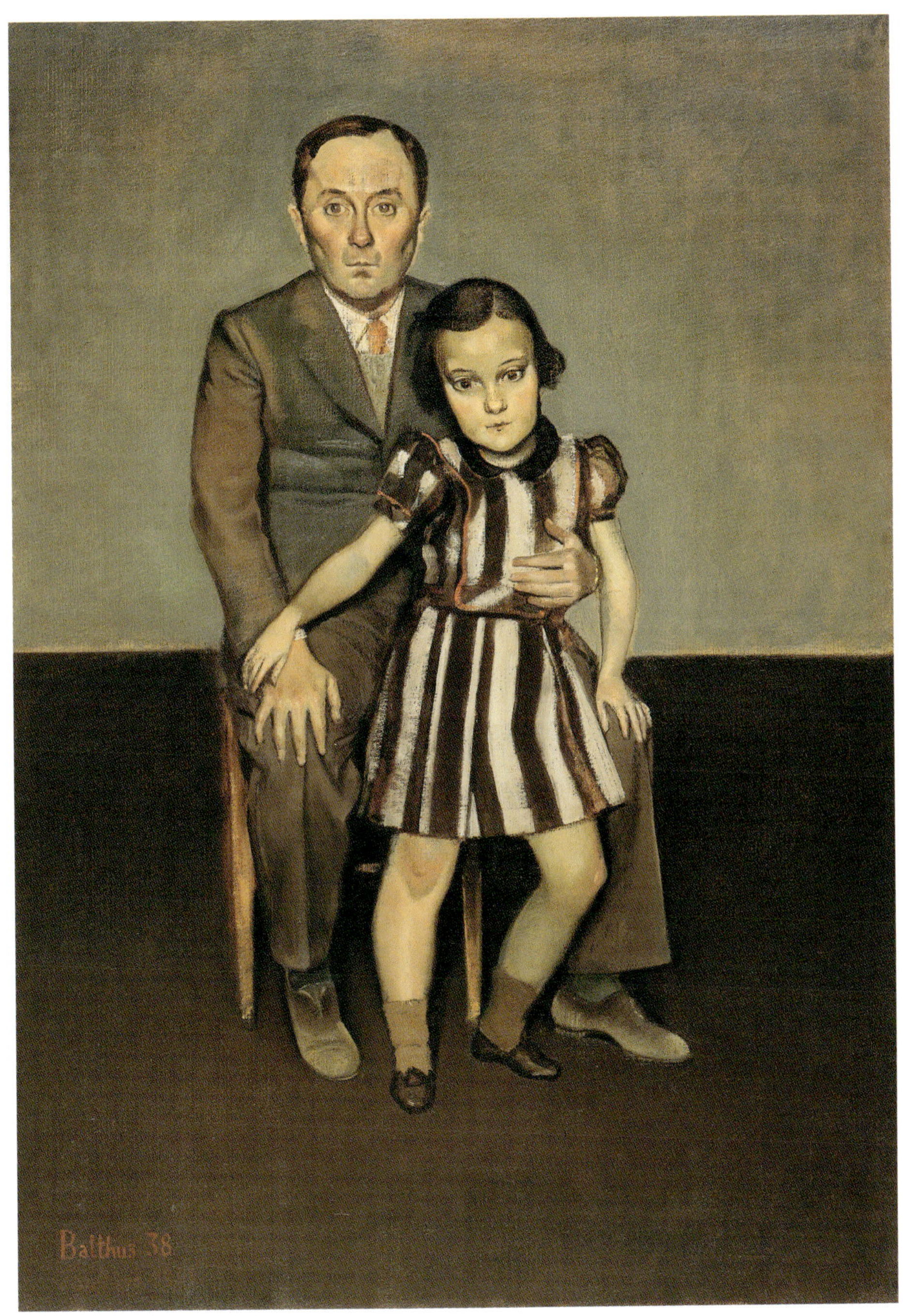
Balthus 38

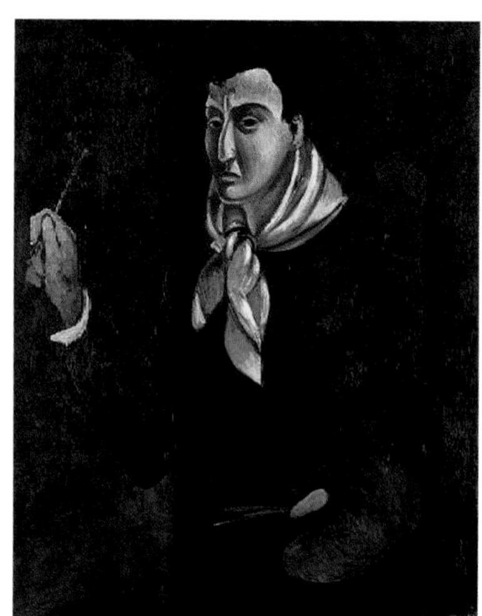

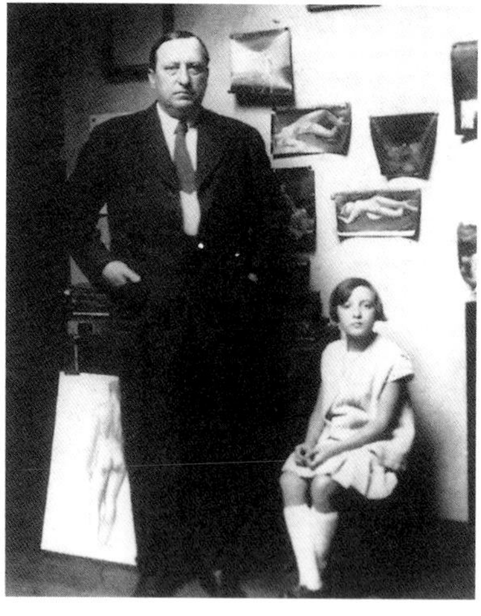

29. Sabine Rewald, another great Balthus specialist (1984; 1998; 2001) has amply written about these works. Her 1998 article details the iconographic allusions to a type of adolescent girls in sexually suggestive positions.

André Derain, *Auto-portrait*, 1913. Self-Portrait. Oil on canvas, 116 x 90 cm. Minneapolis Institute of Art, Minneapolis.

Photo of André Derain with a self-portrait behind him (in Weber p. 339).

Portrait d'André Derain, 1936. Portrait of André Derain. Oil on panel, 112.7 × 72.4 cm. Museum of Modern Art, New York.

The model is painted sketchily, but the chair she sits on is more detailed even than Derain, the main figure. This contrast between the woman and the chair is a statement on the reality status of what we see. Weber is sensitive to the movie-star quality of the model, sitting in a hazy, altogether different luminous space from the large man in the front. Weber notices the fantasy character, the dream image, when he writes:

> The light haze that envelops her [the model]—similar to the way in which dream sequences are rendered cinematographically—, slightly out of focus in contrast to the clarity used for everyday events—supports our impression of her as a fantasy (330).

This division of the image into a competition among rivals and the delight in a fantasized sexuality turns the portrait into something that its genre label might obscure—what I have summed up with the phrase "social conditions". It is with these conditions in mind that I now turn to that hybrid genre for which Balthus is most famous, the scenes that mix the domesticity of genre painting with portraiture, on the one hand, and the nude, on the other. The result is a genre all his own, defined by contradiction and tension. It is the genre that has too narrowly defined Balthus's reputation.

The frankly unappealing figure in front of the woman, who turns her into his sole possession, unavailable to others, in *Portrait d'André Derain,* makes for an exceptional situation. More frequently, the artist uses portraiture to infuse the image with more of that human life, or social conditions, than one would expect, suggesting the contribution of that other genre that the history of western painting has so frankly deployed, the nude. Compare, for example, the portraits of and scenes figuring Thérèse (pp. 84-88).

I present these four works in a more or less chronological order to foreground a development not of the artist, but of the figure of the girl—the girl as figure. I am particularly keen to point out the somber maturity of the face (p. 84). This portrait is painted in loose strokes. The unsmiling demeanor of the girl recurs in a small and sketchy double portrait of the same girl, *Frère et sœur* (Brother and Sister, p. 85) of the same year. Here, the devilish brother, with his nasty grin, small feet and strong arms, affiliated to the dwarf-like monsters that populate Balthus's world, appears to struggle to loosen the iron grip of his sister. She looks away, worried, appealing for help, as if he is about to commit some mischief. His legs indicate that she has captured him. I regard this painting as another case of narrativity without story, and of portraiture with social conditions, unreadable as well as undeniable.

This painting is very sketchy, but done with very effective strokes. Her dark tartan skirt, his striped pullover, the collar only a few strokes of white, and then those four legs, inciting us to tell the story. The attempt at perspective on the floor is soon given up when green and brown mix to form an abstract fresco. In both works from 1936, Thérèse looks much older—and much sadder—than in the *Jeune fille au chat* (Girl with Cat, p. 86) from the following year. As if the work needed the scandalous framing, the latter figured on the cover of the pocket edition of Nabokov's *Lolita*. But let us first look at her face—the portrait aspect of these paintings.[29]

In the 1938 work *Thérèse* (p. 87) the girl sits on an armchair, her legs half-crossed and relaxed. She looks toward the viewer but not at him or her; rather, her pouting mouth and inward-turned eyes suggest boredom. In the earlier portrait I saw grief or at least a

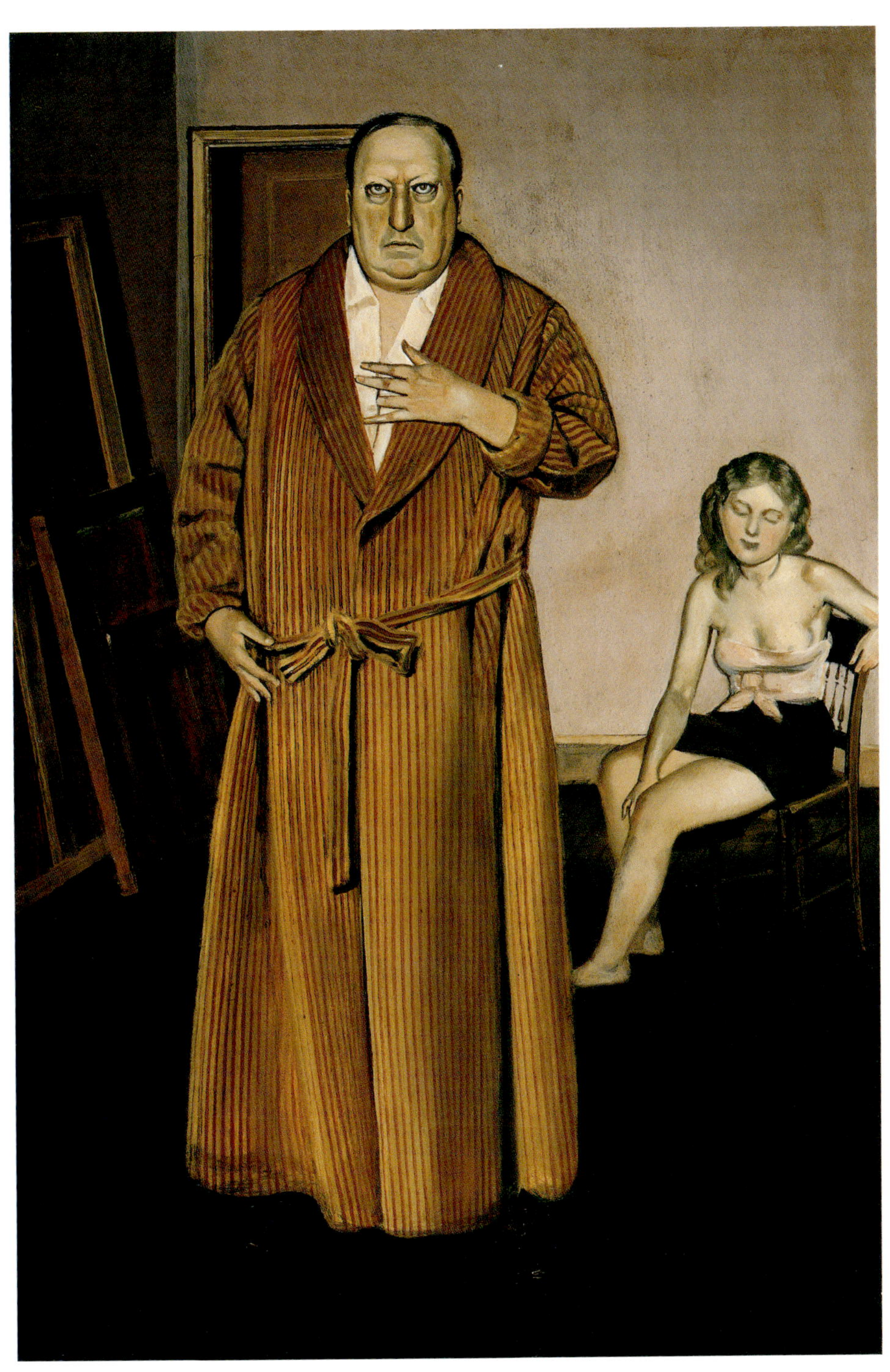

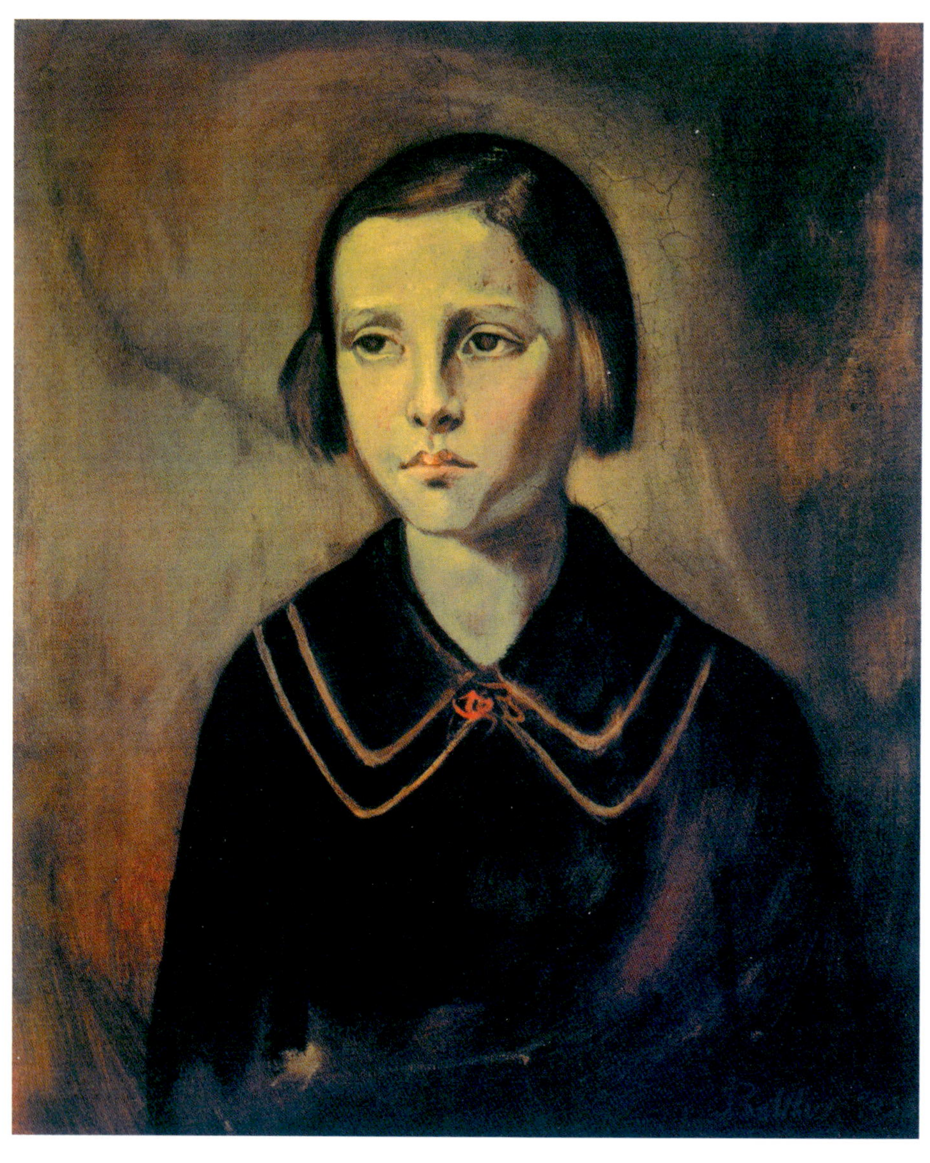

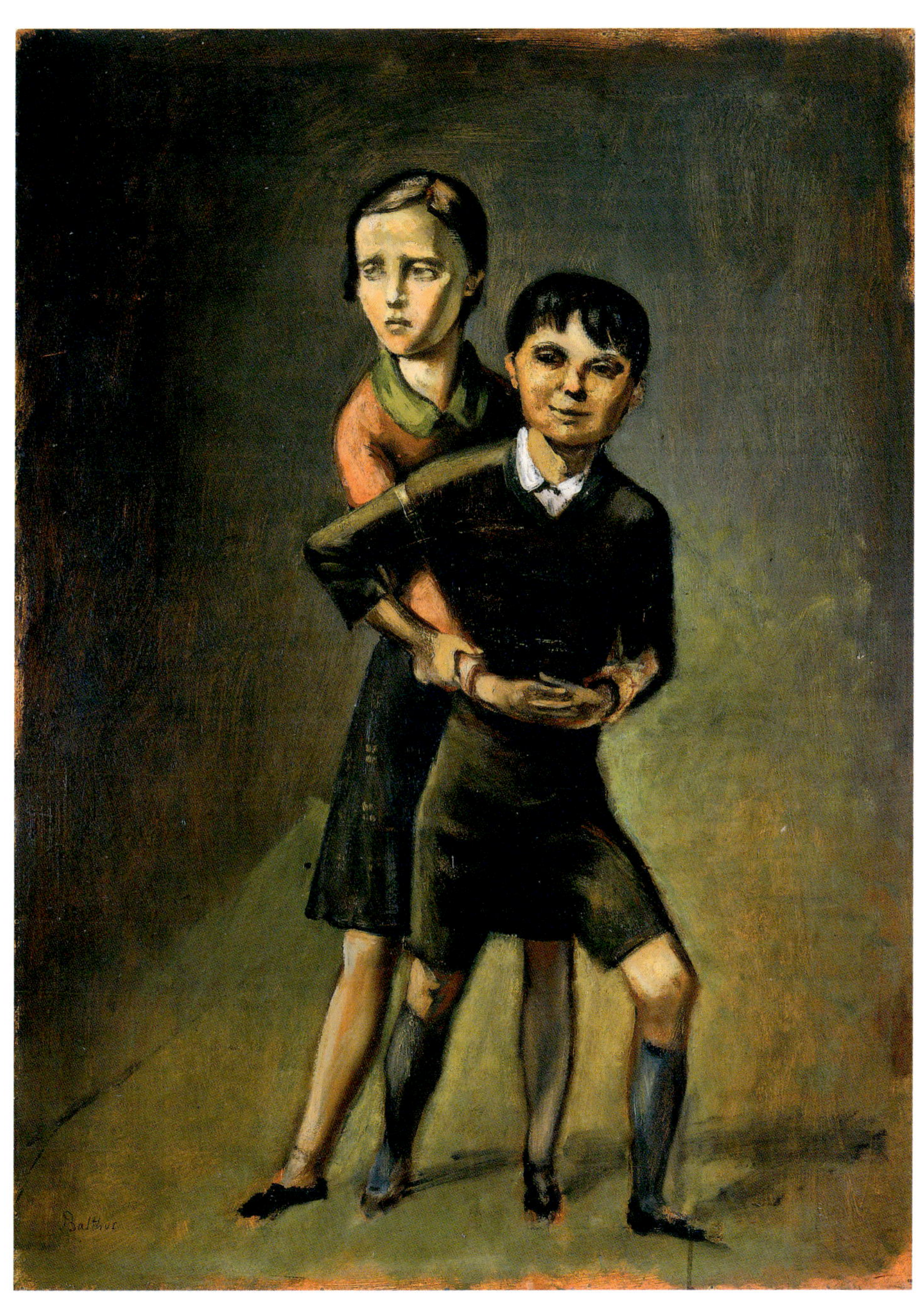

Portrait de Thérèse, 1936.
Portrait of Thérèse.
Oil on canvas, 71 × 62 cm.
Private collection.

Frère et sœur, 1936.
Brother and Sister.
Oil on cardboard, 92 × 63 cm.
Hirschhorn Museum
and Sculpture Garden, Washington DC.

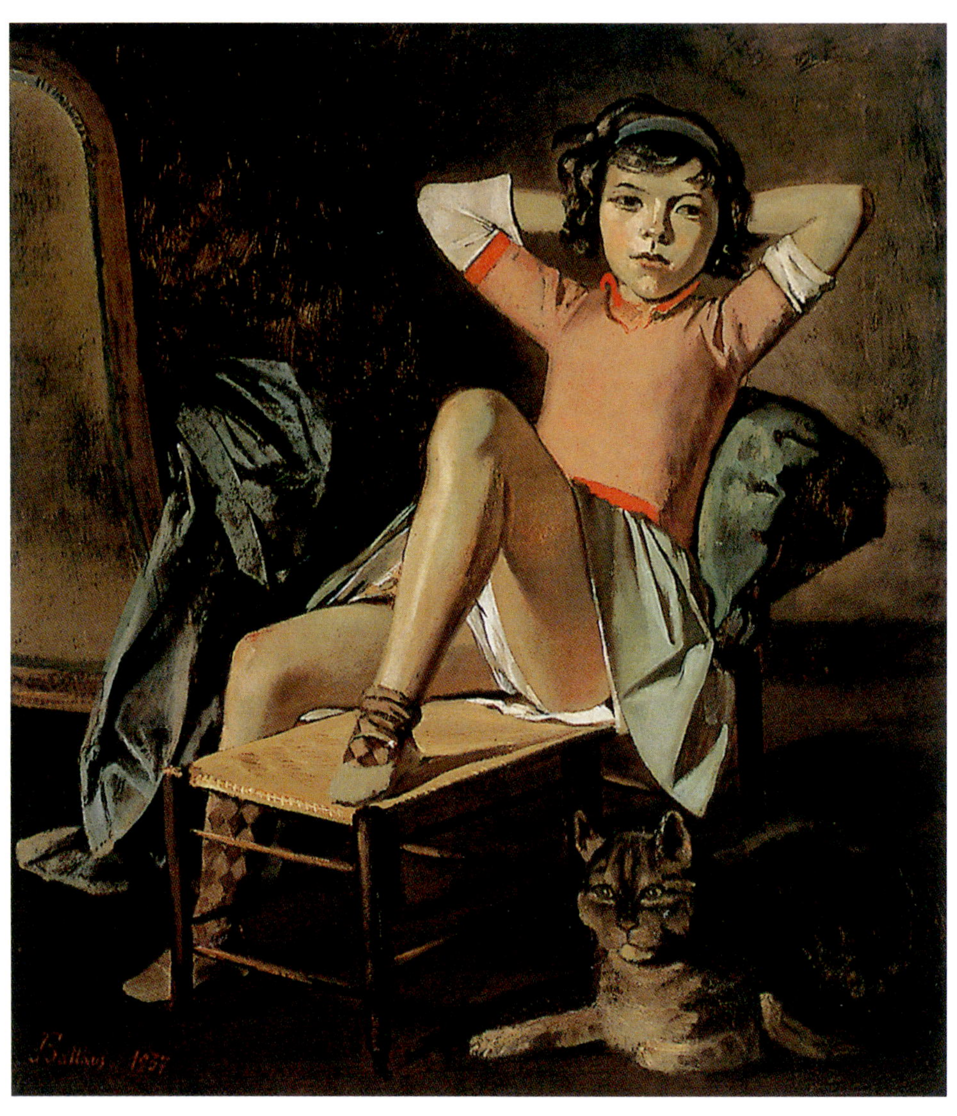

Jeune fille au chat, 1937.
Girl with Cat.
Oil on panel, 87.6 × 77.7 cm.
Private collection.

Thérèse, 1938.
Oil on panel, 103 × 83 cm.
The Metropolitan Museum of Art, New York.

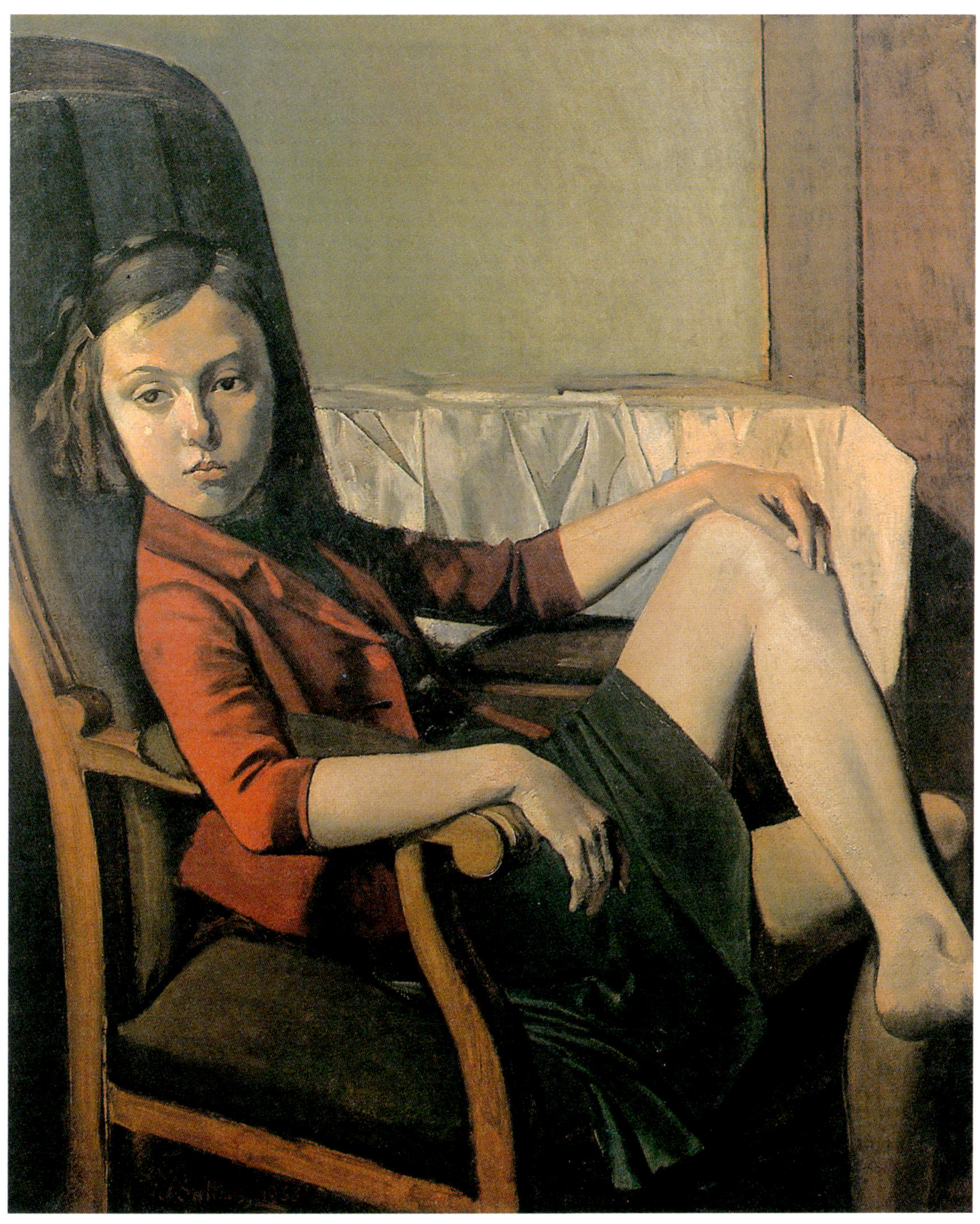

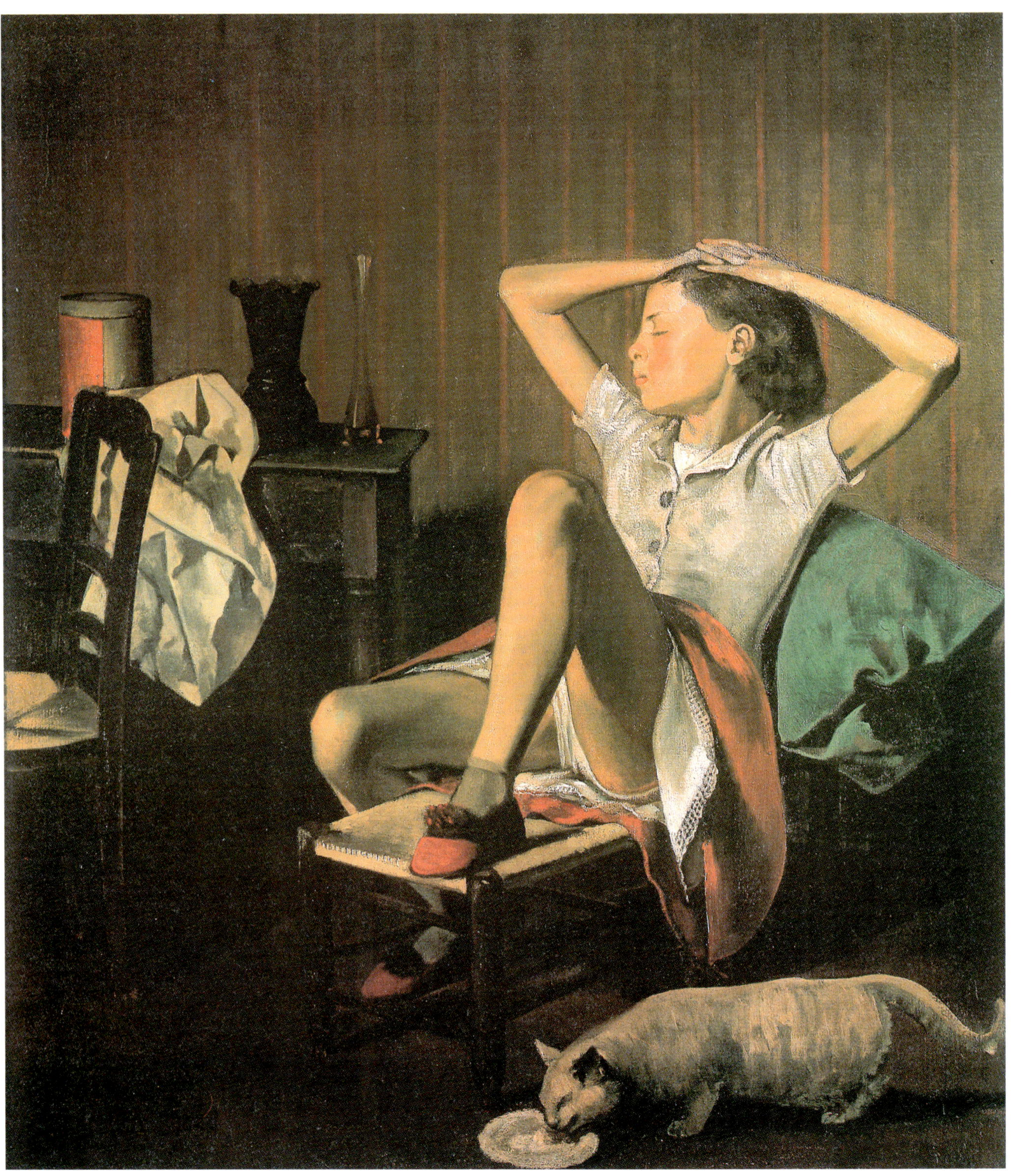

certain sadness, but in this one I do not. Perhaps she refuses to express her feelings. Or perhaps those feelings I do see in other works are entirely the doing of either the artist, his projections, or of the viewer—mine. This reticence to express feelings seems obvious in the Lolita picture, where the miraculously rejuvenated girl, still not smiling, looks frankly at the viewer, her hand raised behind her head enhancing her flat chest, which was much fuller the year before. These are good paintings of perhaps questionable subject matter. They are also portraits ostensibly used to entice.

I am personally most interested in *Thérèse*. To be sure, as a portrait it is only partly successful, but enough to feel that we "know" this girl. She is an individual, sitting as she chooses. The artist has deployed his usual colorist brilliance to the benefit of a suggestive pose, and when, as he apparently does, he denies any eroticism in interviews, to my mind he is disingenuous. He is also jealously denying the viewer the relationality that eroticism simply is. The half-raised skirt, the slightly tight jacket, and the sharply creased tablecloth combine all forms of folds and fabrics a skilled artist may wish to boast with. The old velvet of the armchair, the old wood of its curved legs and back, and the old wood of the door, all conspire to attribute to this painting the old-master qualities that the lively but mute green wall brings us all the way back from fifteenth-century Italy.

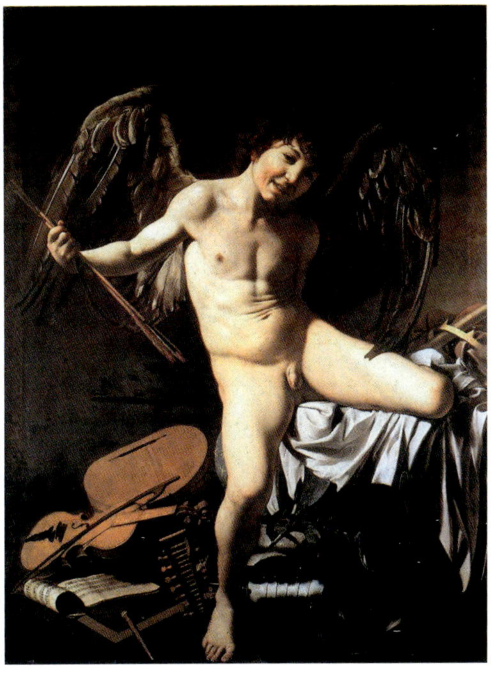

Thérèse rêvant, 1938.
Thérèse Dreaming.
Oil on canvas, 150.5 × 130.2 cm.
The Metropolitan Museum of Art (dépôt), New York.

Caravaggio,
Amor Victorious, 1602-1603.
Oil on canvas, 156 x 113 cm.
Staatliche Museen, Berlin.

Balthus's inspiration comes from Renaissance Italy, classical France, and nineteenth-century France. I find the fabrics, but also the skin texture and the differentiation among all textures to be leading up to a celebration of grumpy adolescent girls in a way Caravaggio celebrated street boys (right). This also fits with the cropped image, the narrow framing of the girl, even the discontented mouth, and the light that illuminates the bareness of her legs. In short, it fits with the Italian painter's pictorial eroticism. There is no doubt that this work merges portraiture, individualizing the sitter, with the tools of erotic imagery that sets her up for visual assessment by a possibly lecherous viewer. I have no problem with that. Not, that is, in general.

Many images are sexually enticing and erotically appealing, and many are suggestive of the possibility that the figure can be appropriated, visually, imaginatively, and some say, in continuity with such imaginings, physically. This image stands in a long line of such works of art, enough to form a genre of their own. Works that, had they been less artistically accomplished, might have been dismissed as pornographic. In the case of Thérèse—and I intentionally call the figure by the name of the sitter, rather than the title of the work—the risk is over-determined by her young age. Can she be a consenting adult? Not really. But consenting to what exactly?

The same girl, made to look younger, less personalized, and more explicitly enticing, sold across the counter of bookstores. Balthus complained about the "idiotic" comparisons between his painting and the novel, but then, we must assume that he granted permission for this use, hence, this is another disingenuous refusal to commit, and therefore I discard it. The comparison between the novel and the painting is all wrong, since, while his inventor did not, the fictional character Humbert Humbert did commit a crime and then another one—murder, and taking sexual possession of an under-age child. Trying to, in fact, because the child was not really for the taking. Balthus did not, and nor did he present before us another Humbert.[30]

30. Weber discusses the Lolita-Thérèse comparison at length, and somewhat more defensively than I do here (390-401, esp. 400 on the comparison with Nabokov).

Is there no problem then? There is, to be sure. But this potential problem cannot be summed up with reference to the erotic. First of all, I am a critic, a mediator between art and its public; not a censor. My task is to propose the elements on the basis of which each viewer may and must judge. I have my own views, and can only share those as opinions. In *Jeune fille au chat* and *Thérèse rêvant*, the artist (and his model) offers us a crotch shot, barely veiled by a narrow band of underpants. In *Thérèse* (p. 87), the pose, although erotic enough, can still be considered ambiguous. *Thérèse rêvant* may be even more disturbing than *Jeune fille au chat*, since there the girl is "asleep" or caught in (possibly erotic) reverie, and the image offered makes us plainly and clearly voyeurs. And if we fail to see the disturbing exposure of eroticism, the gluttonous cat on the foreground to the right—fat, licking, and close to the viewer—seems pregnant, as if to warn us. When I visited the Met, a class of school children marched by, some snickering. This is a more realistic version of what *La Chambre* (p. 70) suggests in a fairy-tale frame. But neither of these two more overtly erotic paintings has cropped the image so closely as in *Thérèse*. This, I contend, makes it both more sharply erotic and at the same time more socially responsible than the other two. As a consequence, I submit, "problematic" and "erotic" are not synonymous concepts.[31]

Putting the adolescent with her semi-bare legs and indifferent look so close to the viewing space, the work enforces, in ways the other two do not, a reflection on where we, as viewers, stand in relation to this picture. In relation, also, to all its predecessors, the countless bathers, rapes of Europe, suicidal Lucretias, sleeping Venuses, and other, nameless figures; and let's not forget, those cuddly little children redeemed as "putti". And perhaps we should, then, also think of the saint Sebastians of the history of art. Balthus's classical style frames his pictures, hence, also his Thérèse pictures, within that legacy. This gives them the prestige as well as the need of viewers to come to terms with subject matter and "great art" together. There is no doubt that, in the West at least, canons of artistic beauty come with canons of human beauty, that the majority of its models are female and white, and that some of them are violated for it. In *Thérèse*, we look into the eyes of an adolescent Olympia—not as naked, but just as insolently indifferent. We are drawn in, enticed to look closely by the textures of all those material things that bring along the texture of the young skin, and so we are invited to become connoisseurs of artistic/female beauty.

Assuming, as I do, that there is nothing wrong with sexual interest, as long as there is no abuse of non-consenting victims taking place, the question becomes, how is the viewer placed in relation to the figure, and what kind of figure is she? This is the question of genres, as well as of eroticism, and of the aesthetic. I have asked around to see what others thought. Some of my friends find Balthus's work "inhospitable to the female viewer". Others find it brilliant and occasionally disturbing, but not objectionable. Others yet see the power of the images to be overruling the possible vulnerability of the figures. These three positions come from friends who, all three, are feminists, intelligent, and interested in women. One of them, when I confronted her with Weber's suggestion that the figure of Heathcliff in *La Toilette de Cathy* (p. 30) is masturbating, (152) exclaimed that to her he looked more like an impatient husband rehearsing a shopping list, or annoyed while his wife took too much time getting dressed for a party. In other words, she found Weber's interpretation a great instance of projection, and offered her own in return. There is nothing wrong with that either, but it is his and hers respectively, not the painting's doing.

In *Thérèse*, the viewer can not escape asking her- or himself such questions; asking, that is, where they wish to stand in relation to this insolent, attractive, adolescent girl, painted and thus, contemplated in a museum. My own line is to do with genre. One reason for my reluctance to be moralistic about this painting is the way the merging of genres liberates the viewer from a pre-established script. As a portrait, the girl gets enough clout, enough insolence, and enough personality to stand up to intrusive viewers. As a domestic scene, it is incomplete, and thus gives the freedom of fantasy to go in as many different directions as domesticity allows. As an interior, it is confining, not only to the back but also toward the picture plane. Thus, it entices the viewer to share the space in which the girl sits. Not to touch her without her consent but to be just as exposed. And let's not forget, she is a flat image, not anyone we could touch. We are exposed, that is, in what we do with conventions, between naturalizing them and accepting whatever the canon offers, and censoring what clearly delights all the people who flock to the museum.

31. Weber (pp. 397-399) offers a nuanced account of *Thérèse rêvant*. He draws attention to her head, oversized, "absorbing us in her thoughtfulness" (399).

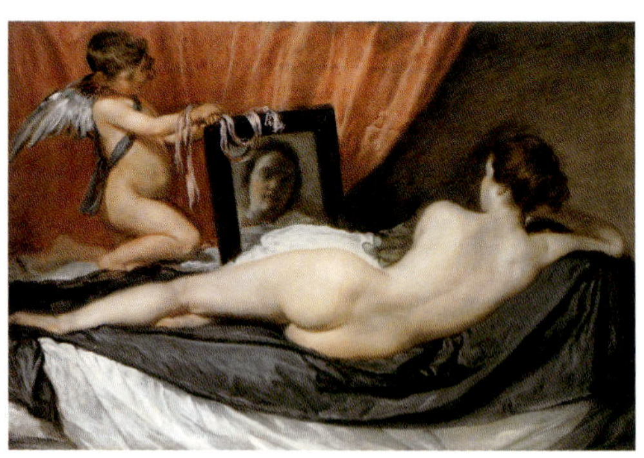

Diego Velázquez,
Venus en el espejo, 1649-1651.
The Toilet of Venus.
Oil on canvas, 122.5 × 177 cm.
National Gallery, London.

Les Beaux jours, 1944-1946.
The Golden Days.
Oil on canvas, 148 × 200 cm.
Hirschhorn Museum
and Sculpture Garden,
Washington D.C.

5. Figures of Visibility

Balthus, the classical painter who was not interested in the fashion of the day, who just wanted to be a new Piero and paint well, shrewdly deployed the classical genres, then blew them up from within. As a result, genre expectations could only deceive. If genres are no longer reliable entrances into images—no longer frames that tell us how to look and what to see—then we can muster other indications. I would now like to look at some of those motives that draw attention to the act of looking and its conditions. Mirrors, windows, and figures depicted in the act of looking; transparent items such as drinking glasses, striking indications of the way light falls and shifts, and details that draw attention to specific modes of looking. I have already mentioned some of these. For example, the painter in *Le Peintre et son modèle* (p. 10) opens the curtain, letting in the light, so that we are led to look at the distribution of light in the studio, and so does the dwarf in *La Chambre* (p. 70). This, in turn, entices us to look at the still life details on the left and right in the one, toward the back in the other painting. Also, we have seen the way the red ribbons on the hat of the woman in *La Rue* (p. 19) fit exactly into a red frame that, in the depicted world, would have to be at least ten meters removed from her. They also form a cross or grid as does the window in *Le Peintre*. This detail, once noticed, tells us to first look at the composition as such, as a structure built up by means of color, before considering this image the depiction of a real street. It is a meta-pictorial element; a detail through which the artist proclaims his artistic program. A manifesto.

Other details fulfill such functions. The most obvious tool to direct ways of looking is the mirror. This motif must be attractive for a painter who believes in the tradition. Mirrors are tools for the self-portraitist, symbols of vanity, hence, mortality as well as conceit, for the iconographer, and doors of access to the self in psychoanalysis. The mirror is an excellent example of Balthus's relationship to the tradition, which is always inflected by a modern sensibility. As we have seen, in Balthus's paintings, mirrors are frequently part of the image, yet equally frequently opaque. This complication makes them more, rather than less significant. Clearly, the artist is interested in this traditional motif, but also in changing the way it functions.

In *La Chambre turque* (p. 28), the mirror does not let us see the face of the woman reflected in it, but the mirror's oval shape multiplies all over the painting, in the woman's face, her belly, the plate with eggs, the eggs themselves, and even the curves of the table legs and the table top made oval by perspective. To realize how quietly radical *La Chambre turque* is in this concealment and dispersal of the mirror image, one only needs to remember Velázquez's classical *Venus* (above). The figure of Cathy in p. 30 shifts the mirror from being a physical object in the image, to a device to call attention to illumination, that is, she changes it into tool of visibility for the viewer (emphatically not for the man who sits in the same space). And Alice, named after the mirror *in* which she is, presents the nude as being (in) a mirror for the viewer (p. 21). This is an indication that we should shift from concrete mirrors to the idea of the mirror, as one among other tools of visibility the artist uses to tell us what his art is all about.

A few pictures contain an unproblematic gaze in the mirror, even if we never get to see the reflection. The young girl in *Les Beaux jours* (The Golden Days, p. 93) pays no attention to the broad-shouldered and strong-backed man who, at the right side of the image, is stoking a fire. His orange shirt has misled critics to assume he is half-naked, and I had been so taken in by this instance of critical projection that I was astonished to see that he is not. (e.g. Weber 1999, p. 413) Nor is there a glow over her, as if in erotic anticipation. She is

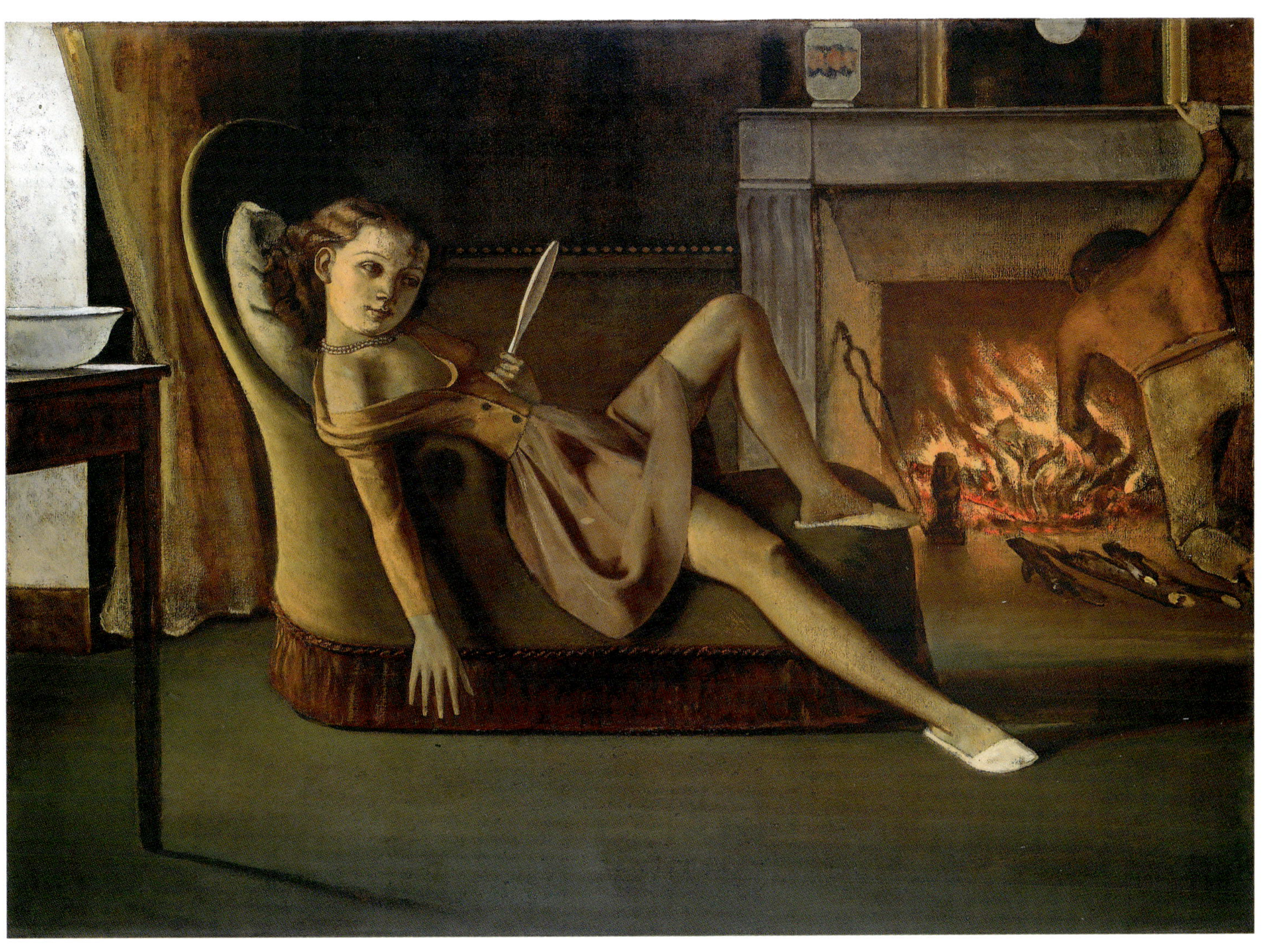

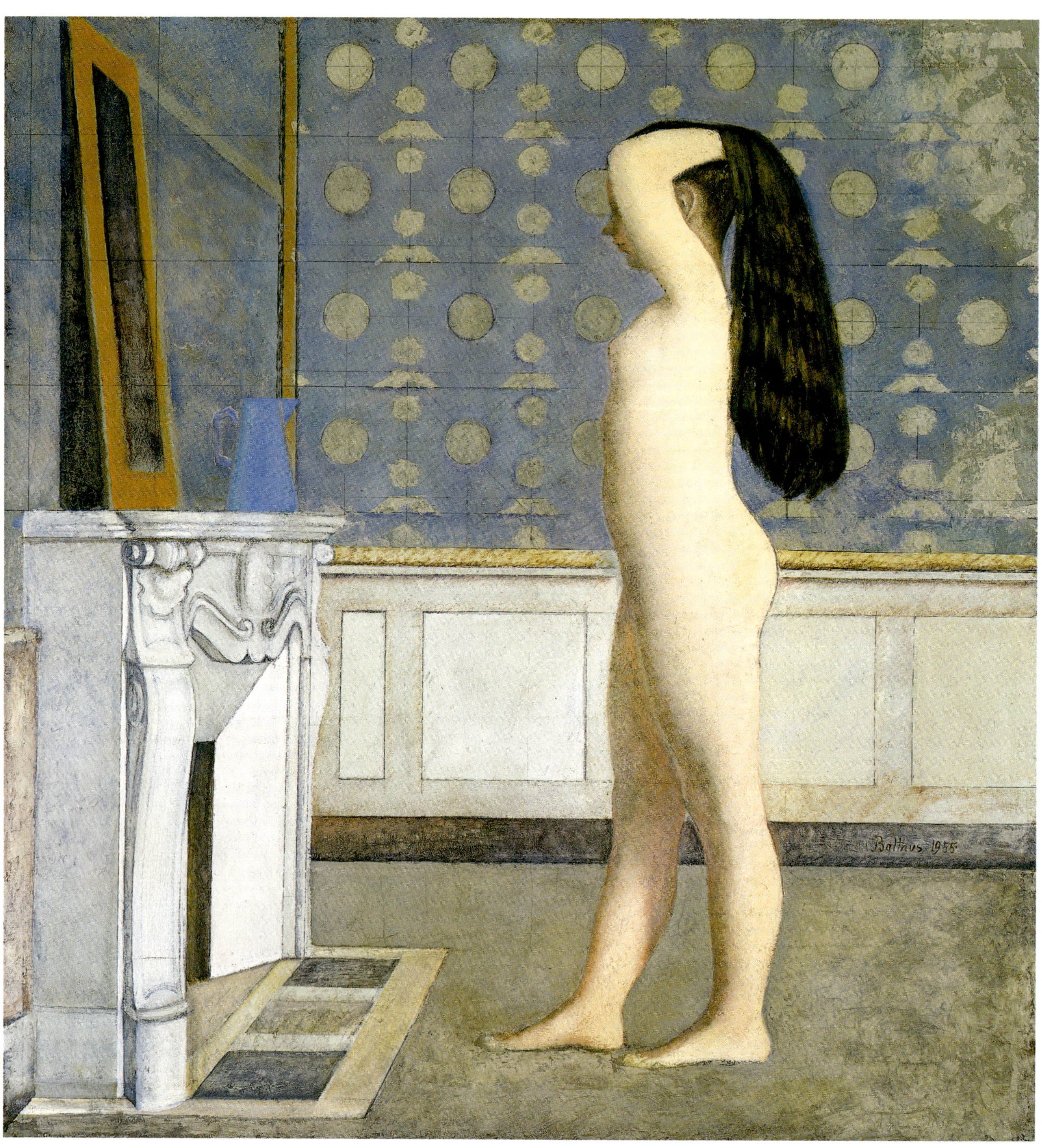
Balthus 1955

looking in a hand mirror instead. But what she sees, supposedly, is not what we see. We only see that she looks into it, that she is self-absorbed in her adolescent relaxation. Daylight lights her face from our side. Her large, flat face, made larger by the massing hair, is wider than her waist. This is in stark contrast to the most emphatic mirror picture, the *Nu devant la cheminée* (Nude in Front of a Mantle, p. 94). Here, the young girl is alone, holding up her hair after a bath. The colors are cool—light blue, yellow, beige, and pale skin tones—and the figure quite sculptural; she has volume but no life. The entire painting is finely drawn, as if exceptionally drawing is the main tool here, rather than color and composition.[32]

Nu devant la cheminée, 1955.
Nude in Front of a Mantle.
Oil on canvas, 190 × 164 cm.
The Metropolitan Museum of Art, New York.

To make sense of the combination of young girls and mirrors beyond the mundane *Nu devant la cheminée* or the dreamy *Les Beaux jours*. I am inspired by what Pierre Klossowski wrote apropos of *Le Chambre* but really, on Balthus's work more in general:

> This painting represents precisely the room I inhabit ... I return home and there is no longer a painting, but now there is a mirror there ... an illusory means to capture the atmosphere to put it out of itself ... but in that respect it is an imperfect simulacrum that our verbal rêverie comes to supplement; between the reflected image and the image of my rêverie the word still insinuates itself indefinitely.[33]

The anecdotal fact that the painting depicts the room where Klossowski continues to live is the occasion for a meditation on the relationship between past and present, painting and dream, image and language. The final word, "indefinitely" brings silence to bear on time, although the time is immeasurable. For the writer, time, self-love, and growing up come together in the image of the mirror as substitute for his younger brother's image of the girl whose nakedness is (about to be) exposed by daylight. This intense image of the mirror—a mirror image—is no longer meaningfully explained with reference to iconographic antecedents, numerous as these may be. Between the Klossowski brothers the specific meaning of the mirror in Balthus comes to the fore. It has to do with self, time, and space.

The self: the motif of narcissism is attached to the mirror. We cannot understand Balthus's work without taking stock of an immense narcissism that gets projected, infused, into the depiction of young girls. If we believe his paintings, Balthus has not only, or simply, an erotic interest in girls; he *is* one. One of the earliest paintings Balthus made was a now-lost copy of Poussin's *Narcissus*, a figure we recognize in the reclining figure in *La Montagne (L'été)* [The Mountain (Summer), p. 97], his huge ambitious work from 1937. Although there is no hint of reflecting water here, the youth is female, and death has become sleep. The identification with Poussin's *Narcissus* (p. 96) is programmatic. The three figures on the foreground of this often-studied painting that merges landscape with scene, take three poses (Klossowksi would call them "excessive poses") that indicate ways of being, physically and symbolically: one reclining, one on his way to standing up, one standing and stretching out. Only the (excessively) standing one is in the light. The symbolism of the poses could be the three stages of life, or it could be the triumph of the girl awake before whom the boy kneels, and of whom the sleeping younger girl is still oblivious. There is no mirror to be seen here at all.[34]

But as before, there is such an ostentatious lack of communication among the figures that the sharp delimitation between shadow and light, or the night of sleep and dreams versus the day of reality, comes to indicate the landscape itself as a mirror. This adventure of mirroring does not concern the tourists in the background. The tourist in the orange shirt with puffed sleeves

32. William R. Herman compares this painting to several traditions, among which the Baroque, Romanticism, and abstraction. (1960) Weber (411-415) finds the painting very sexual, then places the sex in the white bowl on the left.

33. "Ce tableau représente précisément la chambre que j'habite, ... je reviens chez moi et il n'y a plus ce tableau, mais il y a là un miroir ... un moyen illusoire de capter l'ambiance pour la mettre hors d'elle-même ... mais sous ce rapport c'est un simulacre imparfait auquel vient suppléer notre rêverie verbale; entre l'image reflétée et l'image de ma rêverie la parole s'insinue encore indéfiniment" (1983: 81; my translation).

34. *The Mountain* has been studied by many, of which Gaëtan Picon's piece from 1966 (reprinted 1983) interestingly but rather implicitly alludes to Proust. Russell compares the painting to a large Courbet, (1983: 286) a comparison that adds little to our understanding of the work. See also Verschaffel (2004) who fills in the image with autobiographical detail (2004, p. 24). Rewald sees in the closest of the smaller figures the putti on the Poussin (1997).

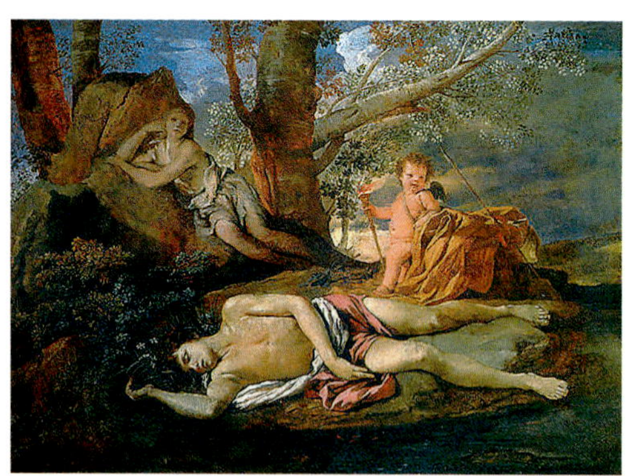

Nicolas Poussin,
Écho et Narcisse, 1628-1630.
Oil on canvas, 74 x 100 cm.
Musée du Louvre, Paris.

La montagne (L'été), 1937.
The Mountain (Summer).
Oil on canvas, 248 × 365 cm.
The Metropolitan Museum of Art, New York.

stops to look just past the strange stretching, while the couple farther back discusses the landscape. Tiny, in this gigantic painting, they are unaware of the drama of self-unfolding that is taking place. Utterly mundane, the man points out something, the woman, wearing a white apron, holds her hat. In the far right an even tinier figure walks away, almost reaching the mountain's summit. Again, like the young man with the baguette in *Le Passage* (p. 12), who is unaffected by the world he just passed through, this lone figure, the characteristic figure of the painter, leaves the frontal poses of the three "stages of man" for us to process. Relaxed, as if he wasn't walking up a steep slope, he has one arm behind his back, holding it with the other hand. But the painter leaves behind what he just created, and us, to reach the peak alone.

The half-kneeling man in traditional mountain dress looks in the general direction of the viewer. So does the stretching blonde. But neither looks either directly at the viewer or at the other. Covered by the eerie shadow, the Narcissus figure with signature bare knees clutching her cane might be dreaming up the others. She is sleeping in the mountain landscape on pumps. Alternatively, the two "main characters" may be offering choices to the viewer for identification. In this sense, the sharp division of the picture plane into bright and dark could be a flat representation of the two sides of a mirror.[35]

This, of course, is hard to see or even to believe. As hard as anything that is a reflection. How, and of what exactly are mirror images reflections? Of the self, and that means, whatever we see in mirrors is a version of ourselves, possibly an amendment, a transformation. And if that is hard to see, this explains the fixed, staring, or dreamy gazes of many of Balthus's figures. The lack of eye contact. The teasingly difficult access the figures give to their souls. Mirrors are not tools, it seems, but motifs that point to, but fail to provide, visibility and its questioning. The young woman stretching out in *La Montagne* embodies above all else, the temporality of the self, the future-oriented existence of desire and ambition. This resembles the arms stretched out, this time sideways, by the fortuneteller of a much later but, if only due to its size, equally ambitious painting *La Tireuse de cartes* (The Fortune Teller, p. 98). She, too, looks straight at the viewer, but with empty eyes. Her real, spiritual gaze, we may assume, focuses on the cards in which the future lies.

The composition is as simple as it is revealing. The "reality" of the room is positioned obliquely; a diagonal structure against which the absolutely horizontal table top and row of cards stands out. The corner of the table is directed straight at the viewer. The very meticulous quality of the depiction of mantle and glass vase, hearth screen and Louis XVI chair, rug and ornate table leg: it all honors and frames the stiff, doll-like figure who is in sole possession of that particular kind of mirror on the table. I see an equivalence with the vertically stretched-out woman in *La Montagne*. That three-way posing, the still of a relentless movement upward, forward, or onward in *La Montagne* is here represented in the still of an arm that just laid out the cards with the skill of a professional of the future.

Figuratively speaking, either the mirror is visible but empty, or it is substituted by something else. The cat, in the three late works with mirrors, can self-reflect, better than his human counterparts, as his bright eyes indicate. The mirror as entrance into subjectivity and self-knowledge seems oddly misdirected (pp. 39-41). In *Paysage de Monte Calvello* (p. 52) the two tiny viewers looking up to the mountain before them, are dwarfed by the landscape. But remember that scale was also a tool for the presentation of perspective. Tininess indicates

35. It is generally known that the blonde woman has the features of Antoinette de Watteville, Balthus's first wife, whom he had been wooing for a long time. This only confirms the merging of desire with identification I have mentioned. In accordance with my own (and Balthus's) repulsion from biographical anecdotes, I will not go into this any further.

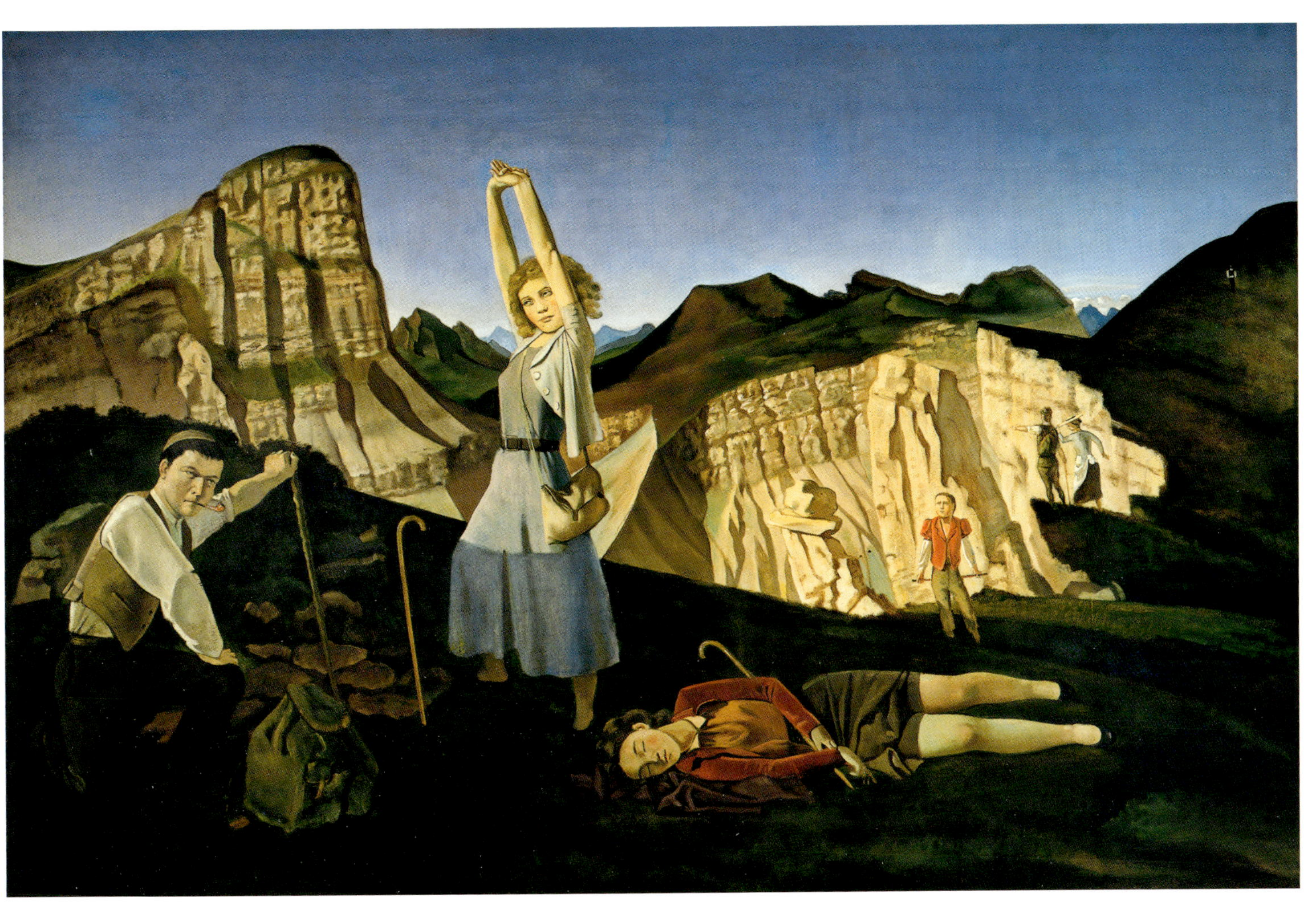

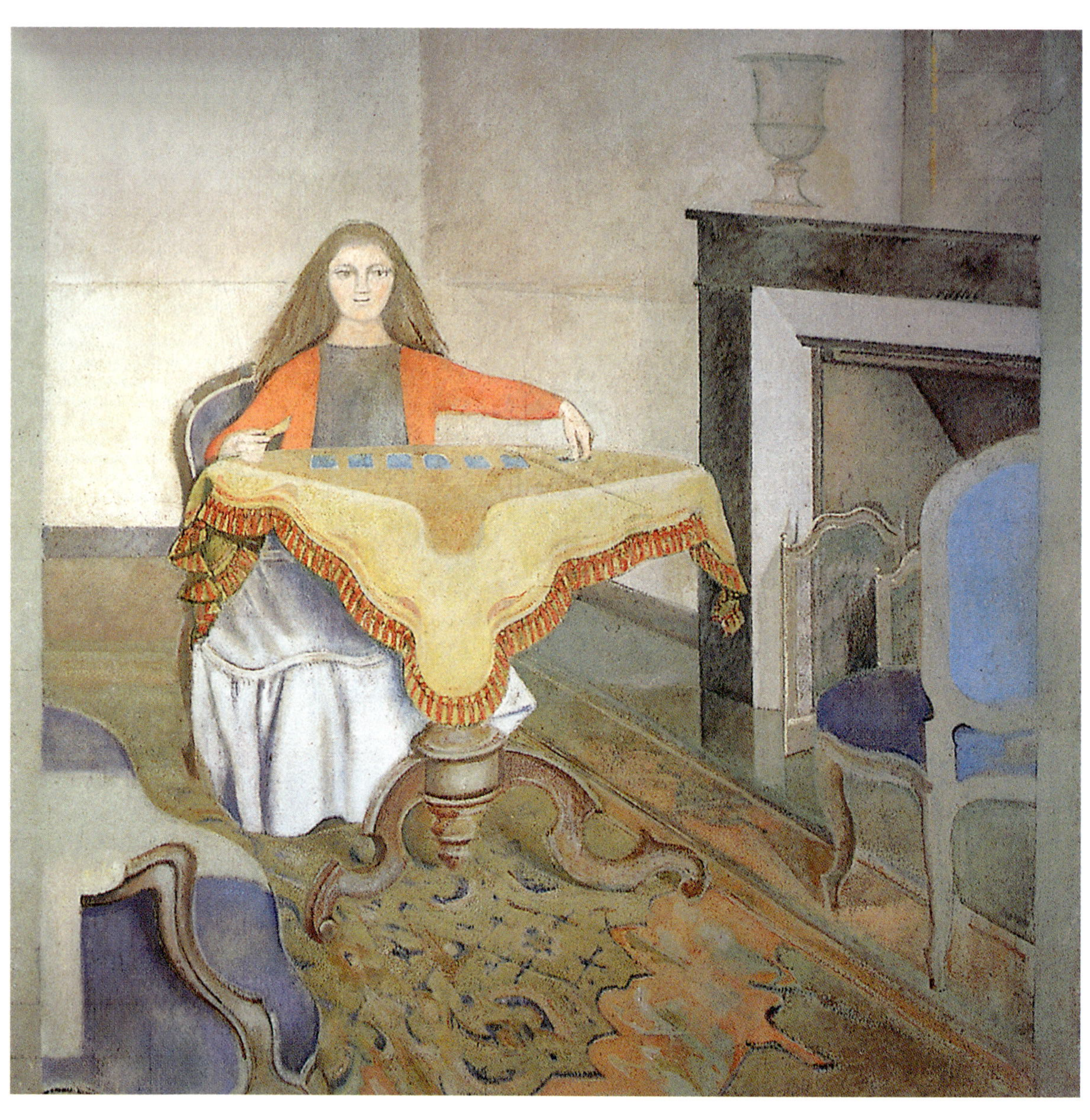

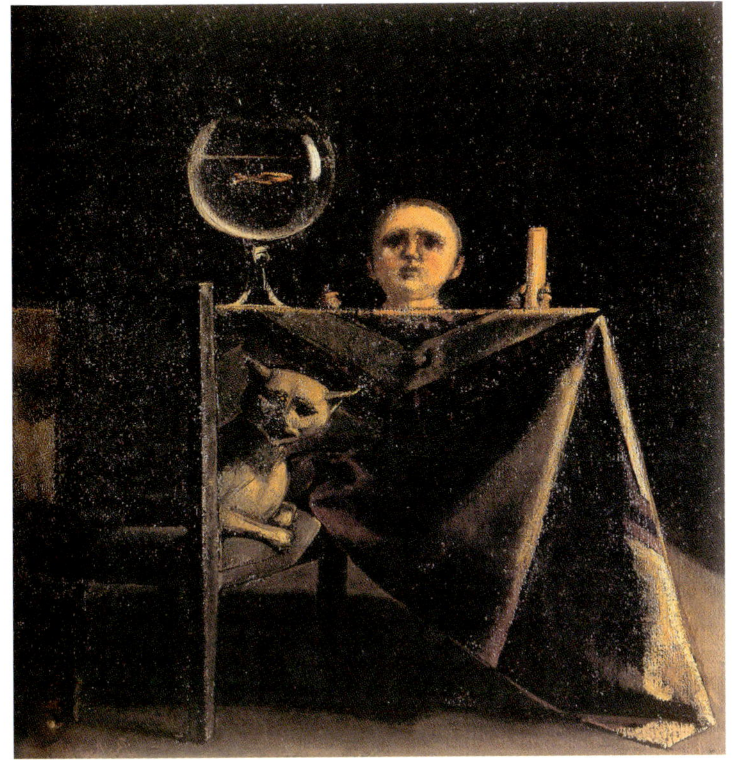

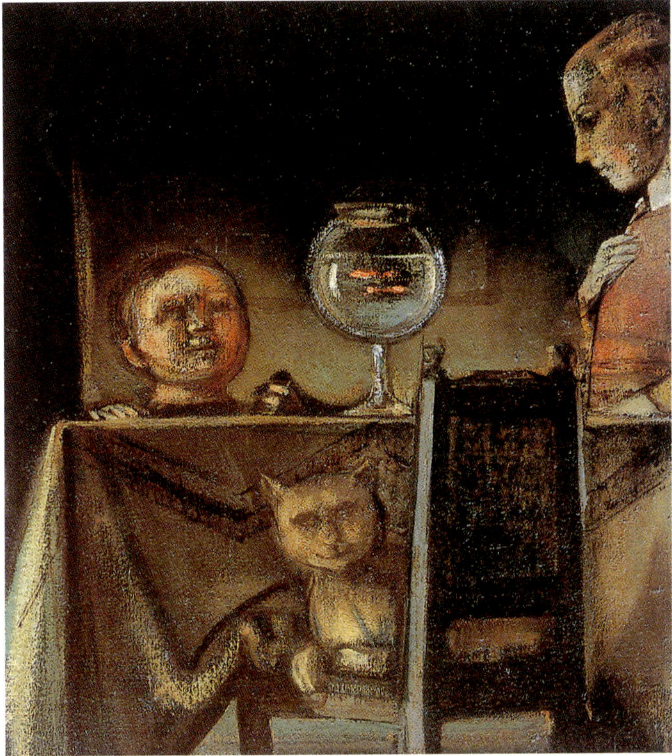

distance in *La Montagne*. But in *Monte Calvello* the tiny figures are closest to the picture plane. They are facing up to the huge landscape that, tilted forward, comes to confront them like a flat image.

In the two strangely flat and childish works *Le Poisson rouge* and *Les Poissons rouges* (The Goldfish, above) the round face we recognize from *La Rue* and *Le Passage* mirrors its shape in the glass bowl, while a very human cat looks at the viewer. In Le *Passage* the round face is doubled: the baby in the window looks exactly like the boy standing in the nearby doorway who looks at us. Round (here), or oval (*La Chambre turque*, *Les Beaux jours*) faces, mirrors, glass bowls: these instances seem to point to a motif that is visual more than semantic, defined by shape, and number, more than by what it represents. And to compound all this, look at the study for a portrait of Claude Hersaint, so different from the finished work (pp. 100 and 101). With even the open mouth made as round as the face which in turn is framed like in a mirror, —it is as if the painter had reached the limit of the socially acceptable—and has gone beyond it. One of the drawings related to this portrait shows the attempt to fit the face in the frame, as well as suggests that the face is less round than in the painting (p. 101, bottom).

Windows are also motifs that qualify visibility, and in Balthus, they don't systematically do that either. Some windows do, some don't; some are allowed to, some not. *La Semaine des quatre jeudis* (The Week of Four Thursdays. p. 102), a painting with affinities to *La Chambre* but much less unsettling, has an absurdly straight diagonal body of a girl as its main figure. The body is

La Tireuse de cartes, 1956.
The Fortune Teller.
Oil on canvas, 208 × 220 cm.
Dolores Kohl collection.

Le Poisson rouge, 1948.
The Goldfish.
Oil on canvas, 82 × 84 cm.
Private collection.

Les Poissons rouges, 1948.
The Goldfish.
Oil on canvas, 62.2 × 55.9 cm.
Private collection.

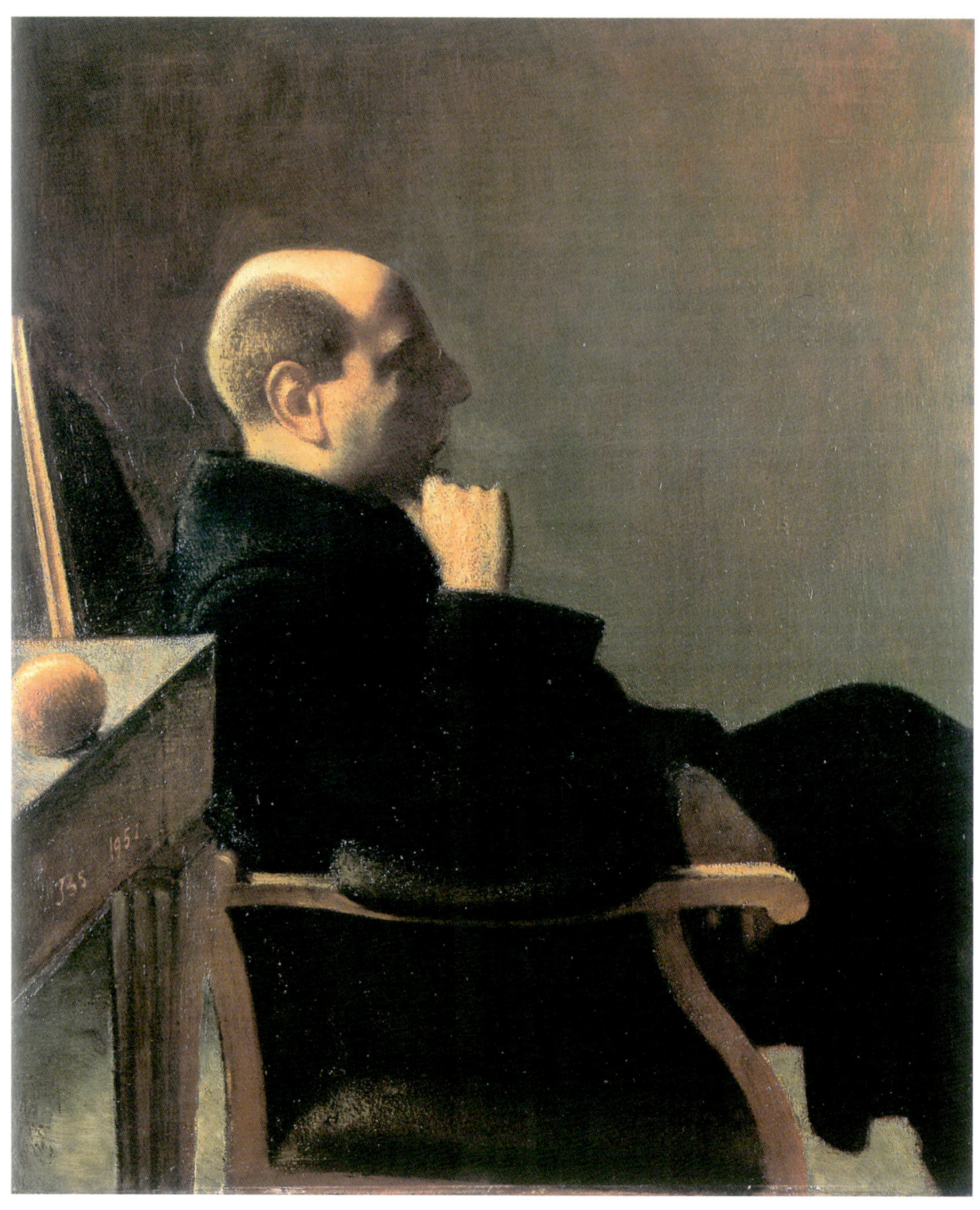

dressed in a bathrobe. By the window stands another girl, in a skirt reminiscent of that of the dwarf in *La Chambre*, but this time she has a normal size and is turning her back to the girl lying so strangely in the forefront. This, and the little symptom of the lifted heel connect this girl to the figure of the painter. We cannot see whether she is opening or closing the window, but we do see some of the shapes of the houses outside. The very simple furniture inside is again meticulously painted, the colors and the light are subtle, and composition through color is based on the alternate use of ochre and yellow on the one hand, and gray-blue on the other.

To draw attention to this, the back of the chair has both, as the center of the image. On more muted tones, this is repeated in the buildings outside, so that interior and exterior are connected, perhaps mirroring. The girl standing there with her heel lifted—her legs are so equal that the lifting of the foot seems a sign more than a representation—is surrounded by the light that comes in from the outside. Her shape is defined by this light. But with all this, the overruling passage is that where the girl stretches her hand up to caress the cat. Her face is round, its eyes are human. She might as well be looking into a mirror.

The interest of this painting for our discussion extends beyond the window, although that has its own interest, as it is an element in a series. But there are many other elements that make this painting a hub in the oeuvre. First, the affiliation with *La Chambre* and that work's unquestionable erotic theme inflects the latter picture. If this one puts visibility on the table, and I contend that it does—namely by means of the window and the roundness—then look again at the way the girl in *La Chambre* is ostensibly hyper-visible in her nakedness, yet crucially not really visible. Not only are her genitals not visible from the viewer's side, but also, her body is so smooth, unreal, and under-developed, that what some had considered the depiction of the violation of a child becomes the resistance of that child to visual appropriation, be it by the dwarf or by the viewer. In view of the idea that the reflection in the mirror, for Balthus, merges subject and object of desire—self and girl—the figure of the dwarf now becomes clearer: the androgyny of the figure says it all.

Second, the girl's round face, enhanced by the round top of the back of the chair and even the atypical round face of the cat with its human eyes, links it to all those pictures where mirror and face mirror each other, so to speak, without reflection ever being visible. The cat, in its interaction with the girl, links it to the three *Le Chat au miroir* (pp. 39-41) pictures, and the girl's apparently—but not necessarily "really"—closed eyes invoke all the sleeping girls that populate Balthus's lazy afternoons. Third, the furniture—its spare simplicity of kitchen tables, its worn edges, and the unadorned yellow tin on the buffet illuminated by the light, resonate with the tables in many images where children while away their time: *Les Enfants Blanchard* (p. 64), for example, or *La Patience* (The Game of Patience, p. 103).

Other window scenes, supplementing the ones already considered (*Jeune fille à la fenêtre*, p. 77), such as *Jeune fille se chaussant* (Girl Putting Her Shoes On), on the other hand, ambiguously connect to things happening between "girls"—children would be the better term—in those closed quarters, and between mundane activities and enigmatic streams of desire. The subject, the artist or the young boy he dreams of remaining, is seldom explicitly in the image, but always in the dream. This would be a gloss to the strangely androgynous old figure behind the girl in *Jeune fille à sa toilette* (Girl at Her Toilet, p. 104) and the equally strangely flattened one in *La Toilette de Georgette* (Georgette's Toilet, p. 105).

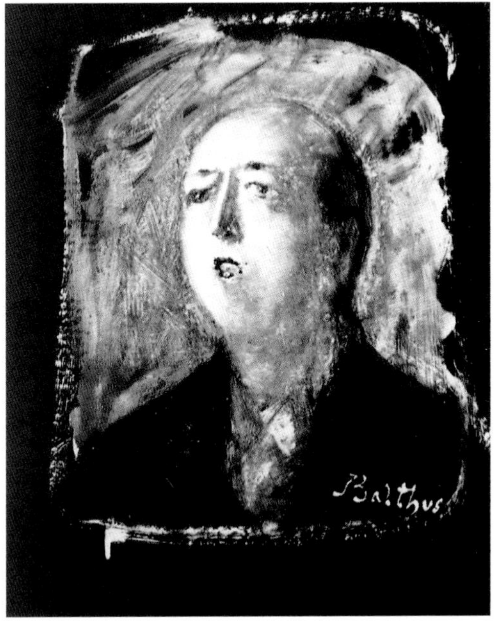

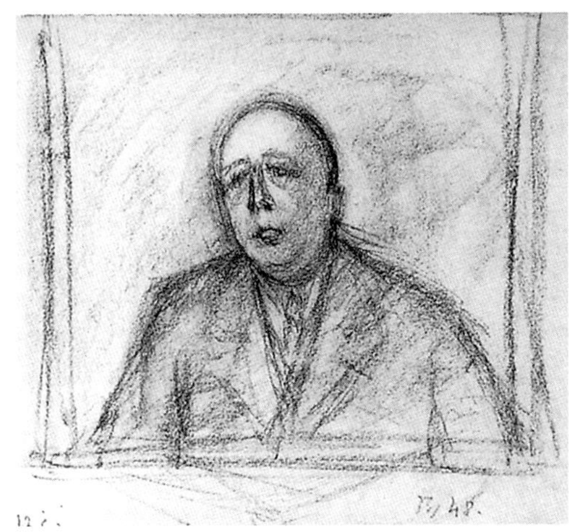

Portrait de Claude Hersaint, 1948.
Portrait of Claude Hersaint.
Oil on cardboard, 92 × 73 cm.
Private collection.

Étude pour un portrait de Claude Hersaint, 1948.
Study for portrait of Claude Hersaint.
Oil.
Private collection.

Portrait de Claude Hersaint, 1948.
Portrait of Claude Hersaint.
Fusain, 24 × 26 cm.
Current location unknown.

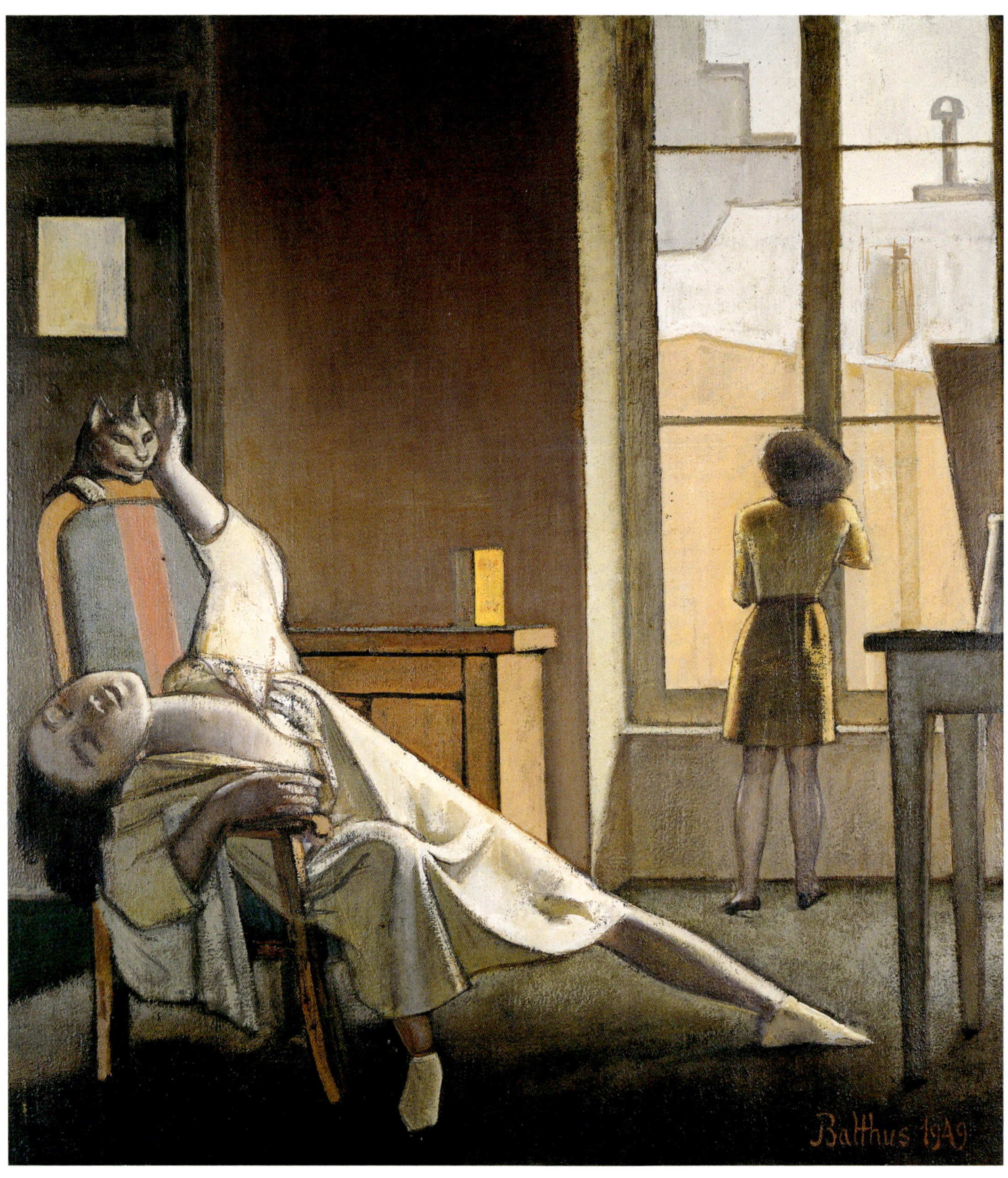
Balthus 1949

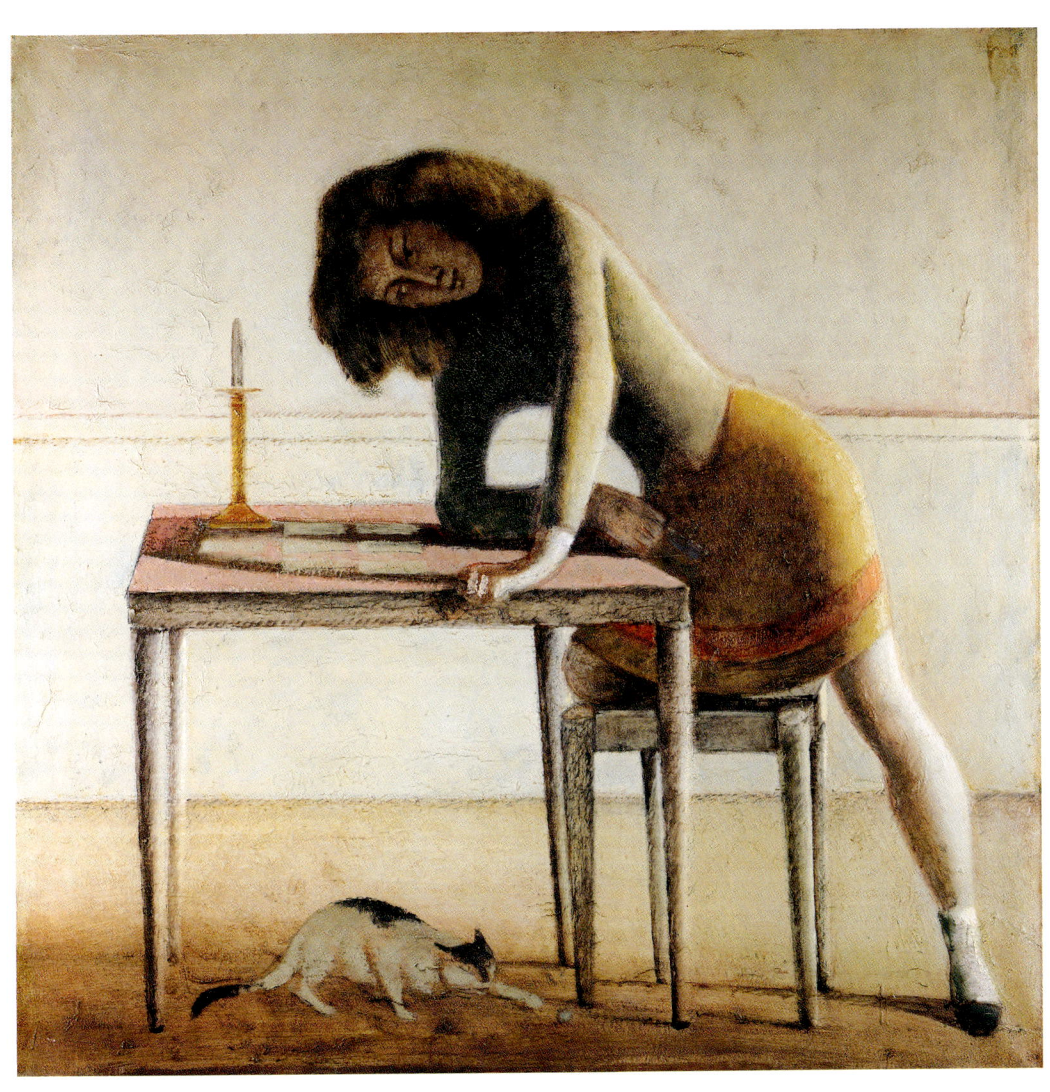

La Semaine des quatre jeudis, 1949.
The Week of Four Thursdays.
Oil on canvas, 97.7 × 83.8 cm.
Vassar College,
Poughkeepsie, New York.

La Patience, 1954-1955.
The Game of Patience.
Oil on canvas, 90 × 88 cm.
Private collection.

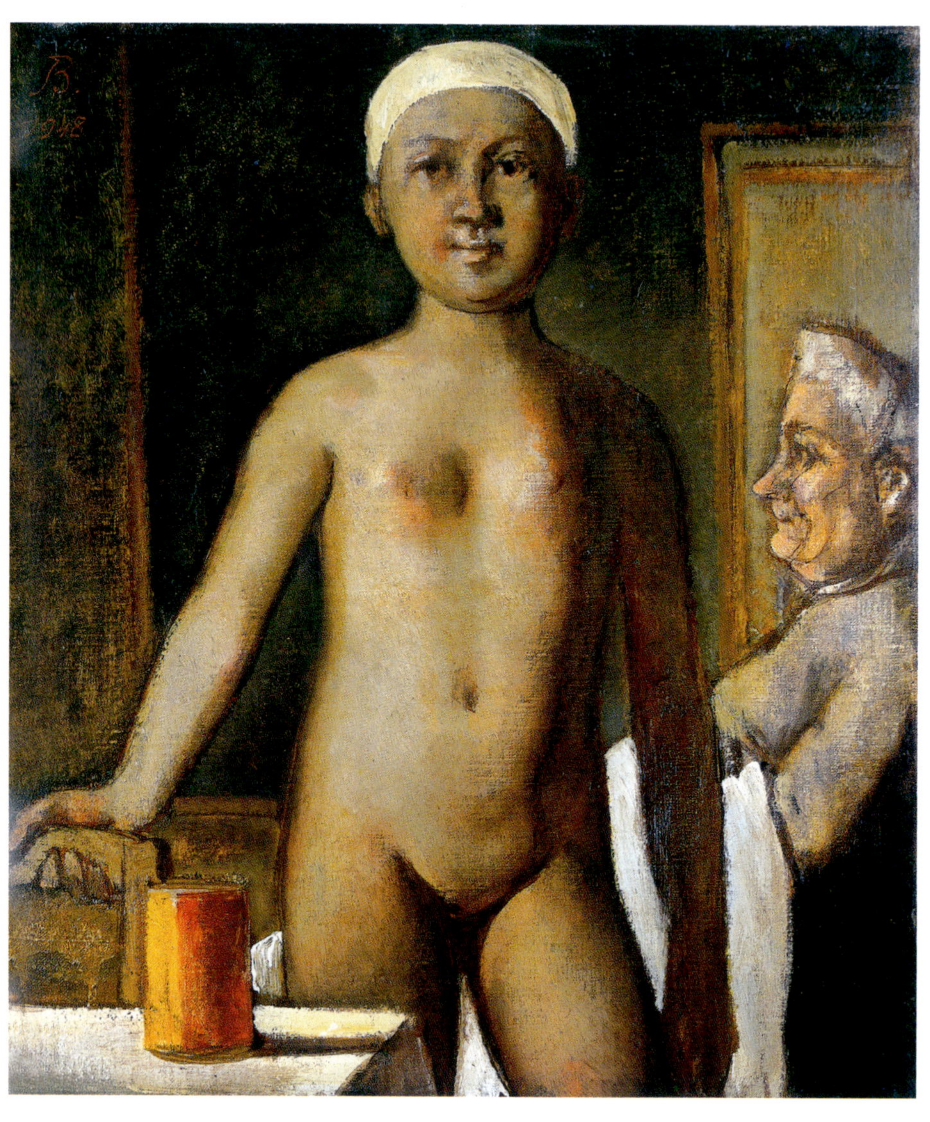

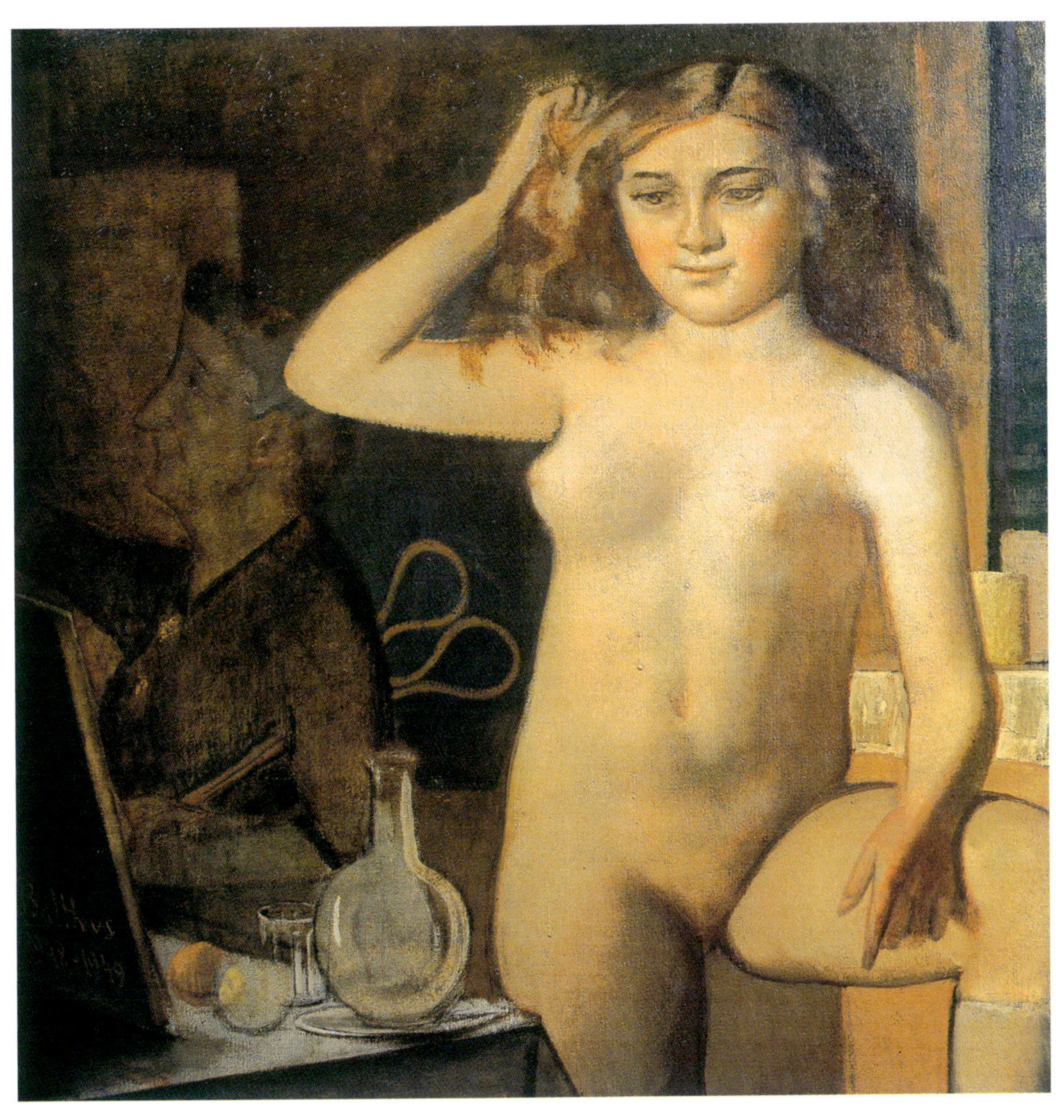

Jeune fille à sa toilette, 1948.
Girl at Her Toilette.
Oil on canvas, 100 × 80 cm.
Private collection.

La Toilette de Georgette, 1948-1950.
Georgette's Toilette.
96.5 × 92 cm.
Elkon Gallery Inc., New York.

La Fenêtre, cour de Rohan, 1951.
The Window, Cour de Rohan.
Oil on canvas, 150 × 82 cm.
Musée d'Art moderne, Troyes.

For me, the most gripping window picture—the picture that sums up Balthus's play with motifs of visibility—is the simple view from the window of his studio in the *La Fenêtre, cour de Rohan* (The Window, Cour de Rohan, p. 107). A merging of color and light holds the composition of oblique and vertical planes together. The salmon color of the walls of the houses opposite the window—but so close!—returns in the table top inside—but so close to the window!—only, the table is the brown color of wood, and the top's pink comes from the light. The image looks so simple, yet, for all its harmony, it is not. The focus of the painting is the still life on the table, to the right edge of the image. A dark container is cropped, a tin jug captures the light on its edges and rim, a knife's blade is a line of light. That knife points to the outside. Next to it, a glass bottle with stopper seems to contain that light, to have captured and imprisoned it.

The glass is one of those small indications of looking. Its transparency is held off; it is not opaque glass as such, yet the image of it is. It concentrates the color that binds the outside to the inside. In this it is a "mirror" à la Balthus: a small thing that tells us how to look. Importantly, what we then do with that looking—seeing the connections between inside and outside—is up to us. Speaking of this painting, Balthus's friend and fellow anti-surrealist, anti-abstractionist, Alberto Giacometti, with the American painter Leland Bell, said that this canvas is entirely sexual. "The buildings across the way reminded him of a woman—as if the dark window openings were female orifices" (Weber 452). Such an association would never have occurred to me. But that is beside the point as well. The glass bottle tells me that the apparent transparency attributed to realism becomes opaque when, focusing on a detail, then going back to the connections, we step inside the mirror. Like inside "Alice" for some, or inside that crossroad where light and color merge, for others.

Figures of visibility abound in Balthus's work. But none of them is more transparent than painting is—which is very little. Especially in the case of the painting of Balthus with its matte surface and frequently cool colors, this means, it is not transparent at all. Even the surface is not reflective. And so, when we are invited to consider the painting "like a mirror" it is never through the seduction of actual reflection that the works convince us. Instead, it is due to the way we see something we can only see when we go along with it, without any appeal to reality.

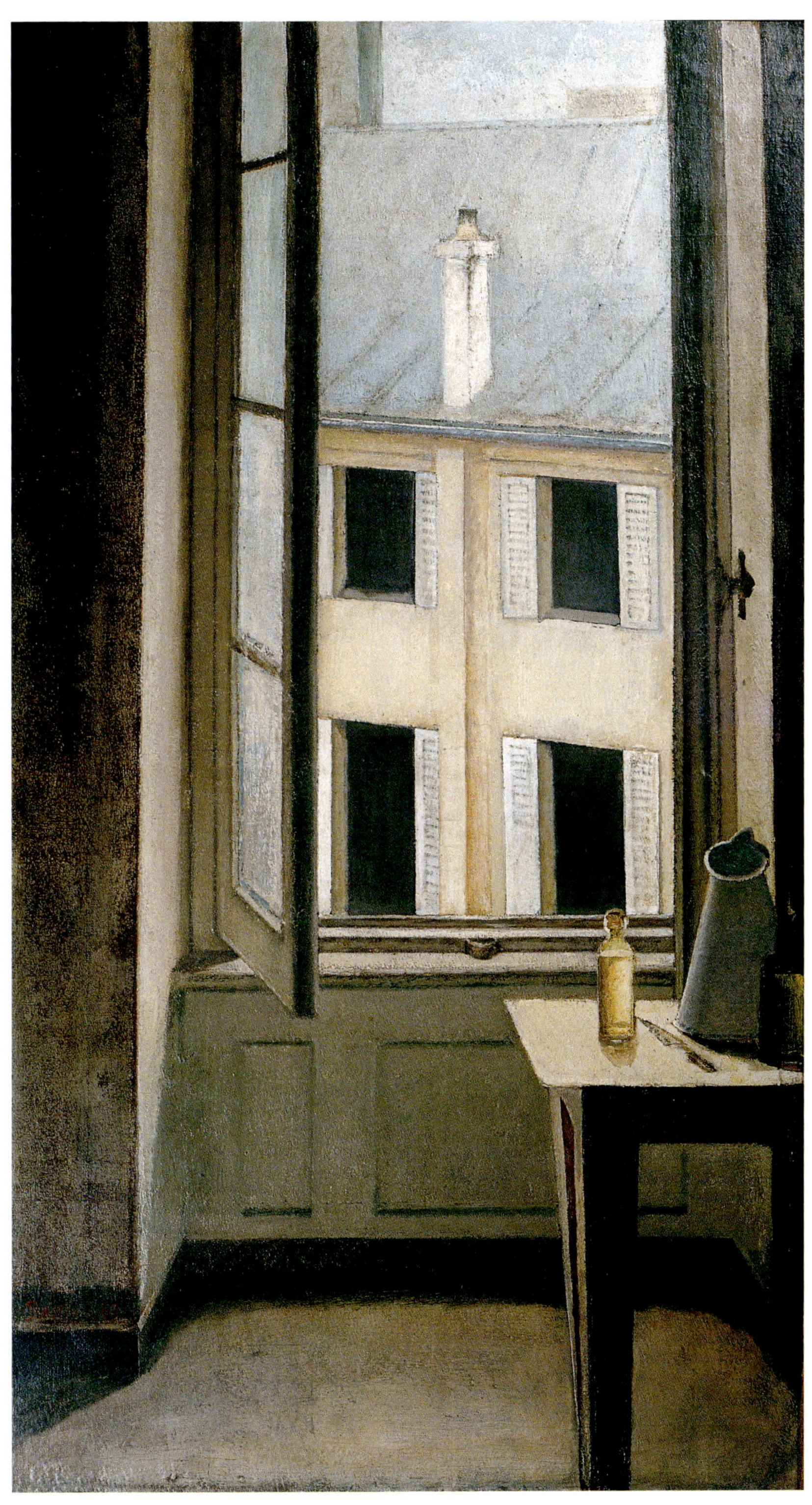

6. Dramaturgy of Dreams

But what is the point of all these strategies to focus on, and then hamper visibility; to complicate vision, and to deploy the most skilled craft of realist painting for the sake of de-realizing vision? They lead us to a domain where vision is paramount but out of reach. Remember *La Semaine des quatre jeudis* (p. 102), the picture with that stretched diagonal body of a girl caressing a cat. Like the girl in *La Chambre* (p. 70) there is something about her pose that strikes me as artificial. The way she is stretched out to form a straight line de-realizes her, so to speak. The woman in *Japonaise à la table rouge* (p. 37) is so uncomfortably stretched out before her mirror that her arm hangs limp. In *La Sortie du bain* (Stepping Out of the Bath, p. 109), the woman who leaves is stepping out of the bathtub in the large, perfectly square, dreamy composition of blue and yellow is in serious danger of falling. No model can long maintain the pose of the girl in the *Le Lever* (The Awakening, p. 110). At a quick glance, the three sisters in the three paintings of that name look like awkward sets of limbs, and one cannot imagine them in *Les Trois sœurs* (The Three Sisters, p. 111), to be immersed in the activities they appear to symbolize rather than exercising. Looking at all three of these versions gives a sense of the seriality so frequently deployed in Balthus's oeuvre. As if he was never content, never convinced—as if his ambition never matched the result; or, as if his fantasy never became visible enough. But the most contrived pose is that of *Thérèse sur une banquette* (Thérèse on a Bench, p. 112).

La Sortie du bain, 1957.
Stepping Out of the Bath.
Oil on canvas, 200 × 200 cm.
Private collection.

This girl seems the symmetrical mirror image of the one, in a comparable pose, also with her eyes closed, in that fantasy piece, *La Semaine des quatre jeudis*. There, what seemed a pose suggestive of looking into a mirror turned out to be playing with a cat. Here, too, the thread she is holding might be teasing a cat, neither visible, nor entirely unimaginable, in the shadow behind the bench. This straight thread is one of those details that must have suggested to Verschaffel his idea of the probing gaze. It is easy to imagine that, in the absence of that imaginary cat, the thread would go straight to her crotch.

With her body resting on only one hand on the floor, the model must become tired and cramped very quickly. The background, the signature fresco mottled green-ochre, leaves very little space, so that the girl seems not only contrived in her pose but also confined in the space. This, again, makes her a flat image, in spite of the detailed and very skilled rendering of the volume of her body. Her left leg is lifted just so that we cannot see beneath the lifted skirt, but barely. The checkered skirt, the orange-red sweater, the elaborate collar and the neat stockings and shoes all indicate a schoolgirl. Just as young as the girl in *Les Enfants Blanchard* (p. 64). But her body is leaner, her pose more provocative, her game more suggestive. If any of Balthus's painting can be called erotic, it is this one. But what does it mean to call an image erotic?[36]

I have mentioned earlier that the eroticism of some of Balthus's paintings is so convincing—so much so that some of his viewers then proceed to see it in rose petals and open windows—because it is, like all eroticism, relational. It is a desire that infuses the image from a source not visible in the picture itself. The making of such images, during which the model is to hold a pose for longer than anyone will care to imagine, is very different from the viewing of it. The pose can only be sustained for a very short time. But the vision can stay. It is the vision, not the girl, that ends up on the canvas. The relational quality of erotic images—as opposed to, say, abusive, exploitative, or, let's say the word, pornographic ones—makes the viewer not only responsible but also aware of his role in the relationship.

36. Here I could cite a range of theoretical discussions, from McKinnon's legal, perhaps a trifle censoring caution (1989) to discussions in film studies that, in the wake of Laura Mulvey's famous analysis of the subject-object division in narrative cinema, vindicate the right to visual pleasure (1975). While I am myself ambivalent enough about these discussions, I reiterate the wish to refrain from moralizing and censoring, and prefer to focus on the way these images transgress, precisely, that dividing line that makes such censoring positions possible: that between subject and object.

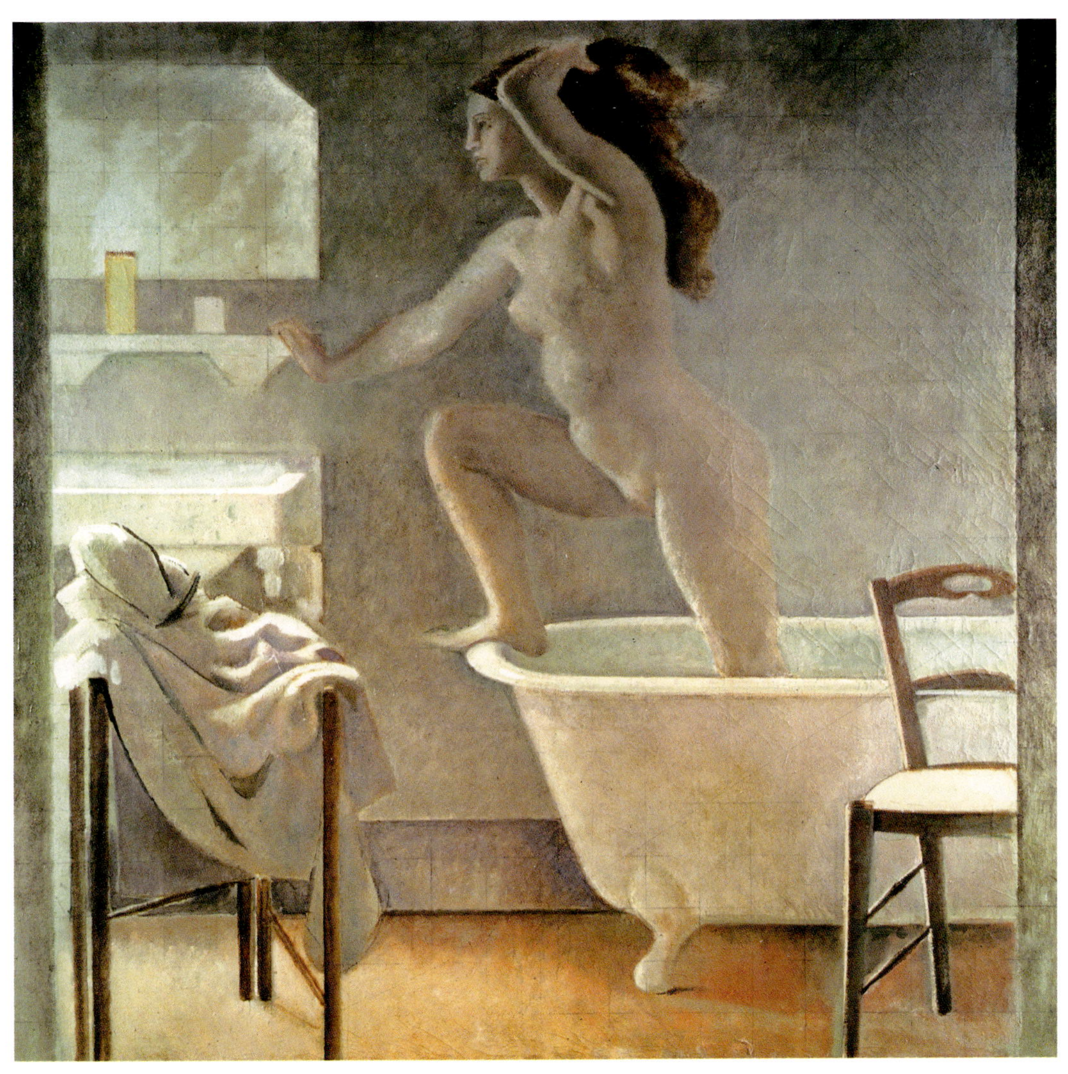

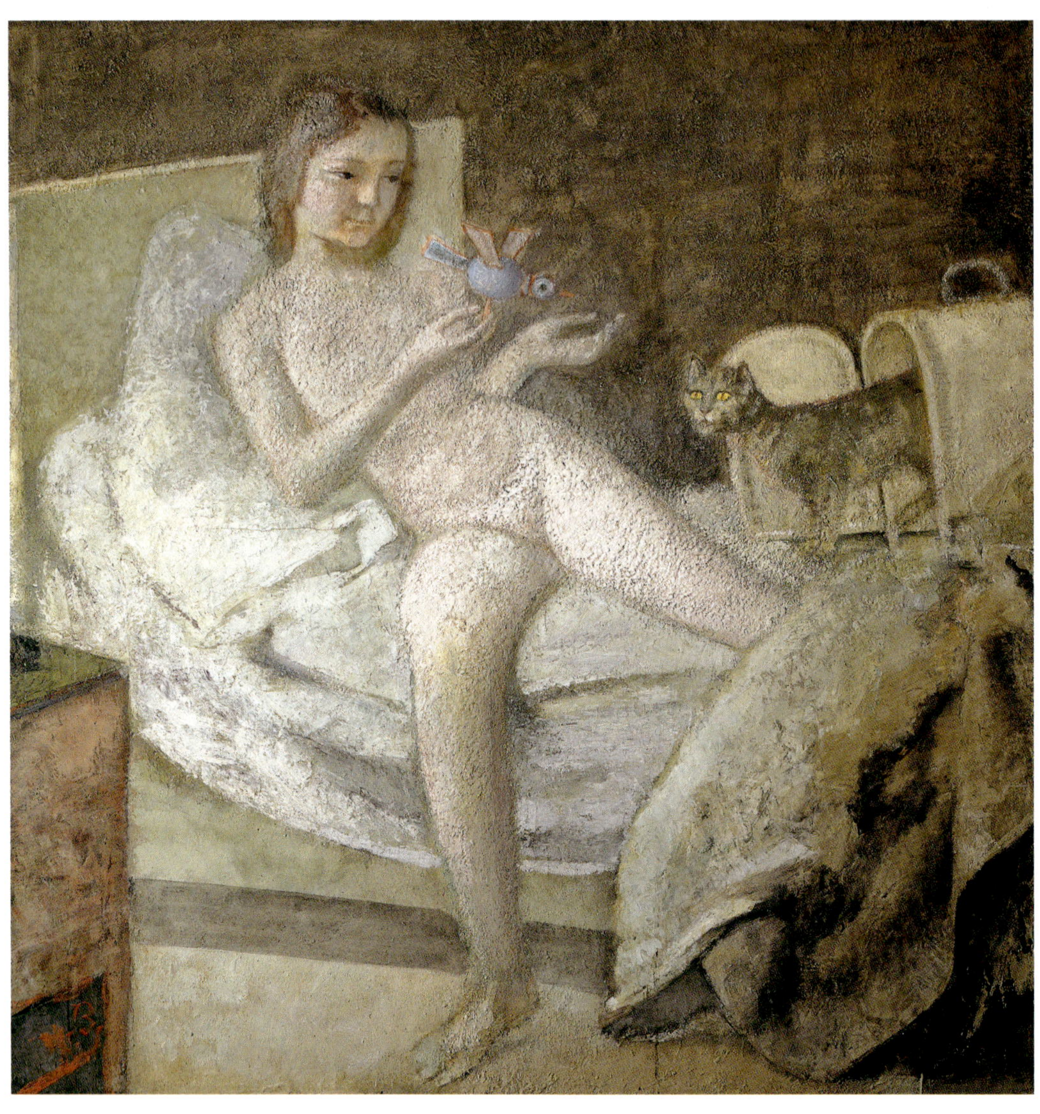

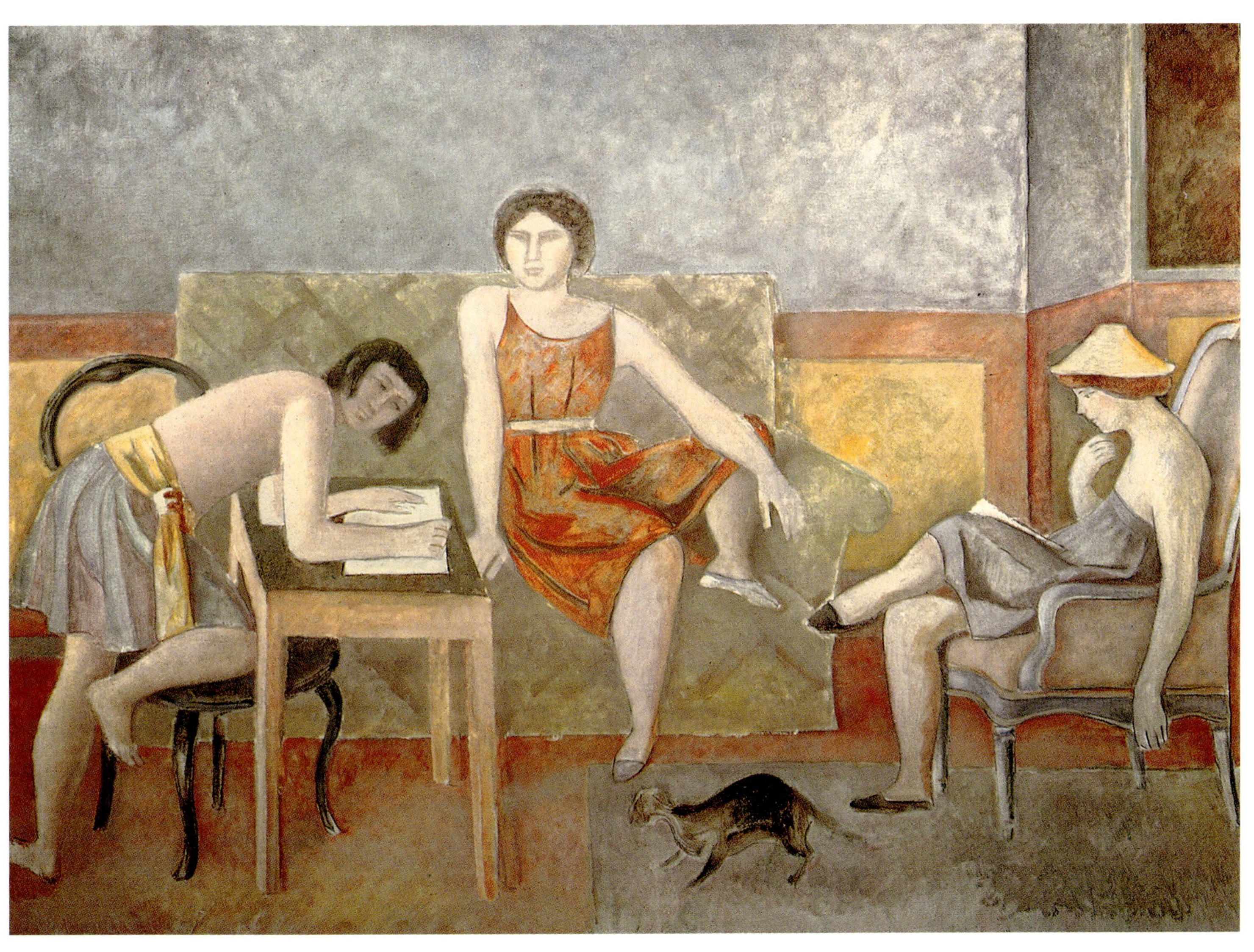

Le Lever, 1975-1978.
The Awakening.
Oil on canvas, 169 × 159.5 cm.
Private collection.

Les Trois sœurs, 1964.
The Three Sisters.
Oil on canvas, 131 × 175 cm.
Private collection.

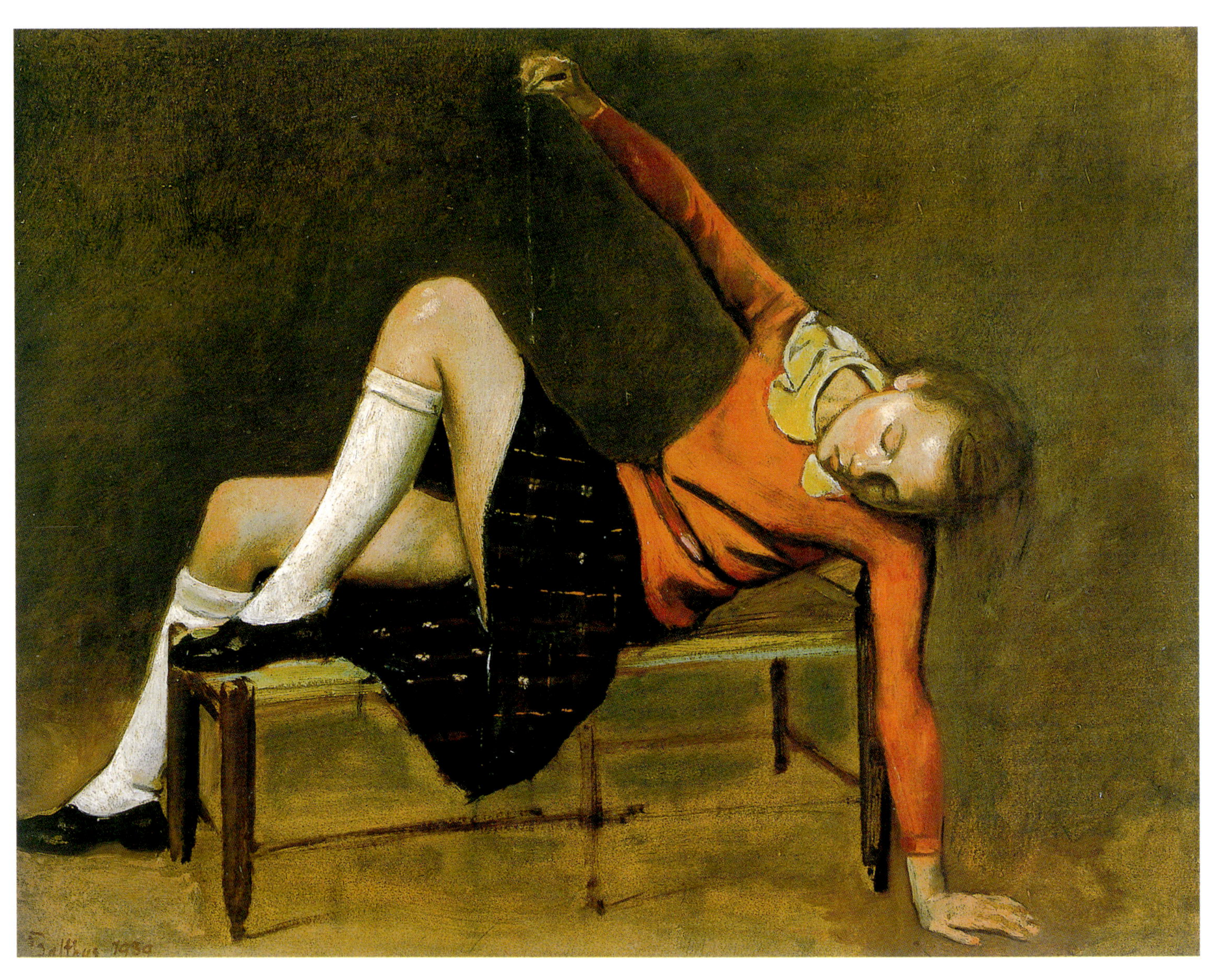

I say this not in order to simply displace everything from the work onto the viewer, from the object in front of us, to the subjectivity that beholds it. What I am trying to say is that what we see is not the girl but the relationship. We see the admiring, loving, desiring, excited and sometimes quite mad look cast upon her, rather than "her". To make the case for this view, I will browse some more in this oeuvre. Compare the implausible, yet (erotically) attractive (for some) image of p. 112, for example with a completely naked figure that is not erotic at all, *Grande composition au corbeau* (p. 23). This is, perhaps, the maddest Balthus image; one that without doubt can only be understood on the model of the dream.

The body is, again, implausibly disposed, in a pose impossible to hold for the length of the sittings necessary to make this complex image. But then, reassuringly perhaps, the legs even more than the arms seem barely attached to the body. The torso, with the small breasts, the round belly, the child's pubis over which a shadow is cast, the round face and the eyes that seem empty, and especially the rubbery skin, all tell us that this is a doll. The painter has applied all the perfectionist effort to the dark fresco wall that ages the painting, and to the pattern in the bedspread, to the furniture and even to the small man standing below the doll, more than to this strange body.

This image does not strike me at all as erotic. Clearly, neither nakedness nor body pose can determine the erotic quality of an image. Much less can straightforward symbols from the Freudian vocabulary. For example, the informal, small still life of p. 114 would be a perfectly Freudian image, so, one may feel free to consider it sexual, but there is nothing erotic about it. Nothing of the nature of eroticism as relational process "happens" between it and the viewer—only, if one wishes, a "translation". Sexuality is situated, here, entirely on the level of meaning, not affect. The *Grande Composition* poses entirely different issues. All interpretations of this painting that consider it erotic miss its point. For, as in other images, this fantastic scene is not to be interpreted at all.

It is neither an image of "possession", as in "the most absolute form of seduction", nor is it a picture of "visual, sensual beauty". It is neither an image of "to seduce and be seduced" nor of the likes of Piero's *Madonna della Misericordia* (right, top), to which only the discrepancies of scale could possibly link it (all in Weber 580-603, who is getting seriously carried away here. If any antecedent makes sense it is Hans Bellmer's series of Poupées (right, bottom). The subject of the raven, unique in this oeuvre, points to literary sources of dream stories, among which Edgar Alan Poe is the most obvious. And in case we don't get it, the fairy animal, neither cat nor rabbit, too large to be either, at the feet of the bed tells us of that most present literary source of all, Lewis Carroll's *Alice*.[37]

At face value, the tiny man with the adult, muscular and perfectly proportioned body brings a cage in which he might either trap the bird, to which he seems to be looking up, or the furry fairy animal below—both fit the size. The size of that green cage is proportioned to the animals, not to the figure that carries it. The arm with which he holds it had to be stretched beyond belief. The scene is filled with elements of stories that we cannot reconstruct. And this is why I find the interpretive exuberance in Weber's pages so excessive. But, as usual, they make a point. The point being, of course, the contagious nature of fantasy.

Fantasy is both contagious, and liberal. The viewer can be sensitive to this or that; to the nakedness that makes Weber imagine seductions and possessions; to the creepy furry thing that cannot be real; to the tiny man with his heavy burden; to the raven, scary or attractive,

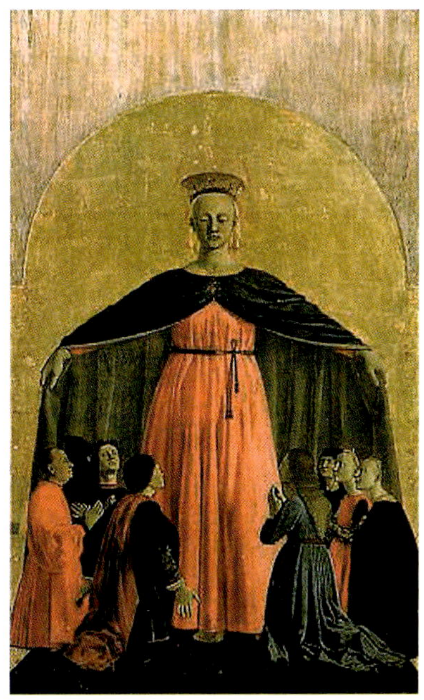

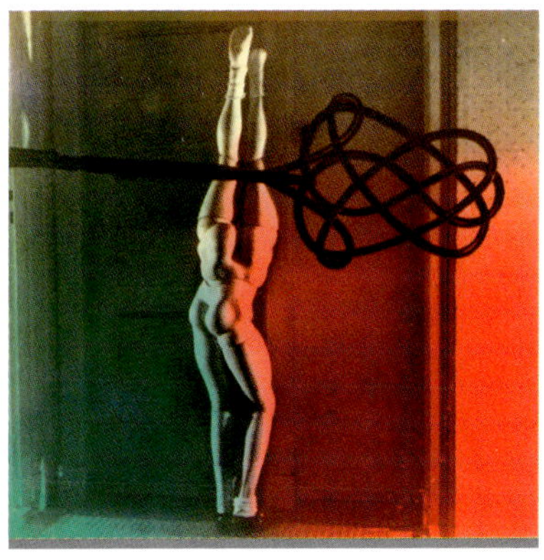

Thérèse sur une banquette, 1939.
Thérèse on a Bench.
Oil on canvas, 71 × 91.5 cm.
Private collection.

Piero della Francesca,
Madonna della Misericordia,
ca. 1460.
Oil on panel, 134 × 91 cm.
Pinacoteca Communale,
Sansepocro.

Hans Bellmer,
Poupée, 1935-1949.
Hand-colored gelatin silver print,
14.1 × 14 cm.
Ubu Gallery, New York.

37. On the Lewis Carroll association, which is rather obvious, see Russell (1983).

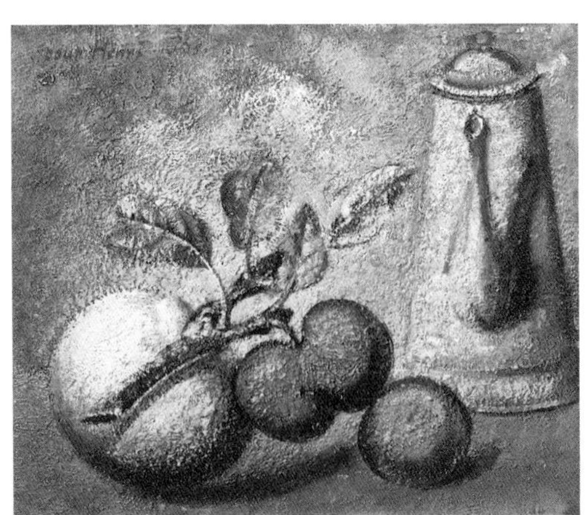

Nature morte, 1958.
Still life.
Oil on panel, 43.5 × 50 cm.
Inventory of Annette Giacometti.

Le Fruit d'or, 1956.
The Golden Fruit.
Oil on canvas, 159 × 160.5 cm.
Private collection.

welcomed or feared by the doll who, being a doll, can do neither. The empty eyes can recall Hoffmann's Sandman, who plucks the eyes out of naughty children and inspired Freud in his theory of the uncanny. The state of the doll, too large to be a dead toy, too rubbery to be alive, can also arouse fantasy theories. The point is not what we fantasize, but that we do.

If we see the painting as a dream, then there must be meaning but that meaning cannot be reconstructed except in "secondary revision", in the awoken state. The dreamer can never be certain that the memory covers what was actually dreamt. The elements of a dream are fragments of a puzzle. And between the words and the images, a relationship much like a rebus pertains. Man, cage, doll, rabbit-cat, raven: the puzzle is yours to play with. But then, do take the title into account: *Grand* (great or grand, or grandiose) *Composition With Raven*. With the raven we make the composition. Grand, or large: the work is not as large as some of Balthus's paintings. But perhaps, as a composition, or composite, it is. Grand also refers to the doll, so out of scale with the man.

Before returning to the idea of the uncanny, which will become more and more relevant, I first wish to pursue the idea that the dream is a key to Balthus's work. I propose to look first at another work that is explicitly about dreams. We have seen in *Le Rêve II* (p. 47) how the dreamer and the dream image are two flat surfaces that overlap a little. *Le Fruit d'or* (The Golden Fruit, p. 115) belongs to the same series. The dreamer is again implausibly positioned, in a pose that should wake her up with cramps. She looks quite like a doll as well, although a different kind, more folkloristic than toy-like, with her old hairdo and plump leg. We can now understand why, as in *Le Rêve II*, the flatness is a meaningful device to bring home the sense of de-reality. The still life on the right of the image reminds us, lest we forget, that we are seeing a painting that uses realism to achieve a dual goal. On the one hand, it inserts the art into its tradition, and on the other hand, by showing off perfection in craft, it shows that this is an image. Not "just" an image—as in a pale reflection of an unfathomable reality—but an image that can, while reality cannot, open the door to fantasy.

In the same series of images of dream and flatness, the girl with her eyes wide open of *La Tasse de café* (The Cup of Coffee, p. 116) must be considered. This girl is not sleeping but nevertheless dreaming. Her pale rosy complexion and the even, soft light suggest as much. But how can you daydream in such a contrived pose, borrowed from Matisse's *Odalisques* (p. 116, left)?. The tension between skillful rendering of three-dimensional volumes and flat surfaces becomes so serious a competition that from this alone a sense of the jigsaw puzzle or rebus emerges. The pale blue sweater, the coffee pot, the blue vase of flowers and the patterned rug compete, in their realistic mode of painting, with the patterns that surround the girl and almost absorb her. She seems caught in the green patterns that surround her, and between the salmon pink above her, from center to left, and the yellow glowing toward orange on her right, the ochre and brown checkered tablecloth below her.

Here is Matisse competing with Delacroix, or Hopper with Picasso, and Balthus with them all, to create an image that is, properly speaking, a dream image: elusive, impossible to grasp in a single look. Just like the image *L'Enfant aux pigeons* (Boy With Pigeons, p. 116), very different in color and mood but made around the same time, of the boy looking at pigeons flying up. Like an illustration for a children's book, this image retains that other side in the plant on the table and the curtain on the right edge. Or the *Le Pigeon* (Pigeon on a Windowsill, p. 117), so different from the *Bouquet de fleurs* (p. 59).

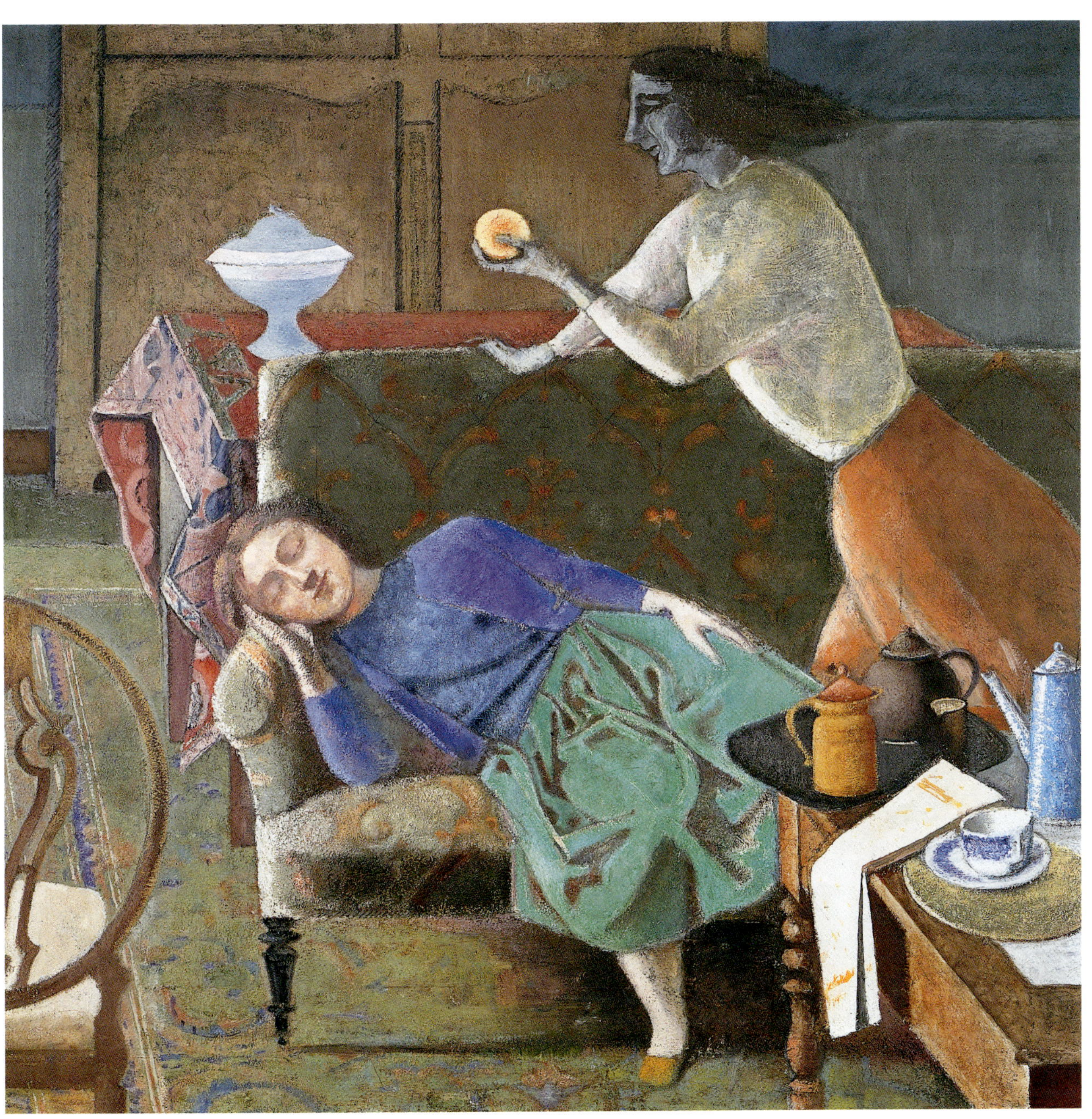

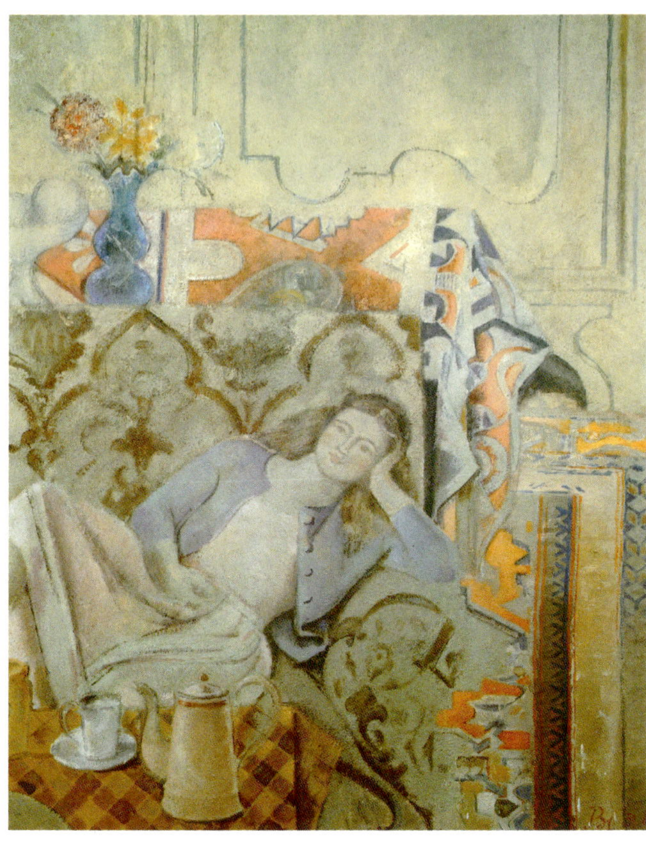

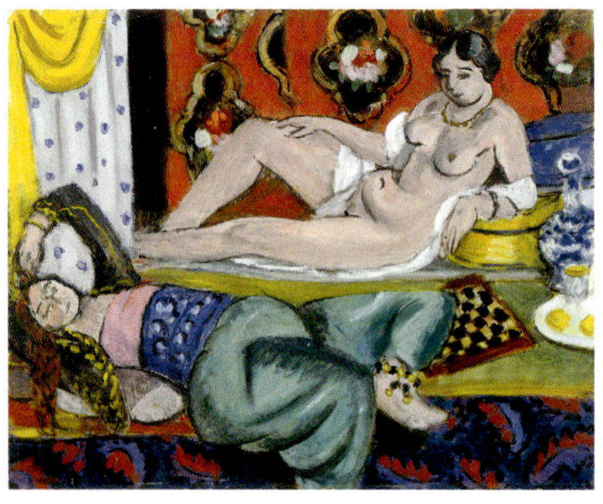

Matisse,
Odalisques, 1928.
Oil on canvas, 54 x 65 cm.
Moderna Museet, Stockholm.

What links these flat images to the dream works is the discrepancy between two-dimensional and three-dimensional elements, as if one were a fragment stuck on the other; a collage without support. This spatial indeterminacy undermines any pretense of realism as a link to reality; yet, the realism of the mode of painting remains present, as if to caution us to not take the image lightly, not to mistake it for "just" an image. Instead, the way the images float without support suggests the fleeting, ungraspable quality of dreams. And dreams can neither be communicated nor depicted.

On the erotic images in Balthus's oeuvre, then, I wish to say the following at this juncture. These images are constructions of fantasies. Everything about them makes us aware of that. At the same time, they can be truly erotic, in the sense of provoking their viewers to fantasize along. As a result, one can enjoy the image, idealize the girl, or partake of an imagined abuse. If one does the latter, the critical indictment concerns the very subject who utters or thinks it. The projected space in which dreams happen is open to all, but how one enters and what one does is up to everyone as well. On the other hand, viewers who are uneasy with sexuality will be uneasy with such paintings. But there is a way in which that, too, is a form of collusion: with a prudish culture that condones violence more easily than allowing sexual pleasure; a culture that, as a result, snickers at sexual fantasy, only to practice it more. But whatever one's position on this, the question of these paintings remains what exactly it is that Balthus offers for visibility.

Somewhere between the painting that proposes these fragments, and the viewer who disposes them into his own dream, the image—not the image as object but as the object's

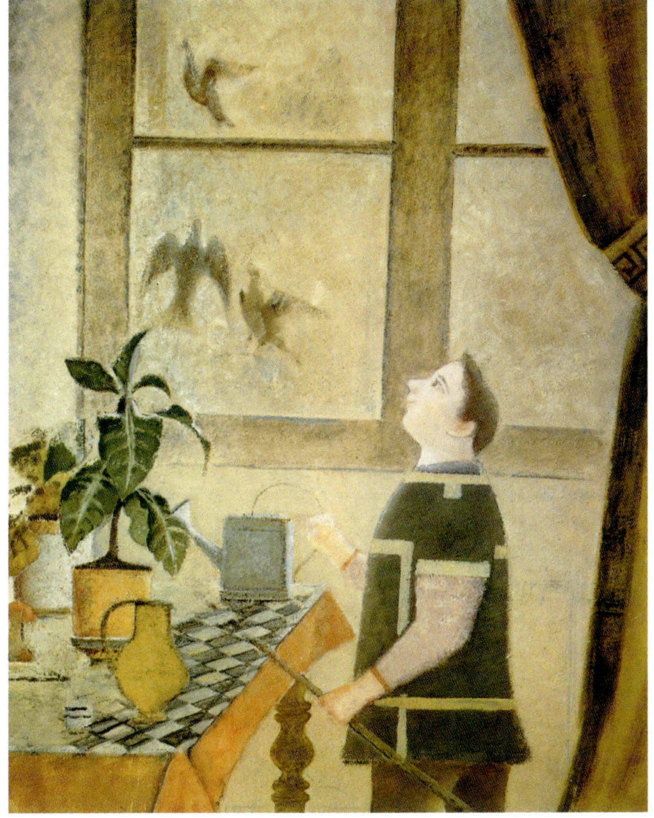

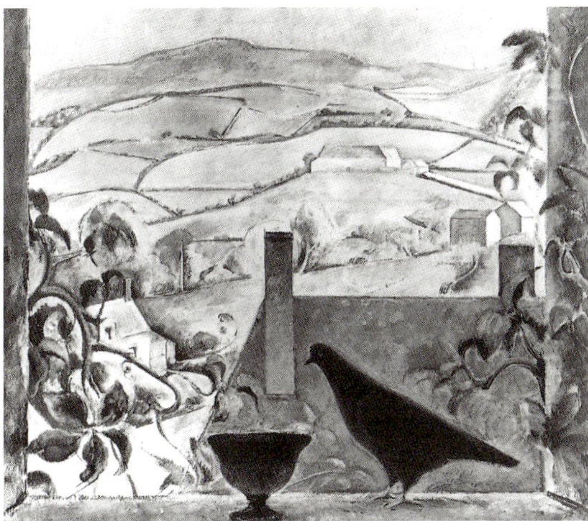

La Tasse de café, 1959-1960.
The Cup of Coffee.
Oil on canvas, 163 × 130 cm.
Private collection.

L'Enfant aux pigeons, 1959-1960.
Boy With Pigeons.
Oil on canvas, 162 × 130 cm.
Present location unknown.

Le Pigeon, 1958.
Pigeon on a Windowsill.
Oil on canvas, 88.5 × 100.5 cm.
Present location unknown.

effect—floats across the divide between that painting made over so much time, and the viewer, in that other world of quick perception.

The painting with which I end this reflection on the construction of fantasy is called *La Chambre* (p. 119), like *La Chambre* (p. 70), that most fantastic dream/nightmare. Again, I feel compelled to translate that title as "*The Bedroom*", not only because that is the specific meaning of the French noun, but also because of the presence of specific still life elements including a water pitcher, and a huge mirror over the mantle. Not, of course, that anything can be seen in that dark opaque surface. This painting is not unlike two I have invoked earlier, *Thérèse* (p. 87) and *La Toilette de Georgette* (p. 105), of large standing nudes. But this one makes explicit what the others intimate: that the nude adolescent girl is a fantasy. Everything, here, stages her as such. To make this clear I must again take issue with Weber's interpretation, for which I wish to offer an alternative.

Balthus's biographer considers the figure "otherworldly, more resurrected than earthbound" (1999: 417) and I concur. He then proceeds to spell out all the oddities in graphic detail. But convinced by the flesh tones and other symptoms of reality, he is satisfied that she is real—at this point, he loses me. The "child who sits on the floor reading", due to her "flattened and oblong" head, and because he finds her face "contorted like a mask", is declared to belong "only to the realm of imagination" (418). On the basis of the same features that Weber rightly finds convincingly realistic I still consider the larger, nude woman a figment of the imagination, of the painter's, or of the viewer's. And the pedestrian but still, also fantastic-looking girl on the floor could be the stand-in for both. Not that she is necessarily a child, nor is she reading.[38]

38. If I mention here that the model is Laurence, Georges Bataille's daughter, it is only to recall that Balthus lived and worked in an environment where his chosen topics were current.

La Chambre, 1947-1948.
The Bedroom.
Oil on canvas, 189.9 × 160 cm.
The Hirschhorn Museum
and Sculpture Garden,
Washington D.C.

The nude figure is oversized and sculptural, and stands very close to the picture plane. Her wide hair floats, and her eyes stare but do not look. The towel draped on her right hand side not only foregrounds her nudity (Weber 417) but also, as if to add the touch of parergon (Derrida 1987), like the drapery of antique sculptures it raises the question whether it belongs to the sculptural body or constitutes its outer limit. The answer, of course, is that it does both. Superimposed on the body it is part of the sculpture. It can hardly be hacked away. And if such drapes tend to foreground nudity even if they cover it entirely but flimsily, this is a statement on the fictional nature of art.

In this painting, the drapery's side effect is to recall the ancient sculpture that venerated the human body. This is why the towel is at the same time part of the picture of the woman, yet different from it, in style and color. In style it belongs to the signature elements of meticulously painted things, on which more shortly. In color, its composition of hues and tones suggesting pristine white set off the flesh tones of the body. In figuration, it allows the arm to be posed so prophetically. Moreover, it can be seen as a literal but reversed quotation of the automaton in *La Rue* (p. 19). The stature of the body, her size, the wide blond hair, and the unseeing gaze all contribute to turn this woman into an ancient Greek *kouros*. It is like a sculpture, a work of art, or like an otherworldly creature, a goddess to whom the girl on the floor looks up. That girl may be a figment of the (artist's) imagination, but the larger woman is a figment of hers, an embedded fiction, so to speak.

In addition to the features that make this figure so emphatically fictional, there is another, very different indication, which leads me back to the dream. Dreams are rebuses, said Freud, loose (mostly) visual elements that hang together due to associations invisible and mostly hard to retrieve from the unconscious. The reason I consider this painting programmatic for the Balthusian mode of dream depiction is the elaboration and placement of the still life elements. The towel's precise rendering already points to the productive ambiguity between sculpture and painting. On the chair next to the kneeling admirer stands a coffee cup. Oversized, it draws attention to itself. On the mantle stands a pitcher. On the right side, next to the nude's elbow, stands a bowl with a lid. And on the floor another pitcher in a typical rustic enamel.

A vulgar kind of psychoanalytic interpretation—frequently let loose on Balthus's still life elements—would see in each four of these objects allusions to female genitals. I do not buy that for a second. There is something else that may be more suggestive when we consider the jigsaw puzzle quality of dreams. The cup and the bowl refer to food, the two pitchers to water. The former two are porcelain, the latter metal. This strongly suggests two pairs, and a systematic disposition on the picture plane. On the surface this painting wants to be, the lines from cup to bowl and from pitcher to pitcher can be considered to form an X, a cross. The two lines cross exactly at the huge nude figure's genitals. The kneeling girl cannot see this. She is too riveted looking at the apparition. But we, the viewers, can.

We don't have to, but we may. This X draws attention to that central element of the female nude. It also draws attention to painting as craft and art, indistinguishable. Moreover it draws attention to itself. The shape of X stands for censorship, for X-rated, for a prudishness disguised as morality. Perhaps Weber is not so wrong, after all, when he attributes to the apparition a "haunting truthfulness". Truthful, as in canny, or Heimlich, as in familiar. Haunting, as in strange, uncanny, unheimlich. Noticing, also, the dispersed elements of the still life, he calls the painting a "mix of the quotidian and the extraterrestrial". All these phrases can be recast as the uncanny.

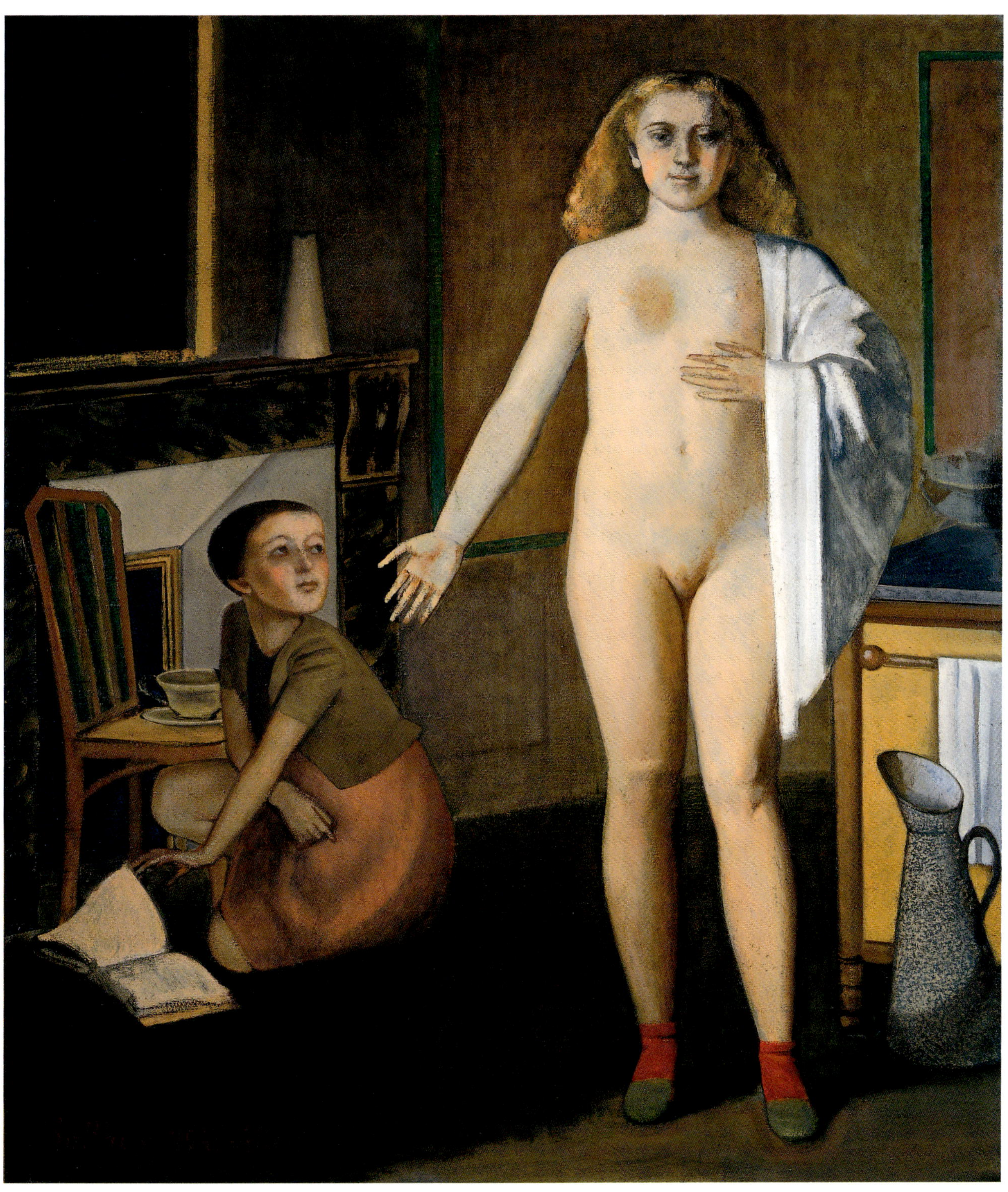

7. Nightmares of History

Dreams, as we have all experienced, have two additional properties. First, they are heavily colored by mood. Second, they are also both starkly visual and de facto invisible. At this point, I wish to "over-interpret" these two aspects of Balthus's painting. The automaton marching toward us in *La Rue* (p. 19), perhaps the most dream-like figure in Balthus's oeuvre, a figure that looks at us with unseeing eyes and moves its arms like a tin soldier, also blushes. This gives him a hint of life in the state of death; a semblance of humanity in a machine-like nature. A living dead, or vampire, or a case of the uncanny—Unheimlich, inquiétante étrangeté. In this respect, but not in looks, style, atmosphere or figuration, his closest peer is the female figure in the *Grande composition au corbeau* (p. 23). Unheimlich: both "Heimlich" and negation, "un-" are important in this phrase. The familiar estranged. It is as if the critics who discuss this painting in the same terms as the frankly erotic ones of the oeuvre, refuse the "un-" part, the estrangement. True, that estrangement, in French "étrangeté", is the more unsettling—"inquiétant"—as it estranges what was, before, familiar. It shifts an opaque but translucent sheet between the subject and the world. What seemed known—"canny"—is suddenly different, and this (un)recognizable vision gives us goose bumps.

Worse, much worse, than frightening but clearly fictional tales of horror occur in our nightly disturbances. Some paintings by Balthus convey this sense of the uncanny, and *Grande composition* is one of them. As is *La chambre* (p. 70), with the angry looking, androgynous dwarf, the witnessing cat with its human eyes and unreliable stillness, and the exposed/hidden girl's body, sleeping or dead, violated or desiring. Or, look again at *Le Passage* (p. 12). Look at the figure at the bottom right, a young girl with an ancient face, who confronts us with the relationship we have with the child, and with the child in ourselves. Between the drawing and the painted study, ages have gone by, all balled together in the finished painting (p. 120). Or the child-man in the sailor costume carried away by a nurse—or is it a bad fairy? He seems to climb up her body rather than being carried around. His face of an adult looks back at us, appealing perhaps. But no, this "baby" is also reading the newspaper. The uncanny is the stuff of dreams that turn into nightmares.[39]

But dreams are not simply products of fantasy. They are produced by the defense mechanisms that the mind provides against all that threatens the well-being of the subject. And the threat that the dream must deal with is triggered by "day rests"—events or impressions of the recent past that set in motion the entire psychic machine constantly in danger of re-activating buried fears and horrors instead of cravings and desires. In dreams these become partly visible, but turned into something else, more bearable, even if, sometimes, only barely. For a painter as meticulous and relatively slow, who spends sometimes years on a single work, the analogy between his works and dreams is tenuous at best. It only makes sense on two conditions. First, the "day rests" must have a longer duration, occupy years rather than days, and for that they must be of great impact. The second condition is that they can only be made visible indirectly, in "moods".

As many critics have pointed out, the classical mode of this painting cannot obscure a very modern sensibility. This means that this fantasy world is not disconnected from the great shocks of modernity and the tragedies that devastated Europe. In what precedes, I have shown here and there clashes between alleged reality and the flat image, between plausible and implausible elements or states, and between viewers' responses and what I see for my own part. With the results of the previous analyses in mind, I would now like to turn to the

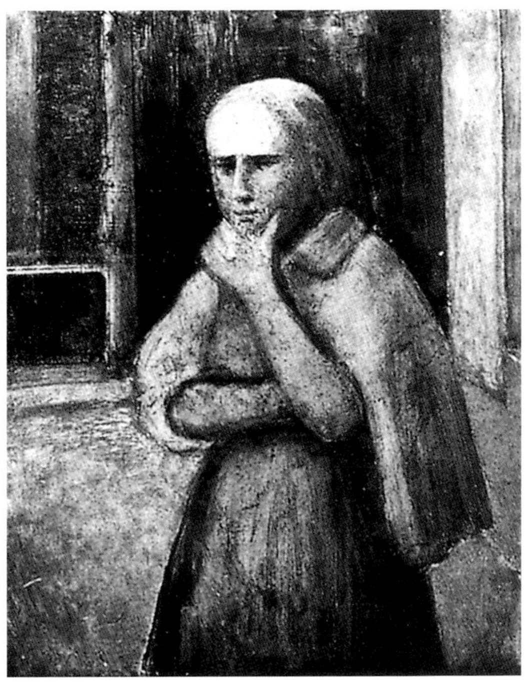

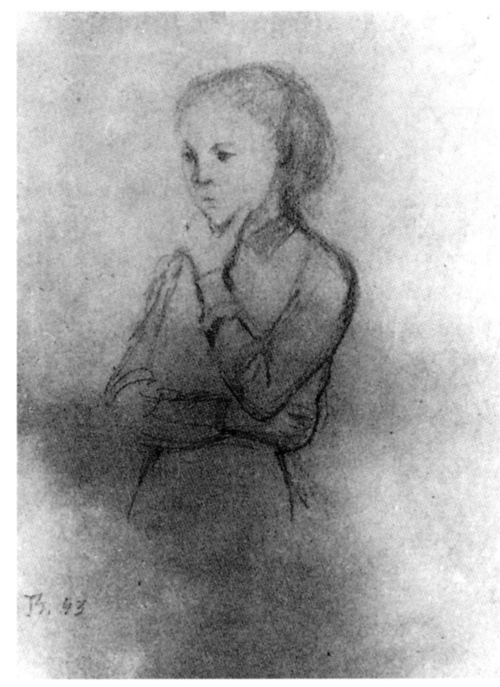

Étude pour «Passage du Commerce Saint-André», 1951.
Study for Passage du Commerce Saint-André.
Oil on cardboard, 92 × 72.5 cm.
Present location unknown.

Dessin préparatoire pour «Étude pour 'Passage du Commerce Saint-André'», 1953.
Preparatory drawing for Study for 'Passage du Commerce Saint-André'.
Lead pencil, 27 × 19 cm.
Present location unknown.

encounter, or the clash, between art and history. This clash takes place in the space where image meets viewer, and where the effects float across that invisible but ontologically absolute divide between painting as object and looking at art as process.

For this examination I am going to isolate a single, relatively short period in Balthus's production—that of the turbulent times of World War II. As an experiment, I will follow the order of the catalogue raisonné, and select images that speak most to me, without giving consideration to subject matter or to how representative they are, nor will I consider links to what I know of the history of that time. During those years of great anxiety and trauma for all of Europe, Balthus painted a great number of extraordinary works. I divide them into three groups, roughly chronologically. The point I seek to make with this selection is not to recuperate chronological art history nor even social art history but, on the contrary, to probe relationships between an art of which I have first established the fantastic character, and the reality in which it was made, in which it functioned, and that in turn, I contend, fed those dreams.

Prelude

The landscape *Larchant* (p. 123) was painted right before the war. A vague sense of an ending, a threat to the world as we knew it, was generally felt in the Parisian art world as elsewhere, although no one knew exactly what was to come. Yet, *Larchant* is "simply" a landscape. A brilliant one, with an insistent horizontality, the horizon lower than half-way, and the sky in turn divided in a cloudy and a blue part, the lower part in a group of buildings around the cathedral in ruins, then below, an even, ochre band with only shimmering nuances, no figuration. Jouve wrote a poem about the painting, and cast it in terms of memory. He described Balthus's painting in 1943 in the following terms particularly apt for *Larchant*:

39. Needless to say, it is worth going back to Freud's texts on dreams and on the uncanny. They contain many examples similar to these.

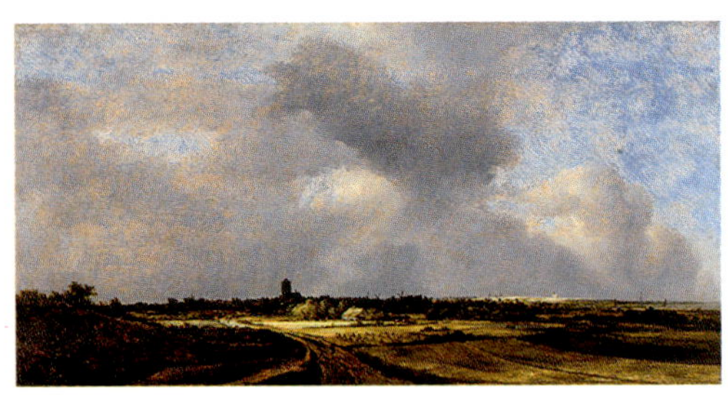

Jacob van Ruisdael, *View of Naarden*, 1647. Oil on panel, 34.8 x 67 cm. Museo Thyssen-Bornemisza, Madrid.

Larchant, 1939. Oil on canvas, 130 × 162 cm. Private collection.

> After a long labor the painter hides the great share given over to metaphysical anxiety underneath quiet forms, heavy, but vibrant, of visual reality.[40]

What Jouve is suggesting here is something that many paintings seem to substantiate, and that may explain the slow pace at which they were made. As Balthus himself often declared, he only depicts what he sees. But, in his vision, or as Jouve suggests, underneath it, is a mood that cannot be unaffected by the world as he lives it.

In an insightful article on Balthus's dramaturgy that focuses on the idea of the "arrested dramaturgy" much as I have used the word "still", Jean Starobinski characterizes the painting as "the painting of meditation before the ordeal of the war".[41] The critic focuses first of all on the ruin of the cathedral. The calm atmosphere of the landscape places the ruin in the temporality of the long duration. In the broad band of sky he sees the union of the land with its light. The distancing allows the particularities of busy and mundane everyday life to be erased while the depiction stays entirely loyal to what is visible. He calls it an "idealist" painting and adds in a footnote that the ruins of Larchant cathedral represented for many, among whom Balthus, the symbol of what was threatened.

Starobinski's description and interpretation sound insightful, yet idealist in themselves. Picon, another contemporary, expresses more of the other side of that positivity. He contends that the artist

> ... inscribed in the infinitude of the horizon the native security of the village. But at the center of that hub of roads, mill stones, roofs, and the traces of labor stands erect the gigantic ruin of the obsolete church. There we could have lived; but no longer... shine the mirages of memory mixed with the shipwrecks of longing, impossible to drown.[42]

These critics, who both lived through the moment in which the painting was made, sense a mood, although not quite the same mood. John Russell, writing in 1968, offers a reading of this painting that fits my earlier analysis of the merging of genres. He associates this work with still life. The field on the foreground would be the tablecloth, falling down from the tabletop, the edge of which would be the horizontal limit of the field. The village stands in for the objects on the table. He also calls it abstract (1983: 288). I think his analysis responds to the huddled togetherness of the houses, hiding under the skirts of a huge protectress. For an analysis of mood, the wavering of scale between distant landscape and still life—a typical baroque phenomenon—indicates a fundamental ontological hesitation that veers toward the uncanny.[43]

I would venture to add that there is something ominous, anxiety-raising, that makes this landscape both familiar ("idealist") and strange ("mirages of memory") so that it becomes uncanny, perhaps nightmarishly so ("shipwrecks of longing"). I see this effect in the remarkable and defining light. With the low horizon and the shifty sky, this is reminiscent of seventeenth-century Dutch landscapes (above). Here, it illuminates small portions and leaves others in the shade. This extraordinary light, in which the long duration to which Starobinski referred and the fleeting shiftiness of change, the fugitiveness of clouds chased by a storm, looks both so "Dutch" and so ominous because the color is. Between white, off-white, and a beige with a nuance of orange, the cloudy part of the sky gives the light in the village its peculiar tone—not quite brilliant, rather hesitant—which makes the cathedral retain the link of its stone. It is that middle band that hides, as clouds tend to do, what the vision can neither encompass nor entirely ignore. The extraordinary quality of this painting lies for me in that

40. [L]a part très grande faite à l'angoisse métaphysique, le peintre la dissimule après un long travail sous des formes tranquilles, pesantes, mais vibrantes, de la réalité visuelle (1983: 55).

41. le tableau du receuillement avant l'épreuve de la guerre (1996: 27). See also Kopp (2001) and Bonnefoy (1983).

42. Inscrit dans l'infini de l'horizon la sécurité natale du village. Mais au centre de cette roue des routes, des meules, des toits et des sillons de labour, se dresse la ruine géante de l'église désaffectée. C'est là que nous aurions pu vivre; mais nous ne le pouvons plus... brillent les mirages de la mémoire mêlés aux épaves insubmersibles du désir (1983: 102).

43. Weber's association, mentioned above, of *Grande composition* with the *Madonna della Misericordia*, which seemed so utterly misplaced there, would work better here, with the houses seeking protection under the church. On uncertainty of scale as a baroque phenomenon, see Bal (1999).

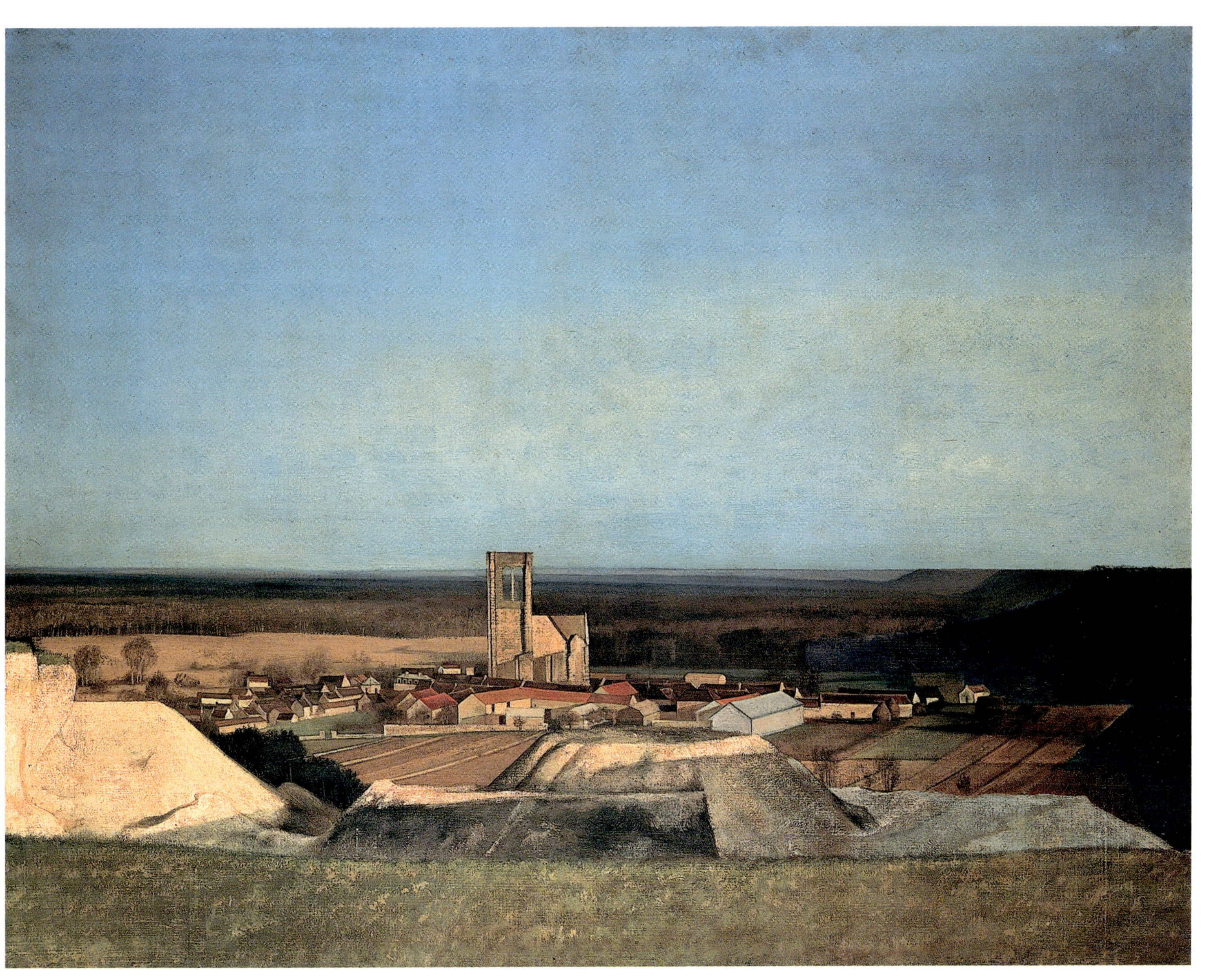

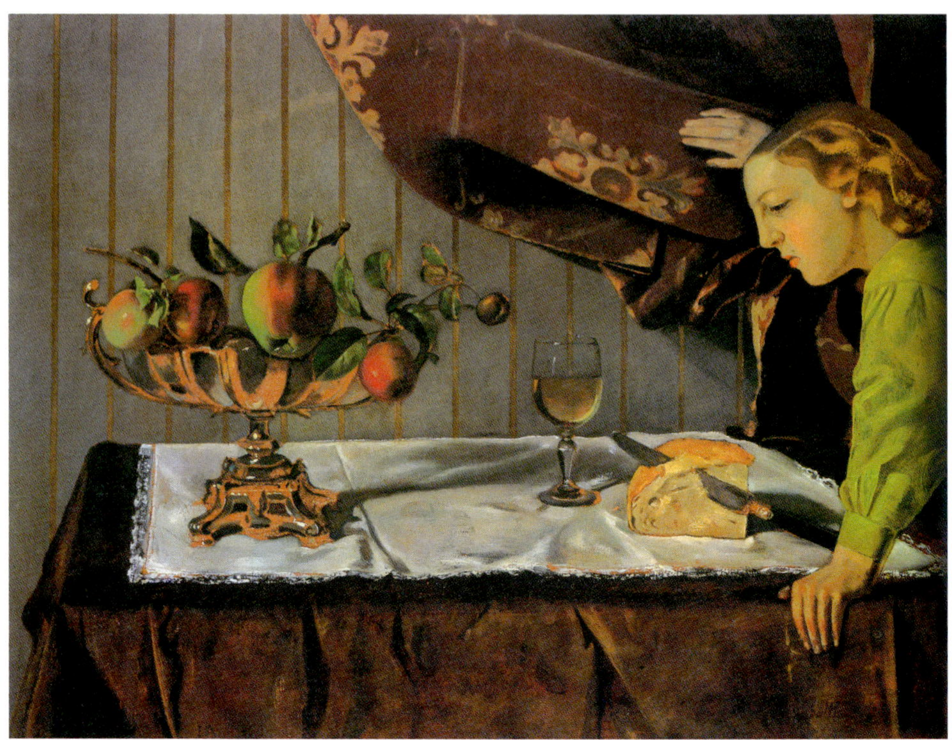

complex duality of mood, to which the extreme realism of the depiction of the buildings, as well as the subtle coloring of the fields contribute, but which these technical achievements do not determine. Beyond the painterly skills there lies a Cassandra-like vision of what cannot be seen but is inexorably already present. This is not even, "simply", a still of a fleeting moment, but a moment with its future as well as the attempt to hold that future at bay by an appeal to the past. The mood is ambivalent, swaying it sways between hope and doom, producing memories of devastation to come; all three critics, thus, captured one element of it.

Act I

A group of paintings that nothing binds together but the hand that made them, the mind that saw their visions, and the moment in history. The self-portrait mentioned earlier changes mood now (p. 33). The set mouth with its corners turned downwards no longer looks disgruntled, as it did when brought in touch with the figure of Heathcliff in *Cathy* (p. 30). The gray-blue-green of his jacket and the yellow-ochre of his pants seem drawn, not without effort, from the wall toward which the man brings his brush. Between his brows is that deep groove of worry, and the eyes look and don't look at us. Nothing in this handsome face betrays any of the Balthusian moods of desire, longing, wit, or ambition. Only the belief in art, expressed in the subject itself as much as in the effort to reach artistic perfection, dominates this painting. And the clutched fist holding a cloth, very unlike the usually failed hands, is more than a virtuoso piece of depicting flesh, muscle, and skin with fabric in folds. It seems to add to that belief: against all odds. It keeps the painting below the threshold of pride. Mood, then, is not depicted; only felt as a motivator.

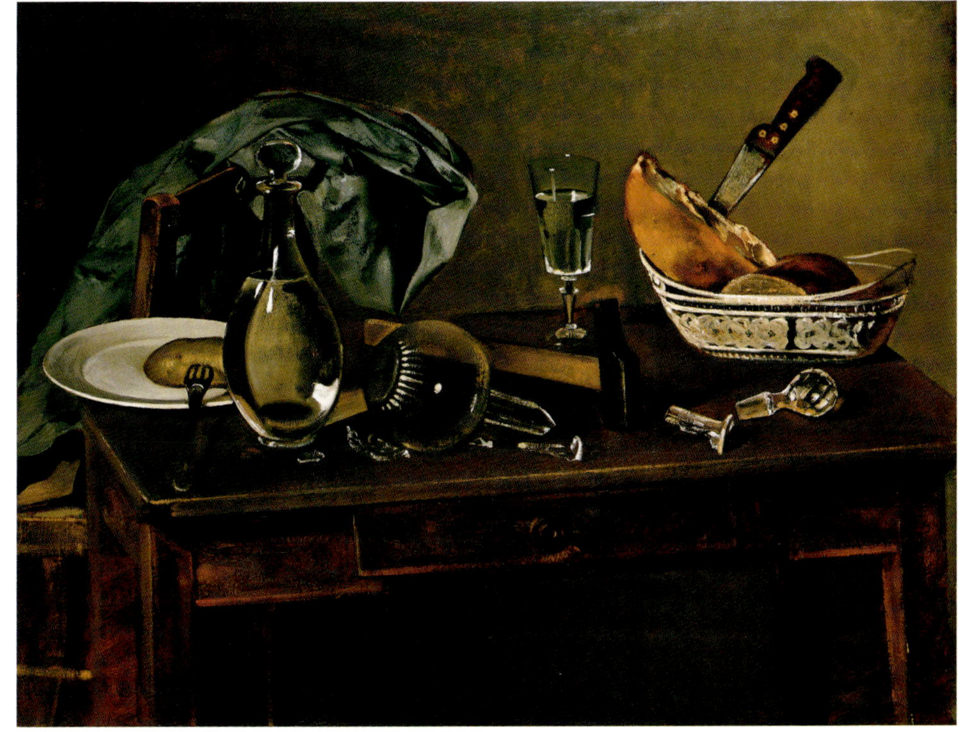

It would be contrived to see anything like this in the figure hovering over food in *Le Goûter* (Afternoon Tea, p. 124) It is just a girl looking at a table. She looks earnest, without a smile, but that happens all the time. She looks both young and old, both a housewife and her daughter. The table is one of those still lives brought to an eerie perfection that one would like to take pages to describe. Take the tablecloth, the thin white cotton cloth covering over it, with its fine lace borders. Or the glass bowl, of which the thickness and transparency set solidity of form over delicacy of surface. The detailed fruits. The glass of water. It is hard to avoid seeing in the coarse country bread with the knife stuck into it, an allusion to the violence, more pronounced, in the 1937 *Nature morte* (Still Life, above), which many critics have suggested could be seen as a prelude of the violence horrors to come.

But then a few details of *Le Goûter* disturb the ease of this picture. The girl is lifting up a heavy Persian rug, magically, with a hand that barely seems to touch it. That rug is more than a theatrical curtain; it is that underneath which things lay hidden, swept underneath it perhaps. Once its heaviness is removed, lightness gets another chance. And what is that apple doing there, floating so high at the edge of the bowl, or the peach and the cherry even outside, escaping it? Is that what the girl is looking at? And the girl is cropped so drastically that she seems bodiless, white enough to seem to be spectral. She appears to prefigure the dream girls in pictures such as *Le Rêve II* (p. 47). For all the realism, the picture loses its reality. The water glass for all its light cannot chase away the shadows cast by the bowl of fruit. These details amount to nothing but a few oddities. Nothing much, just a few oddities. Of the kind of which the stuff of dreams are made.

Le Goûter, 1940.
Afternoon Tea.
Oil on corrugated cardboard,
73 × 92 cm.
Private collection.

Nature morte, 1937.
Still Life.
Oil on panel, 81 × 99 cm.
Wadsworth Atheneum, Hartford.

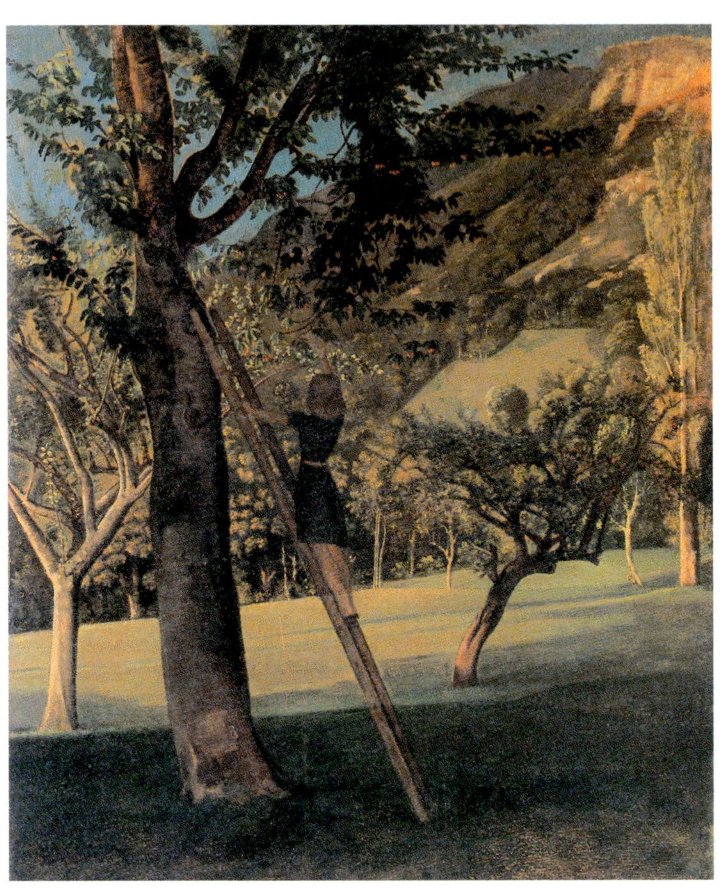

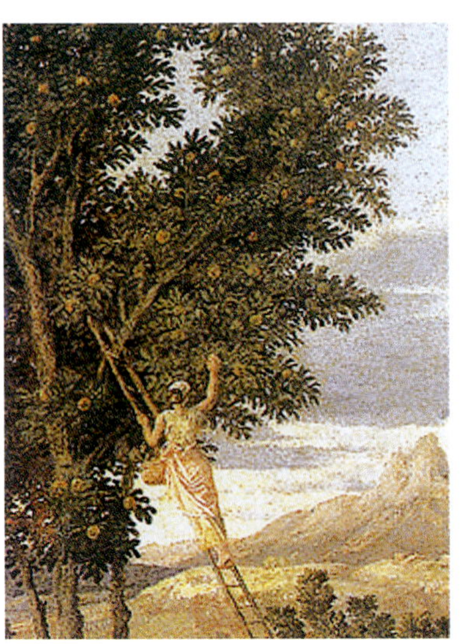

Likewise *Le Cerisier* (The Cherry Tree, above), that fragment cut out of Poussin's *Fall* (left). Especially the leaves on the trees have borrowed their depiction from that Poussin's classical work. Dark and luminous at the same time, offset against the sky yet catching light on the front side. The paint has the quality of enamel. The mountain and the tree in the far right are ablaze with late afternoon light. The girl stands on the ladder without a basket. She picks the cherries only for her own pleasure. The pose allows the depiction of her legs and skirt as elegantly stretched. Poussin depicted busy farmers' life; Balthus, that lone token of human life. In the fragment Balthus selected, the busy life is "momentarily suspended" (Russell 1983: 289).

But this is nothing like the allegory of abundance of Poussin. By isolating the girl from the rest of the scene, Balthus casts his vision on her singular existence. Adolescence now comes to stand for an ambivalent optimism: futurality, the possibility of survival, yet the uncertainty of it, expressed in the darkness that surrounds her in spite of the light at the distance. The sky, as far as there is one, has the color of *Larchant*, a blue that is tainted, here by orange. The idyll can be a distraction from the horrors that rage outside of this orchard. "Damnation to the war, to unhappiness, to History", said the artist to Claude Roy (1996: 130). Fair enough, and in fact, enough to back my interpretation of the mood of these paintings: a

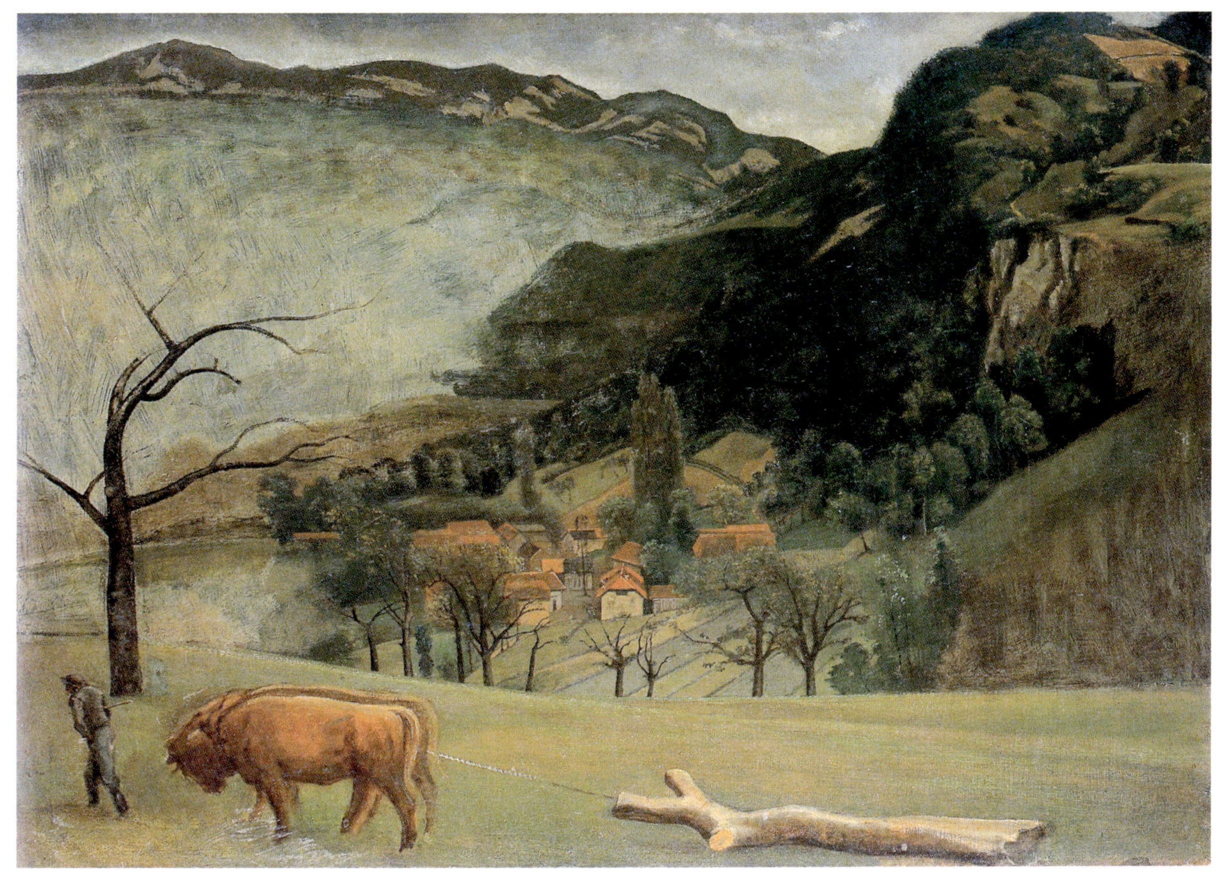

response from within the great art of Europe to the disaster that threatened it (Kopp 2001: Kopp 67, 70-71). Jouve, who was close to Balthus at the time, sees in it the confirmation of disaster by thought (1983: 58).

Two more landscapes in this Act. One of heaviness, where the oxen draw a tree trunk, *Paysage aux bœufs (Le Vermatel)* [Landscape with Oxen, above]. There is nothing here of the ethereal, elegant Chinese lightness of *Grand paysage avec vache* (p. 42). Darkness predominates, and brings this landscape's ambiance close to *Le Gottéron* (p. 133). The right side of the distant mountains is almost black. The farmer leading the oxen, stooped and dark, and almost treading off the picture pane, has just passed a gnarled, dead, entirely black tree. The oxen bow their heads. And while there is that brighter, misty patch on the left mountain to prefigure the *Paysage de Monte Calvello* (p. 52), the dead tree casts its darkness onto it. The hauled tree trunk is oddly cropped at the lower edge, bringing it into the space of viewing, as if we were to share the burden, or at least feel it.

In the context of the works made during this period, the most frequently cited for its paradoxical mood is *Paysage de Champrovent* (p. 25). As a landscape, this is even more perfectly classical. The Poussinian leaves are distributed quietly over the middle part of the

Nicolas Poussin,
Detail of *L'automne*, 1660-1664.
Oil on canvas, 117 × 160 cm.
Musée du Louvre, Paris.

Le cerisier, 1940.
The Cherry Tree.
Oil on panel, 92 × 72.9 cm.
Mr. And Mrs. Henry Luce III.

Paysage aux bœufs (Le Vermatel), 1941-1942.
Landscape with Oxen.
Oil on canvas, 72 × 100 cm.
Private collection.

Portrait de Monsieur L. de Ch. et de ses enfants, 1943.
Portrait of Mr L. de Ch. and His Children.
Oil on wood, 105 × 108 cm.
Private collection.

painting. In the distance, the farthest mountain is blue, rhyming with the dirty clouds above it. Dirty, but with bright white edges, with the silver lining made literal. The modulation of dark and light, green and blue, and sandy brown in horizontal portions produces a landscape of such stillness that we know we have never seen it "really". If there is a connection to the raging violence it must be by counterpoint. If it responds to that violence, it is by refusal. Against disaster, the artist can only posit art. And to demonstrate that he is not alone in this, that there is something bigger to defend, he paints so "Poussinistically". This is not a landscape; it is a willful memory of one.

Nothing suggests that this work was painted after the artist was wounded and demobilized. Nothing, except, perhaps, that excessive calm, that desperate classicism. And that strange, pale creature lying in the foreground. Small, though, for a foregrounded figure. Her legs half bare, and toward the viewer, but so distant, so out of reach. Her skirt is hiked up, but this conveys no elegance, only fatigue and uncertainty as to what to do. The moment is evening. The light, almost horizontal, is still golden; but it is the moment that the trees cast their longest shadows. Casting light in darkness, but barely: the moment of contradiction. As if the desire to oppose the violence by refusal is not quite enough; as if the painter is not quite in mastery, and his mood, as I have been calling it, transpires in spite of him.

Before the curtain closes on Act I we enter the domestic again, with *Le Salon II* (The Living Room II, p. 49). This is one of a series of several studies and two finished works. The girl reading on the floor belongs to the larger series of such girls, such as *Les Enfants Blanchard* (p. 64) and *Le Peintre et son modèle* (p. 10). I have selected this version here over the other *Le Salon I* (p. 48) because both the awkward pose and the self-absorption in the former seem more radical than in the latter. The room, the furniture, the shallow space, and the draped velvet table cloth are all identical in the two paintings, but the girl on the floor now does not even hint at the possibility that she might look up to the viewer. And the sleeping sister is also more radically cut off from the outside. Her head tilted backwards at a painfully odd angle tells us that she is not going to wake up soon; her sleep is deep. The only creature that might connect to the outside world is the cat. But when? His eyes are closed. As was the case before, when violence might threaten to enter the world of the room (*La Chambre*, p. 70), Balthus's favorite and often humanized animal watches out. The silent witness foregrounded by the light that strikes its front and face keeps a watch over these children. But yes, his eyes are closed.

It is impossible to say if and how these pictures relate to the events in history. They most certainly do not represent them, none of them do. There are no war pictures at all in Balthus's oeuvre. But they were made during that time, and, beyond biographical anecdote, that knowledge alone sensitizes us to their potential of uncanniness, their perhaps nightmarish normality against all odds. I submit that there are, here and there, hints of something that might, but does not yet, disturb the stillness that the artist has been seeking in these works. I will refrain from going further than that.

Act II

1943. Yet, the *Portrait de Monsieur L. de Ch. et de ses enfants* (Portrait of Mr L. de Ch. and His Children, p. 129) where all figures look toward the viewer, is so formal, perfectly and uninterestingly so, that it is easy to dismiss it as a commissioned piece without much interest. It has never been exhibited and is not accessible even in a photograph of its

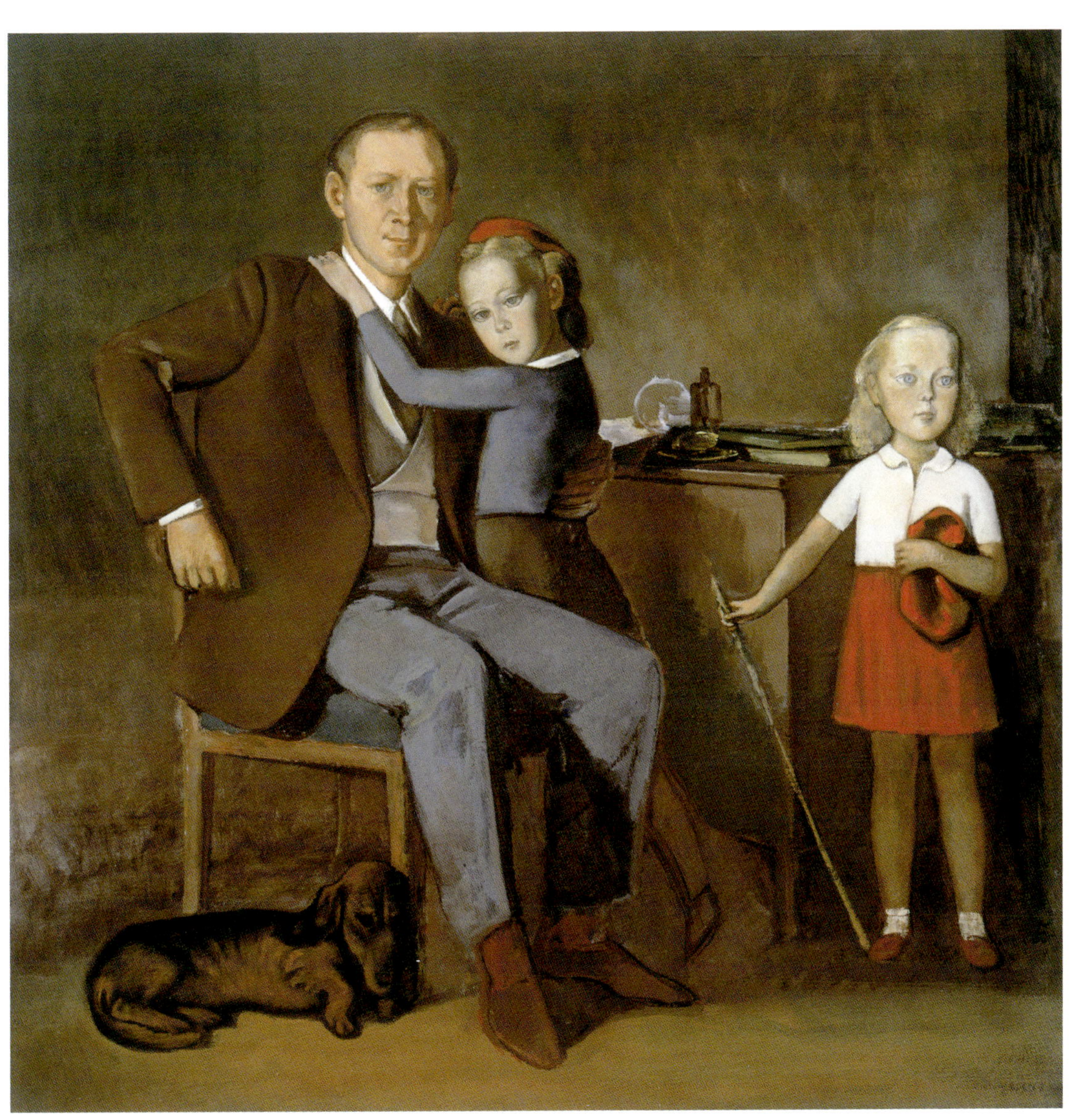

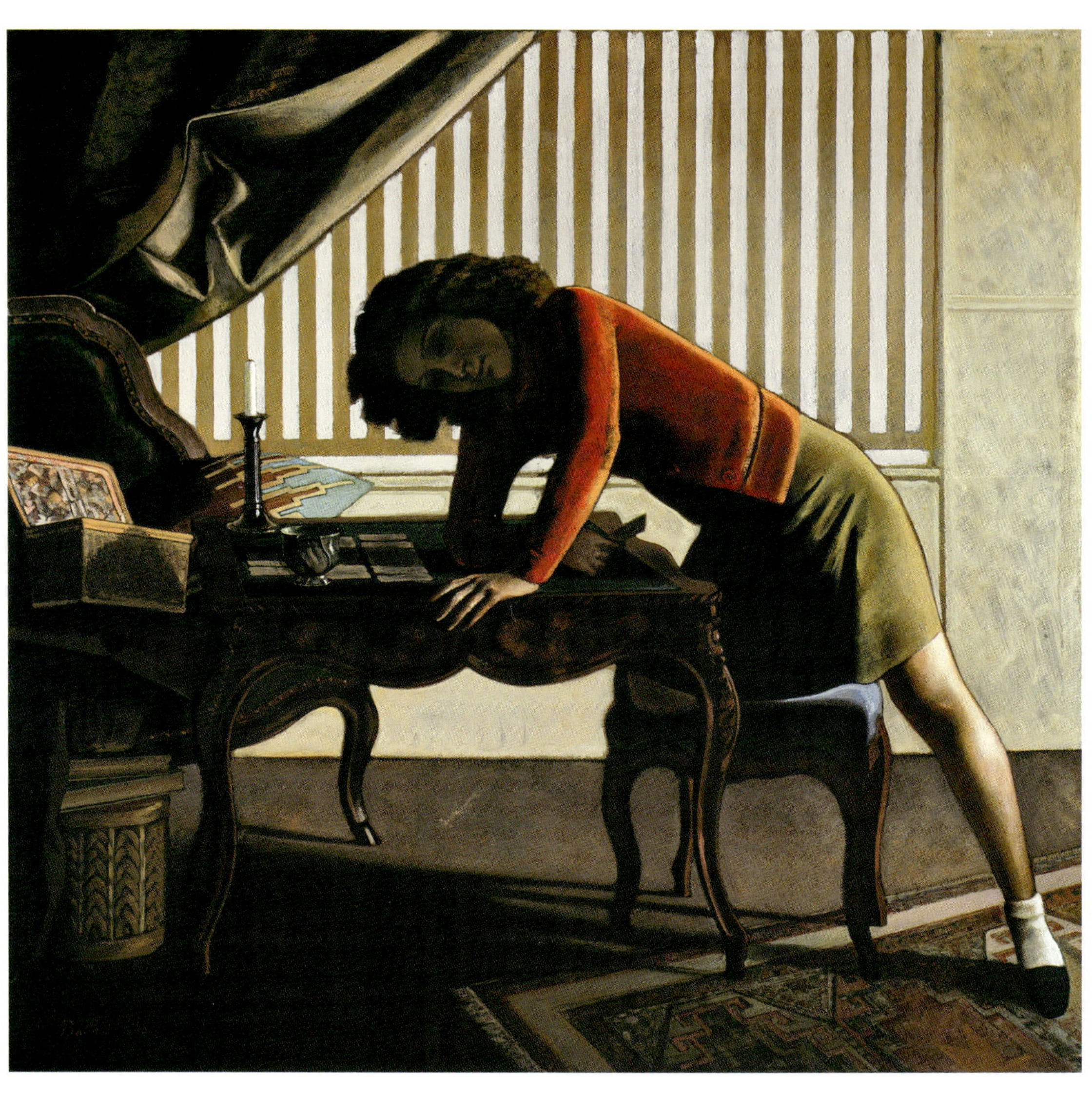

present state. It struck me, though, because of the way the hands give a sense of imminence. Although his arm leans relaxed over the back of the chair, the father's right hand almost makes a fist. His left hand holds the taller girl but barely, as if he must remain ready for change. Her hand touches him equally lightly. The smaller standing child holds a pole in one hand and a cloth in the other. But all these hands do not clutch what they touch. The hands indicate the fleeting quality of time so characteristic of much of Balthus's work. And the unsmiling faces of the two small children look older than that of their father. This mood, I am tempted to say, is the absence of mood, its negative.

This absence of mood might well be characteristic of the interior paintings of this time. These do not convey that sense of desire that infuses so many of the paintings of young girls. Even though the girl in *La Patience* (p. 130) stretches her leg out, her (or his) heart isn't in it. Her large, grave face looks intently at the cards that tell the future. But how different is this painting from that other card reader, *La Tireuse de cartes* (p. 98). This overly large head, emphatically so due to the wide hair, attracts all the attention, in spite of being in the shadow. This darkness defines the painting as a whole. The light may illuminate the outline of her body and allow that color modulation in green and orange to do the compositional work, but even so, it cannot reach her face, nor can the cards that hold the future. Impassible, she is patience.

The interior is ornate, quite classy, and an opportunity for the painter to shine. The elaborately crafted wood carving of the legs of the table finds its equal in the painter who puts before us the difference between the sheen of polished wood and the green felt of the playing surface, the wood and the velvet of the sofa. The plastered, then marbled wall and the green curtain, the oriental carpet, they are all right there for us to see. Except the future, except the face that reads it. Stretching from a small shoe and a child's sock on the bottom right, the girl's diagonal shape grows into an earnest adult before our very eyes. Kopp relates this quiet scene to disaster, Jouve to the dawning of hope, announced by the ray of light that outlines the girl's back. The striped changeant wallpaper seems luminous around her, announcing the apparition of light. It is all possible. None of it is clear. For me, mood itself is suspended. And that alone makes the painting ominous.

The stuff of dreams, of nightmares: how can we see what can only be sensed? We cannot, but what we see, where, how, and when we see it, can affect us with a contagious mood. How can things do that, do anything? Balthus tried hard to probe the strangeness of that affect. The quiet *Jeune fille endormie* (Girl Sleeping, p. 132) certainly doesn't give access to dreaming in the picture. But she is the locus of it. The space is shallow, narrow and short. The shallowness is emphasized in that the simple narrow bed barely fits into the room. The arm hanging out emphasizes the narrowness. And the shortness of the space is evidenced by the girl's head, which is propped against the bed board. All this converges with the physical cropping of the painting that cuts her body in half. Her face is calm, unreadable. Her fully clothed body doesn't give away anything either. No dreams, no nightmares. But sleep. As Jean Clair would have it, A Hundred Years Sleep. As a draughtsman, Balthus worked in very different modes and styles, but as these two exercises in sleep demonstrate, he deployed them all to get at that paradox: to make a sleeping girl speak to us (p. 133). If we follow the sequence, we see an increasing retreat from the clarity of portraiture in the drawing (right, bottom), to immersion in a sleep from which no one should awaken her.[44]

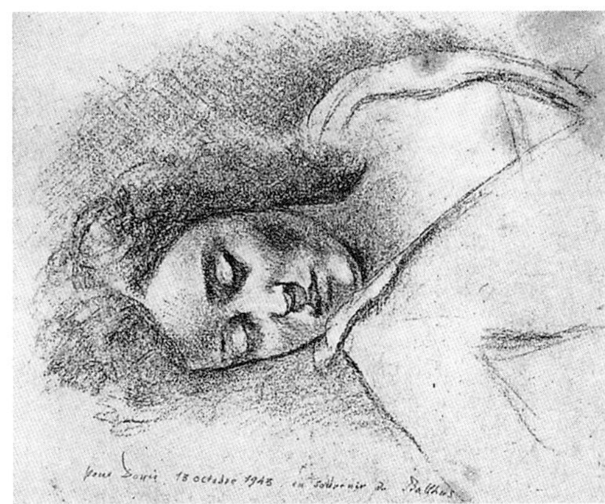

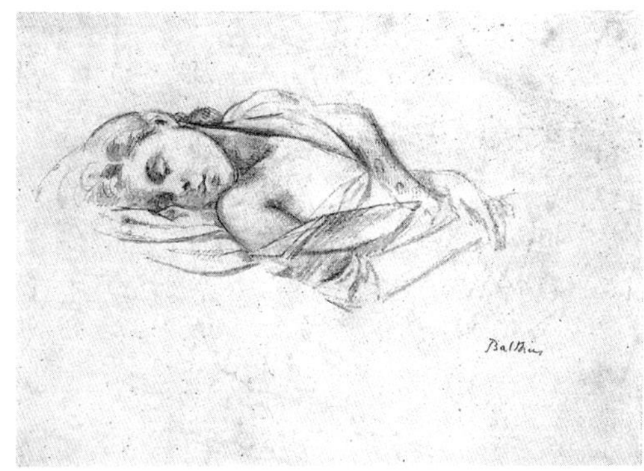

La patience, 1943
(modifed 1946-1948).
The Game of Patience.
Oil on canvas, 161.3 × 165.1 cm.
The Art Institute of Chicago.

Étude pour «Jeune fille endormie».
Portrait de Jeannette, 1943.
(Study for «Girl Sleeping» - portrait of Jeannette).
Pencil, 40 × 40 cm.
Private collection.

Étude pour «Jeune fille endormie».
Portrait de Jeannette, 1943.
(Study for Girl Sleeping - portrait of Jeannette).
Pencil, 30.7 × 41.7 cm.
Private collection.

44. The idea that things such as paintings can actually, "actively", affect their viewers, has been lucidly theorized by Ernst van Alphen (2008).

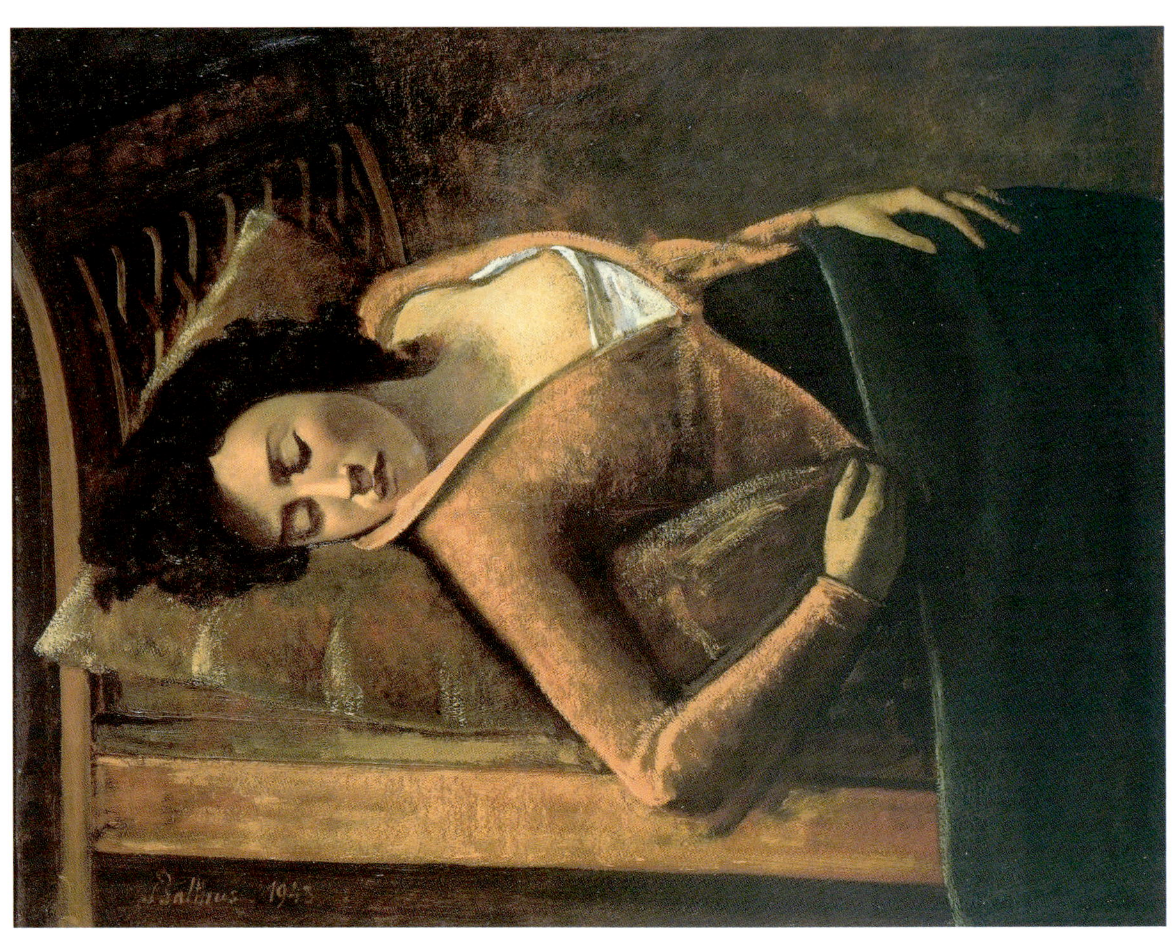
Balthus 1943

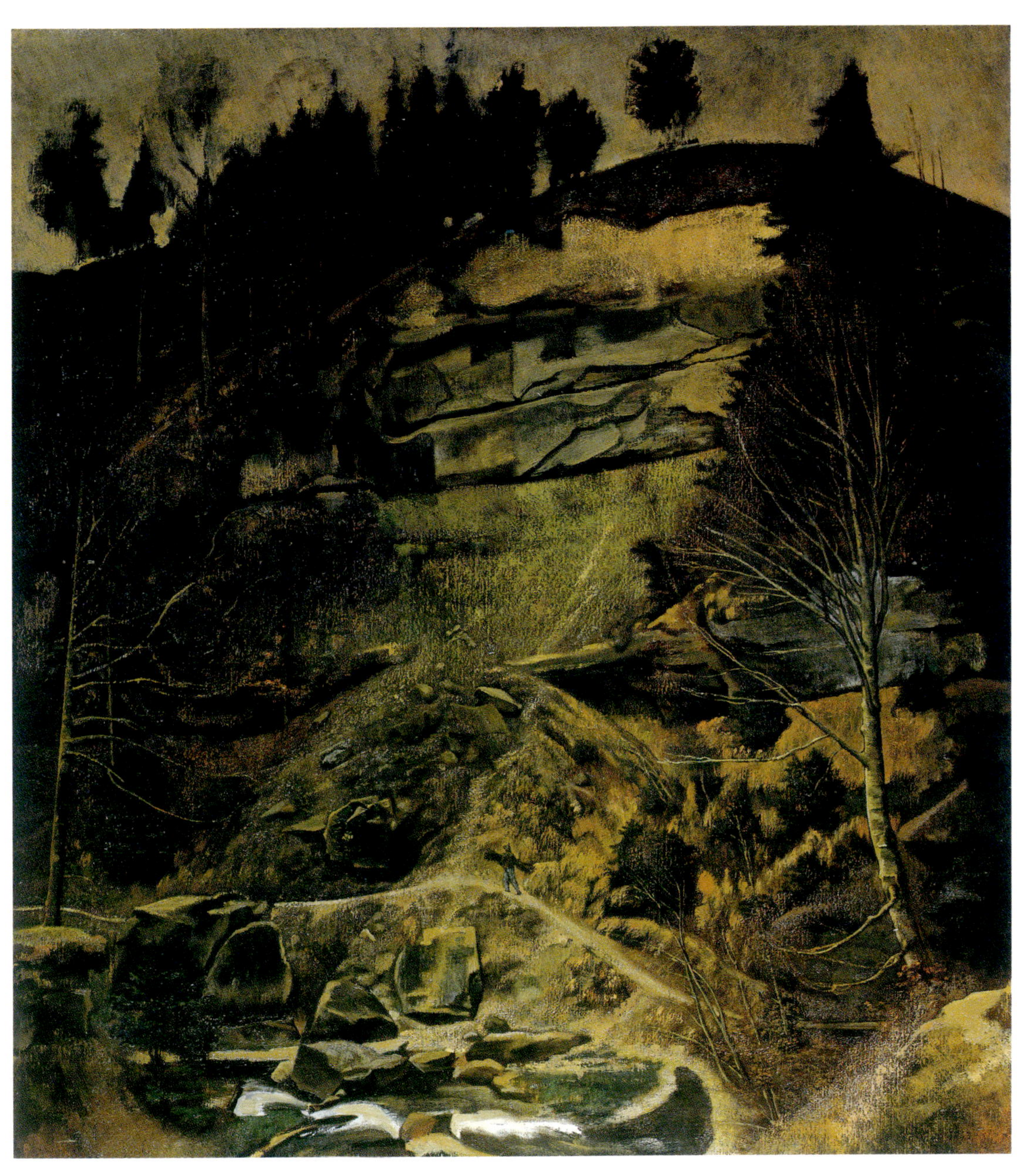

Jeune fille endormie, 1943.
Girl Sleeping.
Oil on panel, 82 × 100 cm.
Tate Gallery, London.

Le Gottéron, 1943
(modified after 1945).
Oil on canvas, 115 × 99.5 cm.
P.Y. Chingchong, Tahiti.

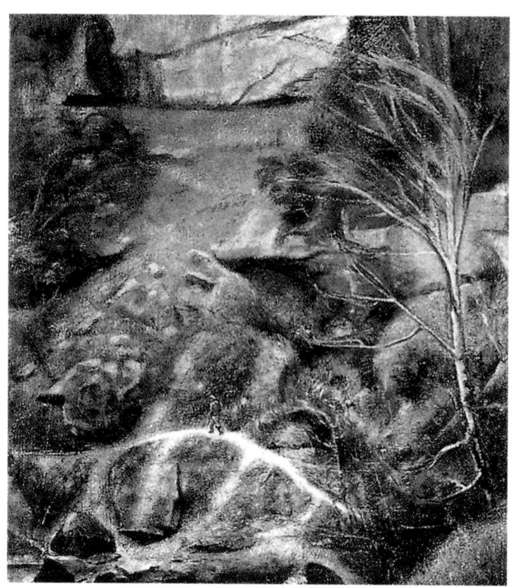

Le Gottéron, 1943.
Oil on canvas, 70 x 62 cm.
Present location unknown.

Jeune fille en vert et rouge (The chandelier), 1944 (modified end 1945).
Girl in Green and Red - the Candlestick.
Oil on canvas, 92 × 90.5 cm.
Former Collection of the Museum of Modern Art, New York.

The landscape of *Le Gottéron* (p. 133), the mountain on which Balthus and his family looked out during those years of retreat, tells us about mood more forcefully than any other painting. Claude Roy calls it "one of the most somber paintings of his oeuvre, somber in all senses of the word" (1996: 130). Roy mentions four such senses. In the first place, the painting is dark in color, with its greens turning to black and ochre. The color of the sky is no different from that of the ground. It is a monochrome of hell. Another version gives us a close-up of this landscape, where the sky is eliminated altogether (left). Second, it is also the representation of a dark landscape. The vertical format makes it not so much Chinese, in this case, but more somber. Endless heights to climb, and when you reach the summit, there is more darkness to be found. Third, it is dark in mood; the mood of the painting, as well as the mood the painting conveys, with which it affects us as viewers. Fourth, it is dark, also, in its emergence from and inevitable immersion in the darkest times of history. How can this painting be called a nightmare of history, while no human figure is represented? Well, this is not quite true.

On the lower part, right above the only small white portion of abstract rough brushstrokes, a path curves, indicating long detours to walk for the worker. On that path, where it begins to ascend, a tiny figure walks carrying a tree trunk. It is on behalf of this figure that the painting and its mountain are so steeply vertical. There are very few workers in Balthus's oeuvre. Granted, we can think of the carpenter in *La Rue*, but that white-clad figure without face and with hands too long seems less real than this tiny figure, whose legs express the great effort of a relentless task. And while the early evocation of city life did affect us with a bizarre sense of loneliness without remedy, here the loneliness of the figure is almost cosmic, physically as well as in mood. Looking at *Les Beaux jours* (p. 93), from the next year, with *Le Gottéron* in our mind's eye, makes the former painting ironic. The hearth becomes ominous, the mirror estranging, the fire dangerous. *Le Gottéron* puts a spell on all other products of that time.

Act III

After this somber painting, all else seems frivolous, and yet overcast; unfitting and nightmarish in that sense. Portraits and other occasion pieces with only the smallest symptoms of something wrong in them. The portrait of a mother with her daughter *Portrait de Madame Matossian et sa fille* (Portrait of Mrs Matossian and her Daughter, 1944) putting a dish on the table would be entirely mundane without the fiercely diabolic look of the child, reminiscent of the dwarf in *La Chambre*. Another girl sleeping, this time seated, and titled "nude", *Petit nu assis* (Small Seated Nude, 1944), although not quite naked, seems a simple exercise. But her cheeks are hollow, her eyes empty, blind rather than closed. And then, there is the *Jeune fille en vert et rouge (The chandelier)* (Girl in Green and Red - the Candlestick, p. 135). And nothing is normal anymore.

According to John Russell this painting was an exercise in achieving a monumentality in intensity through lighting. (1983: 287-288) The invocation of Caravaggio (p. 136 right, top) is certainly appropriate. The voluminous softness of the baroque painter is clearly the object of emulation, and so is the experiment in light coming from the side, as in the sharper focus of Georges de la Tour (p. 136 right, bottom). The two-colored sweater recalls a playing card. Below, the table with the freshly creased cloth, seems white although the colors used to achieve that pristine appearance are a mixture of blue, gray, green, brown, and a little bit of white. In the bread sticks the knife of the violence so easily projected on the 1937 still life. The ornate silver dish completes the elementary adoption of the genre of the still life. The candlestick stands erect, in vain. No flame burns to give the girl's face that golden glow.

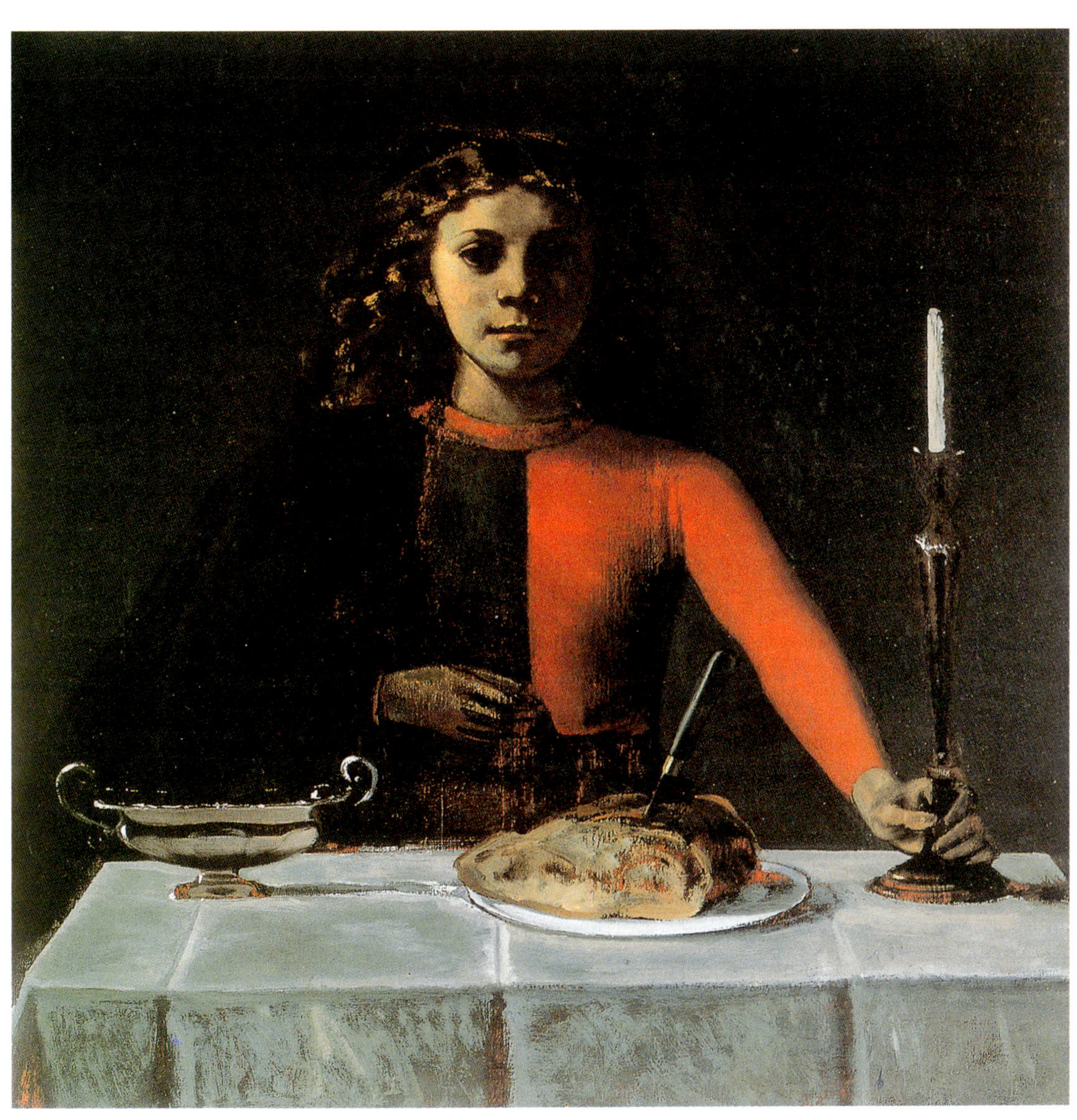

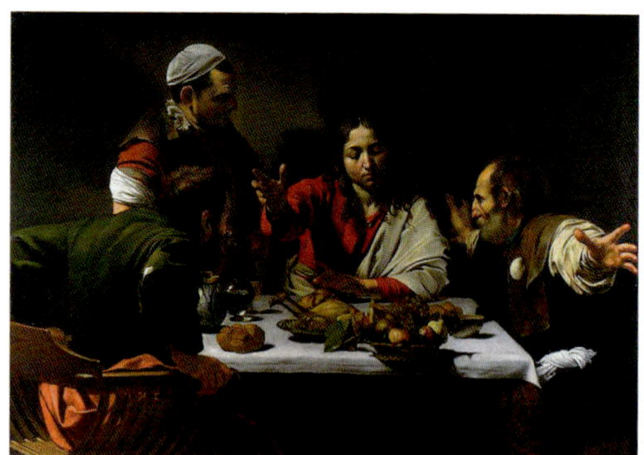

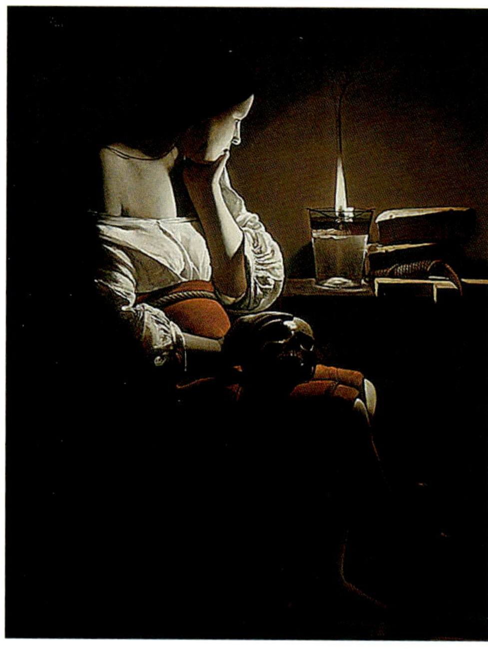

45. See Weber (1999: 310-311). Jouve included the novel in *La scène capitale* (1935), and later, after a fall-out with Balthus made him change the dedication, in the volume *Histoires sanglantes* (1948).

46. Camus published his comments in the catalogue compiled on the occasion of the exhibition in the Pierre Matisse Gallery in New York in 1949.

Caravaggio,
Supper at Emmaus, 1601-1602.
Oil on canvas, 139 x 195 cm.
National Gallery, London.

Georges de la Tour,
La Madeleine pénitente, ca. 1640.
Oil on canvas, 118 x 90 cm.
County Museum of Art,
Los Angeles.

La Victime, 1939-1946.
The Victim.
Oil on canvas, 133 × 220 cm.
Private collection.

The girl looks more monumental than adolescent; and, flattened by the opaque dark background, she looks more like an image than a figure. The arm that stretches to hold the candlestick—supporting it or perhaps seeking support in it—is completely straight. The only other symptom of foreshortening is the over-sized hand. The other hand, very large as well, comes out of darkness to rest on her bust, right above her waist. Compared to all other Balthusian girls, this one is unaffected by anything the painter could have infused into her: desire, hope, violence—nothing. Even the evenly lit, monumental Princess Maria Volkonska, old beyond her years, and just as affect-less, just as staged, has more expression in her face than this figure of cards.

The two most somber paintings of this period, indeed, of the entire oeuvre, *Le Gottéron* and *Jeune fille en vert et rouge (The chandelier)*, were both modified directly after the war. As far as can be deduced from the earlier photographs of them, they were both made darker. The somber mood must have stuck in the memory of the painter, and he must have doubted if that had been sufficiently "painted in". This act of darkening the two paintings into the nightmare images they have become is perhaps the artist's clearest "poetical" act. Not that darkness is to be projected onto all his works, not at all. But the act declares that mood, the mood of dreams, erotic dreams as much as nightmares, of fantasy, of the imagination at its wildest and at its quietest, is the real substance of painting.

Epilogue

This is a useful reminder in the face of one of Balthus's most disturbing paintings. *La Victime* (The Victim, p. 137) was painted in connection with Jouve's novel *La Victime*, in turn based on a story by Edgar Allan Poe. Jouve dedicated the novel to Balthus, who then painted this work in response to it, initially in 1937. It was made over and over again during the entire period of the Second World War, 1939 to 1946. The interest in Sade, which Jouve shared with Balthus's brother Pierre, who wrote a study about the Marquis, was very much in the air in the decade leading up to the War. Jouve's story intimates that spiritual disaster and desire go together. If anything calls for a historical reflection it is this fashion of pain at the eve of the outburst of the most unspeakable infliction of real pain. Here, it is important to qualify the painting of *La Victime* with the understanding that the artist shared this interest with his friends.[45]

Once again, I invoke some critical comments so as to grasp what this painting does to its viewers. French writer Albert Camus commented on this painting by pointing out that in Balthus, there is a knife, but never blood (1983: 77). The knife, indeed, lies on the floor, right before the bed, the blade catching a glimpse of light, the handle cropped. Jean Clair sees in this painting a nude rather than a scene (2001: 24). Somewhat defensively, he can detect no wound and admires the drapery. All true enough. Weber describes the figure as follows: "Seemingly raped, she looks both twelve years old (according to her breast development and lack of pubic hair) and twice that age (based on her face, skin, and size)".[46]

Weber goes to the extreme of consulting a New York public prosecutor specialized in sex crimes, the Chief of the Manhattan District Attorney's Sex Crimes Unit, who also writes mystery novels (which I happen to read). He wanted to know whether "the 'victim' was dead or merely comatose" and whether the crime could be identified. Weber's long biography never quite manages to deal with Balthus's subject matter, wavering between defensive and disturbed. No wonder, with such utterly realistic questions on his mind. There is no crime, no dead body, "only"

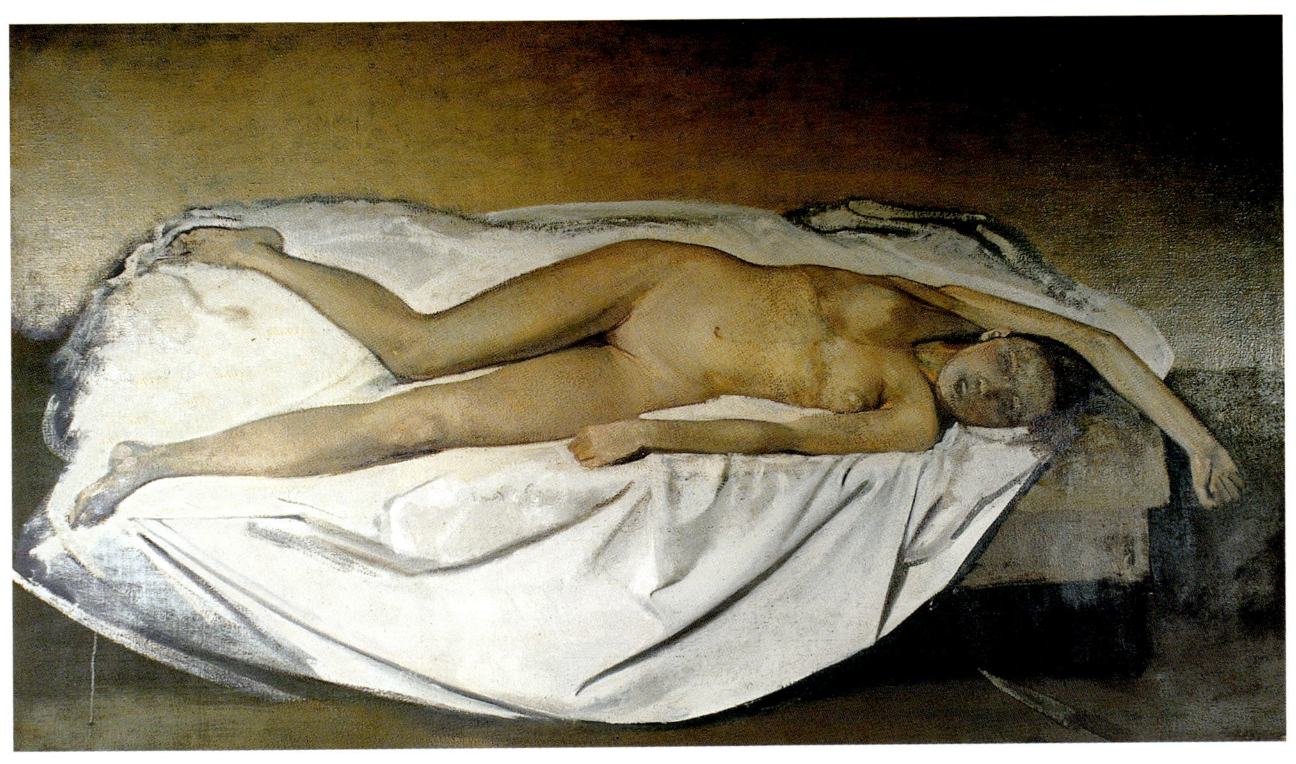

47. This is, roughly, the line of argument of MacKinnon, already mentioned.

Selection from *Mitsou*, 1919 (nrs. I 1512, I 1513 ; then I 1545 - I 1551) > a total of 9]
First published in 1921 by Rotapfel Verlag, Erlerbach-Zürich & Leipzig, preface by Rainer Maria Rilke.

an image of one. The question for me would be whether this representation affects its viewers, and if so, how? In other words, I am more interested in what we do with such a picture, than in identifying the fictive crime. The nightmare is more relevant than the alleged pre-painting event.

The point, for me, is that Weber needed a specialist to reach the conclusion that this painting represents a rape victim. Clearly, this is not visible even for someone with such a fine eye as Balthus's biographer. This undermines the argument that is current enough, which indicts violent imagery for stimulating violence in its viewers. This can hardly be the case if even a connoisseur needs police examination to get it. Seeing violent films across our television screens on an everyday basis, this argument must, at the very least, be historicized and confronted with the medium, as well as the modes of display appropriate for the medium. I would consider the novels of this specialist, Linda Fairstein, where the devastation of sex crimes is described in graphic detail, at least as disturbing in this respect—if not more. There is no violence being committed here. There is the aftermath, the result, a victim. And yes, she looks dead enough to me. But what does that mean?[47]

Indeed, this is a horrible painting. The horror of seeing the image of a naked, dead body is real. We must assume, however, that the model after which this nude was painted was not dead. Instead of turning more realist when the subject matter is more disturbing, I imagine the long duration of the making. For six years, during which millions of real people were turned into real victims, the artist was safely ensconced in his French, then Swiss refuge, vividly evoked by *Les Beaux jours*. Yet, he kept working on a painting called *La Victime* in alleged affiliation with or emulation of a fantastic tale. But when he looked out of the window he saw the dark, ominous mountain *Le Gottéron*. I imagine him turning again and again to this painting.

I see it, therefore, as an ongoing search for the possibility—to represent, rather than merely convey—not the event—neither the war nor the sadistic murder of a young woman—but the *mood* of history at its worst. Perhaps this was achieved, perhaps not quite, because representing this mood is not possible. This doesn't diminish the real possibility of a sadistic imagination quite like that of his fellow artists and writers of the time right before, when he first painted it. It is the ongoing obsession with it itself that I seek to interpret. In this sense—limited as it is—I consider this work the utter nightmare of history.

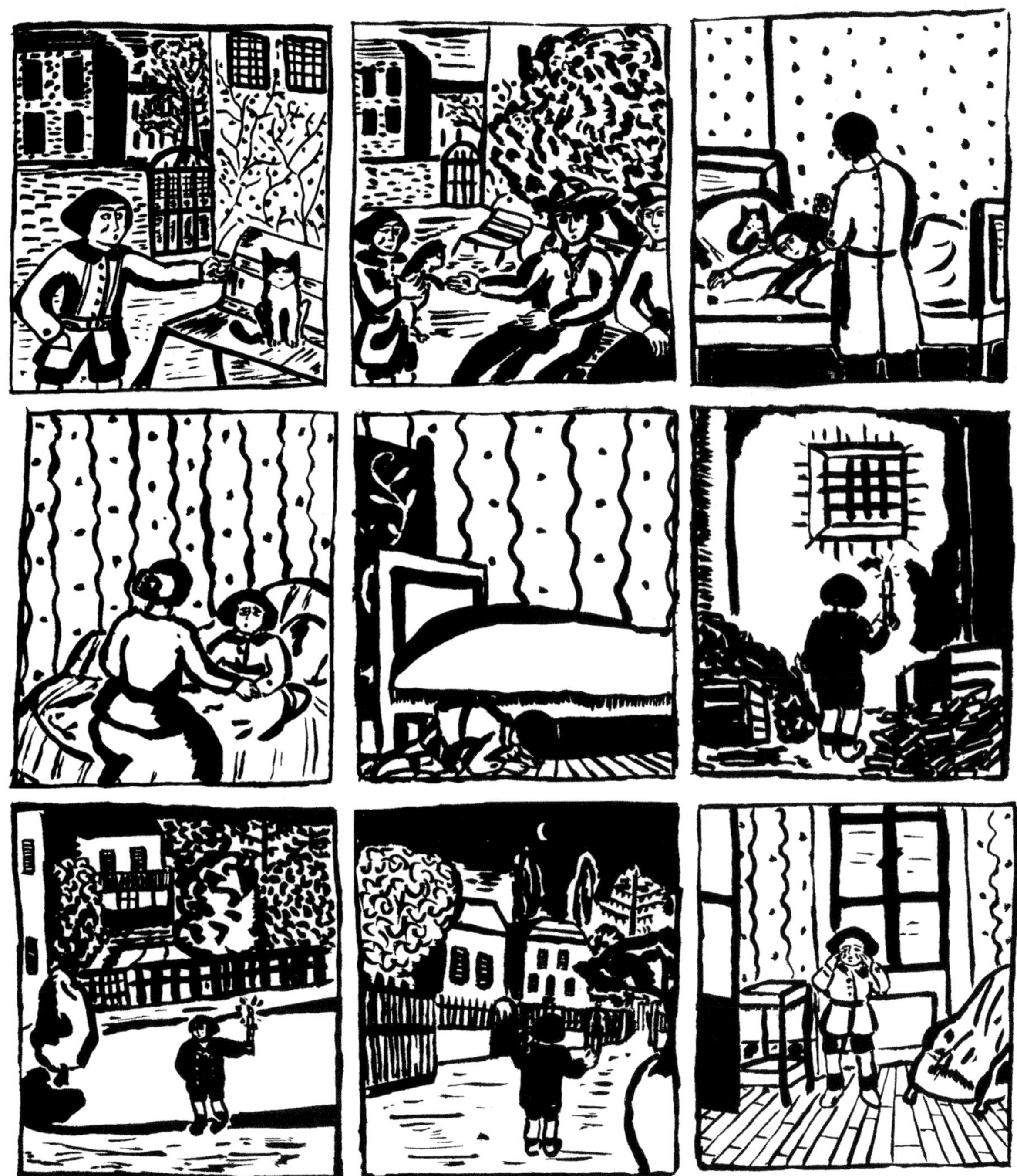

8. Endings

In 1949 Balthus painted a self-portrait (left). Three things struck me when I saw this. First, the colors. The blue painter's smock is almost entirely covered with white. His shapeless hand is a simple blot of white. Both smock and hand are scratched through. Second, the surface. The chest on which he appears to be leaning is visible through the painter's body. Third, the eyes. His eyes are empty, blind, or closed, like a Modigliani figure. This figure is utterly different from the proud, albeit tormented painter of the 1940 *Autoportrait* (p. 33). There, he was tormented, yet "alive". Here, he is a flat image. Even the characteristically large head of the earlier work has vanished; the head is small. The only large surface is his bust, superimposed with the wood.

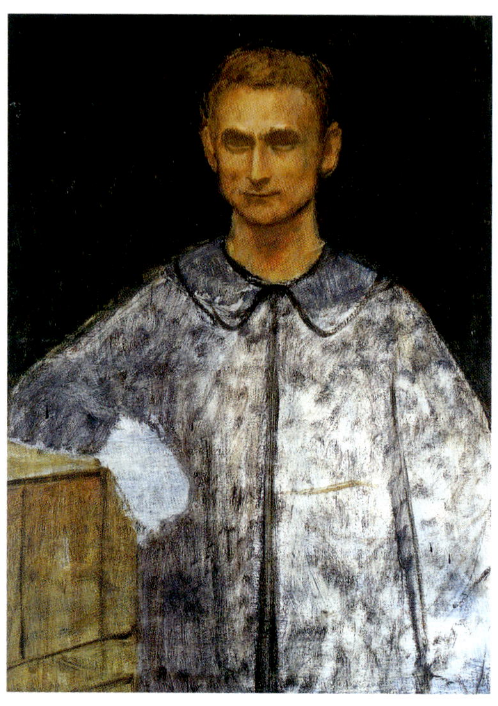

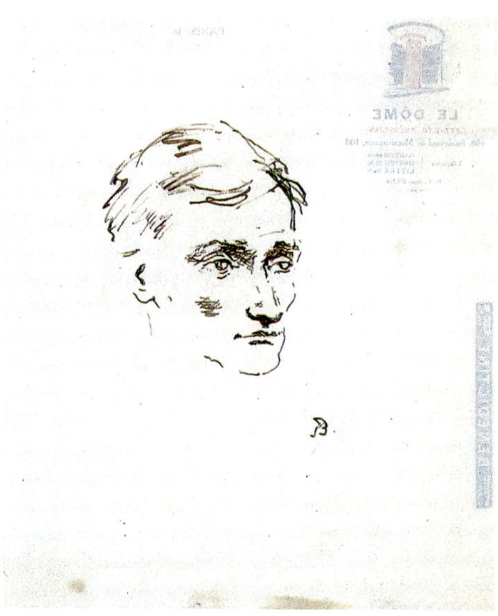

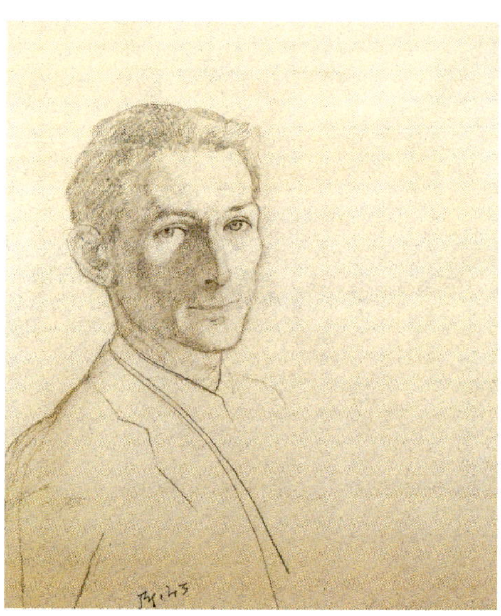

Beyond the experiment with thin paint and the statement on painting as flat as this involved, I propose to see this self-portrait as a statement on presence/absence. As the portrait on p. 33 intimates, the man Balthus was exceptionally handsome; the artist Balthus was told, from his earliest years, that he was a genius. His paintings emulate the greatest artists of the classical Western tradition. It seems safe to assume he had a high opinion of himself. Among his best friends were two people who bore a remarkable resemblance to him. Compare this *Portrait d'Antonin Artaud* (above, left) with the self-portrait from 1943 (above, right). Jean-Louis Barrault, with whom he worked for theater decors, also looked like him. And if they didn't, he made them resemble him; just look at this *Portrait d'Alberto Giacometti* (p. 141, left) and compare it to the self-portrait from 1933 (p. 141, right). I am writing this simply to suggest that the artist, and his sense of his own worth, cannot have been far away when he was painting. Meanwhile, these drawings also convey the clarity and scarcity of means of Balthus's drawings.

But precisely that, his sense of self, his ambition to paint for eternity, seems at odds with the relative scarcity of self-portraits, and the total absence of himself in the scenes he depicted. Or so it seems. This has not always been so. He is the main character in the suite of drawings he made between the ages of 8 and 10. This suite of 40 ink drawings that his mother's lover, the German poet Rainer Maria Rilke, saw in 1919 and published with a preface by his own hand, is more than a child-prodigy's first attempts at creation. It is an accomplished, consistent narrative in ink, in the style of ancient woodcuts. It is also a program for the rest of his life (p. 139).

The narrative tells the simple story of a child who finds a cat, takes it home, and when it disappears, searches the house, the outside, and remains inconsolable. I contend that the totally astounded child of the first images, who finds the cat, and whose delight is complicated by a sense of responsibility, and the totally distraught child of the final image who experiences loss, has never disappeared from the work he made until his very old age.

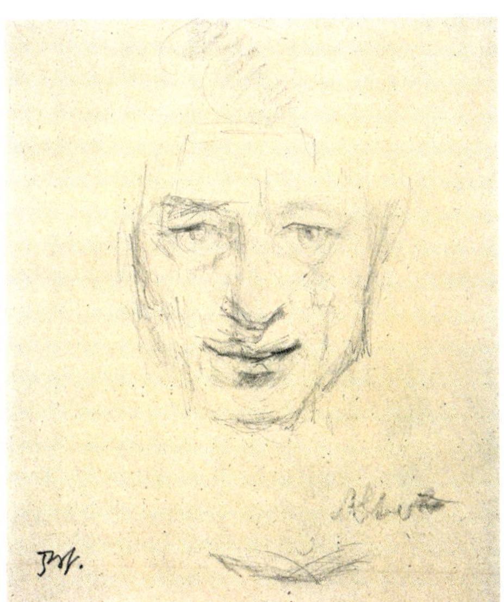

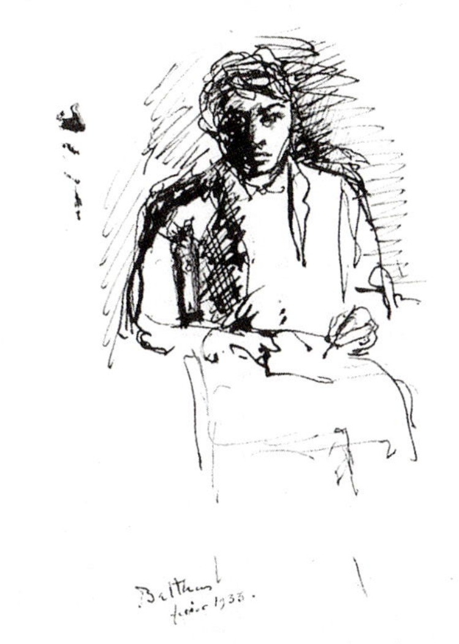

Autoportrait, 1949.
Self-Portrait.
Oil on canvas, 116.8 × 81.2 cm.
Private collection.

Portrait d'Antonin Artaud, 1935.
Portrait of Antonin Artaud.
Ink on paper, 24 × 20.5 cm.
Private collection.

Autoportrait, 1943
Self-Portrait.
Pencil [fusain] on paper,
63 × 45.7 cm.
Private collection.

Portrait d'Alberto Giacometti,
ca. 1950.
Portrait of Alberto Giacometti.
Pencil on checkered paper,
21 × 16.5 cm.
Private collection.

Autoportrait, 1933.
Self-Portrait.
Ink on paper, 22 × 18 cm.
Private collection.

As the visionary maker of the images collected here, he remains a child, and hence his interest in children. All those children are self-portraits as much as portraits of his desire. Not simply his desire to possess, but his desire to be (like) the children he so admires. In every child depicted, there is as much narcissism as celebration of beauty about to erupt. Because in those child's drawings, Balthus was not only the child who experienced love and loss; he was also the cat.

He was an adult, but barely, when at the age of 26 he painted a work he later regretted for its provocative, explicit sexuality. He was heading toward a major solo exhibition, the dream of any young ambitious painter, and since the times were against figuration, he needed a ploy to attract attention. This is how he kept telling the story himself. I believe it, but I find the *La Leçon de guitare* (Guitar Lesson, p. 143) interesting for other reasons. The primary reason for which this seems the right painting to close this book with is the presence of the specter of Balthus. But, obeying one last time Balthus's and my own rule about art writing: let's first look at the painting.

Compared to other paintings, the clarity of this one stops any attempt to cloak the scene in ambiguity—at least, if we see it as a sexual image (only). But it is not. The hand of the figure of the teacher—or why not call her Mistress?—that pulls the hair / presses the cords, much like Nellie the maid in *La Toilette de Cathy* (p. 30), appears to wish to inflict pain,

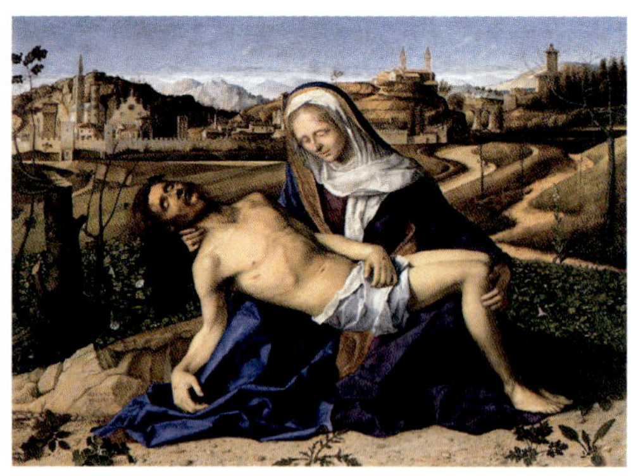

48. Balthus plays with the meaning of shoes elsewhere. In the *Portrait d'André Derain* (p. 83) the dark but shiny shoes of the represented artist belie the suggestion that he just arose from sex with his model, as critics tend to assume.

Giovanni Bellini,
Pietà, 1505.
Oil on wood.
Gallerie dell'Accademia, Venice.

La Leçon de guitare, 1934.
The Guitar Lesson.
Oil on canvas, 161 × 138.5 cm.
Private collection.s

although nothing on the child's face betrays hurt. Her other hand, expertly playing the guitar/ the thigh (not the clitoris) of the girl, has that typical curved pinkie that keeps the guitar player present. The two heads, as large as Balthus's heads always tend to be, express—well, strictly nothing. Neither pain nor pleasure.

All the touching is, literally, beside the point: the mistress's hand close but not on the clitoris, the girl's hand close but not on the nipple. If this painting were to be considered programmatic, Balthus would have done his public the great favor of making defensiveness redundant and censorship ridiculous. Censorship won: the painting was almost acquired by a major museum but one trustee vetoed the purchase (Weber 218). My guess is, this trustee hadn't dared look the painting in the face. How else could he or she so blindly obey the artist's desire to shock, and not see how he uses total clarity to expose the game of ambiguity? One sense—music—traded for another—the pleasures of the flesh. To be sure, there are many reasons why this painting would shock, many of which don't need spelling out. See for yourself.

In addition to the blatant nudity and sexual activity, there is the insult to religion. The iconography turns this into a de-sacralization of the central imagery of grief in the Christian West, of the mother lamenting the dead body of her son—the iconography known as Pietà (left). A traditional image which, in turn, re-sacralized, if I may say so, the ambiguous image of one adult holding another on her lap with a tenderness that opens the door, if ever so slightly, to an erotic imagination. Not only would Balthus not be above such sacrilegious fantasies; he considered all his painting religious. Who is to say, the painting appears to say, that religion must abhor the flesh?

Then, there are those signs of possible sadism, such as the girl's red knees, suggesting all manners of fantasies of a sadistic order. Has the girl been forced on her knees, perhaps to perform unspeakable acts to earn her own pleasure? Has she been exploited for housekeeping chores? Her right hand lays powerless. All this is true, clear, and leaves no doubt. But it does leave alternative thoughts, persistently present even if unable to push the scandalous aspects away. The girl's left hand, baring the pointed breast we also remember from *Cathy*, has the force she needs to perform her agency. As usual, no eye contact occurs. Then, another detail to which we have by now become accustomed strikes. The girl's stockings are prominent, pointing to her young age, and that is the most problematic aspect of Balthus's fantasy images. But visually they lead us to the shoes. While the mistress is wearing shoes, the girl is in slippers. This suggests the beautifully depicted, bourgeois interior is the girl's home, not the teacher's.[48]

The artist designed the painting exactly as it came off. Several studies, mainly practicing the pose of the girl, remain, but one complete sketch shows that the idea was precisely this. Even the faces show the same expressionless intensity (p. 144, top). But fifteen years later, the artist interpreted his own scandal piece, and came out of the closet. Not as a sadist; much as he tried, putting a frantic face on himself, this drawing shows effort, desire perhaps, but nothing beyond that (p. 144, bottom). If anything, the man is having a hard time "getting there". Needing his two hands to bare the body he so wishes to see, his mouth is occupied keeping the fabric away. In a strange conflation of the *La Leçon de guitare* and *La Chambre* (p. 70), this drawing merges sexual desire with the desire to see. If this painting is perverse, then, it is not for being too sexually explicit and homo-erotic at that. It is perverse in the programmatic sense

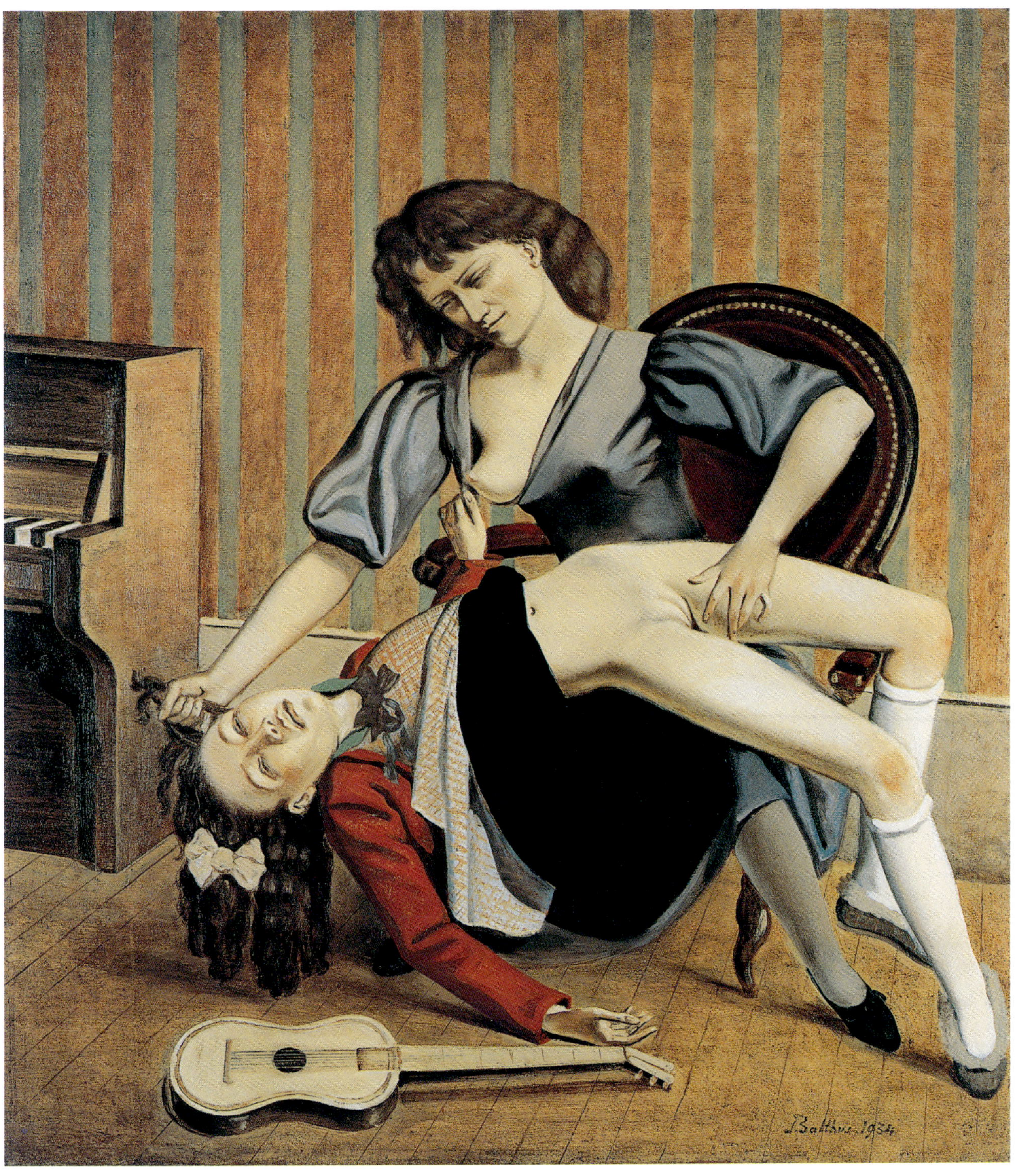
Balthus 1934

of subverting fixed categories. It sets out to undermine, that is, the categories our culture has adopted to reassure us concerning the possibility of perversion as cast out of normalcy. If anything, this subversion constitutes the perversion of these dream worlds and nightmares.

Now that I am ending this essay, let me, for once, confront the painter. In his interviews, Balthus always sounds disingenuous. He vehemently denies the eroticism everyone else sees in the paintings. On *La Leçon de guitare* his well-trained interviewer Costantini tried to obey the artist's rules and ignore what makes the painting so exceptional. When he timidly compares the scandal to the one Modigliani had faced with his nudes, Balthus draws attention to a painting that, in subject matter, is much closer to the *leçon*. "Instead of speaking of Modigliani, it would be more interesting to talk about the *Sleepers* by Courbet". Everyone familiar with that painting can see how it is related, simply for the reason that it is also a lesbian scene. Clearly, in spite of his vehement denials, Balthus does not wish us to ignore the subject matter. Then, with the coyness one expects, the artist continues: "I find the blue of the vase in that painting very erotic". No one will take this as anything else but disingenuous.[49]

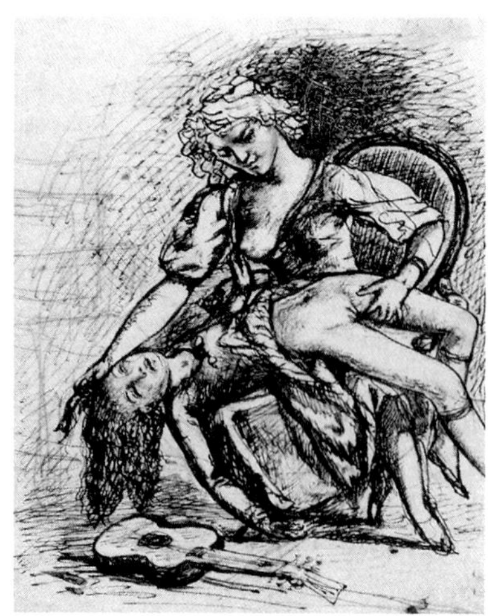

Étude pour «La Leçon de guitare», 1934.
Study for The Guitar Lesson.
Ink on paper, 25 x 20 cm.

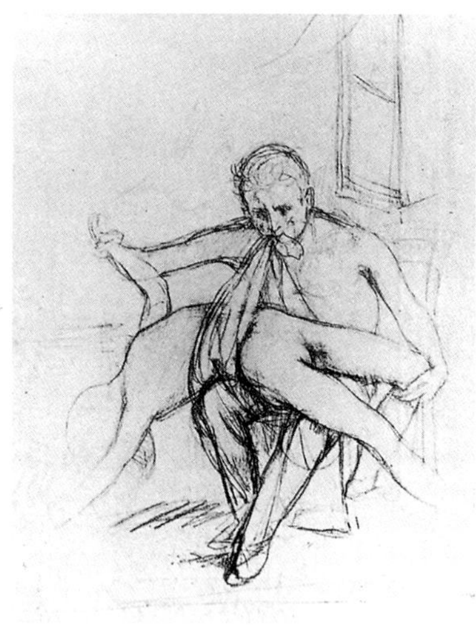

La Leçon de guitare, 1949.
The Guitar Lesson.
Pencil on paper, 29 x 19 cm.
Present location unknown.

And yet, if we go back to the painting, we notice that what seemed a diversion, moving from sex to color, actually makes visual sense, after all. For, there, too, the effort to see is unsuccessful. The mistress cannot see the face of the girl she is teaching/pleasuring. Not only because, as in the drawing from 1949, the girl's face is not available, but also because her eyes are blind. Mere slits, her semi-closed eyes see nothing. Weber (228) considers the teacher a disguised self-portrait. I can see that. He imputes to it a "glorious pleasure". This, I submit, is overlooking the displacements, the shifts, and the other focus, besides eroticism.

That other focus is his artistic program, which is not at all distinct from the subject matter. The task that Balthus had set himself, here and all through his long career, is to depict the invisible. He kept complaining, with what sounds like false modesty in someone so narcissistic, but isn't, that he was never quite satisfied with the result. And color, indeed, is his primary tool, but also, his only consolation. The blue in the vase in the Courbet, which he calls erotic, might well stand for the invisibility of the erotic, in spite of this artist's life-long attempt—practiced, and denied—to make it visible.

This discontent makes sense if we consider what it was he tried to depict. Desire, even lust; grief for the lost cat; repression of a hurtful history; seeing the self in opaque mirrors and through opaque glass; landscapes full of labor, always distanced; flowers about to shed their petals, fruits precariously ripe; bread pierced; people keeping their grief, boredom, and relations of oppression to themselves; moments fleeting past in a split second, and which took years to fix on canvas; moods of wonder and joy sometimes, not often, and motiveless melancholy; loneliness in crowds, or in togetherness. No wonder, then, that he could never quite make it, in his own eyes. Balthus the alleged realist, the figurative painter who braved the fashion of abstraction, spent his long life attempting to depict the invisible.

And that, obviously, is impossible. The next best, he must have thought, would be the traces, the anticipations, and the desires. Some of his paintings are disturbing, most, the large majority, are not. But even the most shocking one—the one meant to shock—cannot hide the specter of the artist who, rather than looking in on someone else's private moment, puts himself at the edge where invisibility promises a glimpse, visible when imagining can transform into imaging, and what happens inside those over-sized heads, presented for us to see, after all.

49. See Costantini (2001: 50). The book of interviews is full of moments where the artist takes over, asks questions himself, and refuses to answer the ones put to him.

Bibliography

Alphen, Ernst van
1997 "The Portrait's Dispersal: Concepts of Representation and Subjectivity in Contemporary Portraiture". In *Portraiture: Facing the Subject*, ed. Joanna Woodall. Manchester: Manchester University Press, 239-256.

2004 "Opgenomen in abstractie". In Windstil, Marian Breedveld (ed.). Staphorst: Hein Elferink, 5-25.

2007 "Affective Operations in Art and Literature". *Res* (in press).

Artaud, Antonin
1983a (1934) "Exposition Balthus à la Galerie Pierre". In Centre Georges Pompidou, 41.

1983b (1936) "La jeune peinture française et la tradition". In Centre Georges Pompidou, 42-45.

1983c (1947) "Balthus". In Centre Georges Pompidou, 46-47.

Bal, Mieke
1997 *Narratology: Introduction to the Theory of Narrative*. Toronto: University of Toronto Press.

1999 *Quoting Caravaggio: Contemporary Art, Preposterous History*. Chicago: The University of Chicago Press.

Benjamin, Walter
1974 *Charles Baudelaire*. Frankfurt am Main: Suhrkamp.

1999 *The Arcades Project*. Harvard: Harvard University Press.

Bonnefoy, Yves
1983 (1959)"L'invention de Balthus". In Centre Georges Pompidou, 86-93.

Bryson, Norman
1989 *Looking at the Overlooked: Four Essays on Still-Life*. Cambridge: Harvard University Press.

Camus, Albert
1983 (1949) "Nageur patient...". In Centre Georges Pompidou, 76-77.

Centre Georges Pompidou
1983 *Balthus*. Paris: Centre Georges Pompidou, Musée national d'Art moderne.

Clair, Jean
1983 "Les metamorphoses d'Eros". In Centre Georges Pompidou, 256-279 .

1999 "The Hundred-Year Sleep". In Clair and Monnier (eds.), 7-59.

Clair, Jean (ed.)
2001 *Balthus*. London: Thames and Hudson.

Clair, Jean and Virginie Monnier (eds.)
1999 *Balthus. Catalogue raisonné of the Complete Works*. Paris: Gallimard.

Costantini, Costanzo
2001 *Balthus à contre-courant. Entretiens avec Costanzo Costantini*. Le Mothâ, Switzerland: Editions Noir sur Blanc.

Dällenbach, Lucien
1977 *Le récit spéculair: Essai sur la mise en abyme*. Paris: Editions du Seuil (English: *The Mirror in the Text*. Trans. Jeremy Whiteley with Emma Hughes. Chicago: University of Chicago Press, 1989).

Davenport, Guy
1989 *A Balthus Notebook*. New York: Echo Press.

Deleuze, Gilles
1993 *The Fold: Leibniz and the Baroque*. Trans. and foreword Tom Conley. Minneapolis: University of Minnesota Press.

Derrida, Jacques
1987 *The Truth in Painting*. Trans. Geoff Bennington and Ian McLeod. Chicago: University of Chicago Press.

Fouilloux, Etienne
1984 "Récupérer Balthus". *Vingtième siècle. Revue d'histoire* 3, 3: 119-124.

Freud, Sigmund
1900 *The Interpretation of Dreams*. SE V: 533-621.

1919 "The Uncanny". SE XVII: 219-256.

Grootenboer, Hanneke
2005 *The Rhetoric of Perspective: Realism and Illusionismin Seventeenth-Century Dutch Still-Life Painting*. Chicago: The University of Chicago Press.

Grossman, Evelyne
2004 *La défiguration. Artaud – Beckett – Michaux*. Paris: Editions de Minuit.

Herman, William R.
1960 "Photographic Realism and Abstract Art". *College Art Journal* 19, 3 (Spring): 231-241.

James, Merlin
2000 "Review: Gwen John and Balthus, New York and London". *The Burlington Magazine* 142, 1162: 59-61.

Jouve, Pierre Jean
1983 (1960) "Le tableau". In Centre Georges Pompidou, 64-65 .

Klossowski, Pierre
1983 (1957) "Du tableau vivant dans la peinture de Balthus". In Centre Georges Pompidou, 80-85.

Kopp, Robert
2001 "Balthus and Pierre-Jean Jouve. Previously Unpublished Documents". In Clair, 61-76.

Lichtenstein, Jacqueline
1993 *The Eloquence of Color: Rhetoric and Painting in the French Classical Age*. Trans. Emily McVarish. San Francisco: University of California Press.

MacKinnon, Catherine
1989 *Sexuality, Pornography, and Method: Pleasure Under Patriarchy*. Cambridge, MA: Harvard University Press.

Mulvey, Laura
1975 "Visual Pleasure and Narrative Cinema". *Screen* 16, 3: 6-18.

Picon, Gaëtan
1983 (1966) "Les dalles de Venise". In Centre Georges Pompidou, 98-103.

Pleij, Herman.
2004 *Colors Demonic and Divine: Shades of Meaning in the Middle Ages and After*. New York: Columbia University Press.

Rajchman, John
1995 "Another View of Abstraction". *Journal of Philosophy and the Visual Arts* 5: 16-24.

Rewald, Sabine
1984 *Balthus*. New York: The Metropolitan Museum of Art/Harry N. Abrams, Inc.

1997 "Balthus's Magic Mountain". *The Burlington Magazine* 139, 1134: 622-628.

1998 "Balthus's Térèses". *Metropolitan Museum Journal* 33: 305-314.

2001 "The Young Balthus". In Clair, 43-60 .

Riley, Charles A. II
2001 "King of the Cats: Balthus". In *Aristocracy and the Modern Imagination*. Hanover and London: University Press of New England, 202-221.

Rilke, Rainer Maria
1921 "Preface". In *Mitsou: Quarante images par Baltusz*. Erlenbach-Zürich & Leipzig: Rotapfel - Verlag.

Roy, Claude
1996 *Balthus*. Boston: Bulfinch Press.

Rouan, François
1993 "Circling Around a Void". Trans. Rosalind E. Krauss. *October* 65, Summer: 77-88.

Russell, John
1983 (1968) "Mais l'Alice de Tenniel". In Centre Georges Pompidou, 280-297.

Salomon, Nanette
2004 *Shifting Priorities: Gender and Genre in Seventeenth-Century Dutch Painting*. Stanford: Stanford University Press.

Starobinski, Jean
1983 "Des peintures de Balthus à la galerie Moos à Genève". In Centre Georges Pompidou, 68-69.

1996 "Dramaturgie de Balthus". *Studi di Letteratura Francese* XXI: 23-28.

Stewart, Garrett
2003 "Painted Readers, Narrative Regress". *Narrative* 11, 2: 125-176.

2006 *The Look of Reading: Book, Painting, Text*. Chicago: The University of Chicago Press.

Stein, Ruth
2005 "Why Perversion?: 'False Love' and the Perverse Pact". *International Journal of Psychoanalysis* 86: 775-799.

Verdi, Richard
1995 *Nicholas Poussin, 1594-1665*. London: Royal Academy of Arts.

Verschaffel, Bart
2004 *A propos de Balthus. Le regard des chats. Le regard sondeur*. Trans. Daniel Cunin. Ghent: A&S Books.

Weber, Nicholas Fox
1999 *Balthus: A Biography*. London: Weidenfeld and Nicolson.

Xing Xiaozhou
2001 "'The Landscape Is Very Chinese at the Moment...': The Influence of Chinese Painting in Balthus's Landscapes". In Clair, 89-102.

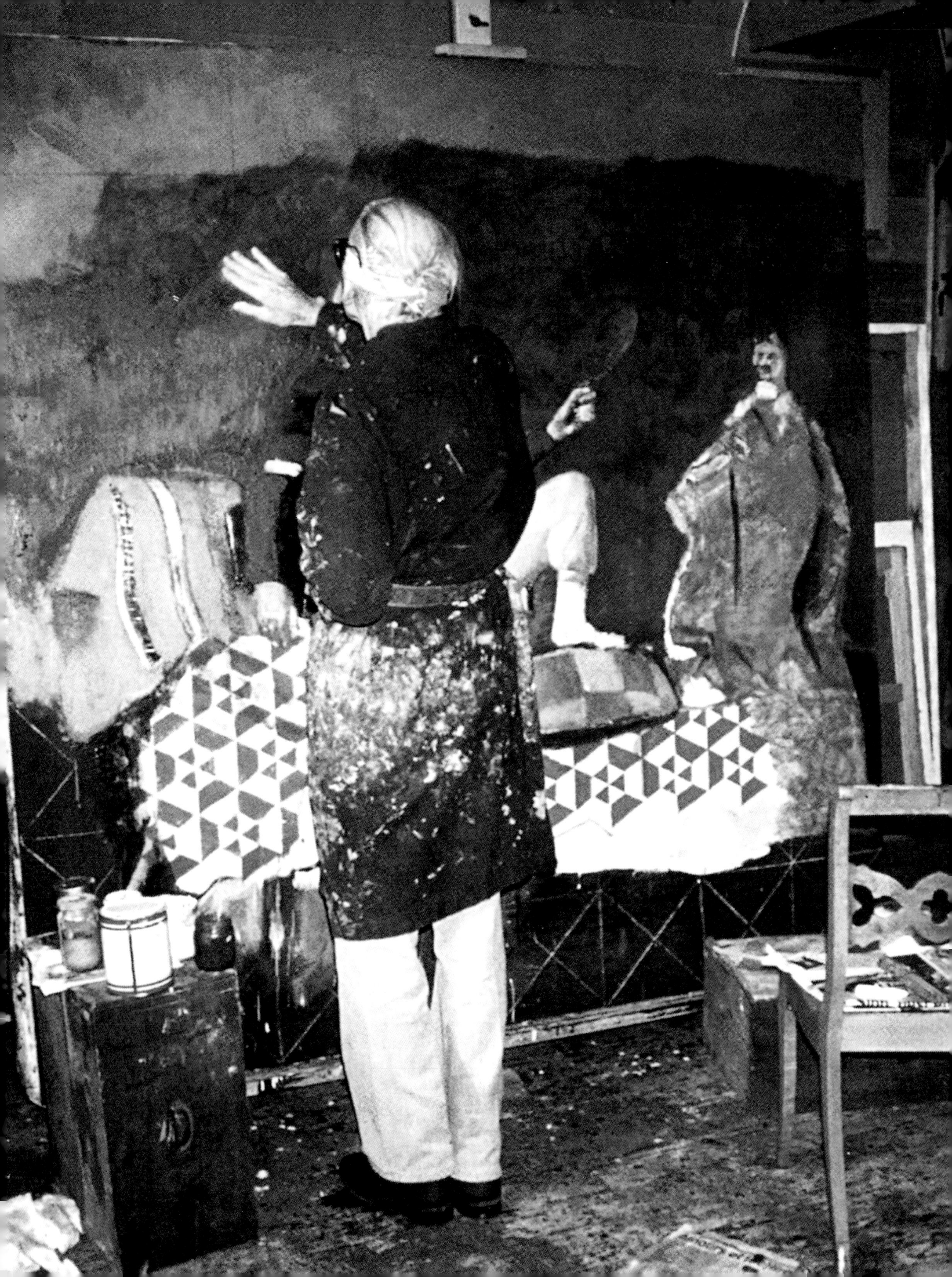

Balthus à contre-courant, 1992

WITH COSTANZO COSTANTINI

Translated from *Balthus à contre-courant. Entretiens avec Costanzo Costantini*, Les Editions Noir Sur Blanc, 2001. Montricher (Switzerland), pp. 61-77.

Costanzo Costantini: In 1933 you illustrated the French edition of Emily Brontë's novel *Wuthering Heights* (published in French as *Les Hauts de Hurlevent*). Was it because you identified closely with Heathcliff, the mysterious boy who refused to grow up, that you made him look like yourself?

Balthus: What do you mean, he refused to grow up? To a certain extent, you have to become what you paint or draw in order to express it better. Great Western Art is not the art that represents things but the one that identifies them. To tell you the truth, I identified a little with all the characters in the novel. I also identified with Cathy.

But Cathy has Antoinette de Watteville's features.

More so in the painting *Cathy at Her Make-up* than in the drawings. This painting is inspired by Antoinette's features; the drawings are completely imaginary. Heathcliff and Cathy are tightly bound together in a kind of symbiosis. Cathy confesses to Nelly "Nelly, I am Heathcliff! He's always, always in my mind". For his part, Heathcliff tells Cathy, "I have not broken your heart—you have broken it; and in breaking it, you have broken mine". At the end of the 15th chapter, when Cathy dies, I found myself facing the problem of illustrating the following events in a style that did not clash with the preceding illustrations. I struggled long and hard to come up with a solution but all my efforts were in vain. In the end, when Heathcliff gives up his plan to seek revenge and to wreak destruction, I decided against illustrating the other part of the novel.

What struck you most in this novel?

The characters' fatalistic nature. But it was above all the landscape that prompted me to do these illustrations. The landscape had fascinated me ever since my time in Leeds with the two young publishers from Leeds, which we talked about earlier.

But isn't there some deeper reason? Did you not identify with Heathcliff and Cathy because they both wanted to remain in the world of childhood forever?

No, that wasn't it... Don't forget that when I illustrated this novel, I was 27 years old, I was no longer a small boy.

But you were a romantic young man, just like the novel *Wuthering Heights* is romantic.

In what sense is *Wuthering Heights* romantic?

In the sense of *Sturm und Drang*, a wild nature and a whirlwind of unleashed passions.

As Lucien Daudet wrote in his preface to the first French edition of *Les Hauts de Hurlevent*, if *Wuthering Heights* is a romantic book, then Shakespeare is the first romantic writer in English literature.

In his preface to *Bleu du ciel*, Bataille asks "How can one waste time on books that the authors were manifestly not compelled to write?" Among the books whose authors were evidently not driven to write them, he cites *Wuthering Heights* ahead of *The Trial, Remembrance of Things Past, The Red and the Black, Eugénie de Franval, Death Sentence, Sarrasine* and *The Idiot*.

It would take too long to discuss the other books that Bataille includes in his list. We could each add to it and subtract from it according to our own preferences. Some of these novels are universally acknowledged as masterpieces or as very important books. *Wuthering Heights* is without doubt an extraordinary, deeply moving book.

Balthus at his studio in Rossinière, 1994.
Photo: Giorgio Soavi.

With regard to your illustrations, mention has often been made of John Tenniel's drawings for *Alice's Adventures in Wonderland* and *Through the Looking Glass* by Lewis Carroll.

Tenniel was a marvelous illustrator. I am a great fan of Lewis Carroll's books.

Where are the originals of your illustrations?

Some of these illustrations were published in the magazine *Le Minotaure*. The originals belong to Duchamp's widow. Her husband made her buy them. The Limited Editions Club in New York published the first edition of these illustrations in English in 1994.

Did you know Duchamp well?

Yes. He was an acutely intelligent man. He was also a great chess player.

What did you think of him as an artist?

Haven't I talked about that enough already?

When did you move into your studio in the Cour de Rohan?

In 1936. I had become familiar with the Cour de Rohan through a friend of Jouve's, the painter Sima, who had a studio up in the garret. The building was once a private mansion. My studio consisted of just a single, though very large, room. It was a simple, unattractive place but I gave it a bit of style by installing a Gothic bed in it. People of all kinds came to see me there: painters, sculptors, actors, bohemians, critics, art dealers. That was where I painted the portraits of Marie-Laure de Noailles, Derain and Miró and his daughter Dolores. In the 1930s, Paris was the centre of the world, the international capital of the arts.

The Cour de Rohan is still famous today. There are still historic spots there such as La Jacobine and the Pub révolutionnaire. The most famous place is still Le Procope café and restaurant, where Robespierre, Danton and Marat used to meet.

I haven't been back there for many years. We used to meet up at the restaurant run by Roger la Grenouille on Rue des Grands-Augustins, where Picasso had his studio. Roger was a very friendly man. I did a portrait of him and his son standing. We also used to get together at Le Catalan restaurant, where Picasso and Greta Garbo, when she was in town, used to go to eat. After the Montmartre era came the 'golden age' of Montparnasse. We'd meet at Le Dôme, La Rotonde, Le Select and La Coupole. Then Montparnasse became passé and it was the era of Saint-Germain-des-Prés, Le Flore and Les Deux-Magots. You used to come across the most bizarre people there, such as the painter Forain, who was always after a bit of money. It was said that one of his favorite victims was Degas. When he'd managed to find some money, he'd get drunk and say that he was a thief. And Degas would say, "It's true, he steals, he steals, but his hands are in my pockets".

Did you know Greta Garbo well?

Quite well. I met her at the home of Marie-Laure de Noailles, who became the mistress of Oskar Dominguez, a very strange character. One evening Garbo was at Le Catalan, her face hidden as usual behind enormous dark glasses. I went over to say hello and then returned to my seat. Marie-Laure and Dominguez then came in and sat at my table. "There's a woman over there who looks like Greta Garbo", said Marie-Laure. Immediately afterwards, Garbo got up to leave and passed right in front of us. "But it's really her!" exclaimed Marie-Laure and she launched into great demonstrations of affection, saying things like "My darling" and "My love" and inviting her to join us for a moment. Dominguez began to touch and caress her, seriously bothering her. "Oskar, you are going too far, this is Greta Garbo", I told him, but he carried on until Garbo suddenly got up and left. He was so drunk that he refused to believe that she really was Garbo. He was mad. He eventually committed suicide. He died drained of blood like a bull.

Acording to some artists who were in Paris in the 1930s, Dominguez killed himself because Picasso made a harsh comment about one of his exhibitions.

That's nonsense. Dominguez killed himself because he was unbalanced. Picasso was very generous and an extraordinary man. He was very interested in other painters, regardless of whether they were any good or not. Despite his fame and success, he was always anxious when he showed his paintings. He had no love for the surrealists either. He invented Cubism with Braque, but to my mind Braque had more of an instinct as a painter. Braque had what he himself termed a 'pictorial sense', which doesn't exist today. He was a great craftsman, a perfect master of the techniques and materials he employed. Among other things, he spoke extremely elegant French and unlike Picasso he was very calm. I learned a curious thing from the catalogue of the exhibition of my work at the museum on Andros in Greece. Masson records in it that Picasso told him one day: "Balthus and I are two sides of the same coin". However, I do not fully understand what Picasso meant by that. In 1941, Picasso bought *The Children* from the Colle & Renou Gallery in Paris, a work I had painted in 1937. It was Giacometti who told me that Picasso had purchased it. Then he gave it to the Louvre and now it is in the Picasso Museum in Paris. I adored Picasso the man.

You did not, however, adore Matisse. Why was that?

I had no love for him because he had a terribly teacherly side to him. When his son Pierre decided to become an art dealer, Matisse told him that he would not give him a single one of his paintings, and he was true to his word. The Matisses that Pierre had in his collection were works that he probably acquired after his father's death.

But did you love him as a painter?

I admired him, though not completely. Some of his paintings were splendid, magnificent, but he over-simplified. I have never loved painters who over-simplify or who paint too fast. I'll accept it in great painters such as Courbet and in certain Japanese Zen Buddhist monk painters such as Sengai, Hakuin and others, who painted very quickly after a long period of meditation and who had mastered their craft. Matisse, however, destroyed the traditional craft of the painter and abolished the use of glaze. I realized this when I was making copies in the Louvre and came to the realization that the *Narcissus* paintings were done entirely with glazes.

Early on, Gustave Moreau had told Matisse while he was one of Moreau's pupils at the School of Fine Arts, "Matisse, you want to simplify painting". Moreau was right, he had fully grasped the temperament of the young Matisse. I really shouldn't say this, but I prefer Tintin to some of Matisse's paintings. Tintin is no less simplified and he's altogether more amusing. No, I'm sorry: Matisse is someone I've merely admired.

In his *Journal,* Gide records that Denis told him the story of Matisse's visit to Rodin to show him some of his drawings and how he had come back furious. Rodin had told him, "Nibble away, nibble away. When you've nibbled away at it for another fortnight, come back and show it to me again".

Amusing.

Derain also painted too fast, yet you liked him.

I liked Derain because he was an extremely cultivated, intelligent man, even though his frame of mind and mood changed with the wind, just as he changed his shirt. He reminded me of G.K. Chesterton's novel *The Man Who Was Thursday*, which I read when I was ten and which profoundly moved me. Derain also painted too fast, but his virtuosity was breathtaking. Despite his corpulence, he came to my studio in the

Cour de Rohan on foot; his studio was a long way away on the other side of Paris. Another remarkable thing about Derain was that he could identify the different accents of Paris and the *quartier* they came from. He sat for me 20 times or so.

I went to buy the dressing gown that he wears in my painting with Madame Kalinska, the famous theatre wardrobe mistress. It was through her, in fact, that I met Derain, and Cassandre. I admired Cassandre's sets for *Don Giovanni* enormously. Derain always made me think of a Chinese general. Sonia Mossé, the woman in my painting with Derain, had often sat for Derain. I put her in my painting without making her sit for me.

Miró and his daughter Dolores also walked to your studio?

Yes. They came to see me on countless occasions over the course of a year or so. Miró had endless patience, whereas Dolores could not keep still, she was mercurial, she was a devil of a girl. One day I tied her up in a coal sack. I remember that she once said to her father, "Papa, why don't you do paintings like Balthus'?" But she had no idea how much effort I went to to produce those paintings. I wasn't like Derain, who painted his works, including portraits, at a single go. Miró, however, would sit and never said a word, like a well-brought-up child. In fact, he was a child. One day, Picasso remarked to him on seeing his paintings, "At your age, Miró, really!" I've only once ever done a portrait at a single go. It was the portrait of Boris Kochno, who, like a good Russian, was constantly drunk. I never once saw him sober. Naturally, he was never in a fit state to sit for a portrait and I did it in a single sitting, if you can call it that.

Boris Kochno has described this historic sitting in an article by Jean Clair printed in the catalogue that accompanied the exhibition at the Pompidou Centre in 1983-1984.

Yes. He recalls that in 1949, when he was artistic director of Les Ballets des Champs-Élysées Company, he asked me to do the sets and costumes for *Le Peintre et son modèle*, a ballet choreographed by Léonide Massine and then, following on from that, I asked him if I could paint his portrait.

For this set, I stripped the entire back of the stage bare, leaving just some of the flies visible. All I used was just a single stage element. I remember that Aragon's wife asked me: "What are you going to put at the back?" "You have the set in front of your eyes", I replied. "What more do you want?"

Coming back to Kochno's portrait, you arranged to meet him at nine in the morning in a café in the quartier of the Odéon, near the Cour de Rohan, and he turned up with Picasso.

He was a close friend of Picasso's, who loved the strangest of people. I had asked him if I could paint his portrait because his face interested me. He had the face of a convict. He was thoroughly fascinating, in the Baudelairean sense of the word.

In his article, Kochno recalls that you had met in the 1930s at the home of Marie-Laure de Noailles, where world celebrities and young artists in the revolutionary mould would gather. He said that of all the people there, you stood out as the "the shadowy handsome man", that you reminded him of Jean-Louis Barrault in the part of Hamlet. He added that you observed this ill-assorted world in silence, but that your malicious expression and ironic smile allowed others to guess what you thought of it.

Barrault and I were very similar, to the extent that we were sometimes mistaken for each other. In 1950, we were together at the Aix-en-Provence Festival, where there was a performance of *Così fan tutte* by Mozart, for which I had done the sets and costumes. One day, a woman approached me and said, "I am one of your greatest admirers". "Jean-Louis Barrault is over there", I replied. She insisted, "Monsieur, do not mock me". I could not believe that I was as famous as Barrault, who was then a great star.

Boris Kochno reports that he came to your studio on 7 November 1951, after breakfast, and that in the evening he was expecting you to say, "Come back tomorrow", when you picked up the portrait and had written at the bottom, "For Boris, [from] his friend Balthus". The portrait was finished.

Picasso liked that portrait too.

Did you see Boris Kochno after that?

No. He died three or four years ago in Munich.

What most interests you in a face when you draw it?

That's a difficult question to answer. A face is an ensemble, a totality. Each of its elements contributes to determining that ensemble, that totality.

But in many portraits from the past, it is one or other of the subject's traits that characterizes his face. Let us consider, for example, two portraits by one of your favorite painters, Piero della Francesca: his portraits of Federico da Montefeltro, Duke of Urbino, and Sigismondo Malatesta. In these two portraits, the face is characterized by the nose rather than by its other traits, isn't that so?

By the nose and by the other traits in an overall vision. Federico da Montefeltro had suffered a wound to his nose. These two portraits are characterized not just by the nose but by the subjects' eyes and gazes. The eyes are no less interesting than the noses. In a face, it is in fact the eyes that hold my attention the most. But I am very slow and it takes me a long time to study a face, just like I need a long time to study the subject, until I come to virtually identify with him.

Do you like Picasso's portraits?

I especially like his portrait of Olga Kokhlova, the mother of his first son, Pablo. Picasso's pencil portraits are marvelous.

Did you know Olga Kokhlova and the other women in Picasso's life?

I knew Olga Kokhlova but not well. I knew Dora Maar very well.

When I interviewed Masson in Rome in 1968, he told me that one day Giacometti had said to him "Picasso's portraits of Dora Maar are merely caricatures". Masson added that Giacometti was right.

I don't know... I couldn't say.

But more than Picasso, wasn't Giacometti your great friend?

Giacometti was six or seven years older than me, whereas Picasso could have been my father. Giacometti and I looked at things in the same way.

Was he the person who gave you the sculpture on a console in the room next door?

Yes, it's a memento from him. I did a pencil portrait of him on graph paper that is here. We were like brothers. I remember that one day we went to meet Mondrian, who had an apartment overlooking the Seine. We were looking through the window and the row of trees on the embankment when he came in and slammed it shut in fury. What a strange man! Perhaps he didn't like trees. Giacometti and I also shared a deep dislike of Le Corbusier. Le Corbusier has destroyed the house. He has done away with its roof, the most fascinating feature of a house. In Paris, one of his projects was for an arena. I told him it looked like a soup bowl. He flew into a rage. But there was something else that brought us closer together, Giacometti and me.

At an artistic level or on a personal level?

On a personal level. We both of us walked with a limp. I was wounded during the war in the Saar by an explosion down a mine. I remember that the newspapers wrote that the pigs were coming. The pigs were us. Giacometti was wounded in a road accident. He was knocked down by an American who was driving while drunk. Once he got over the shock, he disappeared. His brother Diego was desperate. He searched frantically high and low and eventually found him at the Hôtel-Dieu hospital. He had made himself at home there, was enjoying himself and wanted to stay.

Rilke also talks of the Hôtel-Dieu at the start of *The Notebook of Malte Laurids Brigge.*

Giacometti was comfortable there. In any case, as a result of this accident, Giacometti broke off his friendship with Sartre.

Why?

Because Sartre wrote "At last something has happened to him". I don't recall where he wrote it. Giacometti became angry. He said "If a man who has known me for so long and who sees me virtually every day can write such a thing, it means he has understood nothing about me. Things happen to me every day". And he refused to see him again.

Did you know Sartre well?

Quite well, if only because he concerned himself with art, though somewhat badly, it has to be said. As a man, Sartre was extremely pleasant, even fascinating. He was the cousin of the famous Dr. Schweitzer who went off to care for the lepers in Africa. Because of that, people used to say "The devil and the good God". In contrast, Diego Giacometti loathed him, just as I loathed Simone de Beauvoir, who wrote novels in the style of *Marie-Claire.*

It may be true that Sartre concerned himself with art though "somewhat badly", yet in 1987, Jean-Marie Drot, who succeeded Jean Leymarie as director of the French Academy, devoted an exhibition to him at the Villa Médicis entitled "Sartre and Art". The catalogue included the essays that Sartre had written on Giacometti and the portraits—four portraits—that Giacometti had done of him. In one of these essays, Sartre said that Giacometti had attempted to paint the void, to expel the world from his canvases, something that no-one had done before him.

It was Giacometti himself who said that Sartre concerned himself somewhat badly with art and that he had understood nothing about either him or his oeuvre.

Did Jean Genet understand Giacometti better than Sartre had done? The essay-interview that Genet wrote on Giacometti, *Alberto Giacometti's Studio,* is very interesting.

What is interesting about it?

Giacometti told him that he had been very happy when he learned, following the operation after his accident, that he would be left with a limp.

That might seem strange, but he was indeed happy to have a limp.

Genet says that one day, when he had lunch with Sartre, he confessed to Sartre what he would have liked to say to Giacometti—and eventually did say to him—that when he was casting his statues in bronze, it wasn't the statues that were enhanced but the bronze. Sartre replied to him: "That would give him immense pleasure. His dream would be to disappear completely behind the work. For him, it would be better still if the bronze could create itself on its own".

I agree with Sartre in that respect: the artist ought to disappear completely behind his work. It is the work that matters, not the artist. Cézanne said the same thing: you can produce good paintings without drawing attention to your private life, you must stay hidden in the shadows. Once upon a time, the work of art was anonymous and universal.

Genet lays great emphasis on the fact that Giacometti was never happy and that when he was struggling with the face of Yanaihare, Sartre found him a state of veritable despair.

You know, it was Diego who did all Alberto's works. Alberto could not exist without him. He knew what his brother was like, he knew he was bent upon destruction, and he knew everything Alberto did to turn it into plasters or bronzes as required.

True painters or sculptors are always discontented or despairing. Dürer was, and even Michelangelo was. The same is also true of Bacon. Bacon is an extremely gifted painter but one who yields to horror, which I have always shunned.

And you? Are you despairing as well?

Now, when I finish a painting, I am happy and despairing: happy to have finished it; despairing because I feel as if I have expended my last remaining energy on it and I am incapable of doing any others.

Giacometti told James Lord that the more one works on a painting, the more it becomes impossible to finish it.

It's a paradox, but there is some truth in that.

In his book *A Giacometti Portrait*, James Lord records that one day he asked Giacometti whether he had ever thought of suicide, and Giacometti replied that he thought of it every day.

Giacometti had a tremendous sense of humor. I have enormous admiration for him. He turned sculpture into something that was completely new, but he was also an excellent draughtsman. Shortly before his death, he did some magnificent portraits.

Jean Genet said something else that will perhaps give you pleasure, which is that Giacometti's statues seemed to him to belong to a bygone era, which he defined as the "eternity that passes".

Yes, I like the expression "the eternity that passes".

Giacometti once told him that he had thought of making a statue and burying it on condition that it would be dug up later, when no-one remembered either him or his name.

Giacometti had the same concept of art as the Ancients.

But perhaps neither Jean Genet nor Giacometti recalled that, according to Vasari, Michelangelo was in the habit of burying his statues to make them seem older.

I don't want to repeat myself, but true art is always timeless.

Did you know Jean Genet?

Yes, but I don't know whether I saw him in Giacometti's studio. Perhaps I was not in Paris when he went there; perhaps I was at Chassy. But now it's time for me to go and finish *Cat with Mirror III*, even though I prefer to paint early in the morning. I like light that does not move, static light, though it does not last long. In the early hours of the morning, when people are not yet awake, the silence is absolute, and a magical, almost metaphysical atmosphere reigns in Rossinière.

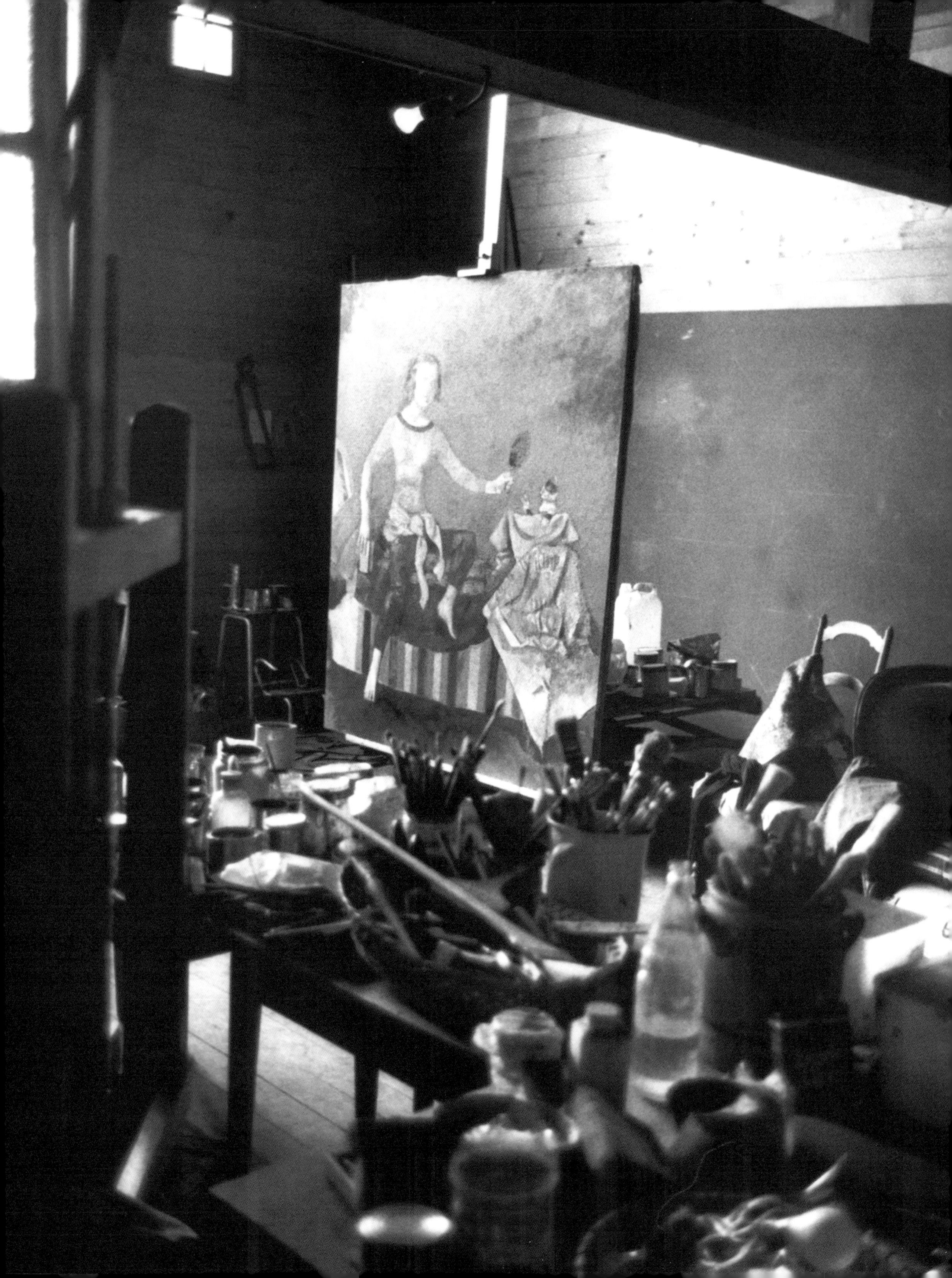

Biography

EDITED BY VIRGINIE MONNIER

Quoted from *Balthus: Catalogue raisonné de l'œuvre complète*, edited by Virginie Monnier and Jean Clair, and published by Éditions Gallimard, Paris, 1999.

1908
29 February: birth in Paris of Balthasar Klossowski, second son of Erich Klossowski (1875-1946) and Elisabeth Dorothea Spiro (1886-1969). Erich Klossowski was a painter and art historian, author of a monograph on Henri Daumier that is still relevant. His wife as well was a painter, known as Baladine. Their elder son, born in 1905, is the writer and painter Pierre Klossowski. Erich Klossowski was of Polish birth, of a family that had taken refuge in Eastern Prussia since the mid-nineteenth century. Baladine was born at Breslau (Wroclaw), in Silesia, a region under Prussian rule at the time. The couple had been living in Paris since 1903, in the district of Montparnasse, and belonged to Pierre Bonnard's circle. They also kept company with some artists and writers who had left Breslau as they had. Among them the painter Eugen Spiro, Baladine's brother, the art historians Julius Meier-Grafe and Wilhelm Uhde.

1914
When the war broke out, the Klossowskis, being German citizens, had to leave France. Their possessions were seized and sold; a small part was kept safe by Pierre Bonnard. Their financial situation was extremely critical. After staying in Zurich as Professor Jean Strohl's guests, they settled in Berlin.

1916
Erich Klossowski designed for Victor Barnowski, who was also from Breslau, and director of the Lessingtheater since 1913, sets and costumes that met with great success.

1917
The Klossowski couple separated. Baladine and her two sons spent a few months in Bern. Contrary to what has been claimed, the boys did not attend school, but it was at that time that Balthus would have met Robert and Hubert de Watteville, brothers of his future wife Antoinette.
In November, Baladine, Pierre and Balthus left Bern for Geneva.

1919
Rainer Maria Rilke, travelling through Geneva, visited Baladine, whom he had met in Paris before the war. Several months later a romance blossomed between the poet, whom she called René and Baladine, become Merline. Balthus was enrolled in the Lycée Calvin. An episode of his childhood—the adoption and then the loss of a kitten—was the origin of the 40 drawings of *Mitsou*. About at that rime Baladine began spending the summer months at Beatenberg, a small but cosmopolitan resort on the shores of the Lake of Thun, with Balthus; there he met Margrit Bay, a woman painter and sculptor surrounded by a group involved in anthroposophy, and would become her assistant in 1922.

1920
Beginning of the correspondence between Rilke and Baladine.
Balthus discovered, through a book, Chinese culture, becoming fascinated by it. He illustrated for Rilke several episodes from the life of the Taoist sage Chuang-tzu, then inventing a "Chinese novel".
Rilke was enthusiastic over the drawings of *Mitsou* and tried to have them published.

1921
Publication of *Mitsou, quarante images par Baltusz*, with a preface by Rilke. During the spring, Baladine and her sons settled in Berlin again where Eugen Spiro took them in.
In the summer, Baladine arranged the castle of Muzot, near Sierre, for Rilke. In November, she returned to Berlin with her sons. Their studies were broken off, because of a lack of means.

1922
Balthus executed some maquettes of settings for a Chinese play he proposed to the Staatstheater in Munich. The offer came to nothing since the play was not staged. At Beatenberg, Balthus painted his playmates, the young local peasants, worked with Margrit Bay and took part in the theatrical activities of her entourage. He spent the fall at Muzot, Rilke being away at the time.
The Klossowski family was back in Berlin for the winter. Balthus failed to be admitted to the Academy of Applied Arts.

1923
In May, Baladine and Balthus left Berlin permanently for Beatenberg. There Balthus painted, for Margrit Bay, a large panel representing the *Madonna and Child* surrounded by Saint John the Baptist and Saint Luke. He had a mural project, that he would have to give up. For Christmas, Rilke sent him a copy of Dante and a work by the art historian W. Worringer and received from him a painting.
Pierre Klossowski moved to Paris, where, at Rilke's request, he stayed at André Gide's.

1924
In the spring, Baladine and Balthus joined Pierre in Paris. During the summer, at Beatenberg, Balthus met Antoinette de Watteville, who was then twelve years old. After returning to Paris in the fall, he sat in on classes at the Academy of La Grande Chaumière. During the same period, he showed his drawings and paintings to Pierre Bonnard and to Maurice Denis, who encouraged him to copy Poussin's paintings in the Louvre.

1925
In the spring, Balthus and his mother were guests in Toulon of the Vulliez couple, whom Baladine had met through Rilke. There Balthus painted the *Paysage Provençal*.
Rilke was in Paris (9 January-18 August), then left for Muzot with Baladine. She came back in the late fall.
In the Louvre, Balthus copied Poussin's *Narcissus* that he sent to Rilke, and painted several views of the Luxembourg garden.

1926
Thanks to a group of sponsors, the most important one being Professor Jean Strohl, Balthus spent part of the summer in Italy. He copied several frescoes of the cycle of the *Legend of the True Cross* by Piero della Francesca at Arezzo and the *Resurrection* at Borgo San Sepolcro, as well as frescoes by Masaccio and Masolino in Florence.
In the fall, he was back in Beatenberg. He may have gone with his mother to Toulon for Christmas. Rilke died on 29 December.

1927
January: Balthus attended Rilke's funeral. During the spring, in the Protestant temple of Beatenberg, where Margrit Bay's father had been minister, he painted frescoes depicting *The Good Shepherd* and the *Four Evangelists*. He had the project of a big painting on the theme of the story of Tobia; that work would never be done. During the fall, he began in Paris a series of paintings and drawings with street scenes and views of the Luxembourg garden. Erich Klossowski moved to Sanary-sur-mer, in the South of France, where he lived with Hilde Stieler, a German journalist.

1928
Balthus stayed in Zurich from February to September. He was a guest of the Müller and Thomann families, and portrayed several of their members.

1929
In April, Balthus was invited to Berlin to stay with the publisher Martin Hürlimann, whose portrait he painted. In September-October, the Forter gallery of Zurich organized an exhibition that showed about ten paintings by Balthus, works by Toni Ciolino and lithographs by Gregor Rabinovitch. It was Balthus's first exhibition.
Back in Paris, he sought, unsuccessfully, funds to rent a studio. He is believed to have destroyed, at the time, a certain number of paintings.

1930
During tbe summer, Balthus spent several weeks with his friends the Wattevilles. He fell in love with Antoinette, and painted her portrait.
In October, he was called up to perform his military service in the French army. He was drafted in the 4e régiment de tirailleurs marocains (Moroccan artillery), at Kenitra, on the Atlantic coast of Morocco. Several sketches and a water color allude to the barrack-room at Kenitra.

1931
February: he had an eight-day leave that he spent in Gibraltar.
August: he was transferred to Headquarters in Fez where he was to stay until the end of his service, in December. A couple of sheets of sketches of Gibraltar and a group of drawings executed in the barracks yard in Fez are all that remain of that period. Later on three paintings would be executed.

1932
Spring: after staying in Zurich, where Professor Jean Strohl tried in vain to find him a job, Balthus went to Beatenberg and then to Bern. He was there from May to October, as a guest of the Watteville family, and executed a series of copies after the cycle of *Swiss Peasants* by Joseph Reinhardt.
Antoinette fell in love with a Belgian diplomat.
Back in Paris in the fall, Balthus shared an apartment with Pierre Leyris (who had been his brother Pierre's school-mate at the Lycée Janson-de-Sailly in 1923) and his young wife Betty. He resumed the illustrations for *Wuthering Heights* by Emily Brontë, begun early that same year. Pierre and Betty Leyris posed for him on several occasions.

1933
March: he rented the studio of the Swiss architect Jeanneret, Le Corbusier's cousin, at 4, Rue de Furstenberg.
He became friends with Pierre Jean Jouve, whom he had met during Rilke's stay in Paris in 1925, and frequently went to see André Derain, who gave him technical advice.
Painted *La Rue* that Jean Cassou put forward for the Grand Prix de la peinture organized by the Bernheims. The painting was rejected because of its size. He then painted *La Caserne*, in memory of Fez, *Alice*, whose model was Betty Leyris, and *La Fenêtre*. He spent the first half of August at Muzot, and then in September went to see his father at Sanary.
In November, collaborated in the sets for Johann Strauss's Junior *La Chauve-souris*, staged by Max Reinhardt at the Théâtre Pigalle. It was his first personal engagement in the theater world.
December: finished *La Toilette de Cathy*. Julien Green came to see him twice and Wilhelm Uhde visited him bringing Pierre Loeb, the young owner of the Galerie Pierre that championed Surrealist painting. Loeb claimed he was very impressed by *La Rue*. An exhibition was considered.

Balthus' studio in à La Rossinière, 1990.
Photo: Martine Franck.

In the following weeks, André Breton visited him along with Paul Eluard, Georges Hugnet and Alberto Giacometti. The Surrealists were highly disappointed to discover he was a resolutely figurative painter, but that would be the beginning of the friendship between Balthus and Giacometti (himself soon a dissident of the Surrealist movement) that was to last for thirty years.

1934
March: Pierre Loeb sought to make Balthus known: the Minister of the Interior Albert Sarraut and Picasso came to see him. April: one man show at the Galerie Pierre. Balthus presented *La Rue, La Toilette de Cathy, La Fenêtre, Alice* and *La Leçon de guitare*, that caused a scandal, as well as two portraits, including one of Antoinette (probably The *Jeune fille en costume d'amazone)*.
The exhibition, that Balthus had meant to be provocative, did create a little social "scandal" but not a single painting sold. Notwithstanding, it drew the attention of several personalities, among whom the famous vicomtesse de Noailles, and especially Antonin Artaud, who praised it in a review in the *N.R.F.*
May: exhibition in Brussels around the review *Minotaure. La Toilette de Cathy* was shown.
June: a stay in Beatenberg. His nerves shattered by the letdown of his exhibition and Antoinette's sentimental vacillations, Balthus alternated between states of exaltation and despair.
July: attempted suicide. During the summer, Pierre Matisse, Henri Matisse's son, who owned a gallery in New York, discovered Balthus's painting at the Galerie Pierre.
August: the famous Berlin stage director Victor Barnowski, for whom Erich Klossowski had worked during the First World War, and who had sought refuge in Paris after Hider's election, asked Balthus to create the costumes and sets for Shakespeare's comedy *Comme il vous plaira* [As You Like It], that he wished to stage. The play was presented at the Théâtre des Champs Elysées in October but was thwarted by the performance held at the same time by Jacques Copeau at the Théâtre de l'Atelier, as well as by the latent antisemitism surrounding Barnowski. Balthus continued working on his illustrations for *Wuthering Heights*. Spent Christmas at Bern at the Watteville's.

1935
February: Antonin Artaud called upon Balthus to design the sets and costumes for *The Cenci*. That tragedy, an interpretation of Shelley's play, was supposed to illustrate Artaud's innovatary conceptions, published in 1932 by the *N.R.F* under the tide "Théâtre de la Cruauté".
The play was sponsored by Iya Abdy, who played the leading role, and whose portrait Balthus painted at the time. Varia Karinska, who made the costumes, introduced him to the poster artist A.M. Mouron Cassandre, from whom he immediately received a commission to do a portrait of his family.
March: Antoinette broke off her engagement.
May: publication of eight of the illustrations for *Wuthering Heights* in Albert Skira's *Le Minotaure*.
Brief stay in London at Herman Shdjver's. Two portraits, including that of *Lelia Caetani*, were shown.
September: stay in Engadine at Pierre Jean Jouve's.
October: Balthus moved into the studio in the Cour de Rohan. Pierre Colle commissioned him to paint the *Portrait d'André Derain* and Loeb advanced him funds so he could begin *La Montagne*. Finished the final version of the illustrations for *Wuthering Heights*.
Attempted to publish a study, the manuscript of which is lost, on nineteenth-century illustrated children's books. That year was also the date of the first painted self-portrait, titled *Le Roi des chats*, the first study for *La Montagne* and a series of social portraits that would support him for two years.

1936
January: began *La Montagne*.
March: exhibited in London his illustrations for *Wuthering Heights*, without succeeding in having them published. A short stay at Hyères at the vicomtesse de Noailles's who cornmissioned her portrait.
April: second stay in London. Painted the portraits of *La vicomtesse de Noailles* and *André Derain* as well as *Roger et son fils*.
August: Balthus traveled with Pierre Jean Jouve to Soglio, in Engadine.
Fall: third stay in London to portray *Lady Schuster and her daughter*. He began a series of drawings and paintings whose models were the Blanchard children. The first portrait of *Thérèse* was bought by Jouve. Executed an illustration for Jouve's poem, *Urne* (CLM, Paris 1926).

1937
2 April: married Antoinette de Watteville. Painted *Les Enfants Blanchard, La Jupe blanche*, completed *La Montagne. La Rue* entered the collection of the American collector James Thrall Soby. Pierre Loeb commissioned him to paint the portrait of *Joan Miró et sa fille Dolorès*, for Miró's fiftieth birthday.

1938
March-April: first exhibition at the Pierre Matisse Gallery in New York. Stay at Champrovent, in Savoie, with Pierre and Betty Leyris. There he painted *La Falaise* and the two versions of *Sous bois*. That was the year of the *Portrait de Joan Miró et de sa fille Dolorès*, the *Portrait de Pierre Matisse, Thérèse rêvant*. The portrait of Miró was received at the Museum of Modern Art of New York.

1939
Painted the view of *Larchant*, a village near Fontainebleau where he had probably been taken by Jouve, who devoted three poems to the church of Saint-Mathurin. In September, Balthus was drafted and sent to Alsace. Wounded or ill, he returned to Paris in December.

1940
In January-February, spent several weeks of convalescence with Antoinette at Sittgriswil, near Beatenberg, then went through Bern where he left Antoinette. At the end of February, was back in Paris where he was demobilized.
June: settled with Antoinette at Champrovent where Betty Leyris had sought refuge since the month of April. He thought of having Jouve come and stay in a nearby property at Chemillieu. Painted an *Autoportrait, Le Cerisier; L'Enfant gourmand* and *Le Goûter*.

1941
Balthus and Antoinette spent the months of March and April in Bern at the Watteville's. May: return to Champrovent without Antoinette. He began the *Paysage de Champrovent*, the different versions of the *Salon*. October: Picasso purchased *Les Enfants Blanchard* from Pierre Colle.

1942
When the Germans entered the South zone, Balthus left Champrovent, and settled with Antoinette at Bern and then Fribourg. Birth of their son Stanislas.

1943
Fribourg. Several commissions of portraits. He painted *La Patience* and *Le Gottéron*. November: gallery Moos of Geneva organized an exhibition of his works.

1944
February: birth of his son Thadée. November: stay in Paris, visited Picasso.

1945
Moved into Villa Diodati at Cologny near Geneva, where he became friends with the publisher Albert Skira, was introduced to André Malraux, and met up again with Giacometti, Jean Starobinski, etc.
Completed *Les Beaux Jours*. Prepared, in collaboration with the French Embassy, an exhibition titled "École de Paris" that would be shown at the Kunsmalle of Bern in the spring of 1946 and where he showed *Les Beaux Jours*. Stay in Paris. Met up again with the artists exiled by the war at the restaurant *Le Catalan*, where he would spend a great deal of time during the years 1948-1950. Publication in the review *Fontaine* of the letters Rilke had written him between 1920 and 1926.

1946
Balthus separated permanently from Antoinette and moved back to Paris.
November-December: exhibition at the gallery Beaux-Arts organized by Henriette Gomès. Twenty-seven paintings were shown, including *La Victime*, begun in 1939 and finished that year, various portraits and landscapes, *Les Beaux Jours* and two versions of the *Salon*.

1947
Summer: trip with André Masson in the south of France. On the Côte d'Azur met up again with Lacan, Sylvia Bataille, Picasso, Françoise Gillot. On that occasion he met Laurence Bataille, of whom he made several portraits.
Balthus became friends with Albert Camus and Paul Eluard.
Painted *La Chambre* and the *Portrait de Jacqueline Matisse*.

1948
Albert Camus asked him to design the sets and costumes for *L'Etat de Siège* directed by Jean-Louis Barrault.
Painted a series of *Nus* and began *La Partie de cartes*.

1949
Balthus designed the sets and costumes for Boris Kochno's ballet, *Le peintre et son modèle*.
Exhibition at the Pierre Matisse Gallery in New York, with a preface by Albert Camus.
Painted *La Semaine des quatre jeudis*, a half-dozen *Nus*, the *Portrait de Rosabianca Skira* and *Le Chat de la Méditerranée*. Death of Erich Klossowski, at Sanary.

1950
With Marie-Laure de Noailles and Jean Cocteau, Balthus was witness to the marriage of Georges and Myrtille Hugnet.
Designed the sets and costumes for Mozart's *Cosi fan tutte* for the Festival of Aix-en-Provence, commissioned by Cassandre.
Painted the first *Étude pour le passage du Commerce-Saint-André*.

1951
During the summer, stayed in Italy, invited by the Caetanis. Went to Rome and to Sermoneta where he painted the *Paysage d'Italie*.

1952
Began the *Passage du Commerce Saint-André* and *La Chambre*. Gave an illustration for *Langue* by Pierre Jean Jouve (L'Arche, Paris 1952).

1953
Balthus left Paris and, thanks to the support of a group of collectors and dealers, settled at the château de Chassy in the Morvan.
Designed the sets and costumes of *L'Ile des chèvres* by Ugo Betti.

1954
Painted a series of views of Chassy, the two portraits of *Colette* and the three paintings portraying *Léna Leclerc*. Completed *La Chambre* and the *Passage du Commerce Saint-André*. Painted the first studies for *Les Trois sœurs*. Frédérique Tison, his brother Pierre's stepdaughter, joined him at Chassy. She would live with him until around 1962. First studies for *Le Rêve I*. Publication of the Rilke-Baladine correspondence (Max Niehans, Zurich).

1955
Painted the first two versions of *Les Trois sœurs*, the *Jeune fille à la fenêtre, Le Rève I, Jeune Fille à la chemise blanche, Nu devant la cheminée.*
In December, spent three months in Paris.

1956
29 February: opening of his exhibition at the gallery Gomès.
Exhibition at the Museum of Modern Art in New York.
Painted *La Tireuse de cartes, Le Rêve II, Le Fruit d'or.*

1957
Exhibition at the Pierre Matisse Gallery in New York.
Painted *Golden Afternoon, La Toilette, La Sortie du bain.*

1958
First exhibitions in Italy, in Turin and Rome.
Le Drap bleu, several still lifes and landscapes.

1959-1960
Le Phalène, several landscapes.
Designed the sets for Shakespeare's *Jules César* directed by Jean-Louis Barrault.

1961
André Malraux, Minister of Culture, appointed Balthus directer of the Academy of France in Rome, Villa Medici, despite the opposition of the Institut of which Balthus was not a member.
His mission was to undertake the restoration of the Villa and update the statutes of the Prix de Rome, so as to open it to researchers, restorers or young authors.

1962
Balthus was sent by Malraux on a mission to Japan; there he met Setsuko Ideta.
In Rome, became friends with Renato Guttuso, Federico Fellini, Valerio Zurlini, several actors and writers.

1963
Resumed *La Chambre turque*, its model being Setsuko Ideta.

1964
Began the series of the *Trois Sœurs*, giving two new versions.

1966
May-June: major retrospective of his work at the Musée des Arts Décoratifs in Paris, then taken to Knokke-le-Zoute in Belgium. Several exhibitions of his drawings in the United States.

1967
Balthus and Setsuko Ideta were married in Japan.
La Chambre turque and *Les Trois sœurs* were shown at the Pierre Matisse Gallery in New York. *La Chambre turque* was purchased by the French state.
Balthus began *Japonaise au miroir noir* and *Japonaise à la table rouge.*
The restoration of the buildings of Villa Medici being completed, he began that of the gardens.

1968
Birth of Fumio, son of Balthus and Setsuko, who would live only two years. October-November: retrospective at the Tate Gallery in London, curated by John Russel.
Began *Katia lisant.*

1969
Death, in Paris, of Baladine Klossowska.

1970
First drawings of Monte Calvello, the medieval castle he bought near Viterbo.

1971
October-November: major exhibition at the gallery Claude Bernard in Paris of drawings executed in Rome, with a preface by Jean Leymarie.

1973
Birth of his daughter Harumi. Exhibition at the Musée Cantini of Marseilles.

1973-1977
Balthus completed *Japonaise au miroir noir, Japonaise à la table rouge, Katia lisant.* Painted *Nu de profil* and *Nu au repos.*

1977
Federico Fellini wrote a preface for a major exhibition gathering works from 1934 to 1977 at the Pierre Matisse Gallery in New York.
La Toilette de Cathy was purchased by the Musée national d'Art moderne of Paris.
Jean Leymarie replaced Balthus as director of the Villa Medici. Balthus moved to Rossinière, in Switzerland, with his wife and their daughter.

1977-1980
Paysage de Monte Calvello, Chat au miroir I, Nu assoupi.

1979
La Rue was bequeathed by James Thrall Soby to the Museum of Modern Art of New York.

1980
Twenty-six paintings were shown in the context of the Venice Biennale.

1981
Balthus was appointed member of the Royal Academy of London. Completed *Le Peintre et son modèle*, which was received in the collection of the Musée national d'Art moderne of Paris.

1982
First retrospective of works on paper at Spoleto, curated by Giovanni Carandente. Publication of *Balthus* by Jean Leymarie, first exhaustive catalog of the paintings (Skira, Genève).
La Montagne was received in the collection of the Metropolitan Museum of Art of New York.

1983
Nu au miroir, Nu au foulard.

1983-1984
Retrospective at the Musée d'Art moderne of Paris, curated by Jean Clair; at the Metropolitan Museum of New York by Sabine Rewald and at the City Museum of Kyoto.

1983-1986
Nu à la guitare, Nu couché, Composition au corbeau.

1987-1990
Chat au miroir II.

1989-1994
Chat au miroir III.

1993
Retrospective at the Musée cantonal des Beaux Arts of Lausanne.

1994
Retrospective of drawings at the Kunstmuseum of Bern.

1995
Traveling exhibition in Hong Kong (Museum of Art), Beijing (Palace of Fine Arts) and Taipei (Fine Art Museum).

1996
Retrospective at the Centro de Arte Reina Sofía in Madrid.

1996-1997
Exhibition at the Accademia Valentino in Rome.

1998
Balthus went to Poland for the first time. He was made *doctor honoris causa* of the University of Wroclaw.
Painted the *Paysage de Monte Calvello II.*

1999
Exhibition at the Musée des Beaux Arts of Dijon, gathering works painted at Chassy. Publication of the *Catalogue raisonné de l'œuvre complet* (Virginie Monnier, under the scientific supervision of Jean Clair, Gallimard, Paris).

2000
A Mid-Summer Night's Dream, a tribute to Poussin, painted for the exhibition "Encountees, New Art from Old", curated by the National Gallery of London.

2001
18 February: death of Balthus at Rossinière, Switzerland.

Selected Bibliography

Writings by the artist

Balthus/Antoinette de Watteville, *Correspondance amoureuse avec Antoinette de Watteville* 1928-1937, ed. by Stanislas and Thadée Klossowski de Rola, Paris: Bucet-Chastel, 2001.

Illustrated books

Balthus, *Mitsou. Quarante images par Balthusz*, preface by Rainer Maria Rilke, Zürich-Erlenbach & Leipzig: Rotapfel Verlag, 1921.

Pierre Jean Jouve, *Urne*, with one drawing by Balthus, Paris: G.L.M., 1936.

Pierre Jean Jouve, *Langue*, a poem with three lithographs by Balthus, Paris: Arche, 1952.

Exhibition catalogues

Balthus Paintings, Pierre Matisse Gallery, New York, 1938.

Balthus: Paintings and Drawings, Pierre Matisse Gallery, New York, 1939.

Balthus, Galerie Georges Moos, Genf, 1943.

Balthus. Peintures de 1936 à 1946, Galerie Beaux-Arts, Paris, 1946.

Balthus, Pierre Matisse Gallery, New York, 1949.

Balthus, James Thrall Soby (ed.), The Museum of Modern Art, New York, 1956.

Balthus, Pierre Matisse Gallery, New York, 1957.

Balthus, Galeria Galatea, Turin, 1958.

Balthus Paintings 1929-1961, Pierre Matisse Gallery, New York, 1962.

Drawings by Balthus, E. V. Thaw & Co., New York, 1963.

Balthus, The New Hayden Gallery, The Massachusetts Institute of Technology, Cambridge, 1964.

Balthus, Musée des Arts décoratifs, Paris, 1966.

Exhibition of Balthus Drawings, Holland Gallery, Chicago, 1966.

Balthus: "La Chambre turque", "Les Trois Sœurs", Drawings and Watercolours (1933-1966), Pierre Matisse Gallery, New York, 1967.

Balthus, John Russell (ed.), Tate Gallery, London, 1968.

Balthus, Donald Morris Gallery, Detroit, 1969.

Balthus: dessins et aquarelles, Galerie Claude Bernard, Paris, 1971.

Balthus, Musée Cantini, Marseille, 1973.

Balthus, peinture, aquarelles, dessins, Galerie Arts Anciens, Bevaix, 1975.

Balthus, Paintings and Drawings, 1934-1977, Pierre Matisse Gallery, New York, 1977.

Balthus in Chicago, The Museum of Contemporary Art, Chicago, undated (1980).

Balthus, Biennale di Venezia, Venice, 1980, preface by Jean Leymarie and Federico Fellini.

Balthus, disegni e acquarelli, Festival di due Mondi, Palazzo Racani-Aroni, Spoleto, 1982.

Balthus, Centre Georges Pompidou - Musée national d'Art moderne, Paris, 1983.

Balthus, The Metropolitan Museum of Art, New York, 1984.

Balthus à la Villa Médicis, Villa Médicis, Rome, 1990.

Balthus dans la maison de Courbet, Musée Maison natale Gustave Courbet, Ornans, 1992.

Balthus, Jörg Zutter (ed.), Musée Cantonal des Beaux-Arts, Lausanne, Geneva: Skira, 1993.

Balthus, Zeichnungen, Kunstmuseum Bern, Basel: Wiese, 1994.

Balthus, Museo Nacional Centro de Arte Reina Sofía, Madrid, 1996.

Ommagio a Balthus, Accademia Valentino, Rome, Milan: Skira 1996.

Balthus, un atelier dans le Morvan: 1953-1961, Musée des Beaux-Arts, Dijon, 1999.

Balthus, Jean Clair (ed.), Centro di Cultura di Palazzo Grassi, Venice, Milan: Bompiani, 2001.

Monographs

Caradente, Giovanni, *Balthus. Drawings and Watercolours*, London: Thames & Hudson, 1983.

Clair, Jean, *Metamorphosen des Eros. Essays über Balthus*, Munich: Schirmer/Mosel, 1984.

Klossowski de Rola, Stanislas, *Balthus: Gemälde*, Munich: Schirmer/Mosel, 1983.

Leymarie, Jean, *Balthus*, Geneva: Skira, 1978.

——. *Balthus*, Geneva: Skira, 1982.

Monnier, Virginie and Clair, Jean, Balthus: *Catalogue raisonné de l'œuvre complète*, Paris: Gallimard, 1999.

Rewald, Sabine (ed.), *Balthus*, New York: Harry N. Abrams, 1984.

——. *Balthus. Time Suspended. Paintings and Drawins 1932-1960*, Munich: Schirmer/Mosel, 2007.

Rilke, Rainer Maria, *Lettres à un jeune peintre Balthus*, Paris: Archimbaud, 1994.

Roy, Claude, *Balthus*, Munich: Schirmer/Mosel, 1996.

Articles

Artaud, Antonin, "Exposition Balthus à la Galerie Pierre", in *La Nouvelle Revue Française* (Paris), no. 248 (May 1934), pp. 899-900.

——. "Les Cenci", in *La Bête noire* (Paris), no. 2 (May 1935), p. 1.

——. "La Pintura francesa joven y la tradicion", in *El Nacional* (Mexico City), June 1936, under the title "La jeune peinture française", also in idem, *(Œuvres complètes*, vol. 8, Paris: Gallimard, 1971, pp. 248-253.

——. Untitled, in *Messages révolutionnaires*, Paris: Gallimard, 1971, pp. 249-251.

——. "Balthus", in *Art Press* (Paris), no. 39 (July-August 1980), p. 4; text written in 1947.

Berne-Joffroy, André, "Balthus", in *La Nouvelle Revue Française* (Paris), no. 41 (May 1956), pp. 929-930.

Bonnefoy, Yves, "L'invention de Balthus", in idem, *L'Improbable*, Paris: Mercure de France, 1959, pp. 49-74.

Camus, Albert, "Balthus", in *Balthus*, exhib. cat., Pierre Matisse Gallery, New York, 1949.

——. "Peut-être", in *Verve* (Paris), vol. 2, no. 27-28 (1952), p. 35.

Carluccio, Luigi, "Balthus", in *Balthus*, exhib. cat. Galleria d'arte Galatea, Turin, 1958.

Cassou, Jean, "Balthus", in *Les peintres célèbres*, Paris: Mazenod, 1964, pp. 50-53.

Char, René, "Balthus, ou le dard dans la fleur", in *Cahiers d'art* (Paris), vol. 20-21 (1945-1946), p. 199.

Clair, Jean, "Balthus", in *La Nouvelle Revue Française* (Paris), no. 314 (March 1979), pp. 92-96.

——. "Le Paris de Balthus", in *Beaux-Arts* (Paris), no. 7 (November 1983), pp. 38-41.

——. "Balthus und die Moderne", in *Du* (Zurich), no. 9 (September 1992), pp. 42-44.

Connolly, Cyril, "Balthus", in *Balthus and Selection of French Paintings*, exhib. cat., Lefevre Gallery, London, 1952.

Courthion, Pierre in *Balthus*, exhib. cat., Galerie Moos, Geneva, 1943.

Eluard, Paul, "Balthus", in *Les Cahiers du sud* (Marseilles), no. 285 (1947).

Fellini, Federico, "Balthus", in *Balthus*, exhib. cat., Pierre Matisse Gallery, New York, 1977.

Gabus, Pierre-Yves, "Qui est Monsieur Balthus?" in *Balthus: peintures, aquarelles, dessins*, exhib. cat., Galerie des Arts Anciens, Bevaix, 1975.

George, Waldemar, "Balthus", in *Le Figaro Littéraire* (Paris), January 25, 1947.

Gendel, Milton, "H.M. The King of Cats, a footnote Interview with Balthus, elusive, uninterviewable artist", in *Art News* (New York), vol. 61, no. 2 (April 1962), pp. 36-38.

Hyman, Timothy, "Balthus, a Puppet Master", in *Art scribe* (London), no. 23 (June 1980), pp. 30-40.

Jouve, Pierre Jean, "Les Cenci d' Antonin Artaud", in *La Nouvelle Revue Française*, Paris, no. 261 (June 1935), pp. 910-915.

——. "Oeuvre peinte de Balthus", in *Lettres I* (Geneva), no. 1 (January 1943), pp. 37-38, without reference to authors.

——. "Balthus" in *La Nef* (Algiers), September 1944, pp. 138-147.

——. "A Balthus" and "Mémoire de Larchant", in idem, *La Vierge de Paris*, Paris: Egloff, 1945, pp. 173-180.

——. "Cosi fan tutte ou le changement des objets", in Aix-en-Provence: Programm of the Third International Music Festival, 1950, a second version under the title "Ironie de Cosi fan tutti", in idem, *Miroir*, Paris: Mercure de France, 1954, pp. 192-200.

——. "Le tableau", "Description", "La douce visiteuse", and "Les Beaux jours", in idem, *Proses*, Paris: Mercure de France, 1960, pp. 21, 30-31, 45-49, 80-81.

Klossowski, Pierre, "Balthus beyond Realism", in *Art News* (New York), vol. 55, no. 8 (1956), pp. 26-31.

——. "Du tableau vivant dans la peinture de Balthus", in *Monde nouveau* (Paris), no. 108-109 (March 1957), pp. 70-80.

Lassaigne, Jacques, "Balthus", in *Arts-Beaux-Arts-Littérature* (Paris), no. 45 (1946), p. 1.

——. "Balthus", in *Peintres d'aujourd'hui France-Italie*, exhib. cat. 7, Turin Biennale, Gallerie Civica d'Arte Moderna, Turin, 1961.

Leyris, Pierre, "Deux figures de Balthus", in *Signes* (Paris), no. 4 (1946), pp. 83-87.

Loeb, Pierre, "La Rue", in idem, *Voyages à travers la peinture*, Paris: Bordas, 1946.

Lord, James, "Balthus: le cas singulier du comte de Rola", in *Commentaire* (Paris), no. 27 (Autumn 1984), pp. 477-494.

Mason, Raymond, "Un témoignange des années 50", in *Balthus*, exhib. cat., Centre Pompidou, Musée national d'Art moderne, Paris, 1983.

Melveille, Robert, "Retrospective at Tate", in *Archives Review* (London), no. 145 (February 1969), pp. 131-33.

Metken, Günter, "Larchant von Balthus-Frankreich am Vorabend des Krieges", in idem, *In Künstlers Lande gehen*, Munich: Schirmer/Mosel 1988, pp. 347-350.

Peppiatt, Michael, "Balthus", in *Réalités* (Paris), English edition, October 1967, pp. 52-57.

Picon, Gaétan, "Les dalles de Venise", in *Balthus*, exhib. cat. Musée des Arts décoratifs, Paris, 1966.

Pieyre de Mandiargues, André, "Balthus, je me souviens", in *XXe siècle* (Paris), no. 44 (June 1975), pp. 62-67.

Rewald, John, "Thoughts on Drawings by Balthus", in *Balthus drawings*, exhib. cat., E.V. Thaw & Co., New York, 1963.

Rewald, Sabine, "Balthus", in *Balthus*, exhib. cat., The Metropolitan Museum of New York, New York, 1984, pp. 9-54.

——. "Some Notes on Balthus's Nonmusical Guitar Lesson", in *Source: Notes in the History of Art* (New York), vol. 11, no. 3-4 (spring/summer 1992), pp. 59-64.

——. "Balthus's Magic Mountain", in *Burlington Magazine* (London), 139, no. 1134, September 1997, pp. 622-628.

——. "Balthus Lessons", in *Art in America* (New York), vol. 85, no. 9 (September 1997), pp. 88-94, 120-121.

——. "Balthus's Thérèses", in *Metropolitan Museum Journal* (New York), 33, 1998, pp. 305-314.

——. "Balthus à Chassy, " in *Balthus, un atelier dans le Morvan: 1953-1961*, exhib. cat., Musée des Beaux-Arts, Dijon, 1999, pp. 17-27.

——. "Balthus's Mountain Guide Revisited", in *Metropolitan Museum Journal* (New York), 37, 2002, pp. 315-319.

——. "Pierre Matisse et Balthus: Une Relation Difficile", in *Pierre Matisse passeur passionné: un marchand d'art et ses artistes.*

Pierre Schneider (ed.), exhib. cat., The Mona Bismarck Foundation, Paris, 2005.

Russell, John, "Master of Nubile Adolescent", in *Art in America* (New York), vol. 55 (November 1967), pp. 96-103.

Russell, John, "Balthus", in *Balthus*, exhib. cat., Tate Gallery, London, 1968.

Soby, James Thrall in *Balthus Paintings*, exhib. cat., Pierre Matisse Gallery, New York, 1938.

——. "The Position of Balthus", in *Saturday Review of Literature* (New York), August 14, 1948.

——. "Balthus", in *Balthus*, exhib. cat., Museum of Modern Art, New York, 1956.

Starobinski, Jean, "Des peintures de Balthus a la Galerie Moos à Geneve", in *Le Curieux* (Geneva), November 13, 1943.

——. "D'où venait l'enchantement", in *Balthus*, exhib. cat., Centre Pompidou, Musée national d'Art moderne, Paris, 1983.

——. "Malraux, Balthus et l'idée du chat", in *Du* (Zurich), no. 9 (September 1992), pp. 18-19.

Waldberg, Patrick, "Balthus ou la ressemblance au désir", in *Preuves* (Paris), October 1966, pp. 64-67.